Jesse James and
the Movies

Jesse James and the Movies

Johnny D. Boggs

McFarland & Company, Inc., Publishers
Jefferson, North Carolina, and London

LIBRARY OF CONGRESS CATALOGUING-IN-PUBLICATION DATA

Boggs, Johnny D.
Jesse James and the movies / Johnny D. Boggs.
p.   cm.
Includes bibliographical references and index.

ISBN 978-0-7864-4788-6
softcover : 50# alkaline paper ∞

1. James, Jesse, 1847–1882 — In motion pictures.   2. Western films — United States — Catalogs.   3. James, Jesse, 1847–1882 — On television.   4. Western television programs — Catalogs.   I. Title.
PN1995.9.J32B65   2011   791.43′65878 — dc22   2011009913

BRITISH LIBRARY CATALOGUING DATA ARE AVAILABLE

© 2011 Johnny D. Boggs. All rights reserved

No part of this book may be reproduced or transmitted in any form or by any means, electronic or mechanical, including photocopying or recording, or by any information storage and retrieval system, without permission in writing from the publisher.

On the cover: Brad Pitt as Jesse James in the 2007 film *The Assassination of Jesse James by the Coward Robert Ford* (Warner Bros./Photofest); (inset) portrait of Jesse James, circa 1876 or 1882 (Library of Congress)

Manufactured in the United States of America

McFarland & Company, Inc., Publishers
Box 611, Jefferson, North Carolina 28640
www.mcfarlandpub.com

For the Western Movie Night Gang:
Tom Clagett, Kirk Ellis, David Morrell and Robert Nott

Table of Contents

Acknowledgments	ix
Introduction	1
One: Jesse James, 1847–1882	7
Two: Jesse James in Pop Culture, 1875–1903	19
Three: The Silent Era, 1908–1927	23
Four: A-List Jesse, 1939–1940	45
Five: Jesse in the B's, 1939–1949	63
Six: The Proliferation of Jesse James, 1950–1960	112
Seven: Oddball Jesse (1965–1969)	181
Eight: Revisionist Jesse, 1972–2010	195
Nine: Euro Westerns, 1964–2009	227
Ten: Made-for-Television Movies, 1970–1999	230
Eleven: Television Series Appearances, 1953–2001	238
Chapter Notes	245
Bibliography	259
Index	265

Acknowledgments

I couldn't have written this book without help from a bunch of people, most importantly, my wife. Other helping hands:

Elizabeth Beckett, Clay County Historic Sites Director of Kearney, Missouri; Kevin Chatham, Meridian-Lauderdale County (Mississippi) Public Library; Scott Cole, Friends of the James Farm, Liberty, Missouri; Paul Andrew Hutton, history professor at the University of New Mexico, film scholar, of Albuquerque, New Mexico; Diane Jones, Lawrence County Public Library in Monticello, Mississippi; Christie Kennard, Friends of the James Farm, Kearney, Missouri; John J. Koblas, Jesse James historian from suburban Minneapolis, Minnesota; Boyd Magers, editor of *Western Clippings* magazine in Albuquerque, New Mexico; Candy Moulton, historian, of Encampment, Wyoming; Robert Nott, film historian, reporter for the *Santa Fe New Mexican,* of Santa Fe, New Mexico; Christina L. Thornhill, The Library, Hattiesburg, Mississippi; Hayes Scriven, Northfield (Minnesota) Historical Society; and the staffs at the Missouri Valley Special Collections, Kansas City Public Library, and the Vista Grande Public Library and Santa Fe Public Library in Santa Fe, New Mexico.

Introduction

"The best movie about Jesse James is *Ride with the Devil*, which isn't about Jesse James, but that's all right because the best movie about George Custer is *Fort Apache*, which isn't about Custer, either, and the best movie about the O.K. Corral is *My Darling Clementine*, which gets almost all of the facts — including the year of the famous gunfight — wrong."

That was the start of a speech I gave in suburban Des Moines, Iowa, in 2006. Hearing that I was writing a novel about the James-Younger Gang's ill-fated bank robbery in Northfield, Minnesota, John J. Koblas, then president of the National James-Younger Gang, invited me to give the keynote address at the group's annual conference. Now, the last thing I want to do when talking to historians and, as in the case of the National James-Younger Gang, descendants of historical figures, is bring up a subject sure to prompt arduous debate. After all, I am, primarily, a novelist, albeit one firmly grounded in history. As I explained to Jack Koblas, I did not want to get into a discussion about who was inside the bank in Liberty, Missouri, on February 13, 1866; how many bandits actually took part in the Northfield raid on September 7, 1876; what brand of revolver Robert Ford used when he shot Jesse James to death at his home in St. Joseph, Missouri, on April 3, 1882; the color of Cole Younger's vest, if he preferred pewter or brass buttons; what cobbler made Jim Cummins's boots; or whether the Pinkertons were nothing more than hired assassins.

So I told Koblas that I would prefer to talk about something light, maybe the movies featuring Jesse James.

Which isn't to say film is immune from controversy. Far from it. My speech led to an article on the same subject for *True West* magazine, which led to a polite though fairly spirited discussion with director Walter Hill during the Western Heritage Wrangler Award festivities at the National Cowboy and Western Heritage Museum in Oklahoma City, Oklahoma, in April 2007. (Hill had directed *The Long Riders*, a 1980 movie I pretty much dismissed in the *True West* article.)

The first movie about Jesse James that I recall seeing is Philip Kaufman's *The Great Northfield Minnesota Raid* (1972), when it aired on network television in the 1970s. The elementary school playground the following week (or weeks) was full of young boys pretending to be Cole Younger, or at least actor Cliff Robertson's version of Cole Younger. As naive, white South Carolinians instilled from birth with a glorious admiration for the War Between the States/War for Southern Independence/War of Northern Aggression/Lost Cause, we loved the movie's line about 1876 not marking our nation's centennial — Yankees had forgotten four years of Civil War — and a lot of us thought that the James and Younger boys were merely carrying on the fight against Yankee tyranny and greedy railroaders.

Jesse James was a savvy hero saving girls from greedy land-robbers, much the same as

Jesse became a pop culture item after his death. This card shows the St. Joseph house where he was killed, the family farm near Kearney, and the Baptist church where his funeral was held (Library of Congress).

Billy the Kid kept riding to the rescue on the pages of Charlton and Dell comics. Later I would grow to learn that the Civil War wasn't so glorious or all that righteous, and neither was Jesse James, although, ever since watching Cliff Robertson on the screen of our Sylvania color television set, I've always had a grudging respect for Cole Younger. The historical researcher and film buff in me — I'll take in a Western at the drop of a hat — kept drawing me to Jesse James.

Other movies about Jesse and "the boys" left memorable impressions on me, including Hill's *The Long Riders*, which I saw at a theater in Florence, South Carolina, as a high school senior in 1980. Many more came along on television or video such as *Jesse James*, *The Return of Frank James* (for my money, no actor could chew tobacco better than Henry Fonda as Frank James), the insipid *American Outlaws* and, most recently, *The Assassination of Jesse James by the Coward Robert Ford*. Others, especially the B movies, I dug up once I started researching my speech to the National James-Younger Gang. More than a few came along when I got the itch to write this book. Some are, unfortunately, most likely lost forever, and a few are about as elusive as Jesse was to the Pinkertons.

I will still argue that the best movie about Jesse James isn't really about Jesse James, but *Ride with the Devil*, director Ang Lee's 1999 film based on Daniel Woodrell's novel *Woe to Live On*. The film superbly captures the turmoil and people along the Missouri-Kansas border, and the events during the Civil War that propelled the real Jesse James to a life of crime.

If any famous Western historical figure is overdue for film analysis, it is Jesse James.

Introduction 3

Eight theatrical movies have been made about the gunfight at the O.K. Corral, most notably the aforementioned *My Darling Clementine*, *Gunfight at the O.K. Corral* (1957), the pseudo-cult favorite *Tombstone* (1993), and a handful more if you include movies inspired by the event, such as *Law and Order* (1932) and *Warlock* (1959). According to historian Paul Andrew Hutton, forty-eight movies have been made about George Armstrong Custer, from Francis Ford's *Custer's Last Raid* (1912) to Arthur Penn's *Little Big Man* (1970), with the fabled "Boy General" appearing in several other films such as *The Plainsman* (1936) and *Santa Fe Trail* (1940) along with cameo and comic appearances in *Won Ton Ton, the Dog Who Saved Hollywood* (1976), *Teachers* (1984), *Wagons East* (1994), etc.[1]

Jesse James has shown up in forty-odd movies, beginning—as far as we know—with *The James Boys of Missouri* in 1908. "At this point, this corner is willing to concede that Frank and Jesse James are among the most photographed characters of our folklore," *The New York Times* reported in 1951.[2] If you take into consideration foreign films, short subjects, and brief appearances in television movies such as *The Last Ride of the Dalton Gang* (1979) and *Belle Starr* (1980), that number grows substantially.

The truth, however, is that because so many silent movies are presumed lost, we may never know the exact number of movies about Jesse and Frank James.

As a cult icon, Jesse has gone even further, popping up in Western television series such as *Bronco*, *Hondo*, *Stories of the Century*, *Tales of Wells Fargo*, *Barbary Coast*, *Little House on the Prairie* and *The Young Riders*. Yet the popularity of the Missouri bandit hasn't been restricted to TV shows with horses and hats. In a 1953 episode of the Walter Cronkite–hosted documentary-reenactment series *You Are There*, an up-and-coming actor named James Dean played Jesse in "The Capture of Jesse James." Jesse has also gotten his due on *The Brady Bunch*, *MacGyver*, *The Dukes of Hazzard*, even *My Favorite Martian* and *The Twilight Zone*.

The only Western outlaw more popular in Hollywood is Billy the Kid. "At least sixty films, both American and foreign, have celebrated the exploits of this dreamscape desperado," writes Hutton of Billy the Kid.[3] Yet most of the movies about Henry McCarty, alias Henry Antrim, alias William H. Bonney, alias Kid Antrim, alias Kid, alias The Kid, alias Billy the Kid, were a series of some thirteen matinee B-movies for Producers Releasing Corporation starring Buster Crabbe (released between 1941 and 1943), and more than twenty other films from 1943 to 1946 in which the name of Crabbe's hero was changed to Billy Carson. Bob Steele also had a run as Billy the Kid with five movies released by PRC in 1940 and 1941.

Hollywood did produce some serious studies of Billy the Kid, including King Vidor's *Billy the Kid* (1930), Arthur Penn's *The Left Handed Gun* (1958, featuring Paul Newman as a brooding Billy) and Sam Peckinpah's muddled *Pat Garrett & Billy the Kid* (1973).

The movies featuring Jesse James also prove to be an interesting mix worthy of discussion, review and analysis. For casting purposes, it is hard to top the fact that Jesse James has been played on screen by his own son, in *Jesse James Under the Black Flag* (1921) and *Jesse James as the Outlaw* (1921). Matinee idol Roy Rogers played him as half of a dual role in *Jesse James at Bay* (1941); Rogers had already played against Don "Red" Barry's Jesse in *Days of Jesse James* (1939). Clayton Moore, of *The Lone Ranger* fame, also got two turns as Jesse in the Republic serials *Jesse James Rides Again* (1947) and *Adventures of Frank and Jesse James* (1948), as did Audie Murphy in *Kansas Raiders* (1950) and *A Time for Dying* (1969),

Murphy's last role. Jesse has shown up in the comedies *Alias Jesse James* (1959) with Bob Hope and *The Outlaws IS Coming!* (1965) with the Three Stooges, and has also had the non-distinction of appearing in one of the worst horror films ever made, *Jesse James Meets Frankenstein's Daughter* (1966).

"By my count, there have been 36 movies about Jesse James and not one has attempted to tell the truth, even though the truth is more exciting than the myths," Judge James R. Ross, Jesse's great-grandson, wrote for the *Los Angeles Times* after the release of *American Outlaws* in 2001. "And the love story of Jesse and his cousin, Zee [Mimms], is more poignant and beautiful than any of the false stories."[4]

Ross went on: "I've spent 50 years opposing the most popular myths associated with my great-grandfather and I challenge anyone to point out any movie that is more exciting than the real story. I hope that one day someone in the entertainment industry will produce an exciting movie of outlaws and gunslinging, filled with a tremendous love story, and yet remain true to the life of Jesse James."[5]

History and entertainment can be a precarious balance. I've often said that two of the most historically accurate films I have seen are the Civil War epic *Gods and Generals* (2003) and *Son of the Morning Star* (1991), the television miniseries about George Custer. As far as entertainment value, alas, those pictures are about as enthralling as watching coffee boil.

Movies aren't made to be historically accurate, but to entertain.

John Wayne is said to have once remarked that shorter stories make better movies, which might explain why Hollywood can produce entertaining films about a 27-second street fight in Tombstone, Arizona, but stumble over the life and times of Jesse James, whose career as an outlaw lasted sixteen years — and even longer if you include his years as a Confederate guerrilla during the Civil War. Such a life is hard to boil down into two hours.

As far as Jesse is concerned, most movies fail to capture the essence of the man, or the times in

In 1902, Zerelda Samuel moved the remains of her son Jesse and his wife to the family plot in Mt. Olivet cemetery in Kearney. The original monument was moved, too, but by the mid–1930s, curiosity-seekers had chipped away pieces until nothing remained.

which he lived, although *The Last Days of Frank and Jesse James*, a 1986 made-for-television movie, and *The Assassination of Jesse James by the Coward Robert Ford* (2007) come close. *The Long Riders* (1980) and *The Great Northfield Minnesota Raid* (1972) deserve points for trying to capture an authentic look. I also find much to admire in *I Shot Jesse James* (1949), Sam Fuller's first movie as director.

Besides, I also believe that some of those B-movies, with no basis or knowledge of history, can be entertaining if you take them for what they are. You can even find a kernel of truth in them, as Frank James (played by Don "Red" Barry) tells a former gang member in *Gunfire* (1950): "The outlawin' died when Jesse died, Matt."

Perhaps the ending of *Jesse James* (1939), arguably the most famous and most popular movie about the outlaw, provides a clue as to the world's fascination with Jesse James. Actor Henry Hull, playing Major Rufus Cobb (a character inspired by John Newman Edwards, the Missouri journalist who championed the real Jesse James), delivers his sermon and eulogy:

> There ain't no question about it. Jesse was an outlaw, a bandit, a criminal. Even those that loved him ain't got no answer to that. But we ain't ashamed of him. I don't know why but I don't think even America is ashamed of Jesse James.... All I do know is he was one of the dog-gonest, goldingus, dad-blamedest buckaroos that ever rode across these United States of America.

Like Billy the Kid, Jesse James is equally a "Dreamscape Desperado." He has ridden the range as hero, villain and impostor in A-list movies and B's, serious studies and simple schlock, and undoubtedly will ride again.

And who knows myth better than Hollywood?

CHAPTER ONE

Jesse James, 1847–1882

On a freezing afternoon, with a snowstorm threatening to blanket much of Missouri, a group of riders — ten to thirteen by most accounts — wearing Union overcoats and trousers, reined to a halt near the Liberty town square. Two swung out of their saddles and entered the Clay County Savings Association, a red-brick structure on the square's northeast corner. It was about 2 P.M., Tuesday, February 13, 1866.[1]

Inside the bank, the two men warmed their hands by the stove after nodding politely to the bank's two employees, cashier Greenup Bird and his eighteen-year-old son, William. One of the strangers walked to the counter and asked William Bird to change a $10 bill. When the clerk approached to help, both men drew revolvers and ordered the Birds to stay quiet and turn over the money. When William Bird didn't move fast enough, one robber hit him in the back with his revolver and prodded him inside the vault, produced a wheat sack, and began filling it with coins.

Meanwhile, the second bandit collected greenbacks and U.S. negotiable bonds from a black tin box — although he missed 519 stamps that would have made the bonds bearable. The robbers then forced Greenup Bird into the vault with his son. Saying, at least according to one story, "all Birds should be caged," the two men shut the bankers in the vault and hurried outside.

Yet the robbers forgot to lock the vault, and the Birds opened the heavy door and rushed to the window to shout the alarm. "Indeed so quiet had the matter been managed," the local newspaper reported, "if the robbers had succeeded in locking the Bank vault on the Clerk and Cashier, and had retired quietly, it would likely have been some time before the robbery would have been discovered."[2]

Across the street, S.H. Holmes and George Clifford "Jolly" Wymore heard the Birds shouting. One robber fired a warning shot and told Holmes and Wymore to stay put, but other shots soon followed. Wymore, a nineteen-year-old student at William Jewell College, fell dead, and a bullet barely missed Holmes.

Screaming Rebel yells, the riders leaped over Wymore's body and galloped out of town, escaping with $20,000 in coin, $14,000 in paper currency and $42,000 in negotiable bonds. A posse followed, but the snowstorm struck, wiping out the trail.

"The murderers and robbers are believed by many citizens, and the officers of the Bank, to be a gang of old bushwhacking desperadoes who stay mostly in Jackson County," the *Liberty Tribune* reported. "But it makes no difference who they are, or what they claim to be, they should be swung up in the most summary manner. Robbing and murdering must be stopped, and if it requires severe medicine to do it, so be it."[3]

The robbery proved historic. During the Civil War, Southern sympathizer Bennett

Young and a dozen or more prison recruits raided St. Albans, Vermont, on October 19, 1864, and looted three banks before making off for the Canadian border with $20,000. But before the Liberty robbery, no one had dared rob a bank in broad daylight while the United States was at peace. Liberty also marked the first post–Civil War crime linked to Jesse James.

Technically, no one can prove Jesse James committed any crime. Robert Ford's 1882 assassination of the outlaw robbed the courts of any chance to convict Jesse; his older brother, Frank, was acquitted in two trials after Jesse's death; and the brothers' associates, Cole, Jim and Bob Younger, swore that Jesse and Frank had not been involved in any other robbery attributed to the James-Younger Gang.

Most of us know better, although Jesse probably wasn't at Liberty on that icy February day. Cole Younger said "[W]hen I saw him early in the summer of 1866 [Jesse] was still suffering from the shot through the lung he had received in the last battle in Johnson County in May, 1865."[4] Jesse might have helped plan the raid, however, and would definitely take an active part in bank and train robberies — and murder — over the next sixteen years.

The James-Younger Gang would not be linked to the Liberty crime until after becoming suspected of the 1869 robbery of the Daviess County Savings Association in Gallatin, Missouri. But Liberty undoubtedly was the gang's first bank robbery.

A photograph of Jesse James taken in 1874 or 1875 in Nebraska City, Nebraska, possibly around the time of his wedding to Zee Mimms (Library of Congress).

Rewards totaling $7,000 were offered for the capture of the thieves or return of the money, but those rewards would never be collected, and no one was ever brought to trial.

The robbery marked the end of the Clay County Savings Association, which suspended operations after the crime and eventually paid depositors sixty cents on the dollar before folding. Jesse James and his companions, however, were just getting started.

* * *

Jesse Woodson James was born on September 5, 1847, the third son of Robert and Zerelda James. (The second child, named after his father, lived just more than a month in 1845.) Alexander Franklin James was born on January 10, 1843, and a daughter, Susan Lavenia, joined the family on November 25, 1849.[5]

Robert James was born on July 17, 1818, in Logan County, Kentucky, and graduated from the Baptist-affiliated Georgetown College in 1843 with a bachelor of arts degree. A licensed Baptist preacher since 1839, he was considered "a high-minded, honest fellow" by his classmates.[6] On December 28, 1841, James married Zerelda Elizabeth Cole, a tomboy

Jesse James was originally buried near the coffee bean tree at the family farm. His wife Zee joined him there after her death. Today, the home is a tourist attraction and museum.

whose family ran a tavern near Midway, Kentucky, and who was attending Saint Catherine's Female School in Lexington.[7]

In the spring of 1842, the newlyweds left Kentucky and arrived in Clay County, Missouri, where Zerelda was deposited with her mother, now living in the area with her second husband. Robert James went back to finish his studies, returning after his graduation, and became pastor at New Hope Baptist Church. In addition to starting a family, he bought a 275-acre farm near present-day Kearney — then called Centerville.[8] The family owned at least seven slaves.[9]

In 1850, Robert James left his family and took off for the gold fields in California. The reason for this decision is up to speculation. On April 14, he wrote his wife from California, ending the letter with, "Give my love to all inquiring friends and keep a portion of it to yourself and kiss Jesse for me and tell Franklin to be a good boy and learn fast."[10]

Four months later, he was dead, succumbing to fever in a gold camp called Hangtown (present-day Placerville).[11]

Zerelda did not remain a widow for long. She married Benjamin Simms on September 30, 1852, but that relationship was strained: Simms' new stepchildren reportedly didn't care much for him. They soon separated. Family tradition has it that Simms was mean to the children. Neither stepchildren nor wife was saddened when Simms died on January 2, 1854.[12]

On September 26, 1855, Zerelda married for a third time, signing a prenuptial agreement with her new husband, Dr. Reuben Samuel, that gave her ownership of six slaves and two hundred acres if the marriage ended. It didn't. Samuel, who had attended Ohio Medical College in Cincinnati from 1850 to 1851, gave up his medical practice to farm, and they would remain married, through good times and bad, until Samuel's death in 1908.[13]

* * *

They called it "Bleeding Kansas."

The Missouri Compromise of 1820 had allowed Missouri to enter the Union as a slave state and Maine to come in as a free state. Slavery would afterward be restricted in the Louisiana Purchase to land below Missouri's southern border. That act was repealed by the Kansas-Nebraska Act of 1854, which let the question of free state or slave state to a vote. Slave-supporting Missourians moved into Kansas in order to vote in the upcoming election. Bloodshed, mob rule, corruption and chaos followed. On May 21, 1856, pro-slavery forces attacked Lawrence, Kansas. On May 23, abolitionist John Brown led an attack at Pottawatomie that left five pro-slavery men dead. President Franklin Pierce had to send in Federal troops in an effort to restore order. Over the next four years, pro-slavery and anti-slavery forces shed blood along the Kansas-Missouri border.[14]

Kansas sent gangs of anti-slavery "Jayhawkers" and "Redlegs" into western Missouri to raid pro-slavery (or suspected pro-slavery) farms and to free slaves. Missourians retaliated with their own raids, sending pro-slavery "Border Ruffians" into Kansas. By the time the Civil War began in earnest in April 1861, Missouri and Kansas had already witnessed much bloodshed. In Kansas, the name of guerrilla leader William Clarke Quantrill would be cursed, as vehemently as Kansas Redleg leader Jim Lane's name was cursed in Missouri. Although Missouri was technically a neutral border state, it would in reality mirror much of the North and South. The state was divided with loyal Unionists and Southern sympathizers. In terms of battles and skirmishes, only Virginia and Tennessee would see more.[15]

It was during this era that Frank and Jesse James, sons of an ardent secessionist mother, came of age.

Some time in the spring of 1861, Frank James joined the Confederate-allied Southern Missouri State Guard. On August 10, 1861, he saw his first action at the Battle of Wilson's Creek near Springfield. That winter he contracted measles and was captured by Union forces, paroled, and allowed to return to his home in Clay County.[16] By the spring of 1863, he was back in the war, having joined the guerrilla forces of Quantrill, whom Frank called "a demon in battle."[17]

On May 25, 1863, a pro–Union militia

Frank James as an older man in this circa 1898 photograph. He lived out his days in peace, dying at the family farm in 1915 (Library of Congress).

force arrived at the farm of Reuben and Zerelda Samuel, hoping to learn the whereabouts of Quantrill. They cursed and shook Zerelda, pregnant then with Fannie Quantrill Samuel, before turning their attention to Dr. Samuel. They threw a rope around his neck and hoisted him off the ground four times in an effort to make him talk.[18]

Local legend has it that the soldiers then chased down young Jesse James, whipping him relentlessly with a rope. Neither the doctor nor the farm boy would talk, and the soldiers left Dr. Samuel hanging there. According to some stories, the doctor survived but suffered diminished mental abilities. In reality, Dr. Samuel broke and talk, leading the Unionists to the guerrilla encampment. He then was taken and jailed in Liberty, but was soon released. Jesse, however, was caught while plowing, dragged and abused.[19]

At some point, Jesse tried to join Quantrill's guerrillas, but was turned down for being too young. He certainly lacked prowess with a revolver, for some time in 1863 or 1864 he lost the tip of his middle finger while cleaning a revolver. He hollered that that was the "dodd-dingus pistol" he had ever seen, and a nickname was born. From then on, friends would call him "Dingus."[20]

In the summer of 1863, Quantrill led his men on a raid that would go down in infamy. Frank James rode with him. So did Cole Younger. By most accounts, Jesse James didn't. On August 21, Quantrill's men sacked Lawrence, Kansas, with one purpose: kill. They did it with reckless abandon, butchering and burning, leaving the city in ashes with at least 150 men and boys — estimates ran as high as 200 — to be buried.[21]

By the fall of 1863 or spring of 1864, sixteen-year-old Jesse James had joined the guerrillas. Most of the guerrillas were young. "If you ever want to pick a company to do desperate work," Frank later said, "select young men from 17 to 21 years old." Murders and raids continued. Some time in August 1864, Jesse was shot in the chest in Ray County, but quickly recovered, so he was able to ride with Bloody Bill Anderson into Centralia on September 27, 1864. After looting the town, Anderson's men forced a train to stop, made the passengers disembark, and found twenty-five unarmed Federal soldiers, most on furlough. They murdered twenty-four before leaving. When a Union force arrived that afternoon, the commander left some men to restore order, and led the remaining after the bushwhackers. Ambushed by Anderson's men, the Federals suffered extensive losses, including 116 killed.[22]

But time was running out for the Confederacy and the Missouri guerrillas. On October 26, 1864, Anderson was killed by Federal forces. His body was taken to Richmond, Missouri, where a photograph was taken of the corpse and it was beheaded. The head was fastened to a telegraph pole, the rest of the body dragged through the streets.[23]

Quantrill led the remnants of his command, including Frank James, out of Missouri and into Kentucky, where he was fatally wounded by Union troops. He died on June 6 in Louisville. Frank James surrendered on July 26, but was soon paroled and allowed to return home.[24]

Jesse's attempt at surrender did not go as smoothly.

In May 1865, Jesse was shot in the lung while apparently — or so he said — trying to surrender to Federal authorities in Lexington, Missouri. He was carried to a hotel room, where he weakly took the oath of allegiance to the Union. Eventually, he was moved to Rulo, Nebraska, where the Samuel family was living in exile after General Orders No. 11. Sinking closer to death, Jesse is said to have told his mother, "Ma, I don't want to be buried

In 1863, Missouri guerrillas led by William Clarke Quantrill left Lawrence, Kansas, in ruins, as illustrated in *Harper's Weekly*. Frank James and Cole Younger took part in the raid. Jesse James, however, wasn't there (Library of Congress).

Jesse James as a Confederate guerrilla during the Civil War (Library of Congress).

here in a Northern state," and so was taken to a boarding house owned by his uncle, John Mimms, in Harlem (present-day North Kansas City). There, his first cousin, Zerelda, who was called Zee, helped nurse him back to health.[25]

* * *

The war was over, but peace had not settled over Missouri. The new state constitution of 1865 did not grant amnesty to Confederate veterans, especially guerrillas, and even prohibited former Southern sympathizers from voting, holding any office or holding a professional position, even in church. Ex-Confederates found themselves persecuted, while carpetbaggers thrived.[26]

That was the situation when ten to thirteen men rode into Liberty, Missouri, on February 13, 1866.

* * *

"Although the James boys participated in hundreds of robberies," the *Los Angeles Times* reported, "it is now generally believed that there were also hundreds of robberies charged up to them of which they were innocent."[27]

Even today, historians are divided over what crimes were really committed by Jesse and Frank James, Cole Younger, and company. For the first few years after the war, the James brothers lived at their mother's Clay County home, but they obviously weren't gentleman farmers.[28]

On October 30, 1866, four men robbed the Alexander Mitchell and Company bank in Lexington, Missouri. An attempt by six men to rob a Savannah, Missouri, bank on March 2, 1867, failed when the banker refused to give the bandits the key to the vault. A dozen men robbed the Hughes and Wasson Bank in Richmond, Missouri, on May 22, 1867, and left three citizens, including the mayor, dead. On March 20, 1868, five men robbed the Nimrod Long and Company bank in Russellville, Kentucky.[29]

Henrietta Younger poses with her brothers Bob, Jim and Cole while the Younger brothers were incarcerated at the Minnesota state penitentiary in Stillwater (Library of Congress).

The James brothers weren't linked to any holdups until the Daviess County Savings Bank in Gallatin, Missouri, was robbed on December 7, 1869. The cashier, Captain John Sheets, was cold-bloodedly murdered, shot in the face and heart; he had apparently been mistaken for Major Samuel P. Cox, one of the men who had killed Bloody Bill Anderson during the war. A lawyer in the bank at the time tried to run and was shot in the arm, but managed to get out, yelling, "Captain Sheets has been killed!" The bandits grabbed $700 and raced outside, where some townsmen fired on them. As one of the robbers tried to mount his horse, his hand was caught in the reins and/or a foot got hung in the stirrup, and he was dragged a ways. He managed to free himself and leapt onto the back of his partner's horse, and the two men escaped, heading toward Clay County.[30]

They had left behind a sorrel mare. That horse was soon traced to Jesse James, and one of the bandits was said to have resembled Frank James. A $3,000 reward was offered for their capture. The law was finally after the James boys.[31]

The brothers didn't slow down. On June 3, 1871, four men — presumed to be Frank and Jesse James, Cole Younger and Clell Miller — robbed the Obobock Brothers' Bank in Corydon, Iowa. As the outlaws left town, legend has it, Jesse interrupted a speech being given by Henry Clay Dean, and told them their bank had just been robbed. Miller was later arrested and tried, but acquitted after several Missourians testified that he was elsewhere on the day of the robbery.[32]

After Miller's acquittal, a letter to the editor from Jesse James appeared in the *Kansas City Times*. He proclaimed his innocence, and concluded: "If times ever get so in Missouri that I can get an impartial trial, I will voluntarily go to Clay County and stand my trial. But I am satisfied that if I was disarmed at present, that those brave Radical heroes in Missouri would try to mob me."[33]

On April 29, 1872, the Bank of Columbia, Kentucky, was robbed by four or five men, who killed the cashier. Five months later, the outlaws tried something new by robbing — in broad daylight — the box office of the Kansas City fair. The latter crime prompted *Kansas City Times* journalist John Newman Edwards, a former adjutant to Confederate General Jo Shelby, to write an editorial titled "The Chivalry of Crime," in which he praised the outlaws for their daring. "What they did we condemn. But the way they did it we cannot help admiring."[34]

A bank robbery in Ste. Genevieve, Missouri, followed on May 27, 1873, and two months later outlaws derailed and robbed a Chicago, Rock Island and Pacific train near Adair, Iowa. The engineer was killed in the wreck. It wasn't the first train robbery committed in the United States, but it was believed to have been the James-Younger Gang's first train heist.[35]

Eighteen seventy-four proved to be a big year for Frank and Jesse. A stagecoach was robbed near Hot Springs, Arkansas, in January, a train was robbed at Gads Hill, Missouri, an undercover Pinkerton agent arrived at the Samuel farm and was promptly murdered, and another train was robbed in Muncie, Kansas. At Gads Hill, one of the robbers wrote in the messenger's receipt book, "Robbed at Gad's Hill." They were also accused of robbing two stagecoaches near Lexington, Missouri, a bank in Corinth, Mississippi, and another stagecoach near Austin, Texas. All of which might have been pretty hard for the brothers to do, especially since they both got married, Jesse to Zee Mimms on April 23 and Frank to Anna Reynolds Ralston, daughter of a respected citizen of Independence, Missouri, on June 6.[36]

The law struck back, with tragic results. On the night of January 25, 1875, Pinkerton detectives made their way to the Samuel farm. What happened next remains open to debate. Shortly after midnight, believing the James brothers were inside, detectives tossed a "flaming fireball" into the house. Whether it was a bomb or something less lethal, Dr. Samuel shoveled it into the fireplace, and it promptly exploded. The end result left Frank and Jesse's half-brother, Archie, dead, and Zerelda Samuel without part of her right arm.[37]

Retaliation was swift and severe. In April, Daniel Askew, a neighbor believed to have assisted the Pinkertons, was killed with three bullets to the head.[38]

By 1875, Jesse and Zee were living around Nashville, Tennessee, where Zee gave birth to a son, Jesse Edwards James, on August 31. Within a week, the Bank of Huntington, West Virginia, was robbed, and again the James-Younger Gang was suspected.[39]

On July 7, 1876, a train was robbed at Rocky Cut, Missouri, but here the gang blundered badly. One of the recruits for the job was an inexperienced outlaw named Hobbs Kerry, who was soon arrested. Kerry not only admitted to taking part in the robbery, he named his accomplices: Jesse and Frank James, Cole and Bob Younger, Bill Chadwell and Charlie Pitts.[40]

That job was possibly arranged to fund the boys' next outing, and the increased heat after Kerry's confession might have sent Jesse and Frank, Cole, Bob and Jim Younger, Chadwell (aka Bill Stiles), Pitts (aka Sam Wells) and Clell Miller north.[41]

On September 7, 1876, the James-Younger Gang made a grievous error when the outlaws tried to rob the First National Bank of Northfield, Minnesota. Bank employee Joseph Heywood was killed, and another resident, Nicholas Gustafson, was mortally wounded in the streets, but the gang made its getaway with less than thirty dollars, and left two of its members on the street dead: Clell Miller and Chadwell/Stiles, the latter a native of Minnesota who knew the area and was supposed to have helped the boys escape.[42]

Minnesotans quickly organized the largest manhunt in state history. The James brothers managed to escape, but on September 21, 1876, a posse surrounded the Youngers and Pitts-Wells at Hanska Slough, near Madelia, Minnesota. The gunfight that followed left the Youngers badly wounded, and Pitts-Wells dead. The Younger brothers pleaded guilty to

For years, Northfield has held a popular, and historically accurate, weekend reenactment on or near the anniversary of the September 7, 1876, crime. "Defeat of Jesse James Days" brings in thousands of tourists each year.

first-degree murder to avoid a possible death sentence, and were sentenced to life. Bob died in prison in 1889, and Cole and Jim were paroled in 1901.[43]

Jesse reorganized a gang, but it wasn't the same. A train was robbed in Glendale, Missouri, on October 8, 1879, and a stagecoach was held up near Mammoth Cave, Kentucky, on September 3, 1880. A federal paymaster was robbed near Muscle Shoals, Alabama, on March 11, 1881, and another train was robbed in Winston, Missouri. In the latter robbery, the conductor, William Westfall, and a passenger were killed.[44]

On September 7, 1881, the gang committed its last known crime when Jesse James and company robbed a train at Blue Cut, Missouri. But the James Gang was no longer invincible. On July 28, 1881, Governor Thomas Crittenden had announced a $10,000 reward for each of the James brothers, half upon capture, the rest on conviction, and $5,000 for other gang members involved in the Glendale and Winston robberies. Bill Ryan was sentenced to twenty-five years for taking part in

Top: Brutally murdered during the James-Younger Gang's failed bank robbery attempt, Joseph Lee Heywood became a martyr in Northfield, Minnesota, and across the nation (Library of Congress). *Above:* In 1881, members of the James Gang boarded a train at this depot in Winston, Missouri, then robbed the train and killed two men on board.

the Glendale train robbery, his conviction secured primarily by the testimony of Tucker Bassham, who had once ridden with the outlaws.[45]

On January 13, 1882, Bob Ford, whose brother Charles had been recruited into the James Gang, met secretly with Governor Crittenden. Bob Ford later testified that Crittenden promised him not only a pardon, but $10,000 apiece for bringing in Frank and Jesse — dead or alive.[46]

Gang member Dick Liddil surrendered to authorities on January 24. On February 11, Clarence Hite was arrested in Kentucky; he was taken to Missouri where he pleaded guilty

Packed in a coffin filled with ice, the body of Jesse James was displayed at St. Joseph inside Sidenfaden's Funeral Parlor (Library of Congress).

to helping rob the Winston train. Hite was sentenced to twenty-five years.[47]

By then, Jesse James was living with Zee and their two children — daughter Mary Susan had been born in Nashville in 1879 — in St. Joseph, Missouri. The Ford brothers were staying with them, and Jesse planned to rob a bank in Platte City, Missouri. He had even given Bob Ford a revolver, one that Jesse had apparently taken off of gang member Ed Miller's body after murdering him.[48]

The Fords said they feared Jesse knew they had been working with law enforcement officers, and that he planned to murder them on the road — the same way Jesse had apparently killed Miller.[49]

On April 3, 1882, the Jameses and Fords ate breakfast, then Jesse and the Fords fed and groomed the horses in the stable outside the house. Returning inside, Jesse complained of being warm and removed his coat, then took off his gunbelt — saying passersby might see it and become suspicious. Jesse noticed a picture or sampler on the wall that needed

A reconstruction of Jesse's original grave marker, at the family farm outside of Kearney, Missouri. Other replicas appeared in movies.

straightening and/or dusting. He stepped up on a chair to attend to it, his back to the Ford brothers.[50]

Bob Ford drew his pistol and put a bullet in Jesse's head. The outlaw fell dead at age thirty-four.

CHAPTER TWO

Jesse James in Pop Culture, 1875–1903

Shortly after Jesse's death, journalist John Newman Edwards, longtime supporter of the James and Younger brothers, negotiated with Governor Crittenden for Frank's surrender. On October 5, Edwards introduced Frank to the governor, and the outlaw handed him his gunbelt, saying, "Governor Crittenden, I want to hand over to you that which no living man except myself has been permitted to touch since 1861, and to say that I am your prisoner." That was impossible, however, since the revolver was a model 1875 Remington.[1]

Frank was brought to trial in Gallatin, Missouri, in 1883 for the Winston train robbery. The trial of the century was a media sensation, with six attorneys heading the state's prosecution, and eight defending Frank James. Perhaps fittingly, the trial was held in an opera house. On September 6, after less than four hours of deliberation, the jury brought in a verdict of not guilty. The following year, Frank was tried in Huntsville, Alabama, for the

This is the jury that found Frank James not guilty of the Winston train robbery in a sensational trial held in Gallatin, Missouri, in 1883 (Library of Congress).

Dime novels about Jesse James became popular shortly after his death. Pictured is one by William Ward, who wrote many cheap books about outlaws around the turn of the 20th century.

Muscle Shoals robbery, and again acquitted. In 1885, the state of Missouri dropped its last case against Frank, who became a free man. He was never tried for the Northfield robbery.[2]

By then, the James brothers were big news.

Shortly after Jesse's death, a song, perhaps written by a minstrel named Billy Gashade, became popular. Its chorus went:

> Jesse had a wife to mourn for his life,
> Three children, they were brave,
> But that dirty little coward that shot Mr. Howard
> Has laid Jesse James in his grave.[3]

Even before Jesse's death, books had been published about him. Edwards's *Noted Guerrillas, or the Warfare of the Border* came out in 1877, two years after Augustus C. Appler's *The Guerrillas of the West; or the Life, Character, and Daring Exploits of the Younger Brothers*. In 1881, the Five Cent Wide Awake Library began publishing stories about the James gang. After Jesse's death, books — often sporting titles like *Jesse James, the Midnight Horseman; or, The Silent Rider of the Ozarks*; and *The James Boys and The Mad Sheriff; or The Midnight Run of '99* — became popular; William F. "Buffalo Bill" Cody was most likely the only actual person who appeared as a hero in more dime novels than Jesse James.[4]

Bob and Charlie Ford appeared in a traveling play, *How I Killed Jesse James*. Zee James and Zerelda Samuel were alleged to have countered by contracting with Frank Triplett for his book *The Life, Times and Treacherous Death of Jesse James*.[5]

By the 1890s, plays about Jesse James, including W.I. Swain's "Western spectacular"

Bob and Charlie Ford weren't the only ones cashing in on Jesse James on stage. Many plays were produced, including W.I. Swain's *Jesse James* (Library of Congress).

Jesse James, were commonplace, and highly fictitious.[6] Even Cole Younger, paroled in 1901, and Frank James got in on the act. In 1903, they toured the country in The Great Cole Younger & Frank James Historical Wild West show.[7]

Few books and plays had any semblance to history. As Frank said: "If I admitted that these stories were true, people would say: 'There is the greatest scoundrel unhung!' And if I denied 'em, they'd say: 'There's the greatest liar on earth!' So I just say nothing."[8]

The same year that Frank and Cole Younger launched their Wild West exhibition, Pennsylvania-born Edwin Stanton Porter, fledgling filmmaker in the fledgling film industry, shot a Western-set motion picture, *The Great Train Robbery*, in New Jersey. Response to the movie was so tremendous that nickelodeons began springing up across the nation.[9] "From then on," film historians George N. Fenin and William K. Everson wrote, "the Western was a genre of the American cinema."[10]

It wouldn't take long before filmmakers decided to spotlight Jesse James.

CHAPTER THREE

The Silent Era, 1908–1927

The number of silent movies about Jesse James will likely never be known. In "A Jesse James Filmography" in his book *Frank and Jesse James: The Story Behind the Legend*, the late historian Ted P. Yeatman lists five — *The James Boys of Missouri* (1908), *Jesse James* (1911), *Jesse James Under the Black Flag* (1921), *Jesse James as the Outlaw* (1921) and *Jesse James* (1927)[1] — but research reveals others.

The problem for film historians is that moviemaking was in its infancy, records are practically nonexistent, and titles weren't consistent from one theater to another.

Essanay, which made the first known Jesse James movie — *The James Boys in Missouri* (1908) — "ground out films week by week like sausages," Chicago historian Arnie Bernstein says. "In a sense, they were creating disposable entertainments and Westerns were a staple. Titles were fluid with some films, i.e. *The Life of Jesse James* could have been *The James Boys [in] Missouri*. However, if the studio latched onto something that audiences liked, they would produce more films along the same line, hence these could be two different movies."[2]

All of Jesse's silent movies — even Paramount's 1927 epic starring the great Fred Thomson — are presumed lost. A 1930 version of *Jesse James Under the Black Flag*, which re-edited two 1921 movies starring Jesse's son, Jesse Edwards James (*Jesse James Under the Black Flag* and *Jesse James as the Outlaw*), can be found on video today.

Some silent movies garnered publicity, although in the early years, that publicity was often generated by controversy surrounding censorship and the glorification of outlaws. For many other titles, however, all we have are newspaper advertisements. Here are the movies I found, although, obviously, there could be many others:

The James Boys in Missouri
(Essanay, April 1908, 18 minutes)

CREDITS: *Director-Producer-Screenplay:* G.M. Anderson.
CAST: Harry McCabe.

Synopsis

Even legendary director Budd Boetticher of *The Tall T* and *Ride Lonesome* fame couldn't make a Western this tight. Jesse James joins Quantrill's guerrillas during the Civil War, leads his gang in the Chicago and Alton Railroad robbery at Glendale, Missouri, and gets shot down by that dirty little coward Bob Ford — all in one reel![3]

Most likely the first motion picture to depict Jesse James, it was sympathetic to the outlaws. "When the actor playing Frank James was shown surrendering to the actor playing the Governor of Kansas, the whole scene was handled with the ceremony and dignity of Lee's surrender to Grant at Appamattox [sic]."[4]

This was Essanay's first Western[5]; not much is known about it. The only cast member cited is Harry McCabe, and who he played is anyone's guess.[6]

It may, or may not, have also been shown under the titles *The Life of Jesse James* and *The Life and Death of Jesse James*. The Trenton (New Jersey) *Evening Times* advertised the screening of *The Life and Death of Jesse James*, "one of the most remarkable motion pictures ever made," in its April 7, 1908, editions,[7] while *The James Boys in Missouri* ("This latest sensation in moving pictures") was playing in Frederick, Maryland, on April 16, 1908.[8] In Elyria, Ohio, a newspaper advertisement promoted *The Jesse James Bandits* "and their thrilling adventures of robbers told in special film."[9]

A circa–1910 herald for *The Life of Jesse James* calls the movie "A Thrilling Photodrama of the World's Most Famous Outlaw, Portraying His Actual Adventures."[10]

Were they the same movie shown under different titles, or different movies altogether?

Essanay film historian David Kiehn notes that the film's official title was *The James Boys in Missouri*.[11]

It may, or may not, have been adapted or at least inspired by a successful play, George

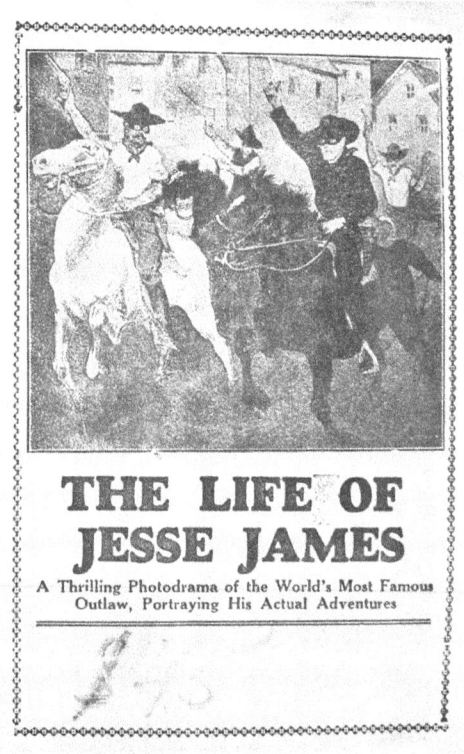

A herald, circa 1910, describes one of many forgotten silent movies about Jesse James. Note the Lone Ranger–Zorro-style masks the bandits wear in the drawing on the right—years before the Lone Ranger and Zorro were created.

The Life of Jesse James

The life and daring deeds of this noted outlaw have a wonderful fascination. The highway robber, road agent or bank plunderer who boldly takes his life in his hands and makes a dash after other people's money at once finds himself a hero.

Jesse James was at large for nearly 20 years, and during that time he and his band of outlaws ranged over a territory embracing half the United States, and for sheer bravery his exploits have never been approached by any one.

Jesse James and his brother Frank were no exception to the rule, and while they were continually hunted by the minions of the law, there were thousands of people who were in sympathy with them and followed their sensational career with the utmost interest, and many gave them assistance which greatly helped them in evading the meshes of the law for so long a period. The lives of these men need no romantic or exaggerated shading to make the narrative remarkable. Their deeds are as prominent in the annals of outlawry as their names are familiar to the people of America.

An authentic history of the most daring and deadly band of outlaws that ever infested the west. No fiction has ever surpassed their exploits and the train robberies conceived and carried out by the James Brothers were startling in their boldness and orginality of method. Their picturesque style of daring was the talk of two continents and their dazzling success in looting vast fortunes made them heroes in the eyes of a vast multitude.

The other side of the herald apparently includes, at left, a still from the motion picture.

Klimpt and Frank A. P. Gazzolo's *The James Boys in Missouri* in which Klimpt played Jesse and "a tall actor with a nasal twang" played Frank.[12] That play—"a 'blood-and-thunder' production having little to do with factual history"[13]—evoked the ire of Frank James when the troupe brought the play to Kansas City in 1902. Frank went through legal channels to stop the performances.

"The dad-binged play glorifies these outlaws and makes heroes of them," Frank told the *Kansas City Star*. "That's the main thing I object to. It's injurious to the youth of the country. It's positively harmful. I am told the Gilles Theater was packed to the doors last night, and that most of those there were young men to see train robbers and outlaws glorified."[14]

The court granted an injunction, but required James to furnish a $4,000 bond in case the troupe appealed and the court's verdict was reversed. Frank wasn't able to meet the court's terms, and the play went on, "but Frank thought the court had vindicated his position."[15]

Following legal advice, Klimpt changed the play's title to *The Blue Cut Train Robbery* and renamed the James brothers Edward and Frank Gorman. Outside of Jesse James country, however, the play reverted to its original title and names, and "played with great success for several seasons."[16]

Legal proceedings would give both film and play much in common: While not much may be known about the actual film, *The James Boys in Missouri* would play a major role in the debate over film censorship when the movie was banned in several U.S. cities, a ban upheld by the higher courts.

The History

Hal Erickson notes in *All Movie Guide* that the film provided "an accurate account of the life and times of these two reprobates and their confederates."[17] Silent film historian Larry Langman agrees, saying that the film "adheres fairly closely to historical incidents."[18] In addition to Jesse's time with Quantrill, the Glendale robbery, the Ford brothers, and Frank's surrender, the movie also depicted the gang's holdup of the Kansas City fair.[19]

If *The James Boys in Missouri* and *The Life of Jesse James* were indeed the same film, then it billed itself as "An authentic history of the most daring and deadly band of outlaws that ever infested the west" that followed "his exploits from Boyhood to His Tragic Death at the Hands of the Traitor, Bob Ford."[20]

Erickson also says the robbery scenes (banks and trains) "were assembled with considerable skill."[21] A newspaper review, reprinted in *Moving Picture World,* called the movie "a thriller from beginning to end and cannot fail to please."[22]

One wonders whether Frank James ever saw the movie. *The James Boys in Missouri* played in Kansas City, prompting the Board of Public Welfare to denounce it. (The board also criticized *Chinatown at Midnight* for its scenes of opium dens and gang violence, and *The White Slave Traffic*, which depicted "country girls being sold into prostitution.") The board went on to propose a censorship law, which Kansas City adopted in 1914. Ordinance No. 7398 banned 13 movies and cut another 170 in its first year.[23]

The Players

Gilbert M. "Broncho Billy" Anderson was born Max Aaronson on March 21, 1880 or 1882, in Little Rock, Arkansas, and spent his first eight years in Pine Bluff, Arkansas. Before becoming a celebrity — the movies' first Western star — he worked behind the camera. He got his taste for moviemaking when he worked on Edwin S. Porter's groundbreaking 1903 picture *The Great Train Robbery*. Afterward, he made some movies for William Selig's Chicago studio, Selig Polyscope. Anderson wrote and directed movies, and in 1907 he partnered with George K. Spoor, "a budding film producer,"[24] to form Essanay Studios — taking the name from the initials of their surnames — in Chicago, Illinois.[25]

Essanay and Selig "built the foundation for an industry that didn't exist before and changed the world," Kiehn says, turning movies into a new art form.[26] Anderson was turning out two films a month in 1907, each running from five to seventeen minutes (a one-reeler). Anderson primarily made comedies — "slapstick was the stock in trade"[27] — which were popular with the new moviegoing public. When Essanay hired E. Lawrence Lee to direct dramas at the end of 1907, Anderson decided to film an ambitious drama himself, this one chronicling the James boys and using Gilbert P. Hamilton as photographer.[28]

Although some sources say the movie could have been partially filmed in Missouri,[29] most put locations at Chicago's Rogers and/or Riverview parks and in Scottdale, Michigan.[30] "Occasionally, Anderson would take a camera crew and his actors down to Starved Rock [a state park in north central Illinois] to film in the rugged landscape," Bernstein notes. "As Selig had learned, audiences were growing more sophisticated about the movies, and authentic backgrounds became a necessity."[31]

Locations weren't the only things authentic. Anderson hired Barney Pierson, owner and manager of Idaho Bill's Cheyenne Frontier Exposition, and filmed performances of the

Wild West show in Scottdale and at Riverview Park.[32] Such authenticity helped make *The James Boys in Missouri*, which was released on April 8, 1908,[33] a hit. But then came controversy.

In November 1907, Chicago approved an ordinance that required permits for any movie before it could be shown in a public place, and the city police had the right to refuse a permit for any film it deemed "immoral" or "obscene."[34] The police refused permits for *The James Boys in Missouri* and another Western, the Kalem Company's *Night Riders*, effectively banning their showing in Chicago. Jake Block and five other owners of "five-and-ten-cent theaters" challenged the law in court. Judge Farlin Q. Ball dismissed the complaint, and Block and his lawyers appealed to the state Supreme Court.[35]

In 1909, *Block v. Chicago* lawyers representing Block argued that the movies were "'reproductions of parts' of plays about the same subject matter that were being staged in Chicago theaters" (giving credence to the theory the movie was based on the play *The James Boys in Missouri*) and that "the acts of criminality depicted in these films were part of the 'American historical experience'...."[36] Also, since the ban was issued before the films could be shown, Block had been deprived "of his property without due process."[37]

The court disagreed. Chief Justice James H. Cartwright held the city law just. It sought "to secure decency and morality in the moving picture business, and that purpose falls within the police power. It is designed as a precautionary measure to prevent exhibitions criminal in their nature and forbidden by the laws."[38] He also noted that those movies "necessarily portray depictions of crime, and pictures of the 'Night Riders' can represent nothing but malicious mischief, arson and murder."[39]

The James Boys in Missouri also sparked outrage from some viewers. *Moving Picture News* reported in 1911 that during a showing, women in the audience said, "I can't stand this any longer!" and "This is too much for me." "Said our informant: 'You couldn't imagine anything very much worse; from murdering the landlord up to wrecking a train, it was all there....'"[40]

Other areas followed Chicago's lead and passed laws implementing film censorship. The Kansas state Legislature passed a bill in 1913, but to fund the Board of Censorship, the law required companies to pay two dollars for each reel inspected. That led Clifton, Kansas, theater operator I.C. Rusher to complain to Governor George H. Hodges, "You can no doubt see at a glance the injustice of this law which if enforced will close every theatre in the small towns of Kansas. I know that there are some Films being shown which ought not to be but this law puts the good pictures out of business as well as the bad. I have several times turned down chances to run such subjects as *The James Boys in Missouri* and would like to see them prohibited but the new law eliminates both good and bad together."[41]

In Belleville, Kansas, the local newspaper editorialized that "vulgar and sensational pictures [should] not be permitted to be put upon the canvass of this community for young minds to witness and absorb lessons from."[42]

Six years after the Illinois high court ruled film censorship legal, the U.S. Supreme Court proclaimed film censorship constitutional. In its 1915 ruling on *Mutual Film Corp. v. Industrial Commission of Ohio,* the court "cited *Block* as having sustained the use of the police power to censor films. Most importantly, the Court determined that the First Amendment did not protect motion pictures because they were 'mere representations of events, of ideas and sentiments published and known, vivid, useful and entertaining no doubt' but also 'capable of evil, having power for it, the greater because of their attractiveness and manner of exhibition.'"[43]

Analysis

The James Boys in Missouri found its place in history not only for being the first known movie depicting the outlaws, but for its impact on allowing film censorship. It's important to note, however, that Chicago theater owner Jake Block's argument eventually won over the courts and the viewing public. "All of Block's constitutional arguments would probably prevail today," historians Edward De Grazia and Roger K. Newman point out in *Banned Films*. "In three cases decided in the 1950s [regarding 1950's *La Ronde*, 1951's *M*, and 1953's *The Moon Is Blue*] the U.S. Supreme Court ruled "that the exhibition of a movie may not be prevented because it is immoral, inasmuch as this term, like some others (not including 'obscene'), is too vague and uncertain a standard for censorship...."[44]

Despite the controversy, however, Anderson's first Western that he directed was a success in 1908.

Essanay immediately followed *The James Boys in Missouri* with *The Younger Brothers*, this one directed by Lee, filmed in Berrien Springs, Michigan, and including actors Harry Clifton, Ben Turpin and Jack Jesperson. Released on June 3, 1908, it likewise ran into problems with censors. Lancaster, Pennsylvania, and other cities banned it. But those productions had whet Anderson's appetite for the Western.[45]

Eventually, hampered by the Upper Midwest winters, Anderson began filming in Colorado—"to film against a bona fide cowboy background"[46]—and later in California, where Anderson built a second studio in Niles.

"But it wouldn't be until 1909 that Anderson started making westerns on a more regular basis, eventually acting as well as directing and becoming known worldwide as Broncho Billy Anderson beginning in 1910."[47]

* * *

Moving Picture World (October 1908): "One can have but little admiration for the pains and time spent in making such films in the first place ... but one can wish heartily that the effort had produced something elevating, or at least harmless, instead of the seeming realism of bloodshed, crime and brutality."[48]

Jesse James (1911) and Other Silents
Credits, Cast, Release Dates and Running Times Unknown

Although film historians George N. Fenin and William K. Everson[49] and Jesse James biographer Ted P. Yeatman cite a 1911 movie titled *Jesse James* (no star, no production company listed), I cannot quite document this movie. Officials at the Jesse James Farm & Museum in Kearney, Missouri,[50] were not familiar with it, and the title does not show up on the Internet Movie Database (www.imdb.com) or in many silent movie reference books.

Newspaper articles and advertisements do mention Jesse James movies, but it's unclear if these are one movie shown under different titles or different films.

On November 22, 1911, the Stevens Point, Wisconsin, paper announced the showing of *Life of the James Boys in Missouri*. "The picture is the greatest ever acted for a moving picture company and is playing to packed houses all over the country."[51]

The movie was reportedly 3,000 feet with 130 scenes, which would translate into roughly a three-reeler of 30 minutes in length — almost twice as long as Essanay's *The James Boys in Missouri*.[52] "Many of the scenes are taken on the identical spot where the original happened," the Stevens Point *Gazette* reported, "and the picture was made at a great cost."[53]

In Xenia, Ohio, the *Daily Gazette* advertised a special feature, *The Historical Life of Jesse James,* noting, "No children will be admitted unless accompanied by parents."[54]

The *Daily News* of Lebanon, Pennsylvania, reported in its November 14, 1911, editions that a movie about Jesse James would be shown at the Academy of Music. "Jesse and his brother are pictured in thrilling scenes, which make the Jesse James novel of yore look tame by comparison."[55]

Theater management was so confident of business that they planned to show the movie, which had employed 250 people and used 50 horses during production, afternoons and evenings.[56] In Racine, Wisconsin, Palace Theatre manager A.G. Grover took out a notice in the local newspaper:

> To the People:
>
> There has been some criticism with reference to a set of Moving Pictures displayed at the Palace Theatre. These pictures show Jesse James and his wild life, ending with his reform and making a good citizen. There is nothing objectionable to the films and they are exhibited at other picture houses. Crowds who attended the show were satisfied. The pictures ended yesterday."[57]

And in Belleville, Kansas, the local paper said, "The Jesse James moving pictures have been suppressed in several Kansas towns by the local authorities, acting under a Kansas statute, or city ordinance. This picture was recently exhibited in Belleville and drew the largest houses of any film in the history of the picture shows of this city."[58]

That falls in line with the comment made by Fenin and Everson in *The Western: From Silents to the Seventies*: "Some advertising for a Western plugging *Jesse James* (1911) were heavily censured...."[59]

Life and Adventure of the James Boys in Missouri (1914)

Credits, Cast, Release Date and Running Time Unknown

In the September 4, 1914, edition of *The Daily News* of Frederick, Maryland, an advertisement appeared for *Life and Adventure of the James Boys in Missouri*, a five-reel feature told in three parts.[60]

At five reels, this could not possibly be the same film as Essanay's *The James Boys in Missouri*, a 1908 movie that ran only eighteen minutes. At the Marvel Theater ads described the movie as "Not a demonstration of crime, but a review of historical facts."[61] The advertisement also proclaim that it was "Positively the only picture in which Frank James personally appears."[62]

Could Frank James have appeared in a movie, or was this a case of shameless false advertisement? Western historian Nancy Samuelson dismisses the claim as highly unlikely, pointing out Frank's age and health. He had turned down offers in the spring of 1912 to serve as a race starter in Oklahoma, citing failing health.[63]

This would not have been the first time Frank was the subject of false advertisement. In 1902, Frank had threatened legal action against a New York theater that was claiming that the former outlaw was appearing in a play there.[64]

"That's a pretty bold claim," Scott Cole, a descendant of Jesse and Frank James and a board member of the Friends of the James Farm, says of the Frederick, Maryland, theater's advertisement. "I personally have no knowledge of Frank ever appearing in a movie. I wouldn't discount the possibility, however, he did seem to be pretty cooperative with visitors to the farm who wanted a photo."[65]

A famous photo of Frank, then about seventy years old, shows him posing in front of the gate to the family farm near Kearney, Missouri. A sign on the fence post reads, "Kodaks bared."[66]

Frank did have experience as an actor, however. He started out as a doorman at a burlesque house in St. Louis from 1894 to 1901, then took minor parts in at least two traveling stock company plays, *Across the Desert* and *The Fatal Scar*, first appearing in *Across the Desert* in Zanesville, Ohio, on November 24, 1901.[67] "I do not expect to become an actor in the true sense of the word," he said. "I do not delude myself with the belief that I have any talent in that direction."[68]

In 1903, Frank joined Cole Younger in The Great Cole Younger & Frank James Historical Wild West, a touring exhibition in the style of William F. "Buffalo Bill" Cody's more famous wild west show. But the two reformed outlaws quickly grew tired of the circus life.[69]

Frank returned to the stage in 1904 in Walter Van Dyke's play *Across the Desert*. Again his role was small. Cole Younger attended a performance in Chillicothe, Missouri. In 1905, when the play was staged in Butte, Montana, Frank's life was threatened but his would-be assassin was arrested before Frank left the theater.[70] So it's not a stretch to believe that Frank could have moved to film.

"If Frank James was in this movie, I'd bet it's archival news footage of Frank," James family chronicler Eric James says.[71]

In 1907, Frank and his wife moved to a farm in Fletcher, Oklahoma, but they returned to the family farm after his mother died in 1911.[72] In November 1914, he was stricken with heart disease.[73]

James gave his last known interview to a *Collier's Weekly* reporter in 1914.[74] He talked about Pancho Villa and the revolution in Mexico, women's suffrage and his past, but did not use the opportunity to promote any movie.[75]

Impostors and false reports also make it hard to keep track of Frank during the last years of his life. The *Washington Post* reported in 1913 that Frank was dying of tuberculosis "in the wilds of the Coeur d'Alene Mountains in Idaho."[76] The newspaper also ran an article from Tacoma, Washington, in 1914, in which a man identifying himself as Frank James, seventy years old, was working as a donkey engineer in logging camps in the winter, and picking berries in the summer. The man also said he had a wife, four married children and a sixteen-year-old daughter."[77] (Frank and Anna James had only one son.[78])

On February 18, 1915, Frank died at his home of a heart attack and possible stroke. He was seventy-two.[79] No obituaries and no biographies have ever surfaced that say he ever appeared in any movie.

The Near Capture of Jesse James
(Luna Productions, 1915, Running time unknown)

CREDITS: Unknown.
CAST: Most likely Dot Farley.

The Near Capture of Jesse James was produced by Luna Productions, a branch of the Los Angeles–based Albuquerque Film Manufacturing Company (distributed through United Film Service) that was formed as a vehicle for its leading lady, comedic actress Dot Farley.[80]

Born in 1881 in Chicago, Farley, who also appeared as Dorothea Farley and Dorothy Farley, made a name for herself in Mack Sennett's Keystone comedies, but she also played in a number of Westerns, including *Romantic Redskins* (1910), *The Ranchman's Vengeance* (1911) and *Peril of the Plains* (1912). She started work with Essanay but moved on to other companies such as American, Universal, and, of course, Keystone and Luna. *Moving Picture World* called her "the charming leading woman and comedienne ... who has won her way into the hearts of thousands of motion picture enthusiasts in addition to her tremendous following of admirers built up during her long stage career which began when she was three weeks of age."[81] Jack Warner, who made a two-reeler around 1912 called *The Covered Wagon*, said she "could ride like Paul Revere."[82]

She had auburn hair, "soulful brown eyes"[83] and was distinguished "by an oversized pair of front teeth."[84] Farley was also an accomplished scenario writer who would have credits for more than 200 movies by 1919; in 1915 she was supplying most of the scripts for Luna.[85] Therefore, it's reasonable to assume that Farley wrote the scenario for *The Near Capture of Jesse James*, and, since her Albuquerque Film shorts for 1915 were comedies, it's also a good guess that, like 1914's *Soul Mates*, *The Near Capture of Jesse James* was a humorous story. Still, Albuquerque Film and Farley did try dramas; Farley earned a writing and acting credit for 1914's *The Lust of the Red Man*. But the *Near Capture* of the title makes one believe this Western was comedic in tone.

Luna released at least ten Farley-starring shorts during the first half of 1915, but the Albuquerque Film Manufacturing Company filed for bankruptcy later that year, claiming fifty-three cents cash on hand.[86] The last Albuquerque Film–Dot Farley movie on www.imdb.com is *Aunt Matilda Outwitted*, released June 5, 1915. Farley's next movie was *Sammy's Scandalous Schemes*, released that December by Vogue Motion Picture Company, which was formed in October 1915 as a production replacement for Mutual Film Corporation's Keystone comedies.[87]

Farley continued acting through the silent era (she had a small role in Cecil B. DeMille's 1927 epic *King of Kings*) and into the 1940s, finishing her career in a series of RKO comedy shorts in which she played Edgar Kennedy's mother-in-law: *Heart Burn* (1942), *Radio Rampage* (1944), *Trouble or Nothing* (1946), *Television Turmoil* (1947) and *How to Clean House* (1948). "Kennedy's death in 1948 marked the end of the long-running series and prompted Farley's retirement."[88] She had appeared in more than 300 movies. She died on May 2, 1971, in South Pasadena, California.

And *The Near Capture of Jesse James*? Presumed lost, it remains an obscure footnote to the Jesse James filmography.

Jesse James Under the Black Flag

(Mesco Pictures, March 1921, Running time unknown)

CREDITS: *Director-Screenplay:* Franklin B. Coates.
CAST: Jesse Edwards James, billed as Jesse James Jr. (Himself/Jesse James Sr.); Harry Hoffman (Cole Younger); Marguerite Hungerford (Zee Mimms); Diana Reed (Lucille James); Franklin B. Coates (Himself); James Neil (Robert Standing); Harry Hall (Charles William Quantrill); Sunshine Baker (Mrs. Sam Clifton); Mrs. Jesse James Jr. (Herself); J.P. McCabe (Bill Anderson); Dan Peterson (Murdock); Hortense Espey (Mrs. Bowman); Ralph Johnson (Judge Bowman); Jack Wall (Captain Andy Clements); Elmo Red Fox (Chief Red Fox).

Jesse James as the Outlaw

(Mesco Pictures, March 1921, Running time unknown)

CREDITS: *Director-Screenplay:* Franklin B. Coates.
CAST: Jesse Edwards James, billed as Jesse James Jr. (Himself/Jesse James Sr.); Diana Reed (Lucille James); Marguerite Hungerford (Zee Mimms James); James Neil (Robert Standing); Ralph Johnson (Judge Bowman); Hortense Espey (Mrs. Bowman); William Baker (Jesse's Stepfather); Mrs. Cart (Jesse's Mother); Frances Coffey (Susan, Jesse's Sister); Elmo Red Fox (Chief Red Fox)

Synopsis

Who better to play Jesse James than the outlaw's own son! Too bad Jesse Edwards James, billed here as Jesse James Jr., was a horrible actor.

Released simultaneously in the spring of 1921, *Jesse James Under the Black Flag* and its sequel, *Jesse James as the Outlaw,* offered a romanticized view of the bandit. Surviving copies of the two movies as originally released are presumed lost, but the two movies were combined and reedited into one picture, complete with sound effects, musical accompaniment, and narration that replaced most of the inter-titles, and rereleased in 1930 as *Jesse James Under the Black Flag.* That version, with a running time of 69 minutes, exists.

In the opening scene — billed as "an authentic portrayal of the life of his father" and "a play based upon facts," Jesse James Jr. is working on a book about his father with Franklin B. Coates when Robert Standing, a New York sportsman making a continental trip by airplane, is forced to land in a nearby field for gas. He meets Jesse Jr.'s daughter Lucille and, according to the narrator, "romance is in the air." Months later, after the book is published, Standing returns and proposes marriage. Jesse Jr. makes him read Coates's book, *Jesse James Under the Black Flag,* to learn the true story about Lucille's grandfather.

Viewers are then taken back in time when young Jesse James Sr., seeking revenge after Union soldiers mistreated his family, joins the band of guerrillas led by Charles William Quantrill. Jesse swears allegiance to the black flag, meaning the guerrillas will give no quarter nor ask for any, and is awarded two revolvers by Quantrill's lieutenant, Bill Anderson.

Cole Younger (Harry Hoffman), left, and Jesse James (Jesse Edwards James) try to get out of Northfield in a scene from *Jesse James as the Outlaw* (1921) (Missouri Valley Special Collections, Kansas City Public Library, Kansas City, Missouri).

Cole Younger, wearing an obscenely large cowboy hat; Jesse, disguised as a federal soldier; and Mrs. Sam Clifton, a Southern sympathizer, visit the Union headquarters to learn of the Federal Army strength, then shoot their way out. Jesse and Cole later take part in the guerrilla attack on the Union encampment in Plattsburg, Missouri, where Jesse risks his life to save a comrade.

Later, Jesse is shot from ambush and taken home to recuperate. During his recovery, the Union Army issues General Orders No. 11— which expels Southern sympathizers from their homes in Missouri's Jackson, Cass, Bates and parts of Vernon counties.[89] Cole Younger's mother and sisters are driven from their home, which is promptly burned. When Jesse learns of this, he sends his family off to safer climes while Cole swears vengeance on the Union Army. Meanwhile, back in camp, a guerrilla named Murdock is kicked out of camp for using Jesse's name, and vows revenge.

As the war draws to a close, the guerrillas find surrendering isn't so easy. Arch Clements and his men are shot upon while attempting to surrender, and later Jesse is again seriously wounded, spending two days at a water hole before a friend takes him to the home of Judge Bowman and his wife, where Jesse receives excellent medical attention. In fact, Jesse spends much of this movie in bed, recovering from wounds. He "dreams of becoming a useful citizen once again," and during a reception thrown by the Bowmans "in honor of Jesse's speedy recovery" (instead of celebrating the war's end), Jesse meets Zee Mimms, and falls in love. Alas, Jesse is "never allowed to lay down his weapons."

Around here is where *Jesse James as the Outlaw* picks up the story. Jesse returns home, taking off his guns and telling his mother that he wants only "to become a useful and law-abiding citizen." Shortly after neighbor Dan Askew warns Jesse that the Liberty bank has been robbed of $70,000 and that Jesse is suspected, the Home Guard arrives, demanding Jesse's surrender. If he gives up, the Home Guard says, he'll be hanged.

That's not much of an incentive to surrender, so Jesse buckles on his gunbelt, kisses his mother and sister goodbye, and escapes.

Meanwhile, Murdock is committing crimes — including the Chicago and Alton train robbery — using Jesse's name. There's a shootout involving Jesse on a steamboat, some palling around with friendly Indians, a rodeo (with archival footage), and a horse race involving Jesse's horse, Stonewall. Outlawed and hunted, Jesse rides across the country on Stonewall and hooks up with a posse after Murdock robs the Corydon, Iowa, bank.

Eventually, Jesse gets the drop on Murdock, who confesses to his crimes and is turned over to the sheriff. Murdock is promptly lynched. Jesse returns to Zee Mimms, assuring her — again! — that his "only wish is to be at peace with the world," and the two are married in the Mimms home. After this, Jesse lives a "quiet and uneventful life" until, perhaps upon finding "quiet" and "uneventful" too boring for a former bushwhacker, he and several gang members rob the Northfield, Minnesota, bank.

The robbery is a disaster, but Jesse and brother Frank manage to escape, leaving the Youngers to be shot down and captured, while Jesse returns to Missouri. He befriends the Ford brothers, and presents Bob Ford with a pearl-handled pistol because he is about to buy a farm where he can "live at peace."

While using a duster to straighten a picture in his St. Joseph home, the unarmed Jesse is shot from behind by Bob Ford, dying in the arms of his wife and children. "This marked the end of America's Robin Hood."

Having finished the book, Robert Standing is given permission by Jesse Jr. to wed his daughter. The last words of the book are:

> In closing, I would like to say — if I have caused you to believe that Jesse James would have lived as God so willed mankind to life — if he had been permitted — then my efforts have not been in vain — then I am fully repaid for my work — and have brought happiness to the heart of the man who bears the name Jesse James, Jr., and his children, who have their lives to live in this world which belongs to you and I.

The History

For the most part, *Jesse James Under the Black Flag* and *Jesse James as the Outlaw* are lousy movies with sorry history.

When he first signed on to play his father, Jesse E. James said, "I will try to show that my father was driven into a life of crime and banditry."[90] The result is a whitewashing of the Jesse James story. "His excuse for attempting to do something in this line was that for his daughters' sake he desired to put the actions of his father, 'Old Jesse James,' in a better light," Thomas T. Crittenden said.[91]

About the only thing missing is Jesse saving a widow from foreclosure by giving her money to pay the banker, then robbing the banker — but that scene would find its way into other Jesse James movies.

Writing and co-starring in a "historical picture,"[92] Franklin B. Coates, "a minor actor"[93] who had appeared in handful of movies (including 1920's *The Revenge of Tarzan*),[94] went on to tell *Moving Picture World*: "We are not making a 'dime novel' sort of story of the life of the outlaw. We have taken care to make the picture accurate in every way."[95]

Accurate? Coates got William Clarke Quantrill's name wrong, calling him Charles William Quantrill. He also misidentifies one of Cole Younger's outlaw brothers as Charlie Younger, instead of Bob or Jim. The Chicago & Alton train robbery at Glendale happens before the Corydon, Iowa, bank robbery, when in fact Glendale was 1879 and Corydon was 1871, and in Coates's version, those crimes were committed by a villain using Jesse James's name. Jesse's son had proclaimed when he first signed the deal, "No scene ... shall portray Jesse James in the perpetuation of any train or bank robbery."[96] That must have slipped his mind when filming the Northfield sequence.

Instead of history, audiences got, as Laura James accurately writes, "a lot of silly propaganda."[97] Yet some scenes did have authenticity. Samuel Anderson Pence recalled that during the scene involving Quantrill's attack on the Federal encampment at Plattsburg, about 100 horses were used.[98] The history of General Orders No. 11 is accurate, but the filmmakers overlooked what led the Union Army to kick non–Unionists out of their Western Missouri homes: The orders were issued four days after Quantrill's raiders massacred more than 150 men and boys in Lawrence, Kansas, and left the city in ashes.[99]

Jesse James was known for his fondness for racing horses, and he did have at least two fast mounts while living in Tennessee, but those horses were named Red Fox and Jim Malone — not Stonewall.[100]

The pursuit of the James-Younger Gang after the Northfield robbery is well-told, and when Cole Younger is informed by a gang member that they are surrounded and had better surrender, Cole says, "Here is where I die." Outlaw Charlie Pitts responds, "Cole, I can die just as game as you can." Which is pretty close to the historical record.

In her book *The Love Pirate and the Bandit's Son*, which tries to prove (unconvincingly, in my opinion, but still a good read) that Jesse Edwards James murdered a gold-digging, ruthless woman named Zeo Zoe Wilkins in 1924, author Laura James says exterior scenes weren't shot in Missouri, but in New Mexico: "The extras weren't Midwestern farmers; they were Mexicans and Chief Red Fox and a small band of Sioux."[101] Film historian Jerry Wayne Williamson also says the movie was shot on a ranch near Albuquerque, and subsequently in four Western states.[102]

Actually, many of the movie's exterior scenes were shot in Missouri. The *Kansas City Star* reported that the scenes would be filmed around Kansas City, and Samuel Anderson Pence wrote on October 22, 1920, that Quantrill's raid at Plattsburg was being filmed near Plattsburg.[103]

In November, shooting moved to Albuquerque and Santa Fe, New Mexico, for about a week. The latter was chosen, Hoffman said, because the city "furnished the right Spanish atmosphere and we feel sure we can get the Spanish characters, men and women of refinement and wealth, needed for portraying certain scenes." Hoffman said about three of the movie's eight reels were to be filmed in New Mexico.[104] Interiors were filmed in Chicago.[105]

The Players

Jesse Edwards James didn't learn that his real name wasn't "Tim Howard" until he was six years old and his father had been shot dead in the Jameses' St. Joseph home.[106] He worked part-time in a Kansas City department store at age eleven, took a job as a timekeeper at the Armour Packing Company in 1891 and opened a tobacco stand at the county courthouse in Kansas City in 1898. In 1899, he was tried for the September 23, 1898, robbery of a Missouri Pacific train near Leeds, Missouri — like father, like son? — but was acquitted; the trial led him to write a book, *Jesse James, My Father*. He closed the tobacco stand to open an ice cream soda parlor, which is where he met Stella Frances McGown. They were married on January 25, 1900. In June 1907, Jesse E. James was graduated with honors from the Kansas City School of Law.[107]

"He was a criminal defense lawyer," recalled his grandson, James R. Ross, an Orange County, California, Superior Court judge. "I kidded him when I was younger by saying, 'With the name Jesse James Jr. you didn't have any problem getting clients.' He would just smile."[108]

When Cole Younger died in 1916, Jesse began to believe that nobody could be hurt by a film version of Jesse's father's life. More importantly, Jesse had four daughters — two in high school, and another at the University of Missouri, and he could use the extra income. So when Mecca Pictures Corporation offered Jesse a five-figure, three-year contract to play his father, he accepted.[109] He was in his mid–40s, too old and too overweight to be playing a teenage guerrilla pistol-fighter, but, then again, that has never stopped moviemakers.

Mecca included Franklin B. Coates, identified in the *Kansas City Star* as vice-president and director general; Bert Hall, president; and R.W. Vail, secretary of the J.R. Crowe Coal Company, apparently secretary of the film company, too. Edwin L. Barker of Chicago was named as one of the company's directors, and L.B. Connor, an Overland Park "farmer and capitalist," was "also interested in the concern." Harry Hoffman, marshal of Jackson County, was also to be in the movie *Jesse James Under the Black Flag*, which Jesse called "a thriller that was sure to go."[110]

That relationship with Mecca didn't last long. Jesse was concerned that Hall and Connor were trying to sell stock in the movie, so Jesse and Hoffman asked a Kansas City detective to help them get released from the picture. "The selling of the stock seemed to be Jesse's chief grievance," Kansas City Police Sergeant Michael Cassidy said. "He believed the concern was to have been financed before he and Harry signed up as actors." Hall and Connor were then summoned to police headquarters, where they released Hoffman and James from their contracts.[111]

"The arrangements with Hall and Connor were unsatisfactory," Hoffman said. "Mr. James wasn't satisfied with the contract. The picture, *Jesse James Under the Black Flag*, will be produced later by a very strong organization, backed by Kansas City bankers and business men."[112]

Coates also resigned from Mecca, and Mesco Pictures was promptly formed with political leader Thomas "Boss Tom" Pendergrast as the head of the company. James hit up family, acquaintances, friends, and Kansas City leaders to invest in Kansas City–based Mesco. The city's former mayor, Thomas T. Crittenden Jr., whose father had been the Missouri governor who helped orchestrate Jesse James's death at the hands of Bob Ford, was vice-president.

Hoffman was general manager, and the company claimed $250,000 in capital, offering 2,500 shares at a par value of $100 each, though the money has been reported to have been as much as $1.4 million.[113]

Soliciting bigwigs made sense. "This was a weirdly ironic (and safe) scenario: the former capitalist enemies of Jesse James were investing their capital to help the bandit's now respectable son romanticize his father's legend in order to certify his own class acceptability to the fine families of the East."[114]

With a contract paying him $50,000, Jesse E. James rented Kansas City's Dyer mansion, renaming it Mesco City.[115] His wife Stella found the idea of her husband playing his dead father "distasteful from the beginning."[116]

Equally distasteful were the amateur actors. The movie company eventually hit Chicago's Rothacker Studios for interior shots, including the filming of Jesse James's death. Jesse E. James fainted twice while filming that scene, but the movie was completed. Then the company ran out of money.[117]

Jesse mortgaged his home. Other investors mortgaged their homes and farms. Jesse agreed to tour with the movie for four months, to be paid a $25 per diem and expenses. The two movies opened in Kansas City on March 21, 1921, and afterward Jesse hit the road, touring across the South and Midwest, giving talks and interviews to drum up publicity for a movie advertised as "Historically Correct in Every Detail." Ads read, "Secrets of his life, which have never before been revealed, are now told for the first time." Theater lobbies were decorated with displays of firearms, spurs and other items reportedly used by members of the James-Younger Gang.[118]

None of it helped. Although the movie "attracted considerable attention in western Missouri," it proved to be a commercial bomb.[119] "His picture went on the rocks," said Crittenden Jr., who partially blamed the movie's failure on Jesse's "poor" acting.[120]

Stella James called it "the last great tragedy" in her husband's life, saying it cost him "in peace of mind and eventually broken health." He returned home "heartbroken and sick," and didn't resume his law practice for more than a year. When he did, "he suffered a nervous collapse."[121]

Paid only $32,400, Jesse E. James had to call his daughter home from college, telling her there was no money for her to continue. All of his daughters were forced to find work; the Jameses had to sell their home and moved into an apartment building in 1923. Director-writer Coates never worked in the movies again.[122]

Six years passed before Jesse James rode again in the movies.

Analysis

The $250,000 budget — in an era during which a Tom Mix Western would cost around $175,000 and low-budget Westerns were being made for $5,000 to $7,000[123] — shows with dozens of horsemen, smoking guns, even that ridiculous shootout on the riverboat.

For all its flaws — and there are many — *Jesse James Under the Black Flag/Jesse James as the Outlaw* has some merit, and a few intriguing scenes. The movie is worth watching today as a gimmick — to see the outlaw's son playing his father — but even that can be hard to take.

As Laura James writes: "Though intended as a biographical epic, it became a tragedy — for the film's star."[124]

38 — Jesse James and the Movies

* * *

Kansas City Post (July 21, 1921): "[I]t is a picture of which Kansas City (and the State of Missouri) may be proud."

Jesse James

(Paramount, October 1927, 80 minutes)

CREDITS: *Director:* Lloyd Ingraham; *Executive Producers:* Jesse L. Lasky, Adolph Zukor; *Screenplay:* Frances Marion, writing as Frank M. Clifton.
CAST: Fred Thomson (Jesse James); Nora Lane (Zerelda Mimms); Montagu Love (Frederick Mimms); Mary Carr (Mrs. Zerelda Samuels); James Pierce (Frank James); Harry Woods (Bob Ford); William Courtwright (Parson Bill).

Synopsis

No one would ever mistake the real Jesse James for a Boy Scout, yet Hollywood's first major production about the outlaw starred a real-life Boy Scout, matinee idol and one of

Shake hands with the Devil: An unidentified actor greets Jesse James (Fred Thomson) in a scene from Paramount's 1927 movie *Jesse James*.

the greatest, albeit now forgotten, Western stars of the silent era. But playing Jesse James was a risky career move for Fred Thomson, and it didn't pay off.

The movie opens during Jesse's days as a guerrilla riding with Quantrill.[125] When the raiders go swimming—almost skinny-dipping—they startle a couple of women, including beautiful Zerelda Mimms (Nora Lane). Jesse and Zerelda are smitten with each other. But there's a war going on, so Jesse and his comrades ride back to Quantrill's camp. Jesse and Zerelda are destined to meet again, at the camp of General Grant, when Zerelda finds Jesse dressed as a Union sergeant. Zerelda threatens to turn Jesse in, but he escapes through a fireplace and rides off on his trusty stallion Silver King (Thomson's own screen mount), sometimes called "Stonewall" in this movie.[126] Quantrill's raiders and Union forces meet in a battle, during which Jesse saves the life of his cousin Bob Ford (Harry Woods).

When the Civil War ends, Jesse returns home to learn that the war really isn't over. His mother's right hand has been blown off by Union fanatics, and a citizen's committee headed by Frederick Mimms (Montagu Love), Zee's father, is threatening to drive the James family from their home. Not only that, Mimms might have been involved in the bombing that cost Jesse's mother her right arm.[127]

That's more than Jesse can stand, so he tries to choke Mimms to death, only to be stopped, captured, tried and convicted of attempted murder. As soon as he's convicted, though, Jesse swings across the courtroom on a chandelier, jumps through a window and onto Silver King—that horse always knows where to be!—and gallops off, now branded an outlaw.

He robs banks, stagecoaches and trains. In one spectacular scene, more than thirty outlaws board a train through car windows as the train rolls along at more than thirty miles per hour.

Meanwhile, Mimms has enlisted the help of Bob Ford to betray Jesse. Jesse and Zerelda run off together, and, during a rainstorm, Jesse robs a stagecoach. What luck! One of the passengers is Jesse's old friend Parson Bill (William Courtwright), who marries the couple.

Yet there's no happy ending for Jesse: The movie ends with his death at the hands of Bob Ford. In the original version, Jesse only imagined his death before he married Zerelda (a brief case of pre-wedding jitters, perhaps). Then he sped off with his bride in the stagecoach. Censors forced Paramount to change the ending so that viewers see Jesse dead. After all, crime cannot pay.[128]

The History

Like *Jesse James Under the Black Flag* and *Jesse James as the Outlaw*, Paramount's version was yet another whitewash. That's no surprise considering Thomson's good-guy image and the fact that Jesse E. James served as a biographer and technical adviser.[129]

When Zerelda shows up where Jesse and Quantrill's guerrillas are bathing, she is wearing a period bathing suit, complete with a parasol, and some of the wardrobe and props were authentic. "Curio collectors would gamble all they own for possession of a group of relics which arrived in Los Angeles a few days ago from Kansas City ... for use in the filming of *Jesse James*," the *Portland* (Maine) *Express* reported.[130]

Jesse actually met his future wife while recovering from a gunshot wound, and her father was far from a Union fanatic. It is highly unlikely that he ever tried to strangle

Zerelda's father, whose name was James, not Frederick. Not only that, Jesse James was neither tried nor convicted of any crime.

Yes, Ulysses S. Grant was a general in the Union Army, but he was never stationed in Missouri or Kansas during the Civil War, and Jesse's mother lost her right hand when a bomb exploded in her home in 1875 — almost ten years after the war had ended.

Born on January 31, 1862, Robert Newton Ford would have been much too young to have been fighting in the Civil War.[131] The Ford brothers are often misidentified as cousins to the Jameses, but there is no evidence that the James and Ford families were related.[132]

The train robbery sequence certainly looks exciting on the screen, yet such a scene always leaves me scratching my head. Bandits are going ride up to train cars, which could be full of armed passengers, and risk getting shot or, perhaps worse, falling underneath the wheels of a speeding train? Wouldn't it make more sense for the bandits to board the train at a regular stop, and then rob it? (That's what happened when the James Gang robbed the train near Winston, Missouri.) Maybe even derail it (as in Adair, Iowa)? Or coerce a signal operator into making the train stop (Glendale, Missouri)?

In Missouri, the state censor demanded that Paramount remove the inter-title in which Parson Bill says, "If this is justice, durned if I'll be a preacher any longer."[133] The sequence involving the almost-nude male swimmers brought about objections from censors in New York and Ohio.[134] The *New York Sun* blamed "Jesse's loving relatives" for "steering the movie along the paths of correct behavior."[135]

Thomson told the *Los Angeles Times*: "Naturally in filming the story we put in episodes to build up the dramatic structure, but never once did we violate the real character of James. We left out many instances of kindness merely because we knew they would not be believed."[136]

The Players

Fred Thomson was riding high after a string of commercial hit Westerns, mostly five- and six-reelers, for Film Booking Offices of America (FBO), including *Thundering Hoofs* (1924), the only complete Thomson Western known to survive. His movies featured as co-star a seventeen-hand dapple gray horse (the color eventually faded to almost completely white) named Silver King that Thomson had purchased from a riding academy in New York, and proved incredibly popular.

"Silver King knows his stuff as a screen actor just as well as any human actor — a great deal better than most of them," *Los Angeles Times* writer Harry Carr once observed.[137]

Likewise, Thomson had a great image: a Presbyterian minister, Boy Scout (his 1926 Western *A Regular Scout* featured a Boy Scout Troop from Los Angeles), World War I veteran (an Army chaplain), and star athlete at Occidental College and Princeton Theological Seminary. That athleticism showed in his movies, and Thomson was more often compared to Douglas Fairbanks than Tom Mix, William S. Hart or Buck Jones.[138]

When Thomson's contract with FBO expired in March 1927, he was in demand. He signed a one-year contract with Famous Players–Lasky to make four pictures at $100,000 a film, with distribution through Paramount. The first was to be *Jesse James*, and it would be big: Paramount executives thought it would gross $1.5 million.[139]

Scenario and writing duties went to Thomson's wife Frances Marion Owens (named

A promotional card from *Jesse James* (1927), this one showing Federal soldiers using bloodhounds to track down a fleeing Jesse James.

after South Carolina Revolutionary War hero Francis Marion), whose scenarios had helped Mary Pickford reach stardom. Frances went on to win Academy Awards for screenplays for *The Big House* (1930) and *The Champ* (1931) and was nominated for a third, *The Prizefighter and the Lady* (1933). Through Pickford, she had met Thomson during World War I, and they wed in 1919. Frances was twice-divorced, so the marriage forced Thomson to quit the ministry.[140] He turned to Hollywood. "The transition from pulpit to studio was not difficult," Frances said, "for in the role of preacher he had to act far more than in the role of actor."[141]

Filming of *Jesse James* began in June 1927. Lloyd Ingraham was hired to direct. Frances supplied the scenario, writing as Frank M. Clifton. Jesse Edwards James was brought in as technical adviser and biographer.[142] He also brought at least two of his daughters, hoping to land one of them, Jessie, in the movie as the outlaw's mother. That role, however, eventually went to veteran character actress Mary Carr, known as "The Mother of the Movies"[143] for her matriarchal roles. The James daughters were eventually given minor roles.[144]

Other frequent Thomson co-stars included Courtwright and Woods. The *New York Times* said, "Nora Lane is quite captivating as Zerelda, and that reliable and competent actor, Montague [sic] Love, does well as Frederick Mimms."[145]

For the role of Jesse's brother Frank, Thomson asked former FBO colleague James Pierce, an All-America center for Indiana University who had played Tarzan in FBO's *Tarzan and the Golden Lion* (1927). A distributor advised Thomson not to cast Pierce, saying "a foolish accident" involving Pierce in the Tarzan movie had "cost the studio a lot of money." Pierce denied that the accident was foolish, and Thomson said, "I didn't believe it in the first place. I had to be sure because the releasing company brought it up." Pierce kept the job — a good one, too, as it was paying him $350 a week.[146]

One scene gave Pierce a scare. A Civil War battle sequence had Quantrill's men charging down a hill to meet the Union Army. Dynamite charges were placed by the special effects department to go off an intervals while the cast charged on horseback. During filming, however, the remote control operator accidentally set off one explosion right in front of the mounted Pierce. "My horse fell and both of us went sprawling," Pierce recalled. "It made a terrific albeit unplanned scene. I was not hurt and neither was the horse, but a second earlier and we would have been blown to pieces. I caught the horse, mounted and rode like mad to catch the rest of the gang, which thundered ahead."[147]

Another scene wasn't quite as dangerous. When Thomson leaped out of the courthouse window onto Silver King, he reportedly had to do five takes before he landed squarely in the saddle.[148]

Location work included Bridgeport, California, and Flagstaff, Arizona.[149] Filming was completed after twelve weeks.

Paramount put out an extensive publicity campaign to market *Jesse James*, including the release of arcade cards and cigarette holder advertising. The shy Thomson gave several interviews to media representatives.[150]

In interviews with *Photoplay* magazine and the *Los Angeles Times,* Thomson said that had Abraham Lincoln not been assassinated, Jesse James never would have become an outlaw. In the *Photoplay* interview, Thomson compared James to Robin Hood: "He was a strong, fearless man without the trace of a mean trait.... Since I announced that I would make a picture on the life of Jesse James, I have been flooded with letters from those who still cherish the memory of him for the many kind deeds that he performed."[151]

Thomson did backtrack a little, saying he did not specifically try to turn Jesse into a hero. "[H]e had enough faults and virtues to make him very human. But he was by no means the villain that he has been pictured."[152]

In an interview with the *Los Angeles Times,* Thomson went as far as to endorse a proposal to erect a monument to Jesse James in Kearney, the outlaw's hometown. The mayor of Kearney did not approve, however, saying, "It would be a slam on the rising generation to erect a monument to a bandit."[153]

The movie was released on October 15, 1927, at a time when theater receipts were dwindling and Westerns were beginning to decline in popularity. The previous month, *Variety* had reported, "With the exception of Tom Mix productions, the average Western is no longer expected to gross over $75,000 in rentals.[154]

Photoplay named *Jesse James* one of the Best Pictures of the Month for October, but the magazine also pointed out that the "exciting film version may seem to whitewash the famous bandit of Clay County." Other reviews were lukewarm at best, and Jesse James faced stiff competition at the box office from the first talkie, *The Jazz Singer.*[155]

The *New York Times* noted, "While the film version of Jesse James's bullet-ridden career is undoubtedly entertaining, chiefly because it gives to the bandit-hero a lightning-like mental equipment and an unrivaled acrobatic ability, it is as a whole disappointing as a character study of the famous outlaw."[156]

Jesse James grossed $1.2 million[157] — good money for times when children could get into a movie for ten cents, but not enough to recoup Paramount's expenses. In *The Filming of the West*, historian Jon Tuska writes, "*Jesse James* finished Fred Thomson in pictures," noting that his next two Paramount releases, *The Pioneer Scout* and *The Sunset Legion* (both 1928), "died at the box office."[158] Cari Beauchamp, however, says that *The Pioneer Scout* did better ticket-wise, and that Thomson's FBO movies were steadily shown in smaller theaters across the United States, keeping the star's popularity healthy. Not only that, but "almost every 'What This Film Did for Me' column in the trades included letters from theater owners praising a Thomson film."[159]

Hit or not, the movie was controversial, and Thomson would take a public relations beating. A theater owner in Chicago allowed free admission to the movie, explaining, "After seeing the picture it was impossible for me to take their money."[160]

Paramount distributed many promotional cards to drum up business for its 1927 film *Jesse James*. Here, Jesse (Fred Thomson) calls on his sweetheart Zerelda Mimms (Nora Lane).

Also upset were Jesse Edwards James and his daughter Jessie, who said they understood Jessie was to have been cast as her grandmother. He filed suit against Paramount for $75,000, for money he said was due him for scenario suggestions, providing wardrobe and props and for the "broken promise" to his daughter. When that suit was dismissed, James filed another suit, this one against Thomson. It also was dismissed. So was another suit that James filed against the Thomson estate after the star's unexpected and tragic death.[161]

Late in 1928, Thomson stepped on a rusty nail near the stables at his home, but ignored the injury. In December, he was admitted to Queen of Angels Hospital, where he underwent surgery for gallstones. He did not improve, and when doctors learned of the rusty nail, they began blood transfusions. They had waited too long, however, and on Christmas Eve, shortly before midnight, Fred Thomson died of tetanus.[162] He was thirty-eight years old.

Analysis

Thomson's untimely death had far-reaching consequences for his legacy. While other silent era stars such as William S. Hart and Tom Mix are remembered today, Thomson is all but forgotten. His career was highly successful, but his status as Western star lasted only five years. After Thomson's death, theater owners withdrew his films from circulation, "considering it poor taste to profit from a deceased star."[163]

All but three of his movies are believed to be lost: Two are early Thomson films, a 1921 Mary Pickford drama, *The Love Light*, Thomson's first movie, and 1923's *A Chapter in Her Life*, in which he had a minor role in his last non–Western. With the exception of the aforementioned *Thundering Hoofs*, available on DVD, modern viewers have few chances to see Thomson's acrobatics and grace. They might blame Harry Joe Brown, the producer perhaps best known for his work with Randolph Scott. Brown also produced several Thomson movies, including *Galloping Gallagher* (1924), of which about 29 minutes of footage survive.

In 1951, Brown was approached by a major network that was interested in buying Thomson's FBO Westerns for television. When Brown admitted that he had burned the negatives, the network officials "nearly swooned."[164]

As far as Thomson's *Jesse James* is concerned, it might not have been a hit, but Hollywood's first major production began a trend of whitewashing Jesse James and turning him into a hero, sometimes misguided, often tragic.

* * *

Variety (October 19, 1927): "It's strictly a film for the roughnecks and the gallery ... an uncalled for, useless and dangerous story of Jesse James."

CHAPTER FOUR

A-List Jesse, 1939–1940

In 1938, 20th Century–Fox began production on a new movie. Jesse James was the subject, but this time, there would be little controversy. The public wouldn't be outraged by this whitewashed account of a notorious murderer and robber. Instead, with the country coming off the Great Depression, they would flock to theaters to see Jesse James — in such throngs that a sequel was ordered.

Jesse James (1939) and the sequel *The Return of Frank James* (1940) would help Hollywood rewrite history, and, for better or worse, change public opinion about Jesse James.

Jesse James
(20th Century–Fox, January 1939, 105 minutes)

CREDITS: *Director:* Henry King; *Producer:* Darryl F. Zanuck; *Screenplay:* Nunnally Johnson.

CAST: Tyrone Power (Jesse James); Henry Fonda (Frank James); Nancy Kelly (Zee); Randolph Scott (Will Wright); Henry Hull (Major Rufus Cobb); Slim Summerville (Jailer); J. Edward Bromberg (George Runyan); Brian Donlevy (Barshee); John Carradine (Bob Ford); Donald Meek (McCoy); John Russell (Jesse James Jr.); Jane Darwell (Mrs. Samuels); Charles Tannen (Charles Ford); Claire Du Brey (Mrs. Bob Ford); Willard Robertson (Clarke); Harold Goodwin (Bill); Ernest Whitman (Pinkie); Eddy Waller (Deputy); Paul E. Burns (Hank); Spencer Charters (Minister).

Synopsis

The movie that defined Jesse James.

After the Civil War, the St. Louis Midland Railroad is buying up farmland at a fraction of what the land is worth; railroad agent Barshee strong-arms anyone who resists. That method works well until he and his henchmen show up at the James farm run by Mrs. Samuels and her two sons, Frank and Jesse James. Frank wallops Barshee; when the agent tries to trim the tobacco-chewing Frank down to size with a scythe, Jesse shoots him in the hand. Jesse summons all the neighbors to discuss a legal way they can protect their land.

All this excitement causes too much exertion for the brothers' mother. She has taken to bed when Major Rufus Cobb, editor of the *Liberty Weekly Gazette*, shows up and tells the two sons that Barshee and the railroad have issued warrants for the brothers' arrest. Frank and Jesse reluctantly take to the hills. When Barshee and the posse arrive, they aren't

Advertisement for a 1951 reissue of 20th Century–Fox's giant hit of 1939, *Jesse James*.

convinced that the boys aren't home, so Barshee throws a bomb through the window. And Mrs. Samuels is dead.

"I'm sorry," Rufus Cobb says over her body.

"I'm sorry, too," Barshee concedes.

"I'm wasn't talking about her," Cobb says. "She's gone. It's you I'm sorry about."

Four. A-List Jesse, 1939–1940

With good reason. Jesse rides into Liberty and guns down Barshee. The St. Louis Midland puts a $1,000 bounty on his head.

The reward will quickly go up, because now the boys and friends are avenging their mother's death by robbing trains. "Don't forget to sue the railroad," Frank instructs passengers as he takes their money.

Jesse is in love with Cobb's niece, Zee Cobb. The Liberty marshal, Will Wright, is in love with Zee, too, but Will's a decent sort. Much more than Jesse, who tells Zee, "When I hate, I gotta do something about it."

Zee tells Jesse that if he sticks to his life of crime, he'll turn into some kind of animal. There's only one way out, she advises him, and that's surrender. The railroad president, McCoy, has written a note promising a minimum sentence for Jesse that won't exceed five years. Wright gives his word to Jesse, and Jesse agrees to turn himself in — if Zee marries him, which she does.

Wright's a man of his word. McCoy isn't. He pulls a double-cross and arranges for a military court that will put Jesse on the gallows. Frank busts Jesse out of jail. They make McCoy eat the note he had written Jesse. The reward is now $25,000 for Jesse and $15,000 for Frank.

Zee sticks with Jesse, but it's difficult. He's seldom home, and when he is, he's paranoid. They move from town to town to town. "We live like animals," Zee wails, "scared animals."

Jesse isn't there when his son is born, and a distraught Zee begs her uncle to let her come home with him. When Jesse hears this — and that Wright has helped her return to Liberty — he starts after them, but stops, realizing it's better this way. For Zee.

He intensifies his raids, takes chances he wouldn't normally take, and pushes his men to the brink of mutiny — especially after he proposes robbing the bank in Northfield, Minnesota.

The governor has declared amnesty for any member of the gang that will turn in Jesse, dead or alive. Detective George Runyan visits the farm of Bob Ford, planting a seed for betrayal. Bob reacts, and lets Runyan know about the planned Northfield bank robbery. The town, and detective, are ready, and when Jesse, Frank and the gang ride into the bank, an ambush is waiting. Two gang members are killed, four others captured, and Jesse is badly wounded. Frank and Jesse barely manage to escape, and Frank has to leave Jesse behind to fend for himself.

When Zee realizes that Jesse's all alone, she knows she must return to their home in St. Joseph. She's there with their son, Jesse Jr., when Jesse arrives. Jesse promises Zee that they'll go to California to start a new life.

Jesse is presumed dead, and Frank is believed to have fled the country. Jesse's ready to leave Missouri when Bob and Charlie Ford show up. Bob tells Jesse that he escaped the Minnesota jail, and that Frank has sent him and Charlie to get Jesse to help pull off a bank robbery. Jesse's torn. He could use the $2,000, and might be leaning toward joining the robbery when he is called outside to help his son. Of course, Charlie points out that he can't go outside wearing his guns, so Jesse takes them off. His son has been playing outlaws with older kids; Jesse Jr.'s has been playing Jesse James. "You're Jesse James," the kids tell him. "You're dead." So Jesse Jr. pretends to be dead, and that's all it takes for Jesse Sr. to realize he can't let his family down. He tells the Ford brothers no thanks, that he and his family are taking the afternoon train to California.

A wounded Jesse James (Tyrone Power), left, and other gang members find Northfield a tough town to rob in *Jesse James* (1939).

Jesse is taking down a sampler from the wall when Bob Ford, with a shaking hand, shoots him in the back. Jesse falls to the floor, dead.

"Jesse was an outlaw, a bandit, a criminal," Rufus Cobb says at Jesse's funeral before unveiling the monument over Jesse's grave. "Even those that loved him ain't got no answer to that. But we ain't ashamed of him. I don't know why but I don't think even America is ashamed of Jesse James."

The History

Nunnally Johnson's screenplay helped propagate the myth that Jesse James was fighting evil railroads. If that were the case, then why did the real Jesse James start his career robbing banks in 1866 or 1867 and not start robbing trains until 1873? The banks and trains robbed in the movie are all St. Louis Midland–owned, but the real Jesse James never singled out any one company.

The movie proved incredibly popular, but its facts were basically nonexistent. Frank and Jesse's mother is identified as Mrs. Samuels, a common misspelling of her actual name, Samuel. She is depicted living alone with her two sons. The boys' stepfather, Dr. Reuben Samuel, isn't around, although in real life he lived until 1908. Nor do we see their sister Susan, born in 1849; stepsister Sallie, born 1858; stepbrother John, born in 1861; stepsister

Fannie Quantrill, born 1863; and stepbrother Archie, born 1866. Another brother, Robert R. James, lived only a month before his death in 1845. Reuben Samuel is also rumored to have fathered a half-black son, Perry Samuel, with one of the slaves.[1]

Jesse's wife was not the niece of Rufus Cobb, a newspaper editor. Her name was Zerelda Mimms, and she was actually a niece of Jesse's mother. Jesse married his first cousin in 1874.[2]

Rufus Cobb — whose editorials always begin, "If we are ever to have law and order in the West, the first thing we've got to do is round up all the [insert lawyers-railroad presidents-dentists-etc.] and shoot 'em down like dogs!" — is a rough characterization of newspaper editor John Newman Edwards. Edwards never worked for the *Liberty Weekly Gazette*, but he did help create an everlasting image of the James and Younger brothers, whom he constantly defended with his "editorial rhetoric: an evocation of popular myth mixed with hyperbole, partisan politics, outright balderdash — and, interestingly enough, some significant fact."[3]

There are no Younger brothers in the movie, but that's all right as there are no James brothers in *The Younger Brothers* (1949). The Northfield raid wasn't an ambush, and Frank and Jesse didn't escape by riding their horses through plate-glass windows and through a store. Nor did they leave town alone. Cole, Jim and Bob Younger and Charlie Pitts-Sam Wells also rode out of town. The movie leaves four outlaws wounded and two dead. By the time the Youngers were captured at Hanska Slough, the tally would actually be three captured and three dead.[4]

Bob Ford introduces Jesse to his brother Charlie. In fact, Jesse most likely befriended Charlie before he accepted Bob, although neither rode with Jesse until around 1880. Bob Ford is also given a wife in the movie and is taking part in the robberies as soon as Jesse and Frank form a gang. Robert Ford wasn't born until January 31, 1862, and was a bachelor when he killed Jesse on April 3, 1882.[5]

Jesse was killed by Bob Ford while either straightening or dusting a sampler. The movie has him shot twice. Bob pulled the trigger only once, and his brother was with him when he fired the fatal shot. Jesse was not preparing to leave Missouri with his family (which also included a daughter, who isn't in the movie) and giving up crime forever. At the time, he was planning a bank robbery in Platte City, Missouri, and told the Ford brothers the night before his death that "he might have to go under eventually, but before he did he would shake up the country once or twice more."[6]

The reward for Jesse never reached $25,000; it was $10,000 at the time of his death.[7]

Jesse's headstone, however, was an accurate recreation of the one his mother had put up beside her home outside of Kearney, Missouri. Yes, it did read (and still does):

"Murdered by a traitor and coward whose name is not worthy to appear here."

Did the movie get anything else right? Perhaps Jo Frances James, Jesse's granddaughter, put it best:

"[A]bout the only connection it had with fact was that there once was a man named James and he did ride a horse."[8]

The Players

Jo Frances James had written a manuscript about her version of her grandfather's life, which she was trying to get published as a book. Her friend, retired Western actor William

S. Hart, had contacted Darryl F. Zanuck about James's manuscript, but the studio head wasn't encouraging. Still, Zanuck was interested in another pitch from Nunnally Johnson, who had based his screenplay on a melodrama he had seen years earlier, the writings of John Newman Edwards (the inspiration of Rufus Cobb), pulp versions of Jesse's life and a play, *The Purple Mask*.[9]

Off camera and out of costume, actors Tyrone Power and Henry Fonda take a break during the filming of *Jesse James* (1939) in the Missouri Ozarks.

Johnson was a prolific Fox writer and producer who had received his first solo screenplay credit for *The House of Rothschild* (1934). A reporter and short story writer, he had "a willingness to tackle a great variety of genres, invariably with success." His earlier writing credits also included *The Prisoner of Shark Island* (1936). After Jesse James, he wrote *The Grapes of Wrath* (1940), *Tobacco Road* (1941), *The Moon Is Down* (1943), *How to Marry a Millionaire* (1953), *The Man in the Gray Flannel Suit* (1956), *Flaming Star* (1960) and *The Dirty Dozen* (1967). He even directed eight films between 1954 and 1960.[10]

"The last major holdout against color," 20th Century–Fox announced in March that *Jesse James* would be filmed in color.[11]

When Fox green-lighted *Jesse James*, director Henry King began searching for a suitable location, logging 15,000 flying miles before choosing McDonald County in southwestern Missouri. The town of Noel would serve as headquarters, but much of the filming would take place in Pineville.[12]

"McDonald County and its natives do not change much," the *Kansas City Times* reported in explaining the location choice. "It is in this respect that it is different from certain other sections of the Missouri Ozarks. Its rolling, heavily timbered hills, its mountain-like cliffs and bluffs along winding, clear streams, its countless natural springs, and its unusually large number of caves, some of which have not yet been entirely explored, are all very much the same as they were in the heyday of Jesse James...."[13]

The movie's pressbook included a note, perhaps apocryphal, that said King and an assistant were riding mules looking for location sites when they came across a roadside cabin. They asked "an elderly mountaineer" if he knew of a place where a stream ran through a clear patch. Asked why, King replied, "We're going to shoot *Jesse James* there." The oldtimer said: "Mean to tell me you fellers don't know Jesse's been shot?"[14]

King was a journeyman director who had been in the business since 1915. "There were times when he was swamped by grandeur, pomp or literariness," David Quinlan writes, "pitfalls into which he seemed doomed periodically to fall. But when he returned to Americana, the simple rural qualities of America in times past, he was well-nigh unbeatable." He would be Oscar-nominated for *The Song of Bernadette* (1943) and *Wilson* (1944) yet overlooked for his two best movies, and two of the greatest of their genres, the World War II drama *Twelve O'Clock High* (1949) and the Western *The Gunfighter* (1950), both starring Gregory Peck. King died in 1982.[15]

Pineville was chosen because it resembled the town of Liberty, Clay County, Missouri. The Clay County courthouse in Liberty had been torn down in 1936; Pineville's was built in 1867.[16]

First, however, the streets had to be covered with dirt; hitching rails, false fronts and boardwalks constructed; and a sheriff's office, newspaper office and the Dixie Belle Saloon created. Cost was estimated at between $20,000 and $25,000.[17] The Washington hand press used in the film by Major Rufus Cobb was the property of Claib E. Duval, the 79-year-old editor of the *Pineville Herald*. He rented the press to the film crew for $50 a week.[18]

When filming began on Monday, August 22, 1938, more than 5,000 spectators were on hand. Cast and crew were put up in homes. "The folks opened their houses for us," press agent Jim Denton said. "Some didn't want to charge at all. They just thought it was the kindly thing to do."[19] Actress Jane Darwell was mobbed while eating lunch at Shadow Lake, but said, "I'm used to it."[20] When Randolph Scott arrived by plane on August 24 —

bringing his rod and reel with him — he seemed more concerned about mosquitoes. "They tell us they're gigantic," he said.[21]

Some actors tried to avoid the locals at first, but not John Carradine. Before launching into Shakespeare, he announced to the throngs: "I am here for a sole purpose: To kill Jesse James."[22]

Noel, normally a town of under 500, had seen as many as 5,000 to 10,000 people descend on the area. "It's a bonanza," one woman told the *New York Times*. "It's like the gold rush to Alaska."[23] The local postmaster reported that the daily average of postcards had jumped substantially.[24]

Other businesses took advantage of the filming in their own advertisements. A Kansas City grocer advertised, "'JESSE JAMES RIDES AGAIN' down at Pineville, Mo. Those movie folks are re-enacting old Mizzou history (but he was a gentleman compared to the European dictators) ... BUT we CONFESS to HOLDUP Quality Foods and plead GUILTY— selling for less. But you're THE JUDGE. That's why your VERDICT SHOULD BE FOR KANSAS CITY'S OWN MERCHANTS Who Say —'*Boost Your City and Help Yourself.*'"[25]

A teletype was set up in an office, and a private plane flew undeveloped film each day to Tulsa, Oklahoma, where it was then transferred to another airplane that flew it to the West Coast.[26]

Heat proved to be a factor during the early days of shooting. Makeup artists worked between takes to keep the perspiration off the faces of actors and actresses, and the sun proved so bright that screens had to be erected over the sets.[27]

While studying the script over lunch, Fonda told Power: "For the luvva Mike ... it says here I'm supposed to pick up Barshee [Brian Donlevy] and throw him ten feet. That guy weighs 180 pounds if he weighs an ounce. And what's more I'm supposed to pick up Mrs. James (Jane Darwell) and carry her across the set. Some fun for a hot afternoon."[28]

Nebraska-born Fonda had started acting in Omaha, moved to Cape Cod and, finally, Broadway. When the Broadway hit *The Farmer Takes a Wife* was filmed as a movie in 1935, Fonda came to Hollywood. He wasn't overly pleased with his early movie career: "I'll admit a few of the pictures were pretty good: *The Lady Eve* [1941], *The Male Animal* [1942], *Jesse James,* and *The Ox-Bow Incident* [1943], but as for the rest," he said, "I wouldn't even want to mention 'em."[29]

He would become one of Hollywood's greatest leading men, and a fine Western hero in *The Ox-Bow Incident, My Darling Clementine* (1946), *Warlock* (1959) and *Welcome to Hard Times* (1967) while also playing villains in *Firecreek* (1968) and *Once Upon a Time in the West* (1968). An incredibly talented actor, he earned Academy Award nominations for *The Grapes of Wrath* (1940) and *Twelve Angry Men* (1957) before finally winning for *On Golden Pond* (1981). He died in 1982.[30]

Following in the footsteps of his actor father and grandfather, Tyrone Power had been acting since age seven, but found mostly bit roles until 20th Century–Fox signed him in 1936. Darryl F. Zanuck saw Power's pretty-boy looks and star potential, and made him a top attraction. He had become the studio's biggest male star by the time *Jesse James* was filmed. He was more than just a handsome face and swashbuckler, however, proving that with stellar performances in *Nightmare Alley* (1947) and *Witness for the Prosecution* (1957). He died of a heart attack while filming *Solomon and Sheba* in Spain in 1958.[31]

Nancy Kelly's mother was actress Nan Kelly Yorke and her brother was actor Jack Kelly.

Nancy had started out as a model while only a baby. She played child roles in more than fifty silent movies in the 1920s, moved to radio, and returned to movies at age seventeen. She was seventeen when production began on *Jesse James*; Power was twenty-four. Her movie career began fading, so she returned to the stage, winning a Tony Award for *The Bad Seed*. When that play became a movie in 1956, she earned an Academy Award nomination for Best Actress. She died in 1995.

Born in North Carolina in 1898, Randolph Scott landed in Hollywood "on a whim" in 1928, and gave Gary Cooper voice lessons for *The Virginian* (1929). He was soon starring in B movies based on Zane Grey novels. Westerns became his bread-and-butter, but he remained a supporting player in A movies like *Jesse James*, or a "good" bad guy in *Western Union* (1941). By the late 1940s, he was exclusively making Westerns. "I have always been a fatalist about my career," he said. "What was to be, was to be." He became an amazingly popular star of Westerns, turning out gems such as *Coroner Creek* (1948), *Hangman's Knot* (1952), *Seven Men from Now* (1956), *The Tall T* (1957) and *Comanche Station* (1960)—plus quite a few stinkers. "His career was about to reach an all-time high, in terms of popularity," Robert Nott writes. "And no one was more surprised by all the hoopla than Randolph Scott himself." Retiring after *Ride the High Country* (1962), Scott died in 1987.[32]

The train robbery scene was filmed in Southwest City in early September. "Henry King has an uncanny ability to discover and uncover things," Power wrote in a "Location Diary" published in the January 1939 issue of *Screenland Magazine*. "Imagine finding a ten-mile stretch of railroad on the old Frisco line...."[33] King, or some of his crew, also found an engine and three passenger cars near Alma, Arkansas, which were then restored in Little Rock, Arkansas, before being shipped to Southwest City for filming.[34] The filming, which involved 100 extras, drew 5,000 spectators. Power (or his press agent) wrote, "I never will forget the thrill of standing atop the coal tender with two big single-action 45s in my hands while the old-fashioned train shook, swayed and rumbled down the track.... Somehow, I didn't feel as if I were making a motion picture today. Instead, I was having the time of my life."[35]

Not all was fun and games. Fonda recalled the jailbreak scene, which King repeatedly reshot as the actors shot handguns in the air, reared their horses, and rode off. "My arm got tired from putting the gun back in the holster, then raising it and shooting it in the air," Fonda recalled. "This one time, I lowered my hand without uncocking the gun, the horse wiggled his rear end, and my gun went off. I'd shot myself! No bullet, but a full charge. I sure as hell had powder burns."[36] In fact, Fonda's leg was so badly burned, he was taken to a Kansas City hospital emergency room for a tetanus shot and dressing.[37]

Most of the actors returned to Hollywood in mid–September, while second-unit director Otto Brower remained behind to film mostly chase scenes.[38]

In January 1939, the American Humane Association slammed the treatment of animals during the movie's production, calling it "one of the most bare-faced wanton attacks of cruelty to animals in the past few years." The association accused producers of "hurling horses over a cliff and violently throwing horses to the ground" and threatened to pressure 20th Century–Fox and the Motion Picture Producers and Distributors of America.[39]

The association charged that one horse was drowned during the scene in which Jesse and Frank leap their horses off a 60-foot-high cliff and into the Lake of the Ozarks. 20th Century–Fox president S.R. Kent denied the charge in a letter to Sydney H. Coleman, president of the American Humane Association: "This organization is not in the habit of inflicting cruelty on dumb animals. All of this type of work is carefully watched, and while in the filming of *Jesse James* we used over 300 horses at various times and while it was necessary for us to secure exciting scenes, there was only one accident. This is unusual and a very good record in a picture of this type."[40]

Responded Coleman: "Our evidence to the contrary is overwhelming — but whether the horse was killed or not is irrelevant. The deliberate sending of a blindfolded, defenseless horse over a specially constructed, greased chute scarcely supports Mr. Zanuck's contention that all care and consideration had been used by director and technicians. It would be almost miraculous if a horse escaped unscathed."[41]

The jump — actually two jumps — was the highest made by a stuntman on a horse, and Cliff Lyons, a veteran who had been in the business since 1922, earned $750 for each jump. According to Zanuck, Lyons testified that the horse wasn't injured in the fall, but when the crew tried to catch it in shallow water, the horse "became excited, floundered, went down and took on a great quantity of water. The fact that the second jump, made exactly as we made the first, went off without a slip, and the horse was led ashore in perfect condition, indicates that the first jump was an unfortunate accident."[42]

"After walking to the top of the cliff and looking down at the lake far below," publicist Don Walker said, "I decided that I couldn't have been persuaded to make the jump, with or without a horse, for a million dollars."[43]

It's unclear if the American Humane Association's charges drummed up added publicity for the movie. Also unclear is if a play that had opened on Broadway in September 1938, Elizabeth B. Ginty's comedy *Missouri Legend* starring Dean Jagger as Jesse, increased awareness of the outlaw and, to an extent, the movie.[44]

By the time the Hollywood production had entirely left Missouri, an estimated $200,000 had been spent locally. It was filmed at a budget of $1.6 million.[45]

What remained to be seen was if the public was ready for another Jesse James movie.

Analysis

Jesse James was a huge moneymaker for 20th Century–Fox in what has been called Hollywood's greatest year. Only *Gone with the Wind* and *The Wizard of Oz* beat it at the box office, as *Jesse James*'s $3 million earnings tied it with *The Hunchback of Notre Dame* and *Mr. Smith Goes to Washington*.[46] Twentieth Century–Fox immediately planned a sequel.

This, of course, was the same outlaw featured in previous movies that sparked outrage from censors and viewers. But by 1939, America had changed. The country, and the moviegoing public, had been pummeled by the Great Depression, and Nunnally Johnson's screenplay was anti-establishment. "Jesse indicted big business," Jon Tuska writes.[47] Jesse was the good guy driven to crime by the St. Louis Midland Railroad, which had killed his mother and which controlled the law. There was no way for a poor farmer to get justice. The idea resonated with moviegoers.

In his masterful book *Showdown: Confronting Modern America in the Western Film*, John H. Lenihan notes the "striking resemblance" between *Jesse James* and 20th Century–Fox's *The Grapes of Wrath* (1940), which also starred Henry Fonda. "The James family and other post–Civil War farmers face land foreclosure by invidious railroad promoters in much the same fashion as [author John] Steinbeck's Joad family and neighboring farmers are displaced by an unfeeling capitalist establishment. Both the James boys and Tom Joad are driven to lawlessness by legal authorities who serve the status quo rather than the popular interest."[48]

Both movies also helped transform Henry Fonda into Hollywood's every-man hero, and made him a major star.

Today, the movie is fun to watch but hopelessly sappy, yet in 1939 it propelled a new trend in Hollywood. Outlaws, it seemed, were a huge hit. Other bandit films quickly followed, among them *When the Daltons Rode* (1940), *Belle Starr* (1941), *Billy the Kid* (1941), *The Outlaw* (1943), *The Doolins of Oklahoma* (1949), *The Younger Brothers* (1949).

Hollywood wasn't done with Jesse James, either. Far from it. Over the next two decades, Jesse James would ride across the silver screen in everything from programmers and serials to a few second-tier movies. Many of those movies, it would seem, got their history straight from Nunnally Johnson's script.

* * *

Los Angeles Times (January 19, 1939): "Historians may be thoroughly irked over much that happens during the unspooling of *Jesse James*.... But the public who is interested in entertainment will find this a rip-roaring melodrama with excitement, thrills and human interest.... The color in this picture is radiant, and the locations unusual."

The Return of Frank James

(20th Century–Fox, August 1940, 93 minutes)

CREDITS: *Director:* Fritz Lang; *Producer:* Darryl F. Zanuck; *Screenplay:* Sam Hellman.

CAST: Henry Fonda (Frank James); Gene Tierney (Eleanor Stone); Jackie Cooper (Clem); Henry Hull (Major Rufus Cobb); John Carradine (Bob Ford); J. Edward Bromberg (George Runyan); Donald Meek (McCoy); Eddie Collins (Station Agent); George Barbier (Judge); Ernest Whitman (Pinky); Charles Tannen (Charlie Ford); Lloyd Corrigan (Randolph Stone); Russell Hicks (Prosecutor); Edward McWade (Colonel Jackson); George Chandler (Roy); Irving Bacon (Bystander); Frank Shannon (Sheriff); Barbara Pepper (Nellie Blane); Louis Mason (Watchman); Stymie Beard (Mose); William Pawley (Actor); Frank Sully (Actor); Davison Clark (Officer).

Synopsis

Frank goes after Jesse's killers in the quintessential morality play.

The sequel to Henry King's *Jesse James* (1939) picks up at the end of the first movie where Bob Ford, assisted by brother Charlie, shoots Jesse in the back.

When Frank learns of his brother's death, he's living on a farm in Missouri's Ozarks, going by the name Ben Woodson, clearing land with the family's former slave Pinky and taking care of a young hothead, Clem, whose father was killed during the James Gang's Northfield raid.

Frank's not concerned. The Ford brothers have been arrested, and Frank believes no

Advertisement for a reissue of *The Return of Frank James*. The 1940 movie was rereleased along with 1939's *Jesse James* in 1951.

jury in western Missouri would let anybody go free, even those that shot a wanted outlaw — unarmed, and in the back. Clem isn't sure, and when Frank learns that the Fords were convicted, sentenced to hang only to be pardoned by the governor, Clem lashes out, "There ain't no law for the poor folk except the end of a gun."

Frank orders Clem to stay behind, tells Pinky to make sure he does, and takes off on a vengeance trail. The Ford brothers, finding their welcome in Missouri non-existent, head west, and Frank decides to go after them.

Of course, he needs money. He won't commit a crime because "Them days are far behind me," but decides robbing the St. Louis Midland Railroad isn't exactly stealing, since it was the railroad's money that killed Jesse, and the railroad that killed his mother, and the railroad that paid the Fords and got them off scot-free. He robs the express, but Clem comes along and, with an accidental gunshot, alerts the town to the robbery in progress. A bullet from the posse kills the night watchman, but Frank and Clem get away. That robbery has the railroad president, McCoy, suspicious and nervous, and he sends the detective Runyan to bring in Frank.

In Denver, Frank and Clem dupe a young reporter, Eleanor Stone, into writing that Frank James died in full glory south of the border. News of Frank's death brings the Fords out of hiding. The Fords perform in a play, *The Death of Jesse James,* and Frank naturally has to catch the show.

Sitting in the balcony, chewing tobacco, Frank watches the sordid melodrama and sure enough, the Ford brothers enter the stage and shoot down the actor playing Jesse James. When Bob Ford looks up, he sees Frank standing in the balcony. In a wild panic, he grabs a lantern and tosses it to the balcony — nice aim!— and starts a fire.

Frank and Clem take off in pursuit. When Charlie's horse stumbles and throws him, he takes to the rocks. Frank's horse also throws Frank, and Frank and Charlie shoot it out. Out of bullets, Charlie slips and plummets to his death.

Runyan visits Eleanor Stone and reveals the truth, that she had reported a hoax, and that Frank is still alive. Of course, sweet Eleanor is smitten by Frank. She tries to warn Frank of the detective's presence, but he gets the drop on Frank and Clem in the hotel room. Clem, however, jerks the rug out from underneath Runyan — literally — and they tie up the detective and leave him in the closet.

When Frank visits Eleanor and tells her the truth, she lets him know that Pinky has been convicted of the robbery and murder in Missouri and has been sentenced to hang. Frank's torn. Can he give up his chase to save Pinky? Eleanor pleads with him, but Frank says he has to get Bob Ford first. When Clem brings word that Ford was last seen in Creede, Colorado, the two take off, leaving Eleanor disappointed but resolved to do what she can to save an innocent man.

Frank can't go through with it. When Clem scolds him, "You're gonna give up on account of a darky?" Frank slaps him, and they head east back to Missouri, arriving at the office of newspaper editor Major Rufus Cobb.

Runyan's there with backup this time, the cuffs are put on Frank, and he's hauled off to jail. Pinky's given a reprieve, and Frank goes on trial for murder and robbery. Rufus Cobb acts as Frank's attorney, and the judge is a fair man. Everybody else, it seems, is owned by the railroad. The trial doesn't go well for Frank, who admits to robbing the express but claims the bullet that killed the watchman was fired from the outside. Rufus Cobb makes an inflammatory closing argument.

Bob Ford comes in to watch the verdict, and sends a note to Frank: "Now it's my turn to sit in the box." But he takes off in a hurry when the jury foreman tells the judge that Frank James is not guilty of *anything*. Frank pursues Ford, but the throng of the crowd, led by Eleanor, stops him. If he kills Ford, Eleanor argues, he'll face another trial. That's when gunfire erupts outside the courthouse.

Frank leads the way and finds Clem mortally wounded. "I tried to get him for you, Frank," Clem gasps, "but it appears he got me." When Clem dies, Frank grabs his pistol, reloads it, and heads to the livery where Ford is hiding. This time, nobody tries to stop him.

Frank James — who has never killed anyone, at least in *The Return of Frank James* and *Jesse James*, or so he says — keeps his record intact. Ford dies in the livery from a bullet Clem put in him.

Frank is granted a full pardon by the governor, and is free to return to Denver and — he hopes — Eleanor.

The History

Although he often used the alias Ben Woodson, Frank James was not clearing a farm in the Ozarks when he learned that his brother had been killed by Bob Ford. A few days

Henry Hull (bearded) and Gene Tierney (in hat) plead with Henry Fonda not to go after John Carradine in *The Return of Frank James* (1940). Other actors are unidentified.

after Ford shot Jesse in St. Joseph, Frank was returning to his home in Lynchburg, Virginia, when his wife ran to him with the *New York Daily Herald* and told him the news. "My God," Frank responded, "where and how and who killed him?"[49]

The movie starts off with a few things that are actually true. A headline in the *St. Joseph Gazette*'s special edition announced "Jesse, By Jehovah!" (though the newspaper in the movie is from Topeka, Kansas), and the series of events surrounding the Ford brothers is basically correct. Bob and Charlie Ford were indicted for first-degree murder on April 17, 1882, pleaded guilty and were sentenced to hang on May 19. Governor Thomas Crittenden, however, quickly pardoned them on the afternoon of the day they were sentenced to death.[50]

After this, however, the facts pretty much disappear from the film. Although he may have wanted to avenge his brother's death, Frank James didn't rob a railroad express office and take off to the Rocky Mountains after the Ford brothers. The Fords didn't head west immediately after their pardon. Instead, their play *The Killing of Jesse James* was performed in the East — including New York City — and the Midwest. The brothers were booed and hissed in Louisville, Kentucky, with shouts of "murderers" and "robbers" bringing the curtain down early.[51]

Charlie Ford didn't fall to his death in a gunfight with Frank; he shot and killed himself in 1884. Bob Ford wasn't killed in Missouri by a farmhand named Clem (entirely fictitious), but was blown apart with a shotgun blast in Creede, Colorado, in 1892, by a man named Ed Kelly/Kelley/O'Kelly/O'Kelley (there's hardly any agreement on the spelling of his last name), who may have been a cousin of the Younger brothers.[52]

Frank surrendered to Crittenden on October 5, 1882. He was tried — not for the fictional robbery and murder as depicted in the movie — in August and September 1883 for the Winston, Missouri, train robbery, which had left two men dead. Instead of one prosecutor and one defense attorney, both sides assembled a virtual "dream team" of attorneys. William Wallace of Jackson County and William D. Hamilton of Daviess County led the prosecution team of four other lawyers. Frank's legal battery included six lawyers, led by John F. Philips and Charles P. Johnson, a former lieutenant governor. The "Sage of Rebel Cove," Henry Clay Dean, also briefly served on the defense.[53]

The sixteen-day trial was a media sensation — the O.J. Simpson trial of the 1880s, if you will — that attracted so many spectators that it had to be moved from the Daviess County courthouse to an opera house in Gallatin.[54]

The movie includes a brief scene in which a former Confederate colonel takes the stand as a character witness for the defense. The actual testimony might have been even more comic than the movie version. General Jo Shelby testified on Frank's behalf, but the Missouri Confederate took the stand while he was inebriated and was fined for contempt of court.[55]

Frank was acquitted on September 5, 1883. The jury deliberated for less than four hours.[56]

Shortly afterward, Frank was arrested and brought to Huntsville, Alabama, to be tried for the March 1881 robbery of a federal paymaster near Muscle Shoals, Alabama. This trial ran for ten days, and when Frank was acquitted after six hours of deliberation, spectators in the courtroom cheered.[57]

On February 21, 1885, Missouri dropped its case against Frank James for the Otterville train robbery; the lone witness for the state had died, and key evidence was missing. Frank James lived the rest of his life a free man.[58] He wasn't granted a full pardon, as is depicted in the movie. There was no reason for a pardon. He hadn't been convicted of anything.

The Players

As soon as 20th Century–Fox realized how big a hit *Jesse James* was, studio executives quickly authorized a sequel. Fritz Lang, under contract to Fox, was hired to direct.[59]

A native of Vienna, Lang had been trained as a fashion designer, painter and graphic artist. He began directing in Germany after World War I — including the classics *Metropolis* (1927) and *M* (1931) — and fled to Paris and eventually America in 1932. His wife remained in Germany and supported the Nazis. They divorced in 1934. "I always made films about characters who struggled and fought against the circumstances and traps in which they found themselves."[60]

He directed only three Westerns — "of dubious quality generally praised by critics," Jon Tuska wrote in *The Filming of the West*:[61] *The Return of Frank James*, *Western Union* (1941) and *Rancho Notorious* (1952). Lang never won an Oscar, but he certainly directed memorable films including *Fury* (1936), *Man Hunt* (1941), *Hangmen Also Die!* (1943), *Scarlet Street* (1945) and *The Big Heat* (1953). His last movie was *The Shadow vs. the Thousand Eyes of Dr. Mabuse* (1960) before failing vision forced his retirement. He died in 1976.[62]

Sam Hellman was hired to write the screenplay for *The Return of Frank James*. A California-born writer who had worked in the silents, Hellman had adapted a Stuart Lake book about Wyatt Earp into *Frontier Marshal* (1939), starring Randolph Scott. (That film served as the inspiration for John Ford's classic *My Darling Clementine*.) Hellman received a "story" credit for Samuel G. Engel and Winston Miller's screenplay.[63]

Filming took place from April to June 1940 on the 20th Century–Fox lot, in Sonora, California, and at Owen's Valley in the Sierra Mountains. The studio hired a railroad and reconfigured the rolling stock to make the train look like a wood-burning locomotive and period cars.[64]

Many actors — Fonda, Hull, Carradine, Bromberg, Meek, Whitman and Tannen — reprised their roles from *Jesse James*. Hellman's screenplay introduced two new characters: Clem, played by Jackie Cooper, and Eleanor Stone, played by Gene Tierney.

Jackie Cooper had been acting in movies since he was three years old, but now at seventeen he wasn't the same cute, crying kid he had been in *The Champ* (1931), for which he had been nominated for an Academy Award as Best Actor.[65]

Andrea Leeds, who had been nominated for a Best Supporting Actress Oscar for *Stage Door* (1937), was to play young newspaper reporter Eleanor Stone but withdrew from the movie, apparently because of a slow recovery from surgery. Darryl Zanuck replaced Leeds with Gene Tierney, fresh off Broadway's *The Male Animal*, to star in her first motion picture. An inexperienced actress — and not yet twenty years old when filming began — Tierney was determined to do a great job. She learned her lines and impressed Henry Fonda.

When Tierney wasn't talking in a scene, she had a tendency to keep her mouth slightly open. During one scene, Lang, thinking she was trying to upstage Fonda, snapped, "You little bitch! When you have no lines, keep your mouth shut."[66] Fonda came to Tierney's defense, barking back at Lang, "Don't you dare speak to that girl in that way!"[67]

Actually, Tierney said she found Lang's instructions helpful. Afterward, she recalled, everyone — Lang included — proved helpful. She developed a crush on Fonda, but it ended when she visited the Fonda home and "I saw him, a happily married man, playing with his two small children, Jane and Peter."[68]

When shooting ended in Bishop, California, the residents presented Fonda with a revolver, said to have belonged to Frank James, which had been given to Bishop's town marshal, Lee Horton, in 1903. The initials "F.J." were on the revolver.[69]

Tierney would get her own award after the movie's release. *Harvard Lampoon* "honored" her as "The Worst Female Discovery of 1940."[70] Tierney said she probably deserved the

Jackie Cooper, right, and his unidentified stand-in-double pose for a wardrobe test shot during outfitting for *The Return of Frank James* (1940).

dubious honor. Embarrassed when she attended the movie's preview in Westwood, California, she sank down in her seat. "I could not believe how high and strident my voice came across," she recalled. "I sounded like an angry Minnie Mouse. 'My God,' I thought, 'if that's really how I sound, I'll never make it.'"[71]

She would make it, however. A Best Actress Oscar nod for *Leave Her to Heaven* (1945) and stellar turns in *Laura* (1944), *The Razor's Edge* (1946), *The Ghost and Mrs. Muir* (1947), *Night and the City* (1950) and *Advise and Consent* (1962) would show her talent and range. Bouts with depression would limit her career after the 1950s, however. She died of emphysema in 1991.

And that "Worst Female Discovery of 1940" distinction? Well, *Harvard Lampoon*'s "Worst Male Discovery of 1940" was the charismatic Robert Preston, who later won a Tony Award for *The Music Man* and an Oscar nomination for *Victor/Victoria* (1982).[72]

Analysis

"The contrast between *Jesse James* and *The Return of Frank James*," film historian Jon Tuska writes, "is quite profound; whereas the former was romantic, the latter is sentimental; while the former was symphonic and lyrical in its progression, the latter was at times crude and dull."[73]

Fonda was fine again as Frank, the Technicolor cinematography was excellent and John Carradine evoked a repulsiveness as slippery Bob Ford. Lang, however, was much better directing film noirs or art films, and Hellman's screenplay is heavy-handed.

The Return of Frank James, like *Jesse James*, helped fuel Hollywood and America's passion for more of the myth of the Missouri outlaw, and not the truth.

* * *

Variety (August 14, 1940): "Film suffers from too much rationalization of the necessity for Frank's wiping-out job and not enough of the old one-two with the six shooter. Makin' bad men good is okay, pardner, but keep the hosses movin' and guns a-blazin.'"

CHAPTER FIVE

Jesse in the B's, 1939–1949

The success of 20th Century–Fox's *Jesse James* made other studios take notice. Even before 1939 was over, Republic had released its take on Jesse James, albeit that one was a programmer starring Roy Rogers.

The next decade would produce an odd collection of Jesse James movies, including one comedy written by Dalton Trumbo, programmers, B-movies with Jesse as a supporting player, and three serials.

Not until the end of the 1940s would a movie take a serious and original look at the Jesse James story, and that would be a low-budget film, too.

Days of Jesse James
(Republic, December 1939, 63 minutes)

CREDITS: *Director:* Joseph Kane; *Associate Producer:* Joseph Kane; *Screenplay:* Earle Snell.

CAST: Roy Rogers (Roy Rogers); George "Gabby" Hayes (Gabby Whittaker); Donald Barry (Jesse James); Pauline Moore (Mary Whittaker); Harry Woods (Captain Worthington); Arthur Loft (Sam Wyatt); Wade Boteler (Dr. R.S. Samuels); Ethel Wales (Mrs. Martha Samuels); Scotty Beckett (Buster Samuels); Harry Worth, billed as Michael Worth (Frank James); Glenn Strange (Cole Younger); Olin Howland (Muncie Undersheriff); Monte Blue (Train Passenger); Jack Rockwell (Thompson McDaniels); Fred Burns (Muncie Sheriff).

Synopsis

The King of the Cowboys, Roy Rogers, goes after the King of the Outlaws, Jesse James, and hardly even sings.

Released on December 20—eleven months after 20th Century–Fox's *Jesse James* premiered—*Days of Jesse James* has Roy hired by a bankers' association to go after the James-Younger Gang, which has been accused of robbing a Missouri bank.

The movie opens with Gabby Whittaker traveling by train with his granddaughter Mary after striking it rich in the California gold fields. The train is robbed by Jesse James, who informs the passengers, "Jesse James never hurts anyone who obeys orders."

Roy Rogers, left, keeps Jesse James (Donald Barry), right, covered as Gabby Hayes checks out the cash situation in *Days of Jesse James* (1939).

Whittaker, never one to trust banks, is carrying his wealth in a valise. When Jesse bends down to open it, out jumps the Whittakers' pooch Whiskers, which jerks down the bandana covering Jesse's face. Mary gets a view of Jesse, and Jesse gets a good view of the money, but decides not to take it. He is, after all, a nice guy. When he visits his mother after the robbery, he gives her some money to pass on to a neighbor because the railroad has cheated him. Yep, nice guy.

That train robbery, however, is enough to persuade Gabby to deposit his $40,000 in Sam Wyatt's bank. Bad move. Wyatt decides to rob his own bank, killing an unarmed black porter in the process, and lays the blame on Jesse.

Enter peace officer Roy Rogers, and a slightly crooked lawman named Captain Worthington, the latter only interested in the reward offered for Jesse James. Worthington thinks Roy is smarter than he acts, and believes that if he watches Roy closely, the bank detective will lead him to Jesse. Then the captain can snatch the outlaw and claim the reward for himself.

Roy meets the Whittakers at their house — it gives Roy a chance to sing "Echo Mountain" to Mary — and learns that Mary is the only person around (other than Jesse's family) who can identify the outlaw. So Roy comes up with a plan and takes Mary and her grandfather to the James farm. But after they lure Dr. Samuels (Jesse's stepfather) out of his home, Captain Worthington and his posse surround the house, and a flare is thrown through the window. When it explodes, it's up to Roy to save Jesse's mother and stepbrother from the burning house.

"I tell you it was an accident," Captain Worthington tells Roy.

"Well, so was this," Roy says, and decks the lawman.

When Jesse learns of the raid on his home, he tells his brother, "We've got work to do," and they decide to rob a bank. The robbery's a bust. Roy manages to save Jesse's life, and even helps the outlaw escape.

Going undercover, Roy and Whittaker join Jesse's gang. Roy's a good doctor, not only mending Jesse's wounded hand, but also helping nurse Jesse's sick wife. Jesse and the boys are so pleased, they offer to send Roy to medical school, and break out their stash of loot.

When Roy sees the amount — nowhere near $40,000 — he reveals his true identity and turns to leave with Whittaker. Shocked, Jesse can't believe Roy would turn his back on him, but Roy explains he did it "to prove to myself you're not the kind to shoot an unarmed bank porter." He promises to leave Jesse alone. "Unless you give me a reason," he says, "I won't be back."

Now Roy and Whittaker head off to capture the real crooks. Sam Wyatt decides to make off with the money he has stolen, but Roy and Whittaker, posing as the James boys, rob the train and steal the money. After Roy adds up the total, which matches the amount stolen from the bank, he has the law waiting to arrest Wyatt in Kansas City.

The James and Younger boys are free, Captain Worthington is foiled, and Roy has the opportunity to sing "Echo Mountain" again.

The History

Before 1942, when Gene Autry joined the Air Force, Roy Rogers's Westerns were fairly low on music. "Gene got most of the songs," Rogers said.[1] And while overly sympathetic to Jesse James, the movie has a few — a *few*— moments grounded in history.

There are no hordes of outlaws riding hell bent for leather to leap from their saddles onto moving trains. Instead, in order to stop and rob the train carrying Gabby Whittaker, Jesse's men pile railroad ties onto the tracks. When Roy and Gabby rob the train — Roy switches to a black hat when he pretends to be one of Jesse's gang members — they herd cattle onto the tracks, forcing the train to stop.

When Roy is given the assignment to track down Jesse, he explains to his boss, "The only thing is I can't figure out how Jesse hops around fast enough to do all the things they say he does. Missouri one day and Minnesota the next."

Then and even today, that statement rings true (although the movie is set before the Northfield bank robbery). In many cases, it was and still is hard to determine how many robberies were committed by the James-Younger Gang and how many were actually done by other outlaws.

One of the more interesting scenes involves Captain Worthington's attack on the James farm. That's based on the Pinkerton raid of January 25, 1875. Worthington lights a fuse to a torch and throws it through a window to light up the inside of the home. The Pinkerton operatives threw a shell inside the house, "filled with Levi Short's solidified coal tar and powder concoction" and soaked in Alfred Berney's 'liquid fire,'"[2] also known as "Greek fire."³ Historian Ted P. Yeatman noted, "Murder may not have been the original intent, but destruction of the house certainly was."⁴

Dr. Reuben Samuel (not Samuels, as depicted in this movie) shoveled the "bomb" into the fireplace, where it exploded. One fragment shattered Mrs. Samuel's right wrist. Another pierced the bowels of their thirteen-year-old son Archie. Jesse's mother had to have her arm amputated just below the elbow. Archie died within the hour.⁵

Of course, you can't depict that kind of tragedy in a Roy Rogers movie, so in *Days of Jesse James*, Jesse's mother and stepbrother (named Buster, not Archie) are burned, but both survive the carnage and keep their limbs intact.

The Players

Once an aspiring cellist, Joseph Kane had worked his way up in Hollywood from title-card writer to assistant director to editor and finally, director. "I love making westerns," he said. "I like the scenery and the outdoors. The sense of excitement. The horses and the cowboys."⁶

He made more than 100 Westerns, most of them B movies starring the likes of Gene Autry, Ken Maynard and Bill Elliott. He had directed Roy Rogers's first star vehicle, *Under Western Skies* (1938).

By the time *Days of Jesse James* appeared, Rogers had already starred in thirteen Westerns. Before that, he had appeared in roughly thirteen movies, usually as a member of the Sons of the Pioneers in films starring Bing Crosby (1936's *Rhythm on the Range*) or Autry (1936's *The Big Show*). A native of Cincinnati (born Leonard Slye), Rogers had ambition. In 1937, when Autry demanded a raise and Republic began seeking a new cowboy movie star, Rogers sneaked onto the lot, got an audition and landed the role in *Under Western Skies*.

He had "a drawl like Gary Cooper," film critic Bosley Crowther said, and "a smile like Shirley Temple."⁷

Yet he could also show his mettle off screen. As his fame and popularity grew, he asked Republic president Herbert J. Yates for help with his fan mail. Yates ignored him, so Rogers filled the back of a five-ton dump truck with fan mail, drove to the studio, backed the truck in front of Yates's office "and dumped the letters on the lawn." Yates increased Rogers's salary $25 a week.⁸

Yates, Rogers said, "was a hard man to do business with."⁹

Filmed at Iverson Ranch, *Days of Jesse James* featured a great cast. Gabby Hayes, who joined Republic in November 1938, became Rogers's sidekick in *Southward, Ho!* (1939), replacing Raymond Hatton. "He was a totally different person when he was not working; he was quite handsome, well dressed, and he was intelligent—nothing like the character you saw on the screen," actress Pauline Moore recalled.¹⁰

The movie also co-starred Houston-born Don Barry, in his first turn as Jesse James. Barry, who was still working his way up the ranks with roles in B flicks like *Wyoming Outlaw* (1939) and A movies like *Only Angels Have Wings* (1939), had played Rogers's brother in *Saga of Death Valley*, released a month before *Days of Jesse James*. Barry also "had a chip on his shoulder," Hayes said. "When he showed up at a party ... everyone would say, 'Look out, there's going to be trouble,' and there usually was. About the only one who could handle him—and get away from a potential fistfight—was me. Only reason for that is that I'm too old for him to hit, heh, heh."¹¹

Regarding his role (and illustrating his massive ego), Barry said, "Tyrone Power had just made a picture as Jesse James, too. I knew Ty well, and this is no reflection on him. But the critics' comparisons between my Jesse James and his were all in my favor."[12]

Harry Woods, who portrayed Bob Ford twelve years earlier in Fred Thomson's turn as Jesse James, landed the role of Captain Worthington. Before earning a reputation as one of Hollywood's meanest bad guys, the Cleveland-born Woods had sold women's hats. Glenn Strange, who went on to fame playing the Monster in *House of Frankenstein* (1944) and *Abbott and Costello Meet Frankenstein* (1948) and is probably best known for his role of Sam the bartender in the *Gunsmoke* television series, played Cole Younger.

Moore played Roy's love interest for the first time. They teamed up in four other movies. Born in Harrisburg, Pennsylvania, Moore seemed to be on the brink of stardom. She played a bridesmaid in Universal's *Frankenstein* (1931) and, after moving to Fox, Ann Rutledge in John Ford's *Young Mr. Lincoln* (both 1939). Yet stardom eluded her.

"I was the girl who was always being discovered by the press," she said. "'Watch this girl!' a reviewer would say, and then forget to. The trouble was, if you were any good at all doing B movies, then the more B movies you did."[13]

Analysis

"The harsh, brittle realities of the [1930s] would so deny historical truth in the Western that Roy Rogers and Gabby Hayes could make *Days of Jesse James* ... with a musical setting and have the matter accepted with nonchalance, even indifference," Jon Tuska wrote.[14]

That's true, but *Days of Jesse James* is what it is, without pretensions, a standard Roy Rogers vehicle that proved highly successful. "Latest cowboy hero to hang up nation-wide box-office records with both his films and personal-appearance tours is Roy Rogers," the *Los Angeles Times* reported while *Days of Jesse James* was playing at the Cinema Theater.[15]

Rogers made such appearances for extra money — $150 a pop[16] — and they boosted his popularity. When *Days of Jesse James* opened (oddly paired with *Shipyard Dally* starring Gracie Fields) in Los Angeles, Rogers "rode his horse Trigger right up on the stage, and then did his vaudeville act, twanging his guitar and singing."[17] The manager of a theater in Waldorf, Maryland, reported standing-room-only attendance for Rogers' appearance promoting himself and *Days of Jesse James*.[18]

Cowboy pictures "were the reliable breadwinners"[19] for Republic, and maybe with good reason. As film historian William K. Everson wrote: "From the beginning, Republic got more excitement into their chases, more pep into their stunts, and more punch into their fights, than any other studio.... Few 'B' Westerns could long escape the taint of standardization, and since the key requirement of the 'B' was action, it hardly mattered that Republic's machinery showed. It was exceptionally well-oiled machinery and operated flawlessly."[20]

Days of Jesse James reaped enough profits for Republic that Roy would return in another Jesse James movie two years later. This time, the King of the Cowboys would get a chance to play the King of the Outlaws.

* * *

Los Angeles Times (February 29, 1940): "*Days of Jesse James* idealizes the James boys a bit, and gives Roy a chance to round up the villains."

Bad Men of Missouri

(Warner Bros., July 1941, 75 minutes)

CREDITS: *Director:* Ray Enright; *Executive Producer:* Jack L. Warner; *Associate Producer:* Harlan Thompson; *Screenplay:* Charles Grayson.

CAST: Dennis Morgan (Cole Younger); Jane Wyman (Mary Hathaway); Wayne Morris (Bob Younger); Arthur Kennedy (Jim Younger); Victor Jory (William Merrick); Alan Baxter (Jesse James); Walter Catlett (Mr. Pettibone); Howard Da Silva (Greg Bilson); Faye Emerson (Martha Adams); Russell Simpson (Hank Younger); Virginia Brissac (Mrs. Hathaway); Erville Anderson (Mr. Adams); Hugh Sothern (Fred Robinson); Sam McDaniel (Wash); Dorothy Vaughan (Mrs. Dalton); William Gould (Sheriff Brennan); Robert Winkler (Willie Younger); Ann Todd (Amy Younger); Roscoe Ates (Lafe); William Gould (Sheriff Brennan); Sonny Bupp (Grat Dalton).

Synopsis

The Civil War is over, and the opening scroll tells us: "Dishonest men exploiting the misfortune of the South were driving the farmers from the land. A few men rebelled. Among them were the three Younger brothers. By their enemies they were called 'Badmen'—Missouri called them heroes. This is their story."

Cole Younger (Dennis Morgan) shows off his hardware in *Bad Men of Missouri* (1941).

Five. Jesse in the B's, 1939–1949

Their story is pure fiction.

Near Chancellorsville, Virginia, Cole, Jim and Bob Younger say goodbye to their fellow Confederate soldiers before making their way home to Harrisonville, Missouri. "Well, I hope you boys find everything just like you left it in Missouri," one Reb says, to which Cole quips, "If we don't, we're gonna make it tough on somebody."

That "somebody" turns out to be carpetbagger William Merrick, a banker who is taking over Cass County farms in the railroad's right of way. Merrick won't even let the Adams family stay until after daughter Martha — Cole's girlfriend — has recovered from some sickness. The displaced farmers end up in a wagon-train camp when the Youngers arrive. Mrs. Dalton, another evicted farmer, tells the Youngers what has been going on, adding that Frank and Jesse James have taken to robbing trains to get even with the authorities. That prompts her son Grat to say, "I'm gonna rob trains, too, when I grow up."

That's an obvious homage to *When the Daltons Rode*, a critical and commercial hit for Universal the previous year. In fact, *Bad Men of Missouri* owes a lot to that George Marshall-directed Western starring Randolph Scott. Both films move at a lightning pace, and both turn their outlaw subjects into heroes fighting injustice. The difference is that *When the Daltons Rode* works on a fanciful, fun (but certainly not historic) level; *Bad Men of Missouri* doesn't.

Poor Martha dies in Cole's arms. His brothers cheer him up (so much for mourning) as they ride home, only to be greeted by gunfire. Their father, Henry "Hank" Younger, is suspicious of visitors these days. With good reason. When the sheriff arrives with an eviction notice, Hank protests, only to be shot down by one of Merrick's henchmen, Greg Bilson, who then murders the sheriff. The boys come out shooting, the home is burned and the Youngers escape. Merrick has murder warrants made out for the Youngers, and makes Bilson the sheriff.

After the Youngers rob Merrick employee Mr. Pettibone of $3,000 of Merrick's money, Jim suggests that they use that cash to help the farmers pay off their debts. Mary Hathaway tries to convince Jim that what he and his brothers are doing is wrong. "You've got to pay when you break laws," she says, but the Youngers don't see things that way.

They rob Pettibone again, this time on a train, and then meet up with Jesse James, who had planned on robbing that train with his gang. Jesse suggests they team up "at least for the big jobs."

"There'll be times I could use boys like you," Jesse says, "and I expect you'll need Frank and me now and then."

Jim is skeptical. "Maybe we ain't after the same thing, Jesse."

"It's money we're all after, ain't it?" Jesse says. "And here's a chance to get a lot of it."

Cole and Bob are ready, and Jim reluctantly sides with his brothers, saying, "We gotta stick together."

More banks are robbed. More chases. More shootouts and daring escapes from the law. When Bob is wounded, Jesse and his gang abandon the Youngers, so the brothers are forced to go it alone.

Merrick and Bilson have Mary Hathaway jailed in an attempt to lure the Youngers to Harrisonville. It works. Jim turns himself in on the condition that Mary is released. Later, Merrick receives a note saying Cole and Bob are willing to surrender if promised a fair trial. Merrick and Bilson agree, but plan a double-cross: When the Youngers ride in with their dusters buttoned, they will be shot down in the streets.

Ah, but those boys aren't fools. They dupe the dumb jailer into admitting them, and when Merrick and Bilson come in that morning, they disarm them and free Jim. Merrick and Bilson are forced to put on dusters and sent onto the streets, where they are quickly cut down by their own men. (Hmmmmm. None of those gunmen seem to question why the duster-clad fellas come out of the jail on foot, when they were supposed to be riding into town.)

The Youngers continue their crime spree. The camera zooms in on maps of Missouri and Iowa. Then the Youngers are pursued — apparently by a Minnesota posse, though there's no map of Minnesota — and shot to pieces. They survive, of course, and wind up in prison.

"Bandits must always wind up in prison, according to the wise edicts of the Hays office," the *Washington Post* noted. "No exceptions to this are the Younger Brothers in *Bad Men of Missouri*. But they inhabit the most comfy calabooses you've ever seen...."[21]

Mary tells the wounded prisoners that Missourians have started a movement to pardon the Youngers. It might take a long time, she says, but "we'll get it done if it takes a hundred years."

"What's a hundred years?" Jim says, and Mary falls into his arms.

The History

Neither Cole, Jim or Bob Younger served in the regular Confederate Army, so that introduction to the brothers in Virginia is complete fabrication. Cole joined William Quantrill's guerrillas early in the war, and Jim did the same around May 1864 when he was sixteen.[22] Bob Younger, however, was only nine years old when his father was murdered — in June 1862, not after the war as in this movie — and was too young to have fought in the Civil War.[23]

Frank James, who does not appear in *Bad Men of Missouri,* knew Cole Younger during the war, and the two would remain friends for life. Yet the Youngers and Jesse are strangers when they meet on that train.

Henry Washington Younger and wife Bursheba Leighton Fristoe Younger had fourteen children together, but only five are depicted in the movie. Two are only "kids," Willie and Amy, names none of the Younger children were given. On the positive side, the Youngers were from Harrisonville, Cass County, Missouri. The film even premiered in Harrisonville.[24]

Poor Mrs. Younger, though. She's not in this film — we can assumed Hank Younger is a widower — but in reality Bursheba died on June 6, 1870, having survived her husband by almost eight years.[25]

When Hank Younger tells his sons why he is suspicious of visitors, Cole says, "War finally came to Missouri, eh?" The real Cole Younger, having spent most of the war in Missouri, would have known that the Civil War came to Missouri, and it came early and in earnest. More than one thousand battles and skirmishes were fought in the state; only Virginia and Tennessee had more.[26]

Mrs. Dalton says Frank and Jesse James were robbing trains, but, in fact, the James-Younger Gang wouldn't rob a train until July 13, 1873, near Adair, Iowa.[27] The Reno Brothers Gang preceded the James-Younger Gang in the train robbery department by almost seven years, pulling off its first heist on October 6, 1866, near Seymour, Indiana. (The first documented train robbery in the United States occurred at North Bend, Ohio, on May 5, 1865, involving neither Jameses nor Youngers nor Renos.[28])

Yet screenwriter Charles Grayson is fairly accurate in his description of Jim Younger as a reluctant gang member. "Jim Younger could always be counted upon to respond to his family's needs," historian John J. Koblas writes.[29]

Jim's true love was not a Missouri farmer's daughter named Mary Hathaway but a newspaper woman named Alix Miller whom he met while in prison in Stillwater, Minnesota. In the summer of 1901, Jim and Cole Younger were paroled after serving twenty-five years for the Northfield bank robbery (brother Bob had died of tuberculosis in 1889). Parolees, however, could not marry, and Jim Younger died of a self-inflicted gunshot wound to the head in October 1902.[30]

"[W]hen he was up, he was way up, and when down, away down," Cole Younger wrote. "There was no half way place with Jim."[31]

The Players

Unless you count the musical *Song of the West* (1930) or his Rin Tin Tin movies of the late 1920s, *Bad Men of Missouri* was the first Western for director Ray Enright, who had made mostly comedies and musicals. He must have enjoyed Westerns, however, because he would make fourteen more between 1941 and 1952, including *The Spoilers* (1942), *Trail Street* (1947), *Coroner Creek* (1948) and *Kansas Raiders* (1950).[32]

Enright became a pretty good director, but his first Western wasn't good at all. "The most interesting factor in Warner Bros.' rousing production, *Bad Men of Missouri*," the *Sydney* (Australia) *Morning Herald* commented, "is the ease with which Dennis Morgan, Wayne Morris, and Arthur Kennedy have adapted themselves to unaccustomed roles as historic desperadoes...."[33]

Wayne Morris, born Bert DeWayne Morris Jr., had made a mark with his performance in *Kid Galahad* (1937). He was usually cast in boy-next-door parts. As a Navy pilot in World War II, he shot down seven Japanese aircraft, contributed to the sinking of five ships and was awarded four Distinguished Flying Crosses and two Air Medals. After World War II, he starred in several B-Westerns, but he certainly wasn't a Western regular when the movie was shot in Sonora, California, in March–April–May 1941.[34]

Likewise, Arthur Kennedy, the best actor in the movie, was not known for Westerns in 1941, but dramas such as *City for Conquest* (1940) with James Cagney and *High Sierra* (1941) with Humphrey Bogart. *Bad Men of Missouri* was only Kennedy's fifth movie but he, too, would go on to make many Westerns, including *They Died with Their Boots On* (1941), *Bend of the River* (1952), *Rancho Notorious* (1952) and *The Man from Laramie* (1955). Even Alan Baxter, who plays Jesse James, was often a bad guy but not often a Western bad guy.[35]

Dennis Morgan's only experience in a Western had been the twenty-two-minute short *Ride, Cowboy, Ride* (1939), yet after *Bad Men of Missouri*, Warner Bros. would put him in a handful of other Westerns, most of them as weak as this one. He could sing, though — he performs "Darling Nellie Gray" in *Bad Men of Missouri*.

It's hard to picture Humphrey Bogart singing "Darling Nellie Gray." Or even playing Cole Younger. Yet Bogart was Warner Bros.' first choice for the role. Bogart rejected it, reportedly with the words, "Are you kidding?"[36] Coming off a powerful performance in *High Sierra*, Bogart was placed on suspension, and Morgan got the job. Things worked out for Bogie, too. When George Raft declined to play Sam Spade for director John Huston,

Warner Bros. lifted the suspension and gave that role to Bogart. *The Maltese Falcon* made Bogart a superstar. Bogart later helped Morgan get another role. In 1945, Bogart turned down the lead in *God Is My Co-Pilot*, and Morgan got the part. Morgan was much more convincing as Col. Robert Lee Scott Jr. than he was as Cole Younger.[37]

Analysis

Bad Men of Missouri moves at a fast pace, and is almost as quickly forgotten. It romanticizes history, but gives the Younger brothers star billing over Frank and Jesse James. Cole Younger would go on get star treatment in *The Younger Brothers* (1949, this time played by Wayne Morris) and *Cole Younger, Gunfighter* (1958, played by Frank Lovejoy).

Besides being a footnote in Bogart's career, the movie has another bit part in pop culture. In his 1990 novel *Wild at Heart*, Barry Gifford has a passage in which a character recalls an argument between his parents:

"I heard my mama ask my daddy if he loved her. They were yellin' at each other, like usual, and he told her the only thing he ever loved was the movie *Bad Men of Missouri*, which he said he seen sixteen times."[38]

* * *

Los Angeles Times (August 1, 1941): "The kids whooped and hollered yesterday at *Bad Men of Missouri*.... This kid didn't; the events moving up there, lickety-split, were too old a story...."

Jesse James at Bay
(Republic, October 1941, 56 minutes)

CREDITS: *Director–Associate Producer:* Joseph Kane; *Screenplay:* James R. Webb.
CAST: Roy Rogers (Jesse James/Clint Burns); George "Gabby" Hayes (Sheriff Gabby Whittaker); Sally Payne (Polly Morgan); Pierre Watkin (Phineas Krager); Ivan Miller (Judge Rutherford); Hal Taliaferro (Paul Sloan); Gale Storm (Jane Fillmore); Roy Barcroft (Vern Stone); Jack Kirk (Rufe Balder).

Synopsis

Stories about good and evil twins (sometimes siblings, other times merely look-alikes with no blood bond) were hackneyed in Hollywood well before 1941, but would remain popular for decades, especially in Westerns.

For some reason, the Jesse James story often attracted this plot device, and *Jesse James at Bay* was the first. Resurrections also appeared in *The Return of Jesse James* (1950) and *Alias Jesse James* (1959). Even Jesse's brother Frank would get a look-alike in *Gunfire* (1950).

"The story that Jesse James was finally killed by a disloyal member of his gang is well-known and believed by many to be factual," a scroll informs the viewer after the opening credits of *Jesse James at Bay*. "But there is another legend — vouched for by many old-timers of Missouri — which goes like this...."

Crooked railroad agent Phineas Krager lures settlers to James County, Missouri, prom-

Lobby card of *Jesse James at Bay* (1941), which gave Roy Rogers the chance to play not only a good Jesse James but a bad impostor. Rogers is shown here with co-stars Sally Payne (left) and Gale Storm.

ising them the option to buy their land cheaply after the Midland and Western Railroad receives its charter. Instead, Krager ignores those options and begins taking over the land of poor Missouri farmers. Judge Rutherford calls the scoundrels "the dad-blamedest swindlers yet unhung," but concedes that the hands of the law are tied. There's only one man strong enough to fight these robber-barons, Sheriff Gabby Whittaker claims, and he sends off a note to Jesse James, who has been hiding out in Nebraska.

Jesse robs a Midland and Western train, then uses money from the heist to buy from Krager the mortgage to one of the farms, giving the deed back to its rightful owner.

While Jesse's performing his Robin Hood–esque deed, Clint Burns rides into town. He is promptly mistaken for Jesse and arrested, reluctantly, by Sheriff Whittaker, who scolds the man he thinks he once rode with: "Are you forgetting I'm the sheriff? Coming into town in broad daylight like this."

Burns, sporting a few days' growth of beard, doesn't fool Krager. He orders Burns ("the best poker player in Missouri") freed from Whittaker's jail. With Jesse continuing his good deeds, Krager hires the unscrupulous look-alike to terrorize James County, and thus turn public opinion against Jesse James. "You furnish the cash," Burns tells Krager, "and I'll furnish the trouble."

Enter two enterprising but rather scatterbrained St. Louis reporters, Polly Morgan and

Jane Fillmore, seeking a scoop on Jesse. They interview Sheriff Whittaker at his home when Clint Burns arrives, knocks out the sheriff, and sets fire to the place. The reporters aren't strong enough to carry Whittaker out of the burning building, but the real Jesse — arriving in the nick of time — is.

Burns continues raiding the county, which brings pressure on Whittaker to capture Jesse. The real Jesse seeds a rumor that he has been injured and is hiding in an old cabin, and Burns and his men head there to kill the real Jesse. But the two reporters arrive first — to warn Jesse. Burns and his men show up next, then Jesse and a friend, then Sheriff Whittaker, a marshal and the posse. Shootouts ensue, and Jesse heads to the cabin to make sure Burns doesn't get away. Helped by Jane's timely warning, Jesse kills Burns, then dons the dead man's coat and hat and takes off. The dead Burns, naturally, is mistaken for Jesse again. "After all the gunfights he's been in, you'd never expect a stray bullet to get him," the marshal says over Burns's body.

Posing as Burns, Jesse gets enough evidence on the villains, but he has to rescue Judge Rutherford and Sheriff Whittaker from Krager and his henchmen. Jesse, the judge and sheriff manage to round up the bad guys, and Jesse is able to return to his place in Nebraska with Jane.

"You mean you're going off with Jesse James?" Polly asks Jane as she and Jesse ride off together.

"I reckon you're a little mixed up, Polly," Whittaker tells her. "Jesse James is dead."

The History

While Rogers's previous attempt at the Jesse James story, *Days of Jesse James*, had a few scenes based on history, James R. Webb's *Jesse James at Bay* screenplay, from a story by Harrison Jacobs, was pure fantasy. Once again, Jesse was fighting the dastardly railroads and protecting the rights of upstanding Missourians.

That said, that opening scroll about another Jesse James "legend" does have its believers.

"In all the vast James apocrypha the most persistent myth is that Jesse was not killed that day in St. Joseph," Homer Croy wrote in 1949. "It sprang up immediately ... and it has been going ever since, for it would seem that the public does not want to believe that a person it has been interested in is no more."[39]

The first man to claim he was Jesse James arrived in Excelsior Springs fifty years after Jesse's death. Another came to St. Joseph in 1934. One popped up in Tulsa, Oklahoma, in 1936. Perhaps the most famous made his pitch in Lawton, Oklahoma, in 1948. This one, J. Frank Dalton, said that after he faked his death, he served as a captain in the Brazilian cavalry, fought in the Spanish-American War, in the Boer War, with Pancho Villa in Mexico and with a Canadian field artillery unit in World War I. Alas, in World War II, "all he could do was to sell war bonds."[40]

When Dalton died in 1951, he was buried in Granbury, Texas, with "Jesse Woodson James" on his tombstone with the epitaph: "Supposedly killed in 1882." In Granbury, Dalton must have fit in, because according to another local legend, John Wilkes Booth was not killed in 1865 but moved to Granbury, where he lived under the name John St. Helen. Granbury is not to be confused with Hico, Texas, about 40 miles southwest. That's where Ollie "Brushy Bill" Roberts is buried. Roberts claimed to be Billy the Kid, even asked New

Mexico Governor Thomas J. Mabry for a pardon in November 1950. He was dismissed as a fake, returned to Texas, and died the following month. Yet today, there's a Billy the Kid Museum in Hico that defends the Brushy Bill story.

Look hard enough, and you can discover legends that Wild Bill Hickok wasn't killed in Deadwood, Dakota Territory, in 1876, that cold-blooded killer Bill Longley wasn't hanged in Giddings, Texas, in 1878, and that even Wyoming assassin Tom Horn faked his execution in 1903. My thoughts? Elvis is dead.

Few "Jesse James Survived" stories have been "vouched for by many old-timers of Missouri." Scott Cole, a board member of the Friends of the James Farm and Jesse's first cousin–four times removed, makes a pretty persuasive argument against Jesse ever faking his death. "Even though he was constantly on the move throughout his career, Jesse went to great lengths to keep his family with him ... often at risk to his own life and freedom. I find it unbelievable that he would simply abandon his wife and children ... and condemn them to a life of poverty."[41]

Regarding other slightly historical portions in *Jesse James at Bay*, yes, Jesse James was looking at buying a Nebraska farm, but that farm was in Franklin, not Eagle Pass as depicted in this movie, and Bob Ford prevented any transaction when he killed Jesse in St. Joseph.[42] Oh, and all those farmers moving to James County, Missouri? There is no James County in Missouri.

The Players

This wasn't the first time Roy Rogers played a dual role. In *Billy the Kid Returns* (1938), Roy was a dead ringer for that storied outlaw. The deputy sheriff then posed as Billy to help out the honest ranchers.

In *Jesse James at Bay*, Roy seems to have fun playing bad-guy Clint Burns, too, and he and Gabby Hayes — in their 19th movie in two years — are fun to watch. Hayes, said to have been taller than Rogers, wore flat heels and perfected his walk so that he appeared shorter than the hero. "The production people wanted me to look shorter than the star," Hayes said. "I was normally taller than [William] Boyd and Roy. But when I was in Duke's [John Wayne's] movies, I could have worn stilts, and he wouldn't have cared ... he's a big'un."[43]

"Everyone adored Gabby, on and off the screen," Roy's adopted daughter Cheryl Rogers-Barnett recalled in her book *Cowboy Princess: Life with My Parents Roy Rogers and Dale Evans*.[44] The feeling was mutual. "I'm very fond of Roy Rogers," Hayes said in 1945. "We have never had a difference between us. Roy's a nice kid to work with."[45]

Texas-born Gale Storm won a talent contest on *Gateway to Hollywood*, a radio show, and after appearing in Los Angeles for the finals, received a film contract. *Jesse James at Bay*, her ninth film, was her first with Rogers. They would also team in *Red River Valley* (1941) and *Man from Cheyenne* (1942). Though she would appear in several other B-Westerns, she conceded that she was scared of horses. "I only rode them," she said, "because that's what you had to do."[46]

Analysis

Though it is often called one of Rogers's "historical features"[47] (along with *Billy the Kid Returns*, *Days of Jesse James*, *Young Buffalo Bill* and *Young Bill Hickok*), *Jesse James at Bay* is without historical basis. It was one of the last Roy Rogers movies that, as historian Jon Tuska points out, was not "overloaded with music and elaborate production numbers...."[48] (In *Jesse James at Bay*, Rogers sang one song, "Just for You," to Gale Storm.[49])

After Gene Autry joined the Air Force in 1942, Rogers's movies became more laden with musical numbers. Rogers told Tuska that the change came about after Republic president Herbert J. Yates saw the Broadway production *Oklahoma!* in New York. "He came back to the studio and put out a memo that from then on, my films were to be made in the mold of *Oklahoma!* He wanted musicals more than Westerns from me."[50]

* * *

Variety (October 22, 1941): "Joseph Kane, director-producer, has paced his yarn with the skill usually found in better programmers, and James R. Webb's scripting is above par."

The Remarkable Andrew
(Paramount, March 1942, 81 minutes)

CREDITS: *Director:* Stuart Heisler; *Producer:* Richard Blumenthal; *Screenplay:* Dalton Trumbo.

CAST: Brian Donlevy (General Andrew Jackson); William Holden (Andrew Long); Ellen Drew (Peggy Tobin); Montagu Love (General George Washington); Gilbert Emery (Thomas Jefferson); Brandon Hurst (Chief Justice John Marshall); George Watts (Dr. Benjamin Franklin); Rod Cameron (Jesse James); Jimmy Conlin (Private Henry Bartholomew Smith); Richard Webb (Randall Stevens); Spencer Charters (Dr. Clarence Upjohn); Minor Watson (District Attorney Orville Beamish); Clyde Fillmore (Mayor Ollie Lancaster); Thomas W. Ross (Judge Ormond Krebbs); Porter Hall (Chief Clerk Art Slocumb); Wallis Clark (City Treasurer R.R. McCall); Milton Parsons (Purchase Agent Sam Savage).

Synopsis

The ghost of Jesse James does his part — a small part, indeed — to help clear an honest bookkeeper accused of embezzling, but he's overshadowed by other ghosts, including George Washington, Thomas Jefferson, Benjamin Franklin, John Marshall and, naturally, the star of the movie, Andrew Jackson.

June 2, 1941, is a big day for young, happy (and overly hyper) Andrew Long. He has to balance the annual books for the Shale City, Colorado, city government before going to a dance with his girlfriend Peggy Tobin. He makes a race out of balancing the books — he's fast but never makes mistakes — but this time, he finds a $1,240 discrepancy. Realizing the city clerk and purchasing agent are attempting to cover up their embezzlement, the honest bookkeeper protests, and is promptly suspended.

In Long's apartment, the ghost of General Andrew Jackson pays him a visit. It seems that Long's great-great-grandfather (he's only Long's great-grandfather in Dalton Trumbo's novel,[51]) Ezdra Long, saved the general's life at the Battle of New Orleans, and wrote Jackson a letter after the general became president. "'General,' he said, 'I want you to look out for my boys,'" Jackson tells Long. "Here I am."

Five. Jesse in the B's, 1939–1949

Cast shot from *The Remarkable Andrew*, a 1942 Paramount release starring Brian Donlevy as Andrew Jackson, William Holden and Ellen Drew as a couple of lovebirds, and Montagu Love as George Washington. That's Rod Cameron, as Jesse James, on the left.

Of course, Long's the only person in Shale City who can see and hear the ghost, and that leads to problems. The general's thirsty, and Long has to charge a $4.85 quart of Old Maryland Rye Whiskey—Long doesn't drink. When Long cancels his date, his girlfriend and another suitor barge in and find the whiskey. She becomes hysterical. Antics ensue.

The next morning, he orders another bottle of Maryland rye, and instructs the clerk at the drugstore to leave a bottle at his apartment every morning. By then, rumors have spread across Shale City of Long's peculiar behavior. As he walks down the street to the mayor's office, talking to the general, townspeople believe he's taking to himself.

Long visits the mayor, who offers Long a raise if he will stop investigating the budget discrepancy. The mayor records the conversation using a recording machine, which the general notices, but Long doesn't. Long refuses the bribe. He goes to see the district attorney, but the corruption has reached the DA, too.

That night, Long is arrested for embezzlement. In jail, he finds the general waiting for him. "You've been trying to keep an honest accounting of city moneys," Jackson tells Long. "You've been dealing with politicians. You've been standing up for your own rights.... Naturally, you landed in jail."

Jackson brings along some top legal advice: George Washington, Thomas Jefferson, Benjamin Franklin, and Chief Justice John Marshall, plus two others, an unknown Revolutionary War soldier named Private Henry Bartholomew Smith and a mustached man in black packing two revolvers, Jesse James. When Jackson asks for suggestions as to how Long might be freed, Jesse says, "Look, Andy, this joint ain't nothing but a shoe box. I can shoot my way out of this tin can."

When Long explains that his fellow city employees have been buying seemingly worthless property, then selling it for a profit after a new street goes in, he is scolded. "Democracy isn't a gift," Jefferson tells him. "It's a responsibility." Long says he didn't want to be a hero, and the others laugh, explaining that they never wanted to be heroes, either.

The trial begins the next day, under the jurisprudence of Judge Krebbs, who wants out but agrees to bail out his colleagues one last time. Meanwhile, the general dispatches his fellow ghosts to find some evidence that will exonerate Long. Naturally, the trial goes badly for young Long, and Jackson heads off to see what's keeping his fellow ghosts. He finds them in the mayor's office, where Ben Franklin discovers the recording device. Jackson shows them how it works, and they hear the conversation in which Krebbs is pressured to make sure Long is found guilty. That riles Jackson, who breaks the record, then tells Marshall, "You've prattled about this great memory you have. Here's your chance to prove it."

Back in the courtroom, without any evidence to present, Long delivers a speech about democracy: "It means that they can do what they wish — all the people. It means that they can worship God in any way that the feel right — and that includes Christians and Jews and voodoo doctors as well.... It means: 'Do unto others as you would have them do unto you.'"

At that moment, the ghosts enter the courtroom, and Marshall dictates to Long the conversation in the mayor's office. Long leaves the judge's name out, and the judge lets him testify. overruling objections from the district attorney. After a recess, the corrupt officials have resigned, charges against Long are dropped, and the judge, who is also resigning, asks if he can marry Long and Peggy.

On their wedding night at a lakeside cabin, Andrew Jackson bids farewell and heads into the night. This time, Peggy can see him, too.

The History

As a fantasy, *The Remarkable Andrew* skims over history. Oh, there's a fun scene where Franklin is playing with a light bulb when he should be helping the other ghosts find evidence; and Private Smith asks Long, while his fellow ghosts are arguing politics, "Now do you see why it took us seven years to win the Revolution?"

Jackson spends much of the movie unsheathing his sword, bellowing out about "rascals and poltroons" and saying the culprits' ears should be cut off. He drinks a lot of Old Maryland rye but advises Long against getting drunk: "Just drink till the tickle comes. Then stop."

Although he was chief justice of the Supreme Court during Jackson's presidency, John Marshall seems an odd choice for Jackson. After all, Marshall and Jackson were on opposite sides during the Cherokee removal. Marshall called Georgia's anti–Cherokee laws "repugnant to the Constitution, laws and treaties of the United States," but Jackson ignored the Supreme Court ruling, reportedly saying, "Well, John Marshall has made his decision, now let him enforce it."[52] In the movie, Jackson's ire is against Henry Clay. "If I were in charge," he tells Long, "I'd do with them what I should have done to Henry Clay." "What's that?" Long asks. "Hang 'em," the general responds.

Jesse James is an equally odd choice for Jackson, too. Basically, all he does is stand guard with two guns in his hands, though in Trumbo's novel, he does explain that he was a reluctant hero as well. "I was just going along, minding my own business, see. Then all of a sudden something happened.... The injustice of everything. So I finally decided to take a hand, and there I was, a hero.... I was forced into it, and don't let anybody tell you different."[53]

Perhaps a better outlaw ghost would have been Billy the Kid. After all, there is no documented account that Jesse James was ever jailed. But the Kid's escape from the jail in Lincoln, New Mexico Territory, on April 28, 1881— in which he killed two deputies — sealed the Kid's reputation as a bold and daring outlaw.[54]

The Players

Although William Holden was a rising star, top billing went to Ohio-born Brian Donlevy, who had been nominated for a Best Supporting Actor Academy Award for his portrayal of Sergeant Markoff in *Beau Geste* (1939). It was Donlevy's second film with Jesse James, following 1939's *Jesse James*. Donlevy went on to make two other Jesse James movies, playing William Quantrill in *Kansas Raiders* (1950) and *Woman They Almost Lynched* (1953).

Donlevy and Holden had become good friends (they also appeared in 1941's *I Wanted Wings*), so when Holden decided to marry Ardis Ankerson (aka Brenda Marshall) in Las Vegas, Donlevy said he and his wife Marjorie "will go along and stand up for you."[55]

Shooting had moved to Carson City, Nevada (locations included the Laxalt Building and the Rinckle House),[56] so Holden chartered a plane and reserved the Congregational church in Vegas and the El Rancho Vegas's honeymoon suite for Saturday, July 12, 1941. Holden and the Donlevys flew out after shooting that day and met Ardis in Vegas.[57]

Director Stuart Heisler, however, kept shooting for two extra hours, forcing Holden and Donlevy to rush to the airport still in makeup. (I wonder if Donlevy was still dressed in his general's uniform?) Bad weather shut down the Carson City commercial airport, but the pilot got permission to land at an unpaved Army base nearby. By the time they made it to the chapel at 4 A.M., it had been closed for an hour, and their honeymoon suite had been released to another couple. Holden woke a reverend and pleaded with him to marry them. "We were married," Ardis said, "in a hotel bedroom, standing at the foot of a double bed, by a one-armed man who held the book with his hand and turned the pages with his chin."[58] A month later, on August 16, Ellen Drew married screenwriter/producer Sy Bartlett in Lake Tahoe.[59]

After playing the villain in 1927's *Jesse James*, Montagu Love got the chance to play the father of our country, George Washington, this time around.

Director Heisler, who arrived in Hollywood in 1913, had worked his way up from editor, second unit director and assistant director. *The Remarkable Andrew* was only his fifth credited director's job, and his first comedy. Critic David Quinlan notes that Heisler's "lesser films are mostly in lighter vein" and that he was "obviously at home ... with heady, dark emotions."[60] Certainly, Heisler's direction of *The Glass Key* (1942) and *Smash-Up, the Story of a Woman* (1947) reinforced that reputation, especially compared with *The Remarkable Andrew*. Then again, aside from a nice cast, Heisler didn't have much to work with, especially — in the way of a script.

"Dalton Trumbo, the young Hollywood writer who a year ago astonished his fellow scenario writers and the rest of the nation with a book called *Johnny Got His Gun*, is probably the most indefatigable pounder of a typewriter in [Hollywood]," United Press correspondent Alexander Kahn wrote in early 1941.[61]

Born in Montrose, Colorado, Trumbo grew up in nearby Grand Junction, but left for Hollywood in the 1920s. Like his first novel, *Eclipse* (1935), *The Remarkable Andrew* was set in fictional Shale City. That first novel, however, had left many Grand Junction citizens bitter. "Children of leading residents whose names had been lightly disguised and who were disparaged in the book tell tales of their parents or grandparents ripping up copies of the novel," the *Rocky Mountain News* reported in 2005, more than thirty years after Trumbo's death.[62]

Hired by Warner Brothers as a reader in 1934, Trumbo worked his way up to screenwriter, first in B's. He wrote for Columbia, RKO, MGM, 20th Century–Fox and Paramount. An Academy Award nomination for *Kitty Foyle* (1940) and publication of *Johnny Got His Gun* cemented his reputation as a leading screenwriter and novelist. Yet he was also earning a reputation as a left-wing political activist and suspected Communist.[63]

Trumbo was shopping his 1938 story "The General Came to Stay" when Paramount producer Richard Blumenthal suggested he expand the story into a novel. Trumbo took his advice, and the novel was published in 1941 with the subtitle *Being the Chronicle of a Literal Man*. With war raging in Europe and China, it was hard for reviewers to separate fiction from politics. "Unlike Survivors Hemingway, Cummings, Remarque, Graves, etc., anti-war novelist Trumbo saw nothing of World War I," *Time* magazine noted. "*The Remarkable Andrew* is a further effort to avoid seeing anything of World War II."[64] Ironically, proceeds from the English publication of the novel, Trumbo said, went to the Relief of Bombed-Out Children of London.[65]

Likewise, Trumbo dismissed the book, writing that "the whole damned book was a fake anyhow" and that it "should have been smothered at birth."[66]

Still, neither novel nor film can be overlooked. As Peter Hanson points out: "*The Remarkable Andrew* is best appreciated as either an exercise in didactic storytelling or as a strangely prescient tract about issues that would later figure so prominently in Trumbo's life."[67]

In 1947, Trumbo and nine other suspected Hollywood Communists were subpoenaed to testify before the House Un-American Activities Committee. Refusing to testify, Trumbo became one of the "Hollywood Ten," was fined $1,000 and sentenced to a year in federal prison (he served ten months).

Blacklisted by the studios, Trumbo wrote the Academy Award–winning screenplays for *Roman Holiday* (1953) and *The Brave One* (1956) using writer friends as "fronts." In 1975, shortly before Trumbo's death, the Academy gave Trumbo the Oscar for *The Brave One*. In 1993 his *Roman Holiday* Oscar was presented to his widow.[68]

Analysis

Fantasy, of course, requires a suspension of disbelief, but not logic, and, logically, *The Remarkable Andrew* is a bust.

Andrew Jackson is summoned to help Andrew Long, but doesn't seem to know a whole lot about what's going on. He's unaware that England is at war against the "Hessians," and that California now belongs to the United States and has become "civilized," but doesn't seem to question why he is in Colorado. He seems surprised to learn that Andrew Long is named after him.

And what of those ghosts the general lines up to help? Franklin, Washington, Jefferson, Marshall and Smith fit in. After all, they were all alive during Jackson's life. But Jesse James? He was born two years after Jackson's death.

The conclusion of the trial is also a stretch, and the movie, and novel, have an abrupt, unconvincing ending. The movie, which could have used Frank Capra's touch, lacks the charm of 1941's *Here Comes Mr. Jordan*.

The Remarkable Andrew received lukewarm to mostly positive reviews when it was released but was ignored by the viewing public. "It will not be an easy one to sell," *Boxoffice* noted before the movie was released.[69] Filmed before Pearl Harbor, the movie was released when the United States was at war, and "in literal-minded, war-concerned 1942 such whimsy mixed in with historical allegory and invisible ghosts ... were a bit too much."[70]

As a Jesse James movie, *The Remarkable Andrew* might be one of the outlaw's oddest — at least until he met up with the Three Stooges and Frankenstein's daughter in the 1960s.

* * *

Time (March 30, 1941): "[This] is a refreshing fantasy. It brings back a posse of Founding Fathers and other once-vigorous Americans to mop up a pack of dishonest, flag-waving, 20th-century politicians."

The Kansan

(United Artists, September 1943, 80 minutes)

CREDITS: *Director:* George Archainbaud; *Producer:* Harry Sherman; *Screenplay:* Harold Shumate.

CAST: Richard Dix (John Bonniwell); Jane Wyatt (Eleanor Sager); Albert Dekker (Steve Barat); Eugene Pallette (Tom Waggoner); Victor Jory (Jeff Barat); Robert Armstrong (Malachy); Beryl Wallace (Soubret); Clem Evans (Bridge Tender); Hobart Cavanaugh (Josh Hudkins); Francis McDonald (Gil Hatton); Willie Best (Bones); Douglas Fowley (Ben Nash); Eddy Waller (Ed Gilbert); Raphael Bennett (Messenger); George Reeves (Jesse James).

Synopsis

John Bonniwell is so tough, he can survive four gunshot wounds and run Superman out of town.

Bonniwell arrives in Broken Lance, "the fastest growing little town in Kansas," moments before Jesse James and his gang ride in to rob the bank. Bonniwell kills most of the bad guys, but is wounded by Jesse (played by an uncredited George Reeves, television's future Superman). Jesse gallops out of town, never to be seen again in this movie.

Banker Steve Barat is so impressed by Bonniwell's actions, he helps get Bonniwell elected town marshal as a write-in candidate. The town is celebrating when Bonniwell finally recovers after being nursed back to health by a beautiful woman named Eleanor.

Richard Dix, right, is a quick-shooting marshal who faced down Jesse James in *The Kansan* (1943).

Barat, a transplanted New Yorker (bad news), wants to control the town, maybe all of Kansas, and do it legally. He's charging tolls over the bridge that leads to Broken Lance, and tolls for cattle to pass through his land to the railhead in town. The idea of paying a toll — a dollar a head — infuriates Texas rancher Tom Waggoner (who looks fatter than most of his cattle), an old friend of Bonniwell.

Waggoner protests, but Bonniwell tells him he must obey the law. Bonniwell, however, isn't the type of lawman who follows the law to the letter. He suggests that Waggoner stampede the herd. Well, that's one way to get the cattle across without paying a toll — even though Steve Barat threatens to sue Waggoner.

Then, who should arrive in town but the Hatton gang, Bonniwell's arch enemies. Backed by Waggoner and his cowhands, Bonniwell arrests them, but not before a wild saloon brawl.

Barat turns against the righteous Bonniwell, the banker's brother Jeff turns against Barat, Eleanor turns against Jeff after falling in love with Bonniwell, and it all ends with a bridge being blown up, Steve Barat arrested (seems he fled New York after being indicted for grand larceny), and the Hatton gang wiped out.

Bonniwell's seriously wounded, however, and winds back in the hospital, where Eleanor cares for him a second time. Outside, people are celebrating in the streets again, this time over Eleanor's engagement to Bonniwell.

Those Broken Lance people. They're always doing things before asking Bonniwell what he thinks. Of course, this time, John Bonniwell doesn't mind.

The History

The only time citizens ever turned back Jesse James was in Northfield, not Broken Lance, Kansas, a fictitious town created by novelist Frank Gruber in his 1939 novel *Peace Marshal*, which screenwriter Harold Shumate adapted.

The movie has no basis on history. Gruber recycled certain plot elements in another novel, *Fighting Man* (1948), which he adapted into the screenplay for *Fighting Man of the Plains* (1949).

The Players

Boston native Harry "Pop" Sherman started out in movies as a theater owner before meeting D.W. Griffith on a trip to Hollywood in 1913. Sherman advanced Griffith money so the director could finish an epic he was filming. The movie turned out to be *Birth of a Nation*. After that, Sherman produced the first motion picture adapted from a Zane Grey novel, *The Light of the Western Stars* (1916). In 1935, he formed his own production company and began producing movies for Paramount.[71]

Sherman produced several Westerns starring Richard Dix for the studio, including *Cherokee Strip* (1940), *The Roundup* (1942) and *Tombstone, the Town Too Tough to Die* (1942), the latter starring Dix as Wyatt Earp.

In 1941, United Artists needed movies and signed an agreement with Paramount to distribute some of the studio's lesser films in 1942. Dix starred in three of those movies, *American Empire* (1942), *Buckskin Frontier* (1943) and *The Kansan*.[72]

"Pop was a dear man to work for," said Jane Wyatt, who had signed a two-picture deal (*Buckskin Frontier* and *The Kansan*). "He was always so considerate of his players."[73]

Dix had been a star in the silents — his best role might be that of the Navajo Nophaie in *The Vanishing American* (1925) — and managed to continue on as a star in the early sound era, earning an Academy Award nomination for his performance as Yancey Cravat in *Cimarron* (1931). Born Ernest Brimmer in St. Paul, Minnesota, in 1894, he planned to become a surgeon until he got the itch to act while in college. In 1919, he made his debut on Broadway and two years later Paramount signed him to a long-term contract. In 1929, he moved to RKO, but got into trouble with the federal government in 1931 when he pleaded guilty to income tax evasion and had to pay almost $90,000 in back taxes and penalties, not to mention a $500 fine. By the 1940s he was acting primarily in B's and minor As. After *The Kansan*, he starred in a series of B's based on the radio drama *The Whistler* before retiring from film in 1947. Two years later, he was dead of chronic heart disease at age fifty-six.[74]

For *The Kansan*, Gerard Carbonara managed to get an Academy Award nomination for Best Music, Scoring of a Dramatic or Comedy Picture, probably because of Beryl Wallace's song-and-dance number "When Johnny Comes Marching Home." The *Los Angeles Times* said Wallace's performance "delivers marked impact."[75] Hey, it was a 1940s Western. You had to include a song-and-dance number in the saloon.

You also needed a mega-brawl in a saloon. Something straight out of *Dodge City* (1939) or *The Spoilers* (1942). Unfortunately, the direction failed in that long fight scene.

Paris-born George Archainbaud emigrated to America in 1915 and began directing movies in 1917, often working with a young David O. Selznick. By the 1940s, he was directing mostly B's. He later found steady work on television before his death in 1959.[76] His lack of attention to detail in the fight sequence was pointed out in a *New York Times* review: "But in one barroom brawl at least, this corner found more than a little evidence of cheating by the extras. There were so many fake body blows, so many haymakers that wouldn't have stunned a fly, that we momentarily expected some fight-fan in the audience to cry, 'We was robbed!' 'What's coming over Westerns anyway?'"[77]

Let's not forget Superman.

Discovered at the Pasadena Playhouse, George Reeves had acted in *Gone with the Wind* (1939), *So Proudly We Hail!* (1943) and others, but was finding good roles hard to come by. Eventually, he moved to New York to act on live television, and that led him to star as Clark Kent–Superman on *Adventures of Superman* in 1952. Typecast while playing that iconic role, he saw his acting career slide and died (apparently of a self-inflicted gunshot wound) in 1959.[78]

Analysis

"This movie could really be reviewed in two words — gallantry and guts," the *Chicago Daily Tribune* reviewed.[79]

How about one word? Lame.

Dix, appearing old and unhealthy, didn't look like a tough gunman, and the movie's a predictable 1940s Western. And modern audiences are likely to cringe at comedic actor Willie Best's stereotypical (ahem, racist) performance as the black hotel caretaker.

In Gruber's novel, everybody shows up in Broken Lance: Bat Masterson, Wild Bill Hickok, and Jesse James. John Bonniwell had met Jesse before coming to Broken Lance, as he explained to Tom Waggoner: "There isn't a man in the West can pull a gun against him. Not that he's so fast, but just because he's the most desperate man in the country. They've been after him so long, he's gun-shy. He'd kill a man who'd snap his fingers unexpectedly."[80]

Shumate decided to replace Jesse James with the Hatton gang, but he did put Jesse in that opening shootout. (In the novel, Bonniwell was wounded five times, instead of the film's four, by rustlers, not Jesse.[81])

Gruber turned out to be quite fond of Jesse. The author brought the outlaw back — in bigger roles — when he adapted two of his own works for the movies: the novel *Fighting Man* into *Fighting Man of the Plains* (1949) and a story into *The Great Missouri Raid* (1951). Those two movies would be better than *The Kansan*, on an entertainment, if not historical, level.

* * *

New York Times (October 1, 1943): "There is the usual crop of corrupt local bigwigs, the fracas over fences, mad pursuits with horsemen thundering across the skyline, and the final free-for-all in a barricaded Main Street — in short, the kind of Western in which the cast decreases almost as rapidly as a pay check on Saturday night."

Badman's Territory

(RKO, April 1946, 98 minutes)

CREDITS: *Director:* Tim Whelan; *Producers:* Nat Holt and Jack J. Gross; *Screenplay:* Jack Natteford and Luci Ward (original), Bess Taffel and Clarence Upson Young (additional sequences).

CAST: Randolph Scott (Sheriff Mark Rowley); George "Gabby" Hayes (The Coyote Kid); Ann Richards (Henrietta Alcott); Ray Collins (Colonel Farewell); James Warren (Deputy John Rowley); Morgan Conway (Captain William "Bill" Hampton); Virginia Sale (Meg); John Halloran (Hank McGee); Andrew Tombes (Doc); Harry Holman (Hodge); Chief Thundercloud (Chief Tahlequah); Lawrence Tierney (Jesse James); Tom Tyler (Frank James); Steve Brodie (Bob Dalton); Phil Warren (Grat Dalton); William Moss (Bill Dalton); Nestor Paiva (Sam Bass); Isabel Jewell (Belle Starr).

Synopsis

The more (bad guys) in one town, the merrier.

The way the narrator, actor Ray Collins, tells it, an oversight let a section of Western land — north of the Texas Panhandle, west of Indian Territory, east of New Mexico Territory, and south of Colorado — become a haven for outlaws since it fell under no state or territorial jurisdiction. "No United States marshal dared venture there," we're told. "It was called 'Badman's Territory.'"

Quinto, the main town in the territory, thrives when the bandits do well, so most merchants don't mind, with the exception of reform-minded newspaper editor Henrietta Alcott. Jesse and Frank James, and a few cronies, leave Quinto to rob the train at Trail Cross, Texas, then head back to Badman's Territory, pursued by a posse led by Captain Hampton of the State Police. County Sheriff Mark Rowley, however, doesn't care much for Hampton or his methods.

Traveling with his recently appointed deputy brother, Johnny, and another deputy, Rowley manages to capture one of Jesse's men, the toothless Coyote Kid. Johnny takes charge of the prisoner while Mark goes off after the rest of the James Gang, only to see outlaw Hank McGee kill his deputy and steal Mark's prize horse. Meanwhile, Hampton tries to take the Coyote Kid as his own prisoner, but Johnny won't have that, and heads off with the Kid, only to be back-shot by Hampton.

Then Jesse shoots the gun out of Hampton's hand, and he and Frank free Coyote. Coyote isn't about to leave the wounded Johnny Rowley behind with the likes of Hampton, so they take him to Quinto.

Hampton tells Mark that Johnny helped the James Gang escape, and that if he sees Johnny again he'll hang him. Mark doesn't believe any of it, calling the lawman a coward.

"Rowley," Hampton says, "it's a good thing I'm not armed."

"Yeah," Mark says, "it is." He takes Hampton's horse and rides into the Indian Lands toward Quinto, where he meets Henrietta, who advises Mark to remove his badge. "The life expectancy of a sheriff can be very short in Quinto."

Mark keeps local hoods from shutting down Henrietta's paper, then finds his brother being mended by a doctor who has fled a federal indictment in Texas, in the company with the Jesse brothers and The Coyote Kid.

Things move fast in Quinto—and in the movie, though the film never seems to be actually getting anywhere. Sam Bass arrives in town, concocts a moneymaking scheme; Mark kills Hank McGee in a gunfight. That earns the sheriff the respect of not only the male outlaws in Quinto, but Belle Starr too. There's a big horse race coming up, and she suggests a friendly side bet with Mark: "Money or marbles or ... moonlight?" Mark replies, "Suppose we just make it a dollar and a half." Henrietta gets a mite jealous.

Ah ... but the horse race. Indians have bet heavily on Belle Starr's horse, Mark prevents an uprising by declaring that Belle's horse won (Jesse backs him) and not Henrietta, and stops Sam Bass from stealing the dough.

That's all for Jesse and Frank. They leave Quinto. "I hope we meet again," Mark tells Jesse.

"I don't," Jesse says with a smile.

As soon as the Jameses depart town, here comes the Dalton Gang. The brothers, former peace officers, bring word that Hampton has issued wanted posters on Mark and Johnny, and Johnny begins wondering if all this righteous law business is worth the trouble. Maybe he should be an outlaw like the Daltons. When the Daltons leave town to pull a "doubleheader"—robbing two banks in Coffeyville, Kansas—Johnny goes with them.

Mark rides after him, but he's too late. The Daltons are shot down by Coffeyville's citizens, and Johnny, who was holding the horses in an alley, is mortally wounded. Mark spirits him out of town.

By this time, Hampton has been appointed U.S. marshal, Oklahoma Territory has been formed and annexed Badman's Territory, and Hampton is on his way to bring his own brand of justice to Quinto.

The rogue lawman arrives to

Badman's Territory (1946) put Randolph Scott up against some of the West's most famous outlaws, including Jesse James (Lawrence Tierney).

a practically deserted Quinto, and tries to coerce Coyote into falsely testifying that Mark Rowley was in on the Coffeyville raid. Coyote tells Hampton he can go "straight to —" but the infuriated marshal kills him, in the nick of time, too, or else Coyote would have cursed on film!

That's too much for Mark to take. He grabs a gun, and in the ensuing gun battle, Hampton is killed.

In a courthouse, Mark Rowley is acquitted. He's free to ride off with Henrietta in a buggy down Quinto's quiet streets as the flag waves above the courthouse. Law has come to Quinto.

The History

In *The Films of Randolph Scott*, Robert Nott writes that *Badman's Territory* "opens with a confusing series of events in which just about the entire cast of characters are introduced in comic-book fashion."

That's what *Badman's Territory* feels like: a comic book, and comic books aren't usually noted for historical accuracy.

When Texas entered the union as a slave state, it had to cede all land north of 36.5 degrees north latitude because of the Missouri Compromise. That left a strip of land — today's Panhandle of Oklahoma — unassigned to any state or territory. Officially known as "Public Land Strip," it earned the nickname "No Man's Land" — not "Badman's Territory," though it was lawless.[82]

"In the late nineteenth century," Timothy Egan writes in his phenomenal book *The Worst Hard Time: The Untold Story of Those Who Survived the Great American Dust Bowl*, "one corner of the Panhandle served as a roost for outlaws, thieves, and killers."[83]

But not Jesse and Frank James, Sam Bass, Belle Starr, the Dalton Gang.... No, the most famous band of outlaws based in the Oklahoma Panhandle was the Coe Gang. Jesse and his gang pull off a train robbery in Trail Cross, Texas, in the movie, but in reality the Coe Gang dressed like Indians and raided wagon trains on the Cimarron Cutoff of the Santa Fe Trail.[84]

As far as Jesse James is concerned, he never robbed any train in Trail Cross, Texas — there is no Trail Cross, Texas — and it would have been mighty hard for him to pull off such a crime as, by the time *Badman's Territory* is set (1890), he had been dead eight years.

There's no Quinto, Oklahoma, either. Beer City — not Quinto — was the first settlement in No Man's Land. It was founded in 1888 because selling liquor in Kansas was illegal, and it lasted only two years. In 1890, the Panhandle became part of Oklahoma Territory[85] (the movie has that part right). Still, screenwriters Jack Natteford and Luci Ward get the gist of the Panhandle settlement right. "No Man's Land had been one of the last places in the United States where a person could hide, and nobody cared enough to come look for them," Eagan writes.[86]

The script is handy with names — although the name of the *Arapaho* chief is Tahlequah, which happens to be the name of the *Cherokee* capital — but it's a little too wild with dates. Hampton is a member of the Texas State Police at the beginning of the picture. The Texas State Police was founded in 1870, dissolved in 1873, and reinstated in 1935.[87]

And those outlaws? Sam Bass? The closest he ever got to Jesse James was when he robbed a Union Pacific train on September 18, 1877, in Nebraska, and Jesse and Frank James and another man were briefly suspected of the crime.[88] But Bass was mortally wounded after a botched robbery in Round Rock, Texas, and died on July 21, 1878.[89]

Belle Starr? She's often associated with the James and Younger brothers (oddly, the 1941 movie *Belle Starr* starring Gene Tierney doesn't include the James-Younger Gang in its cast of characters), but she was shot dead from ambush in 1889. Her killer was never identified.[90]

The Dalton Gang? Yes, some of the Dalton brothers were former peace officers. Yes, they did try to pull off a "doubleheader" by robbing two banks in Coffeyville, Kansas, and yes, they were shot to pieces by town defenders. Emmett Dalton survived the carnage, but that's okay, since there's no Emmett Dalton in this movie. There was a Bill Dalton, but he skipped the Coffeyville raid — good for him — only to be killed near Elk, Oklahoma, in 1894. In *Badman's Territory*, two outlaws riding with the Daltons, Dick Broadwell (Elmo Lincoln) and Bitter Creek (Emory Parnell), also are gunned down in the Coffeyville fiasco. Broadwell was killed in the raid, but history tells us that Bitter Creek Newcomb didn't take part in the robbery attempt, and was killed in 1895. The robbery happened on October 5, 1892.[91]

Which makes it odd that, in *Badman's Territory*, outside the courthouse before Mark Rowley is acquitted, word has come about Jesse James's fate. "Man named Ford killed Jesse," Colonel Farewell tells Doc, "and the law got Frank."

That's an accurate statement, but it seems strange that it took eight or ten years for the news of Jesse's death to reach Quinto.

The Players

RKO used Tim Whelan to direct, an odd choice for a Western. Known mostly for comedies and musicals, Whelan had spent a dozen years in England before returning to Hollywood in 1940 to complete producer Alexander Korda's *The Thief of Bagdad* after the German Blitz forced the move from Britain. *Badman's Territory* was his first Western. He would only direct two more, *Rage at Dawn* and *Texas Lady*, both 1955 releases, and neither very good.[92]

Likewise, much of the cast seemed ill-suited for Westerns. Lawrence Tierney had given a star-making performance in *Dillinger* (1945), so RKO likely figured if he played a 1930s gangster well, he'd be perfect as an 1880s outlaw. Tierney was planned to star in *Step by Step* (1946) and *Born to Kill* (1947), the latter originally titled *Deadlier Than the Male*. "RKO is banking strongly on Tierney for dynamic roles," the *Los Angeles Times* reported after Tierney had been cast in *Badman's Territory*.[93]

Ann Richards was an Australian actress; the script made her character English to explain her accent. She had left Australia on the *Mariposa* when World War II broke out. The ship was believed to have been sunk by Japanese, "so when Richards arrived in Hollywood everyone thought she was dead."[94]

Born and reared on a ranch in Wyoming, Isabel Jewell was likely a more appropriate choice for Belle Starr, but screen audiences hadn't seen her in Westerns. Instead, her highlights included performances as a seamstress headed for the guillotine in *A Tale of Two Cities* (1935), a tubercular prostitute in *Lost Horizon* (1937) and "poor white trash" in *Gone with the Wind* (1939). She was also well under five feet tall, compared to Scott's 6-foot-2 frame.[95]

On the other hand, Scott, Gabby Hayes and — briefly — James Warren were synonymous with Westerns. So were Steve Brodie and Chief Thundercloud.

Though he was certainly better suited in film noirs such as *Crossfire* (1947) and *Out of the Past* (1947), Brodie, playing Bob Dalton in *Badman's Territory,* came back as Cole Younger in RKO's *Return of the Bad Men* (1948). *Badman's Territory* was his first Western, but he'd go on to wear cowboy hats in several movies and television shows.[96]

Chief Thundercloud was a Cherokee from Muskogee, Oklahoma, who came to Hollywood in the 1920s. A singer of tribal folk songs, he worked as a stuntman and double and made his screen debut in *Rustlers of Red Dog* (1935), a serial for Universal. The studio promptly changed his name from Victor Daniels to Chief Thundercloud. In 1938, Republic gave him the part of Tonto in their serial *The Lone Ranger*. The following year, he landed the title role — but not the lead part — in Paramount's *Geronimo*.[97]

Gabby Hayes, of course, was a veteran character actor and sidekick to many Western stars, including Randolph Scott.

Scott had partnered with independent producer Nat Holt in 1946, and the two worked together on seven movies with RKO and 20th Century–Fox. *Badman's Territory* had a budget of $831,211.29. "When a million-dollar movie was considered an A in those times, [*Badman's Territory*] came close to meeting the criteria," Robert Nott points out.[98]

Warren, born James Whittlig, had been an aspiring artist when MGM brought him to Hollywood in 1942. After the studio declined to renew his option, RKO signed him in 1944 to replace Robert Mitchum in the studio's B-budget Zane Grey Westerns. The studio had cut back on its Westerns, however, and when actor Tim Holt returned from a stint in the military, Warren lost his lead-role status in the Zane Grey movies. By the 1950s, Warren left acting and returned to art, moving to Hawaii to focus on watercolors until his death in 2001.[99]

The movie also had Western veteran and future Academy Award winner Ben Johnson in an uncredited role. Johnson played a member of Hampton's posse when the lawmen ride into Quinto. In fact, Johnson spots Randolph Scott sitting in front of the Wade Hotel. Hampton, Johnson and another deputy ride up to the hotel, and all three dismount and head inside with Scott. Yet in the next scene, an interior shot, Hampton has only one deputy with him, and it's not Johnson.

Maybe Ben had to turn back to be a stuntman in *Smoky*.

Analysis

Badman's Territory is weak all the way around, as historical Western, as Randolph Scott Western, and as a Jesse James movie, yet "[w]orking from the theory that a western can't have too many bad guys,"[100] it started a trend at RKO.

Scott was later seen in *Return of the Bad Men* as Vance Cordell, a marshal who runs across the Daltons, the Youngers, Billy the Kid, and a vicious Sundance Kid (Robert Ryan).

In 1951, Ryan moved up to hero status and met Jesse James (Lawrence Tierney again) in *Best of the Badmen*. The reason was simple. *Badman's Territory* had earned a net profit of $557,000. "The whole fandango was hopelessly contrived, but action-loving patrons swallowed it up whole...."[101]

* * *

90 — Jesse James and the Movies

New York Times (May 31, 1946): "[T]he only thing unusual about *Badman's Territory* is its inordinate length. Westerns seem to have a lot more life when told rapidly and concisely."

Jesse James Rides Again
(Republic, August 1947, 13 chapters, 180 minutes)

CREDITS: Directors: Fred C. Brannon, Thomas Carr; Associate Producer: M.J. Frankovich; Screenplay: Franklin Adreon, Basil Dickey, Jesse Duffy, Sol Shor.

CAST: Clayton Moore (Jesse James); Linda Stirling (Ann Bolton); Roy Barcroft (Frank Lawton); John Compton (Steve Long); Tristram Coffin (James Clark); Tom London (Sam Bolton); Holly Bane (Tim); Edmund Cobb (Wilkie); Gene Roth (Sheriff Duffie); Fred Graham (Hawks); LeRoy Mason (Mr. Finlay); Ed Cassidy (Grant); Dave Anderson (Sam).

Synopsis

Before he found stardom as a masked man, actor Clayton Moore played a heroic Jesse James, pitted against a bunch of masked raiders.

Lobby card promoting a chapter of Republic's first serial featuring Jesse James as a good guy, *Jesse James Rides Again* (1947).

After being falsely accused of leading the Northfield bank raid, Jesse James has to flee Missouri ("They won't let a man be honest," he says) with his pal Steve, whose father was killed in the Northfield robbery.

The law is casting a wide net in a relentless search, forcing Jesse and Steve to ride across Kentucky and into Tennessee's Peaceful Valley. Using aliases, they stop by a farm to ask directions, and are in the house with wheelchair-bound farmer Sam Bolton and his daughter Ann when the Black Raiders — mounted men wearing black robes and capes — attack.

Luckily for the Boltons, Jesse and Steve are crack shots who drive the raiders off. When Sam Bolton suggests that Jesse James himself might be leading those bandits, Steve and the real Jesse take offense, and Jesse reveals his true identity. He and Steve decide to investigate.

No one knows what the Black Raiders are after. Well, land agent James Clark knows, but nobody suspects that he's the mastermind. He's trying to drive off the farmers so he can get their land — sitting over a giant oil field — at a cheap price.

Clark sends his henchman Frank Lawton to ram a steamboat into the levy and flood the farms, but Jesse spoils that plan. He saves a farmhouse from being burned. He prevents Ann from being crushed to death by a cotton press. He gets in more fistfights than Gentleman Jim Corbett. Jesse even saves himself when he's swept off a steamboat, and poses as a corpse and ghost to frighten one of Lawton's men into revealing what he knows. Those screenwriters at Republic would throw anything against the wall to see if it might stick.

Eventually, Jesse uncovers the motive of the raiders, and heads to Memphis to return with drilling materials. Of course, Clark is willing to loan the farmers money for their venture, hoping to take over their mortgagees after they can't make the payment.

Things look grim when the oil executive won't pay off until the farmers prove they can get their crude to the refinery. and Clark won't extend the deadline. It's a race in wagons to the refinery. That's the same plot as Republic's *In Old Oklahoma* (1943), and so *Jesse James Rides Again* uses stock footage from it.

Of course, Jesse manages to get the oil to the refinery, collect the payment, and get the money back to Clark with two minutes to spare. Then he kills Lawton and has Clark arrested after the law hears the land grabber's confession.

The History

Odd as it might seem in a low-budget serial, the screenwriters got some facts right, or close to right.

Jesse James did wind up in Tennessee after the Northfield bank robbery. He and his family moved to Edgefield — across the Cumberland River from Nashville — after the 1875 Pinkerton raid on the Clay County farm.[102] The whereabouts of Jesse and Frank after the Northfield robbery are open to speculation, but they might have wound up for a while at the home of their uncle, George Hite, in Adairville, Kentucky. By the summer of 1877, Frank had moved to Nashville and Jesse was living near Waverly in Humphreys County, Tennessee. The movie even gets Jesse's alias partly right, calling him John C. Howard. He went by the name John D. Howard.[103]

All right, Jesse didn't go about helping save farmers from robber barons. Between 1820 and 1840, some wells drilled for brine produced some oil, but no real oil searches were conducted until after the Civil War, and no real searches began until the 1890s, long after Jesse's death.[104]

When Steve volunteers to go undercover with the Black Raiders, Jesse warns him that it will be dangerous. "Remember what we used to do to spies," he says. No kidding. In March 1874, Joseph W. Whicher arrived in Liberty, Missouri, and visited Sheriff George E. Patton. Whicher identified himself as an undercover Pinkerton agent hoping to nab the James boys. He would pose as a laborer and work on the farm, then spring his trap. Patton warned Whicher against it. So did former sheriff O.P. Moss, who told the twenty-six-year-old detective: "The old woman [Jesse's mother] would kill you if the boys don't." Whicher didn't listen. He knew his business. He arrived at the James farm on the evening of March 10. The next morning, his body was found on the roadside near Independence with bullets through his heart and head.[105]

Steve fared much better in *Jesse James Rides Again*.

The Players

Mitchell John Frankovich, a former football player for UCLA (he would be inducted into the UCLA Athletic Hall of Fame in 1986), was no stranger to show business: He had appeared in the Mary Pickford movie *Rosita* (1923), worked in radio after UCLA, and married actress Binnie Barnes in 1940 and returned to Hollywood after World War II. In 1947, Frankovich replaced Ronald Davidson as associate producer of Republic's serials. *Jesse James Rides Again* was his first of four, the other three being *The Black Widow* (1947), *G-Men Never Forget* (1948) and *Dangers of the Canadian Mounted* (1948).[106]

Serials had been a part of the sound era since Universal's *The Indians Are Coming* (1930), and Republic Studios had taken the format "to its highest form in the sound era through judicious application of talent, care, and technical knowledge." The studio produced 66 sound serials—second only to Universal's 69—before the format was abandoned in 1956. After World War II, however, production values had lessened, and "a gradual decline set in...."[107]

In 1947, Republic reduced its serial output by one to three original productions per year (with one re-release). *Jesse James Rides Again* was the studio's first of the year. It was filmed between January 10 and February 5, primarily at Iverson Ranch, and went over its $149,967 budget by $30,530.[108]

Perhaps it was an inside joke, or maybe it was a marketing ploy, but *Jesse James Rides Again* had a "cameo" in Republic's next serial, *The Black Widow*, released in November 1947. A poster for *Jesse James Rides Again* is seen on a wall outside villainess Sombra's lair.[109]

Roy Barcroft played the heavy. No surprise there. The Nebraska-born character actor was always playing bad guys in movies, mostly Westerns, for studios such as Republic (where he'd signed a ten-year contract in 1943). He styled himself after Harry Woods, whose villainous roles included Bob Ford in *Jesse James* (1927) and Captain Worthington in *Days of Jesse James* (1939). Clayton Moore said Barcroft even imitated Woods's voice when acting. For such an on-screen menace, Barcroft was, actually, a softy.[110] "He was a big bear cub of a man," Moore said.[111] Linda Stirling said: "He loved to act. He really enjoyed it. He probably spent more time at the studio than he did at home."[112] True enough. In 1947 alone, Barcroft appeared in seventeen movies.[113]

Stirling was no stranger to serials. Born Louise Schultz in 1921, the "Queen of the Serials" had played the heroine in Republic's *Zorro's Black Whip* (1944), in which she was, for all intent and purpose, a female Zorro (aka the Black Whip). She kept busy in serials such as *The Tiger Woman* (1944), *Manhunt of Mystery Island* (1945) and *The Crimson Ghost* (1946).[114]

"Of the characteristics necessary in a heroine, Linda Stirling possessed all — presence, wholesomeness, beauty and versatility — and any single one would have been sufficient in her case," William C. Cline wrote.[115] Moore agreed, calling her "wonderful to work with, so beautiful and talented."

Jesse James Rides Again, however, would be her last serial. She married Sloan Nibley, a Republic screenwriter, and, after an appearance in Republic's film noir *The Pretender* (1947), retired from movies. She later appeared on several television shows in the 1950s.[116]

Jesse James Rides Again was Moore's first Western, and only the second time he rode a horse for the movies. The first had been in *Perils of Nyoka* (1942), in which he battled a gorilla. Born Jack Carlton Moore in 1914 on Chicago's South Side, the real estate broker's son spent many Saturday afternoons at the city's Devon Theater watching Western stars such as Harry Carey, William S. Hart, Ken Manyard, Tom Mix and George O'Brien. As a kid, he wanted to become a policeman or a cowboy, but his career began in a trapeze act. He also worked as a model before moving to Hollywood in 1937.[117]

Working for roughly $200 a week on *Jesse James Rides Again*, Moore paid attention to details. Serials, and many Western features, often ignore the fact that a six-shooter can hold no more than six bullets. "It always bothered me to see someone fire seven or eight shots from a six-shooter," Moore recalled, "so I kept strict count. Every time I fired my sixth bullet, I would reload."[118] It must have been catching. Moore's Jesse isn't the only one seen reloading on screen. Barcroft does it, too.

Moore also did many of his own stunts. In an early chapter, Moore's Jesse races to stop a burning hay wagon that has been rolled to a farmhouse. He tosses a log in front of the wagon, and flips it over. "The bad part was that it overturned toward me, missing me by only a few inches," Moore said. "After that, I turned the big stunts back over to Tom Steele."[119]

Moore had found a niche in Westerns. In 1949, he found another niche, wearing a mask as television's Lone Ranger.

Analysis

"Obviously the real Jesse James was a vicious outlaw, a bank robber and killer, but audiences didn't seem to mind that we turned him into a sympathetic, law-abiding character," Moore wrote. "After all, it was only a serial and a very exciting one at that."[120]

Jesse James Rides Again was controversial, too. In Memphis, Tennessee, Lloyd T. Binford, chairman of the board of censors for the city and county, banned it. "Nothing about Jesse James can show in Memphis," he said.[121] He hadn't even watched it before making his ruling.[122]

Glorifying an outlaw like Jesse James would cause Republic's legal department headaches in a few years, but not in 1947. *Jesse James Rides Again* became a hit, and it prompted two serial sequels.[123]

* * *

New York Times (December 22, 1946): "Quality films ... may be fine for the big cities, but it's the serials, like *Hap Harrigan, G-Men Never Forget* and *Jesse James Rides Again* that keep the small town operators in business."

Adventures of Frank and Jesse James

(Republic, October 1948, 13 chapters, 180 minutes)

CREDITS: *Directors:* Fred Brannon, Yakima Canutt; *Associate Producer:* Franklin Adreon; *Screenplay:* Franklin Adreon, Basil Dickey, Sol Shor.
CAST: Clayton Moore (Jesse James); Steve Darrell (Frank James); Noel Neill (Judy Powell); George J. Lewis (Rafe Henley); Stanley Andrews (Jim Powell); John Crawford (Amos Ramsey); Sam Flint (Paul Thatcher); House Peters Jr. (Thomas Dale); Tom Steele (Mike Steele); James Dale (J.B. Nichols); I. Stanford Jolley (Ward); Gene Roth (Marshal); Lane Bradford (Bill); George Chesebro (Jim); Jack Kirk (Casey).

Synopsis

"The legend of Frank and Jesse James is recorded in bullets and blood," a scroll informs us after the opening credits, "but this story tells of their fight to right the wrongs committed in their names."

Let the action, and hogwash, begin.

After doing a good turn in Tennessee (in *Jesse James Rides Again*), Jesse returns to Missouri to join his brother Frank at the home of miner Jim Powell and his daughter Judy. Frank thinks that if he and Jesse can pay off the victims of crimes attributed to the James Gang, the outlaw brothers might finally be able to live in peace. They own the mine Powell has been working, and thought it was worthless, but Powell believes it has possibilities. The only problem is a rock fault that has interrupted the silver vein; about $1,000 is needed to resume mining.

Jesse thinks he can get a loan from Allentown banker Paul Thatcher, a family friend, but when Jesse arrives at the bank, Thatcher is cold. That's because a Jesse impostor had tried to extort money from him. The fake Jesse shows up and tries to rob the bank, only to be stopped by Frank and Jesse.

When the sheriff arrives, he asks, "What's going on here?" (One would think, after all those fisticuffs and gunplay, he might have assumed the bank was being robbed.) But no matter ... Jesse and Frank, going by the names John Howard and Bob Carroll, have redeemed themselves, and Thatcher is agreeable to the loan — if mine engineer Amos Ramsey agrees it's a worthwhile loan.

When a blast reveals a huge vein of gold, Ramsey gets greedy, kills Jim Powell, makes his death look like an accident, and keeps the gold discovery a secret. Ramsey hires Rafe Henley to help him out. After all, there might be $1 million in that mine.

Well, that sets up a plot pretty much the same as the one in *Jesse James Rides Again*. Ramsey is the mastermind (instead of land agent James Clark) and Henley the lead villain (instead of Sam Bolton). Judy becomes the heroine (instead of Ann Bolton), who gets in a lot of trouble and has to be rescued.

Five. Jesse in the B's, 1939–1949

In 1948, Republic's second Jesse James serial had buckskin-clad Frank James bringing in his brother (Clayton Moore) to do some more nice deeds.

Instead of a steamboat explosion, a stagecoach plummets off a partially collapsed bridge (but Jesse saves Judy, and one of Henley's henchmen). They manage to get the bad guy to the sheriff, but Henley's men free him. Jesse bulldogs him from the saddle, but the villains trample the bad guy before he can talk.

Ramsey reluctantly issues a favorable report to Thatcher and recommends a $1,000 loan. Naturally, he makes sure that Henley's men steal the money. Judy discovers a map that reveals an abandoned tunnel that leads to the rock fault. Frank and Jesse go to investigate, and Ramsey sends the bad guys to stop them. Frank and Jesse are lucky to escape with their lives after a fiery explosion.

Ramsey resorts to trickery. He sends ore samples to Allentown, then manages a swap, and when the fake ore grades out at eight cents a ton, all seems lost. There's no way the bank will loan another $1,000 for a worthless mine like that. But what luck! There happens to be a stagecoach race coming up, with $1,000 going to the winner, and Jesse "knows more about stagecoaches than anyone in the country."

Only the badmen capture Jesse, and hold him hostage. Frank is forced to start the race, but lassoed out of the driver's boot by Henley's men on the rival stage. Ah, but Jesse has managed to free himself, gallops to the rescue, leaps onto the stagecoach, and wins the race.

More chicanery, fistfights, explosions and gunfights follow, and Jesse survives a harrowing fall off a cliff without a scratch. Instead of a race with oil wagons as in *Jesse James Rides Again*, there's an ambush against freight wagons hauling mining equipment.

To stop the mining, Ramsey hires Thomas Dale to file a prior-ownership claim to the mine, and an injunction is filed. The only way to prove ownership is to show the deed, which has Frank and Jesse's names on it. That could get our heroes arrested. So Jesse goes after Dale, finds him, and brings him back to the hearing — just in time.

Before Dale can talk, he's shot, but isn't killed. The bad guys try an assault to get Dale. Dale dies, but Jesse sees this as an opportunity. He disguises himself as Dale, has Frank and the doctor play dead, and Henley's men come in and take Dale back to their hideout. (Go figure. They'd already tried to kill him to keep him from talking, so why not just finish the job?) Well, Jesse played a corpse in *Jesse James Rides Again*. This time, he gets to play only a wounded villain.

Again, fists fly, and Jesse narrowly escapes death. The villains destroy the water supply on Bald Hill. Judy is kidnapped — and saved — again, and the brothers dig a sluice to provide water.

By now Ramsey has revealed his hand, and Jesse confronts him. Frank kills Ramsey before he can shoot Jesse in the back. With the villains rounded up, money will soon be flowing in. Frank and Jesse, nice guys, arrange for their share go to victims of the James Gang.

The History

Undoubtedly, some crimes attributed to the James brothers were not committed by Frank or Jesse but, as biographer Marley Brant calls them, "copycats."[124]

But as for anything loosely based on history in this serial? Well, there once were a couple of outlaws named Frank and Jesse James.

The Players

Although he wasn't under contract to Republic, Clayton Moore reprised his role as Jesse James. Working there, Moore said, was like a happy family. "The studio didn't have a glamorous reputation, but it remained my favorite place to work. Everyone was cooperative and willing to help you out at all times."[125]

Yet it was a grueling work schedule. The 1948 serial was shot for $149,805 — Republic's cheapest since *Son of Zorro* (1947), and cheaper than the rest of Republic's remaining serial releases. It began shooting on April 5 and wrapped on April 25.[126]

Part of that low budget might be explained by stock footage. Moore's outfit of floppy, wide-brimmed Stetson and batwing chaps looked a lot like the outfit worn by Donald Barry in Republic's serial *Adventures of Red Ryder* (1940). Steve Darrell's outfit resembled the buckskin wardrobe of Hal Taliferro, who played Barry's sidekick in *Red Ryder*. The serial apparently relied heavily on stock footage from *Red Ryder*.[127]

With Linda Stirling's departure from acting, Noel Neill came on board as Judy. She would go on to play Lois Lane in two serials, *Superman* (1948) and *Atom Man vs. Superman* (1950), as well as in the popular television series *Adventures of Superman* (1953–58). Moore remembered her as "a lovely young actress with a great deal of talent."[128]

The real star, however, might have been one of the directors. Yakima Canutt had been a rodeo star and stuntman, "the greatest stuntman with horses and horses and wagons" and a man with "nerves of steel."[129] Perhaps best known for his work with Tom Mix, John Wayne and director John Ford, Canutt had retired from stunt work after *In Old Oklahoma* (1943) and began focusing primarily on second unit and assistant-directing. His best-known work is most likely the chariot race in *Ben-Hur* (1959).

Therefore, the real disappointment in *Adventures of Frank and Jesse James* is the dullness of the stunts. Republic was known for its action-packed serials, but that heyday was fading fast.

Analysis

Yet another glorification of Jesse James, this serial pales in comparison to *Jesse James Rides Again*, and for entertainment and originality, falls between the original Jesse serial and Republic's final effort, *The James Brothers of Missouri* (1949).

There's no history here, and not a lot of entertainment.

* * *

Montana: The Magazine of Western History (October 1967): "This second serialized excursion into the lives of the famous brothers was a rehash of the first."

I Shot Jesse James

(Screen Guild, February 1949, 81 minutes)

CREDITS: *Director-Screenplay:* Samuel Fuller; *Producer:* Carl K. Hittleman.
CAST: Preston Foster (John Kelley); Barbara Britton (Cynthy Waters); John Ireland (Bob Ford); Reed Hadley (Jesse James); J. Edward Brombert (Harry Kane); Victor Kilian (Soapy); Tom Tyler (Frank James); Tommy Noonan, billed as Tom Noonan (Charles Ford); Eddie Dunn (Silver King Bartender); Margia Dean (Saloon Singer); Byron Foulger (Silver King Room Clerk); Jeni Le Gon (Veronica); Barbara Woodell (Zee James); Robin Short (Troubadour).

Synopsis

This is the first movie that took the formula created in director Henry King's *Jesse James* (1939), or maybe even earlier, to task.

Jesse James and his gang, including Bob Ford, are robbing the Cattleman's Bank in Topeka, Kansas, when a teller triggers the alarm. Gunfire erupts, and the outlaws have to leave in a hurry. Ford, wounded, drops the cash, so the outlaws escape with nothing but their lives.

Jesse brings Bob to his home outside St. Joseph, Missouri, where Jesse's living under the name Tom Howard, and nurses him back to health. Six months later, Jesse's wife Zee is sick of Bob and his brother Charles. "He just spells trouble...." Zee says while snapping peas.

Charlie brings news of a possible bank job, and word that Bob's girl, actress Cynthy

Samuel Fuller got his first job as director on *I Shot Jesse James* (1949), which starred John Ireland, behind bars, as Robert Ford, the man who killed Jesse.

Waters, is in St. Joe. That brightens Bob's mood considerably, but Cynthy won't marry Bob until he's "free." And the law says that if Bob surrenders now, he *can* be free — in twenty years.

Ah, but suddenly the governor has announced he will award amnesty, and a $10,000 reward, to any member of the gang that brings in Jesse, dead or alive. That's tempting. When Jesse presents Bob with a loaded single-action .45 while the outlaw leader is taking a bath, Bob is tempted to shoot Jesse in the back. But he can't bring himself to do it and instead *scrubs* Jesse's back. He's tempted again later but still can't murder his friend.

Until one hot morning, while Jesse's kids are at school, and Jesse removes his coat, vest and guns. He climbs onto a chair to straighten a picture, and Bob shoots him in the back of the head.

He's arrested, of course, and sentenced to hang, but the governor pardons him. Instead of collecting the $10,000 reward, the law gives Bob only $500, $100 of which Bob uses to stake Charlie, who wants to get out of town because public opinion is completely against the Ford brothers.

Bob feels he has enough to buy Cynthy a ring, yet Cynthy is repulsed by what he has done. "How could you have done it?" she tells him. "Can't you see how wrong it was?"

Bob doesn't see things that way. He thinks Cynthy refuses to marry him because of a

Colorado miner, John Kelley. After Kelley leaves town, Bob reasons that Cynthy won't marry him until he has enough money.

His first stab at a job is on the theatrical stage, as "a special added attraction" in which he will demonstrate how he shot Jesse. That disgusts Cynthy even further. "Have you lost your mind?" she asks. "How can you put yourself up like a freak?"

"What's the difference?" Bob snaps. "He's dead. I just want a chance to prove that I am no murderer, traitor or assassin."

Yet while treading the boards, he can't bring himself to shoot the actor playing Jesse. He walks off stage, to boos, and heads to the bar, where a troubadour comes in and sings "a song everybody likes." The song happens to be "Jesse James." Writer-director Samuel Fuller said he included the scene to illustrate "Ford's self-hatred."[130]

When the troubadour realizes he's singing to "the dirty little coward," he stops, but Ford orders him to finish the song, then walks out of the saloon.

It seems that everybody in St. Joe is gunning for Bob Ford, so Cynthy talks him into heading to Creede, Colorado, site of a rich silver strike, and Bob rides west. In Creede, he shares a room with John Kelley. He even saves Kelley from a would-be back-shooter after Kelley tangles with some ruffians who are trying to con a local miner, Soapy, out of his claim.

Eventually, Soapy takes on Bob as a partner, and they strike it rich. No such luck for Kelley, so he takes the job as town marshal because a "fella's gotta eat."

Cynthy's in town, on her way to Denver, and Bob again tries to get her to marry him, but by now she's in love with Kelley. Then Frank James shows up, is captured, and put on trial. When he's acquitted — because he's wanted for no crime in Colorado (what happened to extradition?) — Frank gets his revenge by telling Bob that Cynthy is in love with Kelley.

Bob goes gunning for the marshal, but Kelley turns his back, and Bob can't bring himself to shoot him like that. When the lawman finally turns around, Kelley tries to reason with Bob. Bob draws his pistol, wounding Kelley, who blasts Bob with a shotgun.

Dying in Cynthy's arms, Bob makes a final confession: "I'm sorry for what I done to Jess. I loved him."

The History

"The real Jesse James was bisexual," Samuel Fuller wrote in his autobiography, "masquerading as a girl to hold up trains that were carrying medical supplies. The guy was a low-down thief, a pervert, and a sonofabitch. But you couldn't show that stuff on a screen back then, demystifying one of the great American icons."[131]

I don't know any stories about Jesse James masquerading as a girl, but I do know that Sam Fuller wouldn't win any popularity contests with the Friends of the James Farm in Kearney, Missouri.

Yet Fuller's screenplay — certainly containing a "subtle suggestion of a homosexual bond between Ford and James"[132] — was one of the first serious attempts at "demystifying" Jesse James. It also paid reasonably close attention, by Hollywood standards, to history. Stretched history, of course.

The James Gang never robbed a bank in Topeka, and it's debated how many crimes Bob Ford really took part in. His older brother Charlie committed his first robbery with

Jesse on the Blue Cut train job of September 7, 1881. The Ford brothers, along with Dick Liddil and Wood Hite, had previously robbed a stagecoach in Ray County, Missouri.[133]

The song gives Jesse three kids when, in fact, he had only two. The children weren't at school when Bob Ford shot him, but in the house. Jesse did have a beard, as actor Reed Hadley sports, at the time of his death. Charlie Ford was also on hand when his younger brother killed Jesse, but not in this movie.

Bob and Charlie pleaded guilty to killing Jesse, and were sentenced to hang, only to be pardoned by the governor. Thomas Crittenden, however, hadn't advertised that amnesty deal in all the newspapers. On January 13, 1882, Bob Ford had met secretly with Governor Crittenden and Clay County Sheriff Henry Timberlake. According to Ford, Crittenden "told me what he would give for the capture — said he would give $10,000 apiece for Jesse and Frank, dead or alive."[134] A woman's love had no part in Bob Ford's motives for killing Jesse.

Bob Ford didn't collect that ten grand; according to Homer Croy, he got more like $1,200. And he doesn't get the dough in the movie, either.[135]

Also, Ford did tour in a play, *How I Killed Jesse James*, opening in New York City (not St. Joseph) on September 18, 1882.[136] Nor was he winning many popularity contests. "Feeling against him had continued to grow; more and more it was realized what sort of a creature he was," Croy writes.[137]

Charlie Ford committed suicide in 1884 at his home in Richmond, Missouri[138]— left out of this movie — but Bob did wind up in the silver-mining town of Creede, Colorado, after stops in Las Vegas, New Mexico, and Walsenburg and Pueblo, Colorado.[139] There was a man named Soapy in Creede, too, only Jefferson Randolph "Soapy" Smith was no miner, but a con artist who eventually was killed in Skagway, Alaska, in 1898.[140] Frank James never made it to Creede.

Creede was Bob Ford's last stop, although he didn't get there until 1892 — ten years after he killed Jesse James — while in the movie, everything happens in about one year. He was killed by a blast from a sawed-off shotgun on June 8, 1892, not on the streets, but inside his tent saloon. The man who killed him was a (maybe) one-time lawman whose name was Ed — not John — Kelly/Kelley/O'Kelly/O'Kelley. He was sentenced to life in prison in Cañon City, Colorado, but was released in 1902, then wound up in Oklahoma City, where he was gunned down by a police officer on January 13, 1904.[141]

The slayer of the slayer of Jesse James expressed no remorse over the murder of Bob Ford. "I don't pull off women's toenails with pincers," he is reported to have said, "but I can kill such men as Bob Ford."[142]

The motive for the killing of Bob Ford has also been debated. Some said it was over a girl, as depicted in this movie, but others deny that. Homer Croy, whose facts aren't always factual, writes that Kelly and Ford quarreled over a diamond ring (Ford had accused Kelly of stealing it). Fuller, who gave story credit to Croy for his *American Weekly* magazine article "The Dirty Little Coward Who Killed Mr. Howard," uses that in his script. Another theory has it that Kelly came from Harrisonville, Missouri, was related to the Younger family, and killed Bob Ford to avenge Jesse's death. Or perhaps he just wanted the reputation of being the man who killed the man who killed Jesse James.[143]

Whatever the reason, Sam Fuller's script was an intriguing character study, loosely based on facts, and it made interesting cinema to watch Bob Ford's spiral into living hell and his redemption in death. The blend of fact and fiction worked. As the *Christian Science Monitor* reported, "Some of *I Shot Jesse James* ... seems factual. Some of it obviously is romanticized. The combination holds attention better than the baldness of the title might suggest."[144]

The Players

Born March 11, 1909, Robert L. Lippert was left on the San Francisco Catholic Charities Orphanage doorstep, and was adopted by an Alameda, California, couple twenty-two months later. At age fourteen, he was playing a pump organ to provide the music for silent films showing at a local theater. In his twenties, he was promoting sound equipment for the new "talkies," and started a theater chain on the West Coast in the 1940s. In 1945, his Screen Guild Productions began releasing his low-budget films produced by his Action Films, Inc.[145]

A former soldier, tabloid newspaper reporter and pulp novelist, Samuel Fuller had written scripts (1949's *Shockproof*) or had his stories turned into movies, and was looking to direct one himself. Enter Lippert, who tracked down the writer and said he wanted to make a movie from one of Fuller's stories and let Fuller direct it. Lippert passed on Fuller's first idea — a movie about Cassius, who plotted the assassination of Julius Caesar — but was intrigued by another movie about a murderer.[146]

"It's about Bob Ford," Fuller pitched. "Nobody ever made a movie about him."

"Who did he murder?" Lippert asked.

"Jesse James."

"Jesse James! Now we've got a movie."[147]

They worked on a handshake deal. "Making just another Western wasn't going to give me a hard-on," Fuller wrote. "Holdups, revolvers, leather gloves, and galloping horses didn't do anything for me. The real aggression and violence in the film would be happening inside the head of a psychotic, delusional killer."[148]

To play that killer, Fuller cast John Ireland, an actor whose work Fuller had admired in director Howard Hawks's *Red River* (1948).[149] Born in Canada and reared in Harlem, Ireland had started off as a swimmer in a water carnival before moving to "legitimate theater." "Shakespeare became his first love and that led to roles on Broadway," his son, John Ireland Jr., recalled.[150] Shakespearean-trained, Ireland showed an intensity in his early roles: gunman Cherry Valance in *Red River*; the letter-writing infantry soldier in *A Walk in the Sun* (1945); Billy Clanton in *My Darling Clementine* (1946); and he gave searing portrayals in two Anthony Mann–directed films noir, *Railroaded!* (1947) and *Raw Deal* (1948). Shortly after completing work on *I Shot Jesse James*, Ireland played Jack Burden in Robert Rossen's *All the King's Men* (1949), for which he earned an Academy Award nomination for Best Supporting Actor.[151]

Ireland's half brother, Tommy Noonan, got the part of Charles Ford in *I Shot Jesse James*. As far as the other key players, the *Los Angeles Times* noted that Reed Hadley, "looking a bit like Abraham Lincoln with his whiskers, his skinny frame and mournful eyes, also draws sympathy," and that Barbara Britton "is dainty and skillfully convincing as the girl."[152]

Fuller said he hoped to make *I Shot Jesse James* "an *Informer* of the West,"[153] which might be why he cast Preston Foster as John Kelley. Foster had played Irish Republican

Army leader Dan Gallagher in John Ford's *The Informer* (1935), one of Fuller's favorite films. Another reason for the casting was that Lippert demanded a name actor in the movie.[154] Name or not, Foster gave one of the movie's weakest performances. Though only forty-eight, he also looked too old to play twenty-nine-year-old Britton's paramour.

One of the film's best performances came from actress Barbara Woodell, playing Jesse's wife as a weary, edgy woman, and not quite the devoted Zee of previous films.

Lippert rented a frontier street at Republic Studios and gave Fuller ten days to complete the movie in October 1948. "Everything was done on the cheap," Fuller said. "When we ran out of money at the end, we had to film the opening credits on posters tacked to a wall."[155]

Analysis

Although Fuller says critics labeled *I Shot Jesse James* "the first adult Western,"[156] the movie got mixed reviews. The *Los Angeles Times* said, "John Ireland is typed perfectly for the Bob Ford role, and does an excellent job,"[157] while the *New York Times* noted that "since the character study is not particularly interesting, *I Shot Jesse James* is a very mild pretense at being an entertainment."[158]

In his book *Western Films*, Brian Garfield lauds Ireland but says the movie is "hammily acted by most of the players, unevenly written and routinely directed...."[159]

Still, the movie proved successful enough that Lippert distributed the far inferior indie *I Shot Billy the Kid*, starring Donald Barry, the following year. Over the next four years, Lippert produced and distributed a handful of other Jesse James movies.

I Shot Jesse James is remembered mostly as the movie that launched Fuller's directing career, but it's certainly worth another look as a historical film. It could have launched a series of thought-provoking dramas about Jesse James and the boys. Instead, the next decade would bring to the theaters, for the most part, action-driven B-Westerns with little regard for history or character.

* * *

Variety (January 1, 1949): "*I Shot Jesse James* is a character study of the man who felled the west's most famous outlaw with a coward's bullet. It's an interesting treatment that doesn't overlook necessary plot and action."

The James Brothers of Missouri
(Republic, August 1949, 12 chapters, 167 minutes)

CREDITS: *Directors:* Fred C. Brannon, Yakima Canutt; *Associate Producer:* Franklin Adreon; *Screenplay:* Royal Cole, William Lively, Sol Shor.

CAST: Keith Richards (Jesse James); Robert Bice (Frank James); Noel Neill (Pet Royer); Roy Barcroft (Ace Marlin); Patricia Knox (Belle Calhoun); Lane Bradford (Monk Tucker); Eugene Roth (Rand); John Hamilton (Lon Royer); Edmund Cobb (Sheriff); Hank Patterson (Duffy); Dale Van Sickel (Harry Sharkey); Tom Steele (Slim); Lee Roberts (Brandy Jones); Frank O'Connor (Citizen); Marshall Reed (Dutch); Wade Ray (Deputy); Nolan Leary (Pop Keever).

Synopsis

In what sound serial historian William C. Cline calls "a quick warm-over of the first two"[160] Jesse James serials, *The James Brothers of Missouri* actually had a few moments of originality.

Yet another story of Frank and Jesse James' "attempt to live within the law," the serial opens with Jesse, again using the alias John Howard, riding a stagecoach to what he thought "was a peaceful corner of Missouri."

It's anything but.

Frank, under the alias Bob Carroll, has asked Jesse to come to Rimrock, where Ace Freight Lines boss Ace Marlin is using brute force to try to force Royer Freight & Stage Lines out of business. Peg Royer is on the stage with Jesse when Marlin's henchmen, led by Monk Tucker, attack it. They're after the federal contract Peg's taking to her father Lon. Jesse drives off the bandits and brings the stage in after the driver and guard are killed.

The contract thwarts Marlin's attempt to steal Royer's business, but not for long. Lon Royer is murdered, and the contract stolen.

Marlin's tough and smart, but the real brains behind the outfit — in a Republic twist — is Belle Calhoun, owner of the Frontier Belle General Store. There's always a mastermind in these serials, but the identity of him — or in this case, her — is usually not discovered by the heroes until the final episode.

Jesse brings back a duplicate of the contract from St. Louis, but the bad guys attack and, using flaming barrels of coal oil, blow up the Royer freight wagons.

The James brothers underbid Marlin to win a copper mine contract, and win more contracts. Belle tells Marlin that county land recorder Henry Simpson is wanted for forgery under the name Harry Sharkey. They blackmail him into forging a new boundary map that puts the main road on Marlin's property, so Marlin can charge a huge toll that will bankrupt Royer. But Jesse and Frank learn of another road and scout it out. Marlin's no dummy, however. He sends his men to blow up Keyhole Pass, but Frank and Jesse escape with their lives.

Sharkey's killed, and the bad guys burn down the land office, but Jesse manages to save the forged county atlas. Peg tells a sympathetic Belle that her friends are taking the atlas to the territorial commissioner to prove it's a forgery, and Belle informs the villains. The bad guys steal the wagon the brothers are traveling in, but Jesse gets it back, saves the atlas before the wagon blows up. Things are always blowing up in Republic serials.

The commissioner rules Marlin's toll road illegal, and Belle gives Royer a contract to bring in a $3,000 payroll for the miners. But she hasn't really had a change of heart. When Frank and Jesse return to Rimrock, the moneybag is substituted by Tucker, and the boys are accused of robbery. Frank and Jesse escape, although Frank is wounded.

The bad guys follow Peg, who's bringing supplies to Frank, and capture him and bring him to town, where a lynch mob awaits. Jesse manages to get the money back and stops the lynching.

Enough with the soft gloves, Marlin declares, and raids begin on all of Royer's customers. Yet the bad guys keep all of their plunder in a cave, which might be Marlin's undoing — after Frank and Jesse learn its location.

Jesse sends Peg to fetch a U.S. marshal. That's tricky — the lawman might recognize

By 1949, Clayton Moore had become TV's Lone Ranger, so Republic's final installment in its Jesse James serials, *The James Brothers of Missouri*, cast Keith Richards as the good Missouri badguy.

Frank and Jesse — but they have no other choice. They plan to blow up the entrance to the mine to keep Marlin from moving it, but Marlin's men trap the boys and try to bury them alive. Yep, another explosion, and another near-death experience for Frank and Jesse.

Peg brings the marshal, a man named Rand, back to Rimrock. Rand is suspicious of John Howard and Bob Carroll and tells Belle he thinks they are really Jesse and Frank James. Belle happens to know a man named Thorne, whose testimony had apparently put Peg's father, one of the original members of the James Gang, out of the outlaw business. Thorne is brought in to identify Frank and Jesse James, and when the boys enter the freight office, Rand is there to arrest them.

But not so fast. Thorne says he's mistaken, that he has never seen these two men, and Rand apologizes and leaves. Why the change in heart? Seems it had something to do with (in a cute twist) the gun Peg had secretly pressed against his back.

Jesse warns Thorne, "You've got ten minutes to get out of Rimrock, or everyone in the old gang will be hot on your trail."

Frank, Jesse and Rand lead a posse to Marlin's cave, killing Tucker. Marlin hightails it back to Rimrock, where he pleads with Belle for help. Belle has another idea. She thinks she can kill Marlin, get away with murder, and save her own neck. Yet by now, Jesse suspects Belle of conspiracy, and he stops Belle from killing Marlin.

Marlin fights Jesse for freedom. They wrestle for Jesse's gun. Belle tries to get away, but a shot kills her. Then Marlin is shot dead.

There's nothing left for Marshal Rand to do but congratulate Peg. He tells her that her late father made a great decision when he stopped riding with the likes of Frank and Jesse James and took up with a pair of respectable heroes like John Howard and Bob Carroll.

The History

Historical accuracy was never a priority for any Republic Western, especially a serial. As has been noted previously, Jesse James did use the alias of John Howard; however, Bob Carroll is not a known alias of Frank James.

One of the more interesting historical snafus in the movie has Jesse riding to see the territorial commissioner in Santa Fe to prove that a map is a forgery. That seems a long ride to New Mexico Territory. Wouldn't Jefferson City be more logical? After all, Missouri had become a state in 1821.

The Players

With Clayton Moore now playing the Lone Ranger on television, Republic turned to Keith Richards to take over the role of Jesse James. The Pittsburgh-born actor had signed with Paramount in 1941, appearing in *Reap the Wild Wind* (1942), *Wake Island* (1942) and *The Miracle of Morgan's Creek* (1944). A supporting actor, he rarely got lead roles; he was the Phony Drunk in Chapter Seven of *Jesse James Rides Again*. Richards and Noel Neill would also have uncredited bit parts in *The Greatest Show on Earth* (1952). By the early 1950s, Richards was appearing mostly in television series. He died in 1987.[161]

Drawing $150 a week, Neill, another actress who landed mostly bit roles, returned for her second Jesse James serial. She later became Lois Lane on television's *Adventures of Superman* after replacing Phyllis Coates at the start of the second season. Having played Lois in two serials before the TV series, her connection with the Man of Steel continued with appearances in *Superman: The Movie* (1978), *The Adventures of Superboy* (1988) and *Superman Returns* (2006).[162]

"I'll tell you one thing about westerns," Neill said. "I never really met any of the guys. Outside of working with them, I just didn't know them. You come in and you get hairdressing, wardrobe, pages of script maybe, and sit and wait to do your thing and that's it."[163]

Big Gene Roth, originally billed Eugene Stutenroth, was back in his third Jesse James serial, again playing a lawman, having been a sheriff in *Jesse James Rides Again* and a marshal in *Adventures of Frank and Jesse James*. Roth had started out in minor parts in Universal's serials, but saw his screen time increasing after World War II at Columbia and Republic. He had been co-villain with Roy Barcroft in *Ghost of Zorro* (1949); other serial credits include *Pirates of the High Seas* (1950), *Mysterious Island* (1951), *Captain Video, Master of the Stratosphere* (1951), *The Lost Planet* (1953) and *The Great Adventures of Captain Kidd* (1953). Roth died in 1976.[164]

Analysis

The James Brothers of Missouri, shot in twenty-one days in July 1949, cost $164,757 and was the last Republic serial featuring Jesse James.[165] With a few surprise twists, it seemed to move at a much livelier clip than the first installments, perhaps because Republic had trimmed all of its serials from thirteen chapters to twelve after *Adventures of Frank and Jesse James*.

Boyd Magers calls *The James Brothers of Missouri* "well-staged," but notes the studio's budget cuts, reliance on stock footage, and "dependence on only one director."[166]

Keith Richards also lacked the charm and grace of Clayton Moore — though neither was any great shakes as an actor.

The reason there were no more Jesse James serials, however, couldn't be pinned on budget cuts and mediocre actors. First, censorship groups had lobbied hard against Hollywood's glorification and glamorization of notorious outlaws — especially in programmers and serials whose audiences were mostly children. PRC had even changed Billy the Kid's name in its kiddie programmers to Billy Carson to sidestep that issue. Memphis, Tennessee, had even refused to show Republic's first Jesse James serial *Jesse James Rides Again*.[167]

More importantly, television, and simple economics, would bury the serial. "[Television] literally absorbed the serials," historian Richard Maurice Hurst wrote.[168]

Still, Republic left behind its own legacy to the sound serial. "Considered the best sound serials ever made," historian Jack Mathis wrote, "the Republic cliffhanger exhibited that intangible asset of production values which combined with a genius for organization to produce polished products which belied their cost."[169]

The James Brothers of Missouri isn't Republic's best serial, but it does have moments, and marked a fitting end to Jesse James's reign as sound serial hero.

* * *

Montana: The Magazine of Western History (October 1967): "Again, there was no justification for making it."

Fighting Man of the Plains

(20th Century–Fox, October 1949, 94 minutes)

CREDITS: *Director:* Edwin L. Marin; *Producer:* Nat Holt; *Screenplay:* Frank Gruber.

CAST: Randolph Scott (Jim Dancer); Bill Williams (Johnny Tancred); Victor Jory (Dave Oldham); Jane Nigh (Florence Peel); Douglas Kennedy (Ken Vedder); Joan Taylor (Evelyn Slocum); James Todd (Paul Hobson); Rhys Williams (Chandler Leach); Barry Kelley (Bert Slocum); Berry Kroeger (Cliff Bailey); Dale Robertson (Jesse James); Paul Fix (Yancey); James Griffith (William Quantrell); James Millican (George Cummings).

Synopsis

Fighting Man of the Plains opens with Confederate guerrilla William Quantrill's August 21, 1863, raid on Lawrence, Kansas (Quantrill's name is spelled with an "e" instead of an "i" in the credits). When guerrilla Yancey (Paul Fix) raises his revolver against Evelyn Slocum (Joan Taylor), who's trying to protect her father, Jim Dancer (Randolph Scott) intervenes, only to be reminded by Quantrell (James Griffith): "Have you forgotten Independence? That's the man that killed your brother!"

In *Fighting Man of the Plains* (1949), Randolph Scott played a former guerrilla mistaken for a peace officer. Jesse James (Dale Robertson) saves his hide at the end.

In a chilling scene, Dancer turns, ignoring the girl's pleas, and the camera focuses on Dancer's revolver as it fires a fatal round into Theodore Slocum.

"The bloody war between the states finally came to an end," the viewer is then informed, "but on the border the hatreds had been too great. Men continued to ride and fight and die. The name of Quantrell was heard no more, but new names were whispered, names of men who had ridden with Quantrell and were outlaws."

Wanted for murder, Dancer is pursued by Pleasanton Detective Agency operative George Cummings (James Millican) for 18 months until we finally see the detective has got his man, and is taking Dancer, handcuffed to the saddle horn, to the agency's Kansas City office.

When Dancer asks about this murder charge, Cummings explains that Dancer killed the wrong Slocum in Independence. Bert Slocum is the man Dancer thought he had killed, the man who killed Dancer's brother in Independence.

Desperate to reach Kansas City, Cummings forces a ferry operator to take them across a raging river, the detective and outlaw now handcuffed to each other. Bad mistake. A rearing horse kicks Cummings in the head, and he falls, dead, into the river, taking Dancer with him. When they are found by travelers on a stagecoach, including Dave Oldham (Victor Jory) and Florence Peel (Jane Nigh), Dancer introduces himself as Cummings, and a pocket knife is produced to cut off the dead man's hand and free Dancer.

Dancer arrives at the Kansas City office, still impersonating Cummings, and quits. We next see him arriving as a railroad worker in Lanyard, Kansas, where he kills a rough cowhand who was assaulting Evelyn Slocum, who fails to recognize the man who killed her father back in Lawrence. The citizens demand that Dancer, aka Cummings, become town marshal, and Dancer accepts — urged on by Oldham and Peel, who know Dancer's true identity, both having realized that Dancer's right hand had been handcuffed to Cummings's left back on the riverbank.

Dancer cleans up Lanyard, much to the displeasure of Bert Slocum (Barry Kelley) and his hired gunhand Johnny Tancred (Bill Williams). Slocum has been buying up a lot of land around town, which he plans to fence in and then charge outrageous fees for anyone wanting to pass through his property to reach the railhead.

A whistling Jesse James (Dale Robertson) shows up in Dancer's hotel room, but decides not to rob the bank after talking with his old friend. "I hate to think of you and I looking at each other across guns," Jesse says, but as he leaves the room, adds, "I might be back sometime. You might not always be marshal."

Yancey is now working for Slocum, but can't quite remember where he has seen Dancer. When Yancey and his men raid a store and kill the owner, Dancer captures them. At the trial, Yancey remembers and identifies Dancer. Dancer quits as marshal and stoically faces Evelyn Slocum in the street; she lashes him across his chest with a quirt before Peel, who's in love with Dancer, intervenes. Evelyn bursts into tears.

By now, Bert Slocum decides to unleash Johnny Tancred on the town. The gunman kills a judge and prosecutor and frees Yancey and his men; they go after Dancer to hang him. Dave Oldham and Peel try to stop them, but Tancred slaps down Peel and kills Oldham. A kangaroo court convicts Dancer and sentences him to hang, and Tancred and his gunmen take Dancer to an oak tree to lynch him. That's when Jesse James and the boys show up. When Tancred announces his plans to rob the bank after disposing of Dancer, Jesse intervenes. "A hanging's one thing, mister," Jesse says. "That may be your line of work, but holding up banks is mine." Jesse has positioned himself on horseback so that Dancer can draw one of his revolvers, and in the melee that follows, Dancer kills Tancred, who accidentally guns down Slocum, and Jesse kills Yancey. The other outlaws quit, saying, "I ain't fighting Jesse James," and are run out of town. Dancer thanks Jesse, who says this might make up for the time Dancer saved his life in Baxter Springs, and rides out. Dancer walks toward Florence, but the end credits run before they can embrace and kiss.

The History

Between 150 and 180 men and boys were murdered at Lawrence by more than 450 of Quantrill's raiders, who also destroyed $1.5 million worth of property and left the city in charred ruins. "I cannot describe the horrors," one witness said.[170]

"None of us're proud of that day," Jesse tells Dancer in the hotel room. Most historians, however, don't think Jesse was at Lawrence, although they put Frank James and Cole Younger there. Younger remembered Lawrence as "a day of butchery."[171] In a rare display of Hollywood paying attention to history, costume designer Marcia Donovan put replicas of Quantrill's "guerrilla shirts" on the raiders, and most of the revolvers are also historically correct.

Lanyard, Kansas, is "a composite of Abilene, Dodge City and other towns"[172] on the Chisholm Trail, a subject screenwriter Frank Gruber was familiar with. His novel *Fighting Man* was the source material, and many of the subplots of the novel could be found in his previous novel *Peace Marshal*, which became the 1943 movie *The Kansan* starring Richard Dix. Jesse was in that one, too.

Jesse is first seen robbing a stagecoach in 1870. Historically, it's hard to say which robberies were committed by Jesse James and which were by his myriad imitators, but only four stagecoach robberies have been credited — by at least some historians — to Jesse: a January 15, 1874, holdup about five miles east of Hot Springs, Arkansas, in which five outlaws made off with more than $2,000; an April 7, 1874, robbery near Austin, Texas, in which five masked men made off with more than $3,000; an omnibus robbery near Lexington, Missouri, on August 30, 1874, in which three men robbed passengers of an undisclosed amount; and a September 3, 1880, robbery near Mammoth Cave, Kentucky, in which two men stole between $800 and $1,200.[173]

The movie was released shortly after the state of Kansas repealed its prohibition laws, a fact noted and lauded by the movie's pressbook. Hollywood filmmakers, the book says, had "been the target of 'you-pulled-a-boner' letters every time a period picture showed the least bit of liquor in a Kansas locale."[174] Maybe so, but enforcing prohibition laws in a trail town was "bad for business," historian Wm. B. Shillingberg says. "If a county attorney in Ford County (home of Dodge City) tried to enforce that, well, he wouldn't be county attorney any more."[175] Of course, the liquor served in the saloons in *Fighting Man of the Plains* was nothing more than iced tea, the pressbook said, the actors being "far to[o] busy to have anything stronger."[176]

The Players

Fighting Man of the Plains was the second of three pictures that Randolph Scott made — for $130,000 a film — for 20th Century–Fox and producer Nat Holt,[177] and it is the best of the three. Which isn't saying too much because 1949's *Canadian Pacific* is perhaps Scott's worst Western, and 1950's *The Cariboo Trail* isn't much better. Holt and Scott had teamed up for three films (1946's *Badman's Territory*, 1947's *Trail Street* and 1948's *Return of the Bad Men*) while Holt was on staff at RKO, and Scott had started out in the film business with Holt's father.[178]

Edwin L. Marin, "one of Scott's favorite directors,"[179] was hired to direct. Film historian David Quinlan writes that the "competent" Marin "never managed to make a memorable film.... But he had a sure visual eye that often produced pleasing results, notably in some of the Scott Westerns."[180] Marin had started out for Paramount's Famous Players Studio as an assistant cameraman, and worked his way up to directing for Sono Art-World Wide and Monogram before being hired by MGM in 1934, directing Philo Vance mysteries and four *Maisie* comedies starring Ann Sothern. His first true Western was 1944's *Tall in the Saddle*, starring John Wayne, for RKO, after he had done some comedy Westerns including 1940's *Gold Rush Maisie* and 1939's *Henry Goes Arizona*.[181]

Victor Jory, who played the heavy in *Canadian Pacific* and *The Cariboo Trail*, gives a nice, understated performance as a good guy, Jim Dancer's gambler friend Dave Oldham, in *Fighting Man of the Plains*. Jane Nigh — reportedly discovered by press agent Arthur S. Wenzel while working on the swing shift at Douglas Aircraft during World War II[182] — is pleasing as Florence Peel. Holt took credit for discovering Joan Taylor (Jory apparently arranged the interview, however) and cast her as Evelyn Slocum in her first film role.[183] "Likable"[184] Bill Williams got his first turn as a heavy, and the movie introduces Dale Robertson as Jesse James. The native Oklahoman's accent, grin and ease behind the camera serve him well playing a charming Missouri bandit.

Much of the movie was shot on a fifty-acre set in California's San Fernando Valley, complete with "a huge Western street," circa–1873 locomotive and a herd of 750 cattle.[185]

When the movie premiered in Topeka, Kansas, on October 13, 1949, Scott, Hayes, Jory and Robertson, along with Joan Taylor and Marty Stuart, were on hand to promote it. The actors took part in a parade; attired in "black Western garb," Scott was the only actor who rode a horse, accompanied by "the Kansas Peace Officers Association, the Topeka Round Up Club, students from Haskell Institute, the Topeka High School band and others."[186]

Analysis

There's a surprising element of savagery to *Fighting Man of the Plains*, from the opening scene in which Dancer cold-bloodedly murders Theodore Slocum. (Scott, per the Hollywood code, explains this away as, "That was during the war," but the Lawrence raid was nothing short of murder. "The butchery of Lawrence shocked the whole nation," historian Richard S. Brownlee writes.[187]) Dead detective George Cummings's hand is cut off with a pocketknife, albeit off-camera, and Randolph Scott pulls a couple of unheroic moves when he pulls a gun on Tancred after the latter has killed a Texas drover, and fires him. "You can't fire me," Tancred says. "Maybe not," Dancer replies, "but I can kill you." When Dancer travels to the cabin where Yancey and his colleagues are hiding out after murdering the Lanyard shopkeeper, Dancer grabs Yancey and uses him as a shield, forcing the other outlaws to give up.

Solid scenes all, which might have shocked audiences in 1949, and Scott, always under-

Five. Jesse in the B's, 1939–1949

rated as an actor, is in command of his character. Yet the movie relies on too many coincidences. We're supposed to believe that Evelyn Slocum can't recognize Jim Dancer after only nine years — and Gruber's script quickly falls apart after starting off with such promise. Jesse James, of course, tags along only to add his name; "another example of Gruber's name-dropping,"[188] notes film historian Bob Herzberg, who will never be mistaken for an admirer of Gruber's prose.

Yet *Fighting Man of the Plains* played well to its audience. A *New York Times* film critic noted, "Judging by the eager-eyed audience yesterday at the Rialto ... thundering hooves and barking six-shooters can still fill a theatre when all else fails." And when Jesse saves Dancer at the movie's end, the reviewer went on, "The general yell that hit the Rialto ceiling on that one as enough to make the original outlaw sit up in his grave and take a bow."[189]

* * *

Los Angeles Times (October 14, 1949): "Fans that hanker to see firstrate ridin' and shootin' will go for *Fighting Man of the Plains* and Randy Scott...."

CHAPTER SIX

The Proliferation of Jesse James, 1950–1960

The period of 1950 to 1960 would see a wide range of Jesse James movies, although he again was relegated to mostly second-feature status. Jesse was seen everywhere, in biopics and comedies. He would also be turning up on television in guest roles on Western series (see Chapter Eleven).

The Missouri bushwhacker became so omnipresent in movies that in 1950, *Boxoffice* magazine ran a feature story headlined, "Anyone Who Hasn't Played Jesse James Please Step Up."[1]

By the time 20th Century–Fox released *Young Jesse James* in 1960, what more could Hollywood have to say about the outlaw?

Gunfire
(Lippert Pictures, August 1950, 59 minutes)

CREDITS: *Director-Producer-Screenplay:* William Berke.
CAST: Don Barry (Frank James and Bat Fenton); Robert Lowery (John Kelly); Wally Vernon (Clem); Pamela Blake (Cynthy); Claude Stroud (Jim Mundy); Leonard Penn (Dan Simons); Steve Pendleton (Charlie Ford); Tommy Farrell (Lerner, Money-Wagon Driver); Dan Riesner (Mack); Paul Jordan (Johnny James); Steve Conti (Matt Riley); Roger Anderson (Bob Ford); Gil Fallman (Bank President); Kathleen Magginetti (Amy James).

Synopsis

One of *Gunfire*'s taglines was, "HUNTED ... by the James Gang because he was a Dead Ringer!"

Not quite. The dead ringer winds up being hunted, separately, by the real Frank James and a stalwart Colorado lawman.

Gunfire opens with outlaws Matt Riley (Steve Conti) and Bat Fenton (Donald Barry) arriving at the home of Frank James (Barry, in a dual role), who's living peacefully near Creede, Colorado. Matt hopes to talk Frank into heading down the owlhoot trail again, but Frank's health is poor (he has a persistent cough throughout the movie), and he's focusing on his family and religion. "It's the first real home Frank and I have ever had," Frank's wife Emily (Barbara Woodell, uncredited in the movie) tells Matt.

Six. The Proliferation of Jesse James, 1950–1960

Frank declines the offer, even after Matt tells him he'll be seeing Bob and Charlie Ford, now living in Creede. Apparently Frank wasn't aware that the men responsible for his brother's death have moved nearby.

Outside, Matt laments to Fenton that Frank "has turned into a Bible-readin' family man," then notices that if Fenton grew his beard out, he'd be a "dead ringer" for Frank James. Odd. You would have thought Matt might have noticed that before.

The two outlaws ride into the deserted streets of Creede just as town marshal John Kelly (Robert Lowery) steps outside and is challenged by Bob Ford (Roger Anderson), who tells the shotgun-toting lawman to turn around and be killed. "Why don't you shoot me in the back — like you did Jesse James?" Kelly says. Kelly tries to avoid the gunfight, which is over a girl named Cynthy (Pamela Blake), but is forced to kill Ford, taking a flesh wound in the process.

Matt and Fenton strong-arm the spineless Charlie Ford into joining up with them. Their plan is simple: They'll rob mining payrolls, banks and trains, never staying in one place too long, but always letting someone get a good look at Fenton's bearded face. The gang first hits a silver wagon; when the driver sees Fenton unmasked, he believes he has been waylaid by Frank James and a new James Gang.

Gunfire quickly turns into a routine chase movie across the oft-used California location

(Don Barry) in *Gunfire* (1950).

of Vasquez Rocks and the Iverson ranch.² Marshal Kelly, skeptical that Frank was in on the robberies, chases the bandits. Naturally, Frank is forced to ride off after the gang alone, to prove his innocence and avenge Jesse's death, informing Emily that there will be "no peace for any of us as long as Charlie Ford's alive."

It's a pretty good bet how the movie will end. Sure enough, Kelly and Frank eventually join forces after Fenton kidnaps Cynthy, and they attack Fenton's hideout. In the ensuing gunfight, Fenton's men are shot up; Cynthy miraculously escapes unhurt. As Fenton makes a made dash on horseback for freedom, Frank draws two pistols and kills him. The dead ringer, at last, is dead. The remaining outlaws surrender.

The History

Wisconsin native William Berke, who produced, wrote and directed the film, certainly mixed entertainment with a small dose of history. A very small dose, that is. The killer of Jesse James, Bob Ford, was indeed killed by a shotgun, by a man named Kelly, in Creede, which was a booming silver-mining town, but that's all there is historically to *Gunfire*. In reality, Bob Ford was shot dead in a saloon on June 8, 1892 by Ed Kelly/Kelley/O'Kelly/O'Kelley. But company head Robert L. Lippert must have believed Samuel Fuller's script for his 1949 production *I Shot Jesse James* was pure gospel. The killer of Bob Ford, again, becomes John Kelly.

What's wrong with the name Ed?

Ford's brother Charlie had contracted tuberculosis, become addicted to morphine and, allegedly grief-stricken over his role in Jesse's death, killed himself in 1884, although in *Gunfire* he outlives his more famous, more hated brother.

Also, Frank James, a free man from 1885 until his death in 1915, never went to Creede, Colorado; and his wife was named Anna, not Emily. Even as an outlaw, Frank was well-versed in both the Bible and Shakespeare, and he had only one son, Robert. The film gives him two cute kids named Johnny and Amy.

The Players

Since appearing as Jesse James in Republic Pictures' 1939 oater *Days of Jesse James* with Roy Rogers, Barry's career had taken off ... and fizzled out. In 1940, he starred as Red Ryder in the serial *Adventures of Red Ryder*. Bill Elliott, Allan Lane and Jim Bannon would have more roles as that Western hero, but Barry would take on the character's name. With the success of *Adventures of Red Ryder*, Barry often became known as "Red" Barry, although he was also billed as Don or Donald, *sans* nickname.³

"He really didn't want to do the *Red Ryder* serial," recalls Boyd Magers, a Western film historian and author who publishes the Albuquerque, New Mexico–based magazine *Western Clippings*. "He felt he wasn't right for it. He stormed into [studio head] Herbert Yates's office and said, 'I'm not going to do this.' Yates said, 'I'm not going to pay you.' Barry said, 'Okay, I'll do it.' He did, and twelve weeks on the screen made him a star."⁴

Yates dreamed that the small-in-stature Barry (his height has been reported from 5' 4½" to 5' 9"),⁵ might become Republic's answer to James Cagney (short, feisty, full of on-screen charisma), and cast him in a series of low-budget Westerns. What Barry lacked in stature, alas, he made up for in ego. Full of charisma? Barry was equally full of himself.

"He had a monumental ego," Magers says. "A feisty little guy. Everybody I ever knew who talked to him, knew him, said the very same thing.... But he was a good little actor."[6]

Not everyone thought Barry was good. In *The Filming of the West*, Jon Tuska calls Barry "a second-rate talent."[7] Nor was he always popular on the set. Vivian Austin, Barry's co-star in *Red Ryder*, said, "He wasn't a very nice fellow when we worked together,"[8] and director Budd Boetticher disliked Barry, saying "he was lucky to get the part" in 1956's *Seven Men from Now*.[9]

Although Barry could be a fine actor (catch his performance as Lieutenant Peter Vince in 1944's *The Purple Heart*), by 1950 his star was waning. His company, Donald Barry Productions, latched onto the *Gunfire* project, which would be released by Lippert Pictures.

In the spring of 1949, Robert L. Lippert reorganized Screen Guild Pictures as Lippert Pictures, Inc., which would produce B-movies until 1955.[10] Lippert was known as the Quickie King for producing movies on the cheap in rapid-fire succession. Julie Adams (then billed as Betty Adams) recalled working simultaneously on six Lippert Westerns that starred James Ellison and Russell Hayden and were released in 1950. All over a five-week period! "We had six different scripts — but we shot all the scenes of the stagecoach together, then all of the ranch scenes, whatever — all at the same time.... It was economical to do it that way," Adams said, "but I never could remember who I was."[11]

No doubt about it: In 1950, Lippert was one busy man. *Gunfire* was the fourth of five movies produced by Donald Barry Productions in 1949 and 1950, distributed by Lippert, and all starring Barry. Barry looked at the Lippert films[12] as a comeback opportunity, but by the 1950s, the B's were beginning to run out of public favor.[13]

Barry had often taken on non-traditional roles in his B-Westerns. "He was not the B-Western typical hero at all," Magers says. That certainly was the case in *Gunfire*, which gave him the chance to play two roles: an unrepentant, rotten-to-the-core bad guy and a reformed rotten-to-the-core bad guy. As much as he was unsuited for the role of the tall, rawboned Red Ryder, Barry was also a physical opposite of tall, lanky Frank James. Yet he was a perfect fit as a short, cocky (and often stereotypical) Western villain, à la Bat Fenton.

Barry must have had a soft spot for comedians, casting Tommy Farrell (whom he had seen performing at a nightclub) as the wagon driver waylaid by Fenton and Company,[14] and former vaudeville veteran Wally Vernon as Cynthy's drunken Uncle Clem.

Barry and Vernon were quite the team, appearing in twelve movies together, including four in 1950. Vernon's slapstick in *Gunfire* quickly wears thin (although he is nowhere near as annoying as when he plays the Mexican associate of Barry's Billy the Kid in *I Shot Billy the Kid*). Vernon worked into the mid–1960s. He was killed in 1970 in a hit-and-run accident while crossing a street in Van Nuys, California.[15]

Of her co-stars, Blake said Lowery was a "better actor than he ever got credit for." Of Barry, she noted: "Don had problems, but I wasn't really aware of it until" Barry's suicide in 1980.[16]

Analysis

The death of Jesse, specifically the way he was killed, is considered nothing short of murder by the principals in *Gunfire*. Although the law may have defended the Ford brothers, Fenton tells Charlie Ford (Steve Pendleton, credited as Gaylord Pendleton), "It didn't give

Bob the right to kill Jesse." After Kelly kills Bob Ford, Cynthy says, "Everything I ever felt for Bob died when he shot Jesse James." Cynthy is a former actress who traveled across the West in a troupe with her whiskey-sodden Uncle Clem. What brought any of them to Colorado is never revealed.

Trying to prove his innocence and avenge his brother's death, Frank typically shows up too late, asking about Charlie Ford, yet no one tries to arrest him. In one town, a bartender recognizes Frank and asks what he wants with Charlie Ford.

FRANK: "I want to kill him."
BARTENDER: "Well, that's fine. I'll tell him you was around."

Humorous exchanges like that are few, however, and repeated chase scenes at Vasquez Rocks emphasize the movie's low budget.

Historically skewed, *Gunfire* is what one would expect from Lippert Pictures. It's fast-moving, loaded with action with limited locations, easy to watch, and equally easy to forget. Yet there is a moment of truth in the picture when a weary Frank James tells Matt that "the outlawin' died when Jesse died." For the real Frank James, that was about as accurate a statement as Hollywood ever produced.

* * *

Variety (July 19, 1950): "Gunfire is more outdoor melodrama than oater and crowds a lot of characters into a short 59 minutes.... It measures up as acceptable supporting fare for secondary situations."[17]

The Return of Jesse James

(Lippert, September 1950, 75 minutes)

CREDITS: *Director:* Arthur Hilton; *Producer:* Carl K. Hittleman; *Screenplay:* Jack Natteford.
CAST: John Ireland (Johnny Callum); Ann Dvorak (Sue Younger); Henry Hull (Hank Younger); Reed Hadley (Frank James); Hugh O'Brian (Lem Younger); Clifton Young (Bob Ford); Tommy Noonan (Charlie Ford); Victor Kilian (Westfield Sheriff Rigby); Barbara Woodell (Ann James).

Synopsis

Another look-alike for Jesse James?

One month after Lippert Pictures released *Gunfire* (with a Frank James double), Lippert sent out another mistaken identity story, reassembling much of the cast from the darker, more historical *I Shot Jesse James*.

Outlaw Johnny Callum, "down to my last dollar," arrives in Clay County, Missouri, in 1883 to rob the bank, but first stops for a drink at Bob Ford's Saloon, where Bob and brother Charlie are living off their reputation for killing Jesse James. Bob even has the gun he used to kill Jesse on display, and proudly shows it off.

Callum isn't impressed. "Must have taken a lot of nerve to shoot an outlaw like him ... in the back," he says.

He's more impressed with blackjack dealer Sue Younger. Her father Hank and brother

Lem notice something familiar about Callum. He's not the spitting image of Jesse, but he sure enough looks like him. Odd ... you would think Bob Ford might have noticed that resemblance, too.

When Callum tries to rob the bank, Hank Younger stops him, then takes Callum to the Younger farm and gives him some advice. He lets him try on Jesse's coat and hat, saying, "When Jesse went into a bank, he looked like he had legitimate business there." Younger, who had ridden with Jesse, has an idea. Bring Jesse back, using Callum. After all, Jesse's name had often been all the gang needed to rob banks and trains successfully.

They rob the Bank of East Kansas, and start a crime wave, putting Jesse James back in the headlines. That isn't good for Frank James, who has hung up his guns and is living with his wife and children on a Lebanon, Tennessee, farm under the name Ben Woodson. Frank rides back to Missouri, and tries to talk Hank and Callum into quitting this charade, but Callum has an ego problem. He wants to one-up Jesse. "Where he took a licking, I'll make a cleanup," Callum tells Frank, "and there's nothing you can do to stop me."

Wanna bet?

When Callum and the gang rob the Liberty bank, and Callum cold-bloodedly murders the bank president, Frank knows the fake Jesse will eventually try to rob the bank where the real outlaw took his biggest licking: Westfield, Minnesota.

Lobby card for *The Return of Jesse James*, a 1950 release that starred John Ireland — who played Bob Ford in 1949's *I Shot Jesse James*— as an outlaw who looks just like Jesse James.

Meanwhile, Missouri authorities have threatened the Ford brothers with a hangman's noose unless they can stop this new Jesse. The law has also reissued amnesty rewards for whoever turns in Frank or Jesse James, so Frank's back on the trail of the fake Jesse.

Bob tries to talk Sue Younger into betraying her father and Callum, and that's fine with Sue. She'll do anything for a buck. When Callum walks into the saloon, the Ford brothers mistake him for the real Jesse, and Callum guns down the dirty little cowards. That really one-ups the dead Jesse.

Callum is living high, but when his bankroll runs out, Sue talks him into robbing the $100,000 in Westfield. Hank, sick of the whole Jesse James business he started, tries to talk Sue into persuading Callum to call off the robbery. All it will take is just one word from her, and Callum will quit, but Sue's greedy. When Hank says he'll give her all his money if she'll just stop Callum, she laughs at him. "Chicken feed. Small change for beer. I'm playing for champagne."

The outlaws ride to Westfield. Frank James, however, is already there, and has warned the law. The town has even put out a coffin on a boardwalk with the sign: "Reserved for Jesse James." Of course, a week later, most people think this man who had warned them is crazy, but when word comes that Jesse James is riding to town, the streets are cleared and an ambush is set up. When Callum and the gang try to rob the bank, they are shot down. Only three — Hank, Lem and Callum — make it out of town, and Lem is mortally wounded.

Hank decides it's up to him to stop Callum, and the two shoot each other. Hank's dead, and Callum's badly injured. He rides back to Sue, who isn't happy that all the bank's money was left on the streets of Westfield. When Frank James arrives, Sue runs out to him, saying she has kept Callum for him and wants to claim the amnesty and reward. Disgusted, the dying Callum blows her away.

The History

As is often the case with films about Jesse, historical inaccuracies abound. The movie opens in 1883 when Jesse, Callum says, has been "dead for six months." Jesse was killed in April 1882. Six months later would make it October 1882.

Bob Ford did own several saloons — in New Mexico and Colorado, but never in Clay County, Missouri,[18] and though Henry and Bursheba Younger had fourteen children, none was named Lem. Besides, Henry Younger never rode with Jesse James, since he was killed in 1862.[19]

There is a *West*field, Minnesota — a township in the Rochester metropolitan area — but that's about an hour's drive southeast of the bank the James-Younger Gang robbed in *North*field in 1876 — not in 1881, as the movie suggests.

Yet some of the movie is relatively faithful to history. A Missouri detective laments how hard it is to pin a crime on the James boys: "Every suspect has nine witnesses to prove he wasn't at the crime." That was certainly the case in the 1870s and 1880s. Testimony like that helped get Clell Miller acquitted after he was charged with the Corydon, Iowa, bank robbery, and would help acquit Frank James of the Winston train robbery. Jesse was often writing letters to newspapers saying he, and other witnesses, could prove he wasn't at certain robberies.[20]

Frank James, in fact, did live under the alias B.J. Woodson in Tennessee. Of course, there's no documentation that he ever hid out in Lebanon, Tennessee; in fact, at the time of his brother's death, he was living in Lynchburg, Virginia, using the name James Warren. The movie mentions Frank and Ann's "children." They had only one child, a son named Robert, born February 8, 1878.[21]

The method of operation depicted in the scene where Callum and Hank Younger rob the Bank of East Texas—first asking the teller to change a bill—was an accurate recreation of the James-Younger Gang's often-used MO. In Liberty in 1866, the bill was a $10 note. In Gallatin, Missouri, in 1869, they made it $100.[22]

Charlie Ford laments that people in Clay County look at him and his brother as if they were "Judases," accurate enough. Bob's dismissal of the fake Jesse James—"There have been a half dozen since we killed the real one"—is also partially true. Homer Croy notes that the myth that Jesse wasn't killed "sprang up immediately."[23] One of those impostors, in fact, might have fueled the imagination of Carl K. Hittleman, credited with the original story, and screenwriter Jack Natteford, and led to *The Return of Jesse James*.

The Players

J. Frank Dalton, probably the most famous Jesse poser, made national news after being "discovered at a tourist camp at Lawton, Oklahoma."[24]

"'Jesse James Is Alive! In Lawton!' I know that I will never write another eight-column headline that gave me the thrill the above headline did on May 19, 1948," city editor Frank O. Hall wrote in *Editor & Publisher*, "and I am quite certain I'll never write another one that created such a furore [sic] among the reading public."[25]

Although Dalton was dismissed as a fraud (admittedly, many still believe he was indeed Jesse James), his story could have sparked Hittleman's story idea. The producer turned the project over to a screenwriter who was certainly familiar with Jesse James and impostors.

A movie writer since the early 1920s, Natteford's credits included *Days of Jesse James* (1939), *Badman's Territory* (1946) and *Return of the Bad Men* (1948). He had also created a Billy the Kid look-alike in Roy Rogers's *Billy the Kid Returns* (1938).

Likewise, Lippert and Hittleman assembled a cast already familiar with Jesse James. Reed Hadley signed on as Frank James. He played Jesse in *I Shot Jesse James*. Barbara Woodell played Frank's wife Ann. She had played the same role in Lippert's *Gunfire*, when she had been married to Don Barry's Frank. She was Zee, Jesse's wife, in *I Shot Jesse James*, a role she would revisit in Lippert's *The Great Jesse James Raid* (1953). Tommy Noonan—John Ireland's half-brother—returned as Charlie Ford, reprising his role from *I Shot Jesse James*. (This time, he gets killed at the hands of Johnny Callum while reaching for the gun Bob used to kill the real Jesse; the real Charles Ford killed himself.) Henry Hull landed the part of Hank Younger. Hull had played Major Rufus Cobb, loosely based on real-life newspaper journalist and Jesse James promoter John Newman Edwards, in *Jesse James* (1939) and *The Return of Frank James* (1940). In fact, Hull has a line in *The Return of Jesse James* that sounds like an inside joke. After Callum murders a bank teller, Hank says the law will "hunt us down like dogs," a throwback to Hull's oft-used "shoot 'em down like dogs" lines from *Jesse James* and *The Return of Frank James*.

Despite strong performances in *Red River* (1948) and *All the King's Men* (1949), Ireland's career had never really taken off, despite strong performances in the late 1940s. His starring roles in the 1950s were typically in B-movies like *The Return of Jesse James*, and by the 1960s — despite a good supporting role in *Spartacus* (1960) — his career was in steady decline. In 1987, he paid almost $2,000 to run an advertisement in an industry newspaper that read, "I'm an actor. PLEASE ... let me Act. John Ireland." He died of leukemia in Santa Barbara, California, in 1992.[26]

Likewise, Ann Dvorak's role of Sue was "a clear indication of her waning status."[27] After earning critical notice in movies such as *Scarface* (1932) and *Three on a Match* (1932), she always seemed on the brink of stardom, but never quite reached that status. In 1940, she joined her husband, actor-director Leslie Fenton, in England and drove an ambulance during the Blitz. The marriage ended in 1946, after they returned to America ("Put it down to a war casualty," she said). She landed good parts in Westerns such as *Flame of Barbary Coast* (1945) and *Abilene Town* (1946), but again stardom eluded her. She made her Broadway debut in 1948 to great reviews, but her marriage to Russian dancer Igor Dega was breaking up (they would divorce in 1951), and she looks bored in *The Return of Jesse James*.[28]

Dvorak went out on a high (if obscure) note playing the repressed Rachel in a quirky, feminist *noir* Western, *The Secret of Convict Lake* (1951), starring Glenn Ford, Zachary Scott, Ethel Barrymore and Gene Tierney. "It was a great, neurotic way," Laura Wagner wrote, "to end a movie career."[29] Dvorak died of cancer in 1979.

Analysis

Of Robert Lippert's three Jesse James follow-ups to *I Shot Jesse James* (*Gunfire, The Return of Jesse James, The Great Jesse James Raid*), *The Return of Jesse James* is the best.

That's not saying much. Often described as a *noir* Western, it probably could have used a better director. This was only the second movie-directing gig for Arthur Hilton (following 1950's *The Misadventures of Buster Keaton*), who took the director's chair for several movie and television projects between 1950 and 1960. Most likely he preferred working as an editor. Nominated for an Academy Award for his editing of *The Killers* (1946), Hilton continued editing up until his death in 1979.

Ireland was always watchable as melancholy gunmen — Cherry Valance in *Red River* (1948), Bitter Creek in *The Doolins of Oklahoma* (1949) — and Henry Hull seemed to enjoy himself playing the same role in movie after movie. Bored as she seems, Dvorak gives the movie a slight lift, and Hugh O'Brian shows his stuff — five years before television's *The Life and Legend of Wyatt Earp* made him a household name.

By no means is *The Return of Jesse James* a great movie, but what was about to come along would certainly make it seem like a classic.

* * *

Variety (September 5, 1950): "Slightly off the beaten track for a Lippert oater, *The Return of Jesse James* proves a successful experiment for the company. Original yarn by Carl K. Hittleman injects the needed action and includes some finely developed characters and a slight psychological overtone which holds interest."

Kansas Raiders

(Universal-International, November 1950, 80 minutes)

CREDITS: *Director:* Ray Enright; *Producer:* Ted Richmond; *Screenplay:* Robert L. Richards.

CAST: Audie Murphy (Jesse James); Brian Donlevy (William Clarke Quantrill); Marguerite Chapman (Kate Clarke); Scott Brady (Bill Anderson); Tony Curtis (Kit Dalton); Richard Arlen (Union Captain); Richard Long (Frank James); James Best (Cole Younger); John Kellogg (Red Leg Leader); Dewey Martin (James Younger); George Chandler (Willie); Charles Delaney (Pell); Richard Egan (First Lieutenant); David Wolfe (Rudolph Tate).

Synopsis

The slaughter of the Civil War — shown in vivid Technicolor (well, actually it was stock footage from Universal-International's 1948 production *Tap Roots*[30]) — was not limited to the North and South. "There was a war-bred outlaw army of guerrillas masquerading under the flags of both sides," the narrator says, "pillaging, burning and killing for private gain."

Kansas Raiders (1950) provided a young Audie Murphy (right) with his first chance to play Jesse James. Murphy would return as Jesse in a cameo in his last film, *A Time for Dying* (1969).

Maybe that explains why such a good-looking group of nice boys want to join up with the "most ominous" of those renegades, William Clarke Quantrill.

Jesse and Frank James, Cole and Jim Younger and Kit Dalton ride into Lawrence, Kansas, where they are taken prisoner by redleg soldiers who have in mind to lynch the strangers. After all, as the redleg leader informs the boys, "In the border country you're either a Union man or a spy." A Union officer stops the hanging and sends the boys on their way. They join up with Quantrill, but not until they stop a runaway buckboard carrying Quantrill's woman, Kate. "More recruits for the butcher brigade," she says upon learning the boys' intention.

Quantrill has his third-in-command, Rudolph Tate, pick a fight with young Jesse, and it's a gory affair. The two men hold a bandana in their teeth, and go at each other with knives. Jesse kills Tate, which impresses Quantrill. "The kid meant it when he said he wanted to fight," Quantrill remarks.

Jesse has reason to join the guerrillas: His Missouri farm has been burned. Quantrill sees a young kid he can manipulate, which disgusts Kate. "You have a winning way with children, colonel," she tells him sarcastically.

"Thank you, Kate," he says, with a slight bow.

It doesn't take long until Jesse realizes that Quantrill isn't the man he thought he was. The young farm boy is disgusted by the pillaging and outright murder committed by Quantrill's men.

Jesse keeps trying to quit, but just can't do it. Same with Kate. Besides, Quantrill has promised his men will be on good behavior when they raid Lawrence, Kansas. Jesse believes him, until he witnesses the brutality. When Quantrill's second-in-command, Bloody Bill Anderson, brings a Union prisoner, partly blinded, Jesse frees the officer and kills Anderson, then registers a complaint with Quantrill, who is taking "contributions" from the surviving Lawrence citizens. Quantrill suggests Jesse file his complaint with Anderson. Jesse can't do that, he says, since he just killed Anderson.

Union forces turn up the heat after the raid, and pretty soon all of Quantrill's men have deserted him except for the James brothers, the Youngers and Kit Dalton. They decide to hightail it to Quantrill's hideout in Kentucky, but first they need to pick up Kate. Soldiers come by, and Quantrill is blinded by a bullet before the guerrillas drive off the Yankees.

They hole up in a burned-out wreck of a cabin — the cabin Quantrill had burned on Jesse's first raid — but soon the Union captain arrives with his men, surrounds the house, and demands their surrender.

Jesse's in a fix. He sends his brother and pals out to make their escape, but he won't — can't — abandon Quantrill. Quantrill and Jesse decide to sneak out the back door, the same as the others have done. Hey, you would think the Union commander would be watching the back door, not just the front.

Quantrill shoves Jesse out the door, then goes out the front door, where he's gunned down. He has sacrificed himself so that the others, including Kate, can escape.

Kit Dalton has learned enough to be an outlaw, and the Youngers decide they'd like to ride along with Jesse and Frank. And Kate? She says goodbye to Jesse, knowing he won't see her the same after the war finally ends. They kiss farewell; Kate goes her way and Jesse rides away to join his friends, "whose warped lives were to be a heritage from their teacher, William Clarke Quantrill."

The History

Born in Dover, Ohio, in 1837, William Clarke Quantrill had tried teaching school and gambling before he settled in Kansas in 1857. Initially, he spoke out against slavery, then concocted a profitable scheme. First, he helped Kansas Jayhawkers free slaves. Then, he helped "border ruffians" captured the runaways and turn them in for the reward money. When the Civil War broke out, Quantrill rode briefly in the Cherokee Nation with a half-breed Confederate sympathizer, then joined Sterling Price's Confederate army, then returned to Kansas, where he began recruiting his own pro–Confederacy army. To win the loyalty of his men, Quantrill told recruits that Jayhawkers had ambushed him and his brother on the Santa Fe Trail, and left his older brother dead. He said he had then joined the Union Army and killed all but two of his brother's murderers. Quantrill actually had no older brother.[31] Brian Donlevy's interpretation of Quantrill as part-con artist, part-manipulator is dead-on.

By 1862, Quantrill had been commissioned as a Missouri Partisan Ranger captain and soon had a band of over 300 guerrillas. He was brutal and relentless, and by 1863 his acts were deemed "little removed from that of the wildest savage."[32]

It all came to a head in the early dawn of August 21, 1863, when Quantrill and a band of 400 partisans attacked Lawrence, Kansas. The movie depicts residents defending themselves, opening fire, even shooting down some of Quantrill's men. It didn't happen that way. "It was a day of butchery," Cole Younger remembered.[33]

"Kill every man big enough to carry a gun," Quantrill ordered, and his men did just that. Men, and boys, were chased down and murdered. Others were dragged out of their homes and killed before wives and children. Some were burned inside their homes. By nine o'clock that morning, at least 150 men and boys had been killed. Quantrill's men suffered no casualties during the raid, and lost only one man — a drunken partisan named Larkin Skaggs who stupidly stayed behind (or was too drunk to ride a horse) and was shot dead by an Indian.[34]

Jesse James wasn't there. By most accounts, he wouldn't join a partisan group until 1864, and would spend most of his guerrilla days riding with Bloody Bill Anderson.[35] The reason James gives in the movie for wanting to join Quantrill, however, is partially right: "I came home to find our house burned [wrong], Ma with her arm shot off [amputated after a bomb exploded inside the house, actually, but not until 1875], and Pa hanging from a tree by Redlegs [close enough]."

Bloody Bill Anderson was, at one point, Quantrill's second in command, but he wasn't killed by Jesse James at Lawrence. The Missouri State Militia killed him on October 26, 1864. Soldiers were so happy the scourge was dead, they hauled his body to Richmond, Missouri, and propped it in a chair for photographs. Not satisfied, they then decapitated the corpse, put the head on a telegraph pole, and dragged the torso down the streets. Eventually, the body was buried in an unmarked grave outside of town.[36]

Jim Younger wasn't at Lawrence, either. He didn't join the guerrillas until May 1864.[37] Yet by most accounts, Cole Younger and Frank James were at Lawrence, Younger having enlisted with Quantrill either in the winter of 1861 or in August 1862, and James joining, by his own admission, in May 1863.[38]

And what about Kit Dalton? In 1914, Captain Kit Dalton had a book published by

Lockhart Publishing Company of Memphis, Tennessee, *Under the Black Flag*, detailing his services under Quantrill and his years as an outlaw. The book has even been used as a source in other histories.

After his death in Memphis on April 3, 1920—the thirty-eighth anniversary of Jesse's death—the *New York Times* noted that "the sole survivor of the Jesse James band of outlaws, the Quantrell raiders and Sam Bass Texas band of outlaws, died here tonight. He did not die with his boots on. He succumbed to an illness which extended over four years."[39]

There was just one thing about Kit Dalton and his book:

"One cannot understand why a writer like this one, supposedly writing about his own life, could possibly make the statements he does, unless in his dotage his memory has turned to fantastic hallucinations," Ramon F. Adams wrote in *Six-Guns and Saddle Leather: A Bibliography of Books and Pamphlets on Western Outlaws and Gunmen*.[40] Dalton Gang historian Nancy Samuelson was a little more blunt, calling Kit Dalton's book "completely fictitious."[41]

Oh, well. So much for Kit Dalton. But he had a great name.

Costumer Bill Thomas provided Quantrill's men with "guerrilla shirts," and indeed they were known for their shirts, low-cut in the front, with four large pockets, sometimes in brilliant red colors, other times in drab butternut. "They were made by the mothers, wives, and sweethearts of the guerrillas, and many were elaborately decorated with colored needlework."[42]

Quantrill did have a mistress (some say they were actually married), Sarah "Kate" King, who went by the name Kate Clarke.[43] At the end of the movie, Kate tells Jesse that "in a few years, the war will be over." Quantrill was shot on a farm near Taylorsville, Kentucky, on May 10, 1865—a month after Robert E. Lee surrendered. Frank James was there (the Youngers and Jesse weren't). The bullet paralyzed the guerrilla leader. Before he died in Louisville, Quantrill told a priest that a woman was holding money for him, and that the priest should find her, use part of the money to pay for a cemetery plot, and give the rest to Kate Clarke. On June 6, Quantrill died. He was twenty-seven years old. Donlevy was forty-nine when *Kansas Raiders* was filmed.[44]

Maybe the movie's most striking resemblance to history was its casting of Universal's young actors as guerrilla warriors. "[T]here has never been a more reckless lot of men," Frank James recalled of his guerrilla company. "Only one or two were over 25. Most of them were under 21. Scarcely a dozen boasted a moustache."[45]

The Players

Texas-born Audie Leon Murphy, a Medal of Honor winner and the most decorated American soldier in World War II, had signed with Universal-International in 1950.[46]

"It wouldn't be at all surprising to see Audie Murphy as Joaquin Murietta one of these days," one newspaper journalist noted, "since Hollywood apparently has a predilection for casting the young actor in desperado roles."[47]

Murphy had played a juvenile delinquent in Allied Artists' *Bad Boy* (1949), his first starring role, and Billy the Kid in Universal-International's *The Kid from Texas* (1950). (Billy the Kid, by the way, wasn't from Texas.) Murphy was an outlaw again in *Kansas Raiders*, but not a bad guy. "For a change Murphy plays a nice fellow," the *Los Angeles Times* reported. "He's coming back from Texas especially for this role."[48]

Murphy never really lost his boyish good looks, but he was obviously suffering from Post Traumatic Stress Disorder.[49] James Best saw that during the filming of the scene in which Murphy's Jesse guns down Scott Brady's Bloody Bill: "I saw a man who went through World War II and had killed a lot of guys. He was killing Scott Brady. His looks chilled me. The hair on the back of my neck stood up because I saw a man who enjoyed killing."[50]

Budgeted at $609,156, *Kansas Raiders* was filmed in May and June 1950 on Universal's backlot and at the Jack Garner Ranch and Johnson Flats in Idyllwild, California. Some of the filming at Idyllwild had been planned for June 5, but grasshoppers cut a swath five miles long, forcing a delay. The crew returned to shoot the scenes on June 12.[51]

Second-billed Brian Donlevy earned $37,500 for his role, while Murphy earned $12,500. Quantrill was suddenly becoming a hot property in Hollywood, as *Boxoffice* magazine reported: "Quantrill, a blood-letter par excellence in his day, hasn't been quite so popular with the filmmakers — up to now. But Hollywood wouldn't be Hollywood without a cycle...."[52]

The cycle started with *Kansas Raiders*. Hal B. Wallis was to produce a movie titled *Quantrell's Raiders* for Paramount. Burt Lancaster was originally thought to get the role of the guerrilla chieftain. Wendell Corey refused to do the film, which eventually became *Red Mountain* (1951) and starred Alan Ladd as Captain Brent Sherwood and John Ireland as Quantrill. MGM's *The Outriders* (1950) had Joel McCrea and Barry Sullivan as two of Quantrill's raiders, though Quantrill didn't appear in the movie. The best Quantrill movie might be Republic's *Dark Command* (1940), with Walter Pidgeon playing a schoolmaster-turned-renegade named William Cantrell. Donlevy would return as Quantrill for Republic's *Woman They Almost Lynched* (1953), and the often-cast villain Leo Gordon would play the guerrilla bad guy in Allied Artists' *Quantrill's Raiders* (1958).[53]

Analysis

Kansas Raiders is probably best viewed to watch the early performances of stars-in-the-making. James Best would manage a lengthy career as a character actor before retiring and becoming an artist. Richard Long would find stardom on television, specifically for his role as Jarrod Barkley on TV's *The Big Valley* (1965–69). Dewey Martin would have a brief fling with stardom when Howard Hawks cast him in prominent roles in *The Thing from Another World* (1951) and *The Big Sky* (1952). Richard Egan would win a Golden Globe as Most Promising Newcomer — Male in 1954 after his performance in *The Glory Brigade* and would play Elvis Presley's older brother in Presley's first movie, *Love Me Tender* (1956).

Tony Curtis, of course, would become a major star, while Murphy would be relegated, for the most part, to B-Westerns. But few can deny Murphy's staying power, or popularity. As *The Washington Post* noted: "This is a good enough Civil War action yarn — in Technicolor — but Audie's next role, the young soldier in *The Red Badge of Courage*, should mean a lot more to his career."[54]

As history, well, Bob Larkins and Boyd Magers likely sum up *Kansas Raiders* best when they call it "a whitewash job regarding Jesse and his companions...."[55]

* * *

Hollywood Reporter (November 8, 1950): "The competent direction by Ray Enright sustains all the excitement in the raids and killings, brings out the human interest in the yarn, and gives his players every opportunity to display their acting abilities."

The Great Missouri Raid

(Paramount, February 1951, 85 minutes)

CREDITS: *Director:* Gordon Douglas; *Producer:* Nat Holt; *Screenplay:* Frank Gruber.
CAST: Wendell Corey (Frank James); Macdonald Carey (Jesse James); Ellen Drew (Bee Moore); Ward Bond (Major Marshal Trowbridge); Bruce Bennett (Cole Younger); Bill Williams (Jim Younger); Anne Revere (Mrs. Samuels); Edgar Buchanan (Dr. Samuels); Lois Chartrand (Mary Bauer); Louis Jean Heydt (Charles Ford); Barry Kelley (Mr. Bauer); James Millican (Sgt. Trowbridge); Guy Wilkerson (Clell Miller); Ethan Laidlaw (Jim Cummings); Tom Tyler (Allen Parmer); Paul Fix (Sgt. Brill); James Griffith (Jack Ladd); Whit Bissell (Bob Ford); Steve Pendleton (Arch Clements); Paul Lees (Bob Younger).

Synopsis

History recreated! And rewritten.

When Union soldiers hunting Frank James threaten to hang the guerrilla's stepfather, young Jesse James intervenes, and is lashed by the relentless Sergeant Trowbridge.

Frank and other Quantrill raiders arrive in the nick of time, and drive off the Union soldiers, but not before Jesse shoots down Trowbridge in self-defense. Having "killed a bluecoat," Jesse is forced to join up with his brother, and they continue raiding until the Civil War has ended and the South is vanquished. Amnesty is being offered, even to partisans, so Frank rides to Independence to make sure the offer is on the level.

It is—and it isn't. The commander is Major Trowbridge, whose brother was killed by Jesse James. Trowbridge gets his soldiers drunk and has them try to ambush the guerrillas when they ride into town to surrender. Jesse is badly wounded in the ambush, but the Yankees get the worst of it. That's all Trowbridge needs, however, and the James boys and the Younger brothers are now wanted—dead or alive. Jesse, sent to Nebraska to mend, falls in love with his nurse, Bee Moore.

Trowbridge is making things rough on the boys, so they decide to rob the bank in Liberty. Afterward, it looks like the boys are committed to a life of crime, although Frank wants to live in peace. Trowbridge sends a spy to the James farm, but the spy doesn't fool Jesse, who shoots him down in self-defense.

The James and Younger boys rob more banks, derail a train, and then make a career blunder when they try to rob a Missouri Central train. Bob Younger is seriously wounded, and Jesse and Frank leave the Younger brothers in the wilderness, attempting to draw the posse away. That doesn't work. Trowbridge and his posse surround the Youngers and shoot them to pieces. The Youngers survive, but they're "full of lead."

Meanwhile, Frank brings Jesse back to the Missouri farm where Frank has been work-

Six. The Proliferation of Jesse James, 1950–1960 127

Lobby card for the 1951 release *The Great Missouri Raid*, starring Wendell Corey as Frank James, Macdonald Carey as Jesse James, and Ward Bond as the man out to get 'em.

ing — and falling in love with the farmer's daughter, Mary. When another farmhand gets the drop on Frank, Jesse guns him down. Frank is forced to leave, but Mary comes along with him, and they marry.

Jesse's new gang members — Ed Miller, Charles and Bob Ford, and Dick Liddil — aren't quite the Younger brothers, and Bee's none to happy about it. "The neighbors are already avoiding me because this trash just happens to drop by," she seethes.

Then Liddil kills Miller, and turns himself in — fearing Jesse's revenge more than he fears the law. Trowbridge visits Liddil in jail, and learns that "Bob Ford's your man" to kill Jesse. Trowbridge makes a deal with Ford, $10,000 and a pardon if he kills Jesse. Even after Trowbridge is killed (off-screen) by "a cheap pickpocket," Bob Ford is still intrigued by the idea of killing Jesse. After all, Jesse doesn't think too much of the younger Ford brother.

Frank has had enough, and leaves with his wife. Jesse decides to quit, too. He and Bee will move to Europe. He starts to get the luggage outside, but Bob warns him that he can't be seen wearing guns. Jesse takes off his rig, saying he might as well get used to it. After he leaves, Bob takes Jesse's revolver from the holster.

When Jesse returns inside, and stops to straighten a picture on the wall, Bob asks to take over the gang. After all, Jesse's leaving. "You, Bob?" Jesse says with a smirk. "You think you're big enough for that?"

Bob shoots Jesse in the back, and the Ford boys flee. Bee runs downstairs and cradles Jesse in her arms. Jesse's dying words are an apology:

"I didn't make much of a life for you."

The History

The movie opens on a historical note. During the Civil War, Union militia arrived at the James family farm searching for Frank and information. They tied a rope around the neck of Dr. Samuel, Jesse's stepfather, and jerked him up four times in an attempt to make him talk. They verbally abused Jesse's mother. They found Jesse in a cornfield and whipped him.[56]

"After painstaking research involving little known records, correspondence and newspaper accounts," the movie's pressbook proclaimed, "producer Holt has placed before his camera the authentic history of America's most sought-after outlaws."[57]

And: "To set matters right, top historical novelist Frank Gruber performed extensive research before he committed the screenplay to paper.... The result is a startling historical revelation, as well as spine-tingling proof that truth is more stirring than fiction."[58]

Not exactly.

Frank James and his guerrilla comrades didn't run off the Union soldiers and save Jesse and his family. That said, the whipping and abuse his family took hardened Jesse, and he later joined the guerrillas, although he would ride with Bloody Bill Anderson and not Quantrill.[59]

Jesse was reportedly wounded while trying to surrender — in Lexington, not Independence — and take the oath of allegiance in May or June 1865, but he wasn't with Frank. Frank had been with Quantrill in Kentucky when the guerrilla was killed, and Frank surrendered on July 26, 1865, and was paroled. Cole Younger wasn't there, either, but in California. Jesse was moved, first to Nebraska, then Missouri, to recover from his wound, and, indeed, he fell in love with his cousin Zerelda. She was called Zee. Not Bee. Her last name was Mimms. Not Moore. Frank's wife was named Anna. Not Mary. Both couples were married in 1874.[60]

In the movie, bushwhacker Arch Clements is killed during the ambush while trying to surrender. In reality, Archie Clement was shot down by Union authorities in the streets of Lexington, Missouri, in December 1866. As he lay dying, he told a friend, "I've done what I always said I'd do — die before I'd surrender."[61]

The raiders are also shown dynamiting buildings during the Civil War, but the explosive wasn't patented until 1867.[62]

Although it is doubtful that Jesse took part in the job, the February 1866 robbery of a bank in Liberty was likely the first robbery performed by the James-Younger Gang. The gang did derail a train in a robbery near Adair, Iowa, in 1873, although that heist wasn't quite as spectacular or fiery as the one in the film.[63]

James Andrew "Dick" Liddil did kill a member of Jesse's gang, but he shot — perhaps with Bob Ford's help — Wood Hite, one of Jesse's cousins. Not Ed Miller. Jesse killed Ed Miller. And Hite wasn't killed in Jesse's home, but at the home of Martha Bolton.[64]

Liddil surrendered to Clay County Sheriff James H. Timberlake on January 24, 1882. Major Trowbridge, obviously, is a composite of Allan Pinkerton and Union and law-enforcement officers who helped bring about Jesse's downfall. Liddil would even testify against Frank James in trials in Gallatin, Missouri, and Huntsville, Alabama. Not that it did any good. Frank was acquitted both times.[65]

As has been previously noted, the James-Younger Gang did not perform the first train robbery, but perhaps the movie's most surprising rewrite of history is turning the Northfield bank robbery into a robbery of a Missouri Central railroad. Jesse and Frank did leave the Younger brothers after the bank robbery, and the Youngers were shot "full of lead" by a posse, pleaded guilty and were sentenced to life sentences in the Stillwater, Minnesota, prison.

Why change Northfield to a train? Perhaps Holt, Gruber and Douglas felt the outlaws had already pulled off too many bank robberies, and they wanted to showcase Smoky Sue, a circa–1869 locomotive that had hauled cargoes on California rails before taking on bit parts in movies for twenty years. "[T]he strain of making the exciting robbery scene ... proved too much for a woman of eighty-two," and Smoky Sue was to be retired after shooting of *The Great Missouri Raid*.[66]

The Players

Gordon Douglas had started in movies, appearing as an extra and an actor in films as early as 1912 as a toddler. An assistant director on Laurel and Hardy comedies, he moved up to director on *Our Gang* shorts, but is probably best-known for his sci-fi classic *Them!* (1954). He proved himself a capable director of Westerns, including the unheralded *The Charge at Feather River* (1954) and *Rio Conchos* (1964). He certainly made his share of bad films — *Only the Valiant* (1951) comes to mind — and he knew it. "Don't try to watch all the films I've directed; it would turn you off movies forever," he said. By the time he made *The Great Missouri Raid*, he had already directed a near-miss Western, *The Doolins of Oklahoma* (1949), starring Randolph Scott.[67]

Ward Bond spent much of the movie chewing up scenery and overacting tremendously as Major Trowbridge. Apparently, it came naturally. Macdonald Carey later wrote: "Ward Bond, who plays the representative of the establishment who is always pursing the James brothers in the picture, in real life is such a rabid anti–Communist that he almost froths at the mouth when he sees red."[68]

Wonder how Bond got along with Anne Revere. She played another strong mom (historians are unanimous in their consent that Jesse's mother was one tough woman). Revere, who had won the Supporting Actress Oscar as Elizabeth Taylor's mother in *National Velvet* (1944) and had been nominated for her matriarchal performances in *The Song of Bernadette* (1943) and *Gentleman's Agreement* (1947), would be blacklisted in 1951 after refusing to testify before the House Un-American Activities Committee. Perhaps that explains why she and Bond have no scenes together.[69]

Carey recalled that he and Wendell Corey were often mistaken for one another. At one time, Carey and Corey even lived on the same street, and they had another thing in common: Both were alcoholics, and they had company during *The Great Missouri Raid*. "The whole company drinks together each night," Carey recalled.[70]

During the filming in and around Sonora, California, both actors would have something else in common. They'd each be slightly injured — in odd ways.

Advertisement for *The Great Missouri Raid* (1951), Paramount's first biopic about Jesse James since the 1927 Fred Thomson silent movie failed to make a profit.

Seated in a wagon, Corey snapped the reins in a scene in which he was supposed to escape Union soldiers. The horses hitched to the team took off at a gallop, and instead of turning down a road, took the wagon down a rocky hillside. Corey pulled the brake, but the handle broke in his hands, and the old wagon fell apart as it went down the hill. He kept his seat, and escaped with only bruises.[71]

Carey's injury came while playing slots in Jamestown, California. A waiter accidentally hit Carey's arm, and his hand crashed through the machine's glass window. The cut was treated, and then "camouflaged" by a makeup artist for filming.[72]

Carey worked well in Westerns. William Holden had taught him how to ride when the two were filming *Streets of Laredo* (1949) in Gallup, New Mexico. He later starred in the underrated *Stranger at My Door* (1956).[73]

Corey was better suited in supporting roles, and more convincing in non–Westerns such as *Rear Window* (1954). Yet after the end of the first week of shooting, producer Nat Holt came up to Carey and said, "I made a big mistake. Wendell should be playing Jesse and you should be playing Frank."[74]

"Since the picture is about Jesse in the main," Carey wrote, "this is not the highest of compliments. Just another example of the Corey-Carey confusion."[75]

Analysis

The Great Missouri Raid is an action-filled movie that doesn't quite work. For the most part, it's a repeat of director Henry King's 1939 version about Jesse, though this one is somewhat more grounded in history: The railroads aren't the villains, and Jesse's mother isn't killed in the raid on the farm.

Yet the movie overlooks logic. When Bee returns to Missouri, soldiers laugh at Frank and Jesse, and pick a fight with him, but make no attempt to bring him in. Hmmmm. What happened to those Wanted: Dead or Alive posters on Jesse and Frank? During one robbery, the local lawman is seen being held at gunpoint, but when the outlaws make their getaway, the lawman is seen firing at the fleeing bandits. Wouldn't Jesse disarm the lawman before riding away? When Dick Liddil guns down Ed Miller in Jesse's home, Charles Ford goes outside to make sure nobody heard the shot. That makes sense, but wouldn't Bee James — inside the house — have heard?

Yet some moments ring true, as when a bitter, tired Frank tells Jesse: "We've never enjoyed one cent of the money we've stolen." As loose as Gruber played with the facts, *The Great Missouri Raid* would still prove to be the last serious study of Jesse James for a long, long time.

* * *

Variety (December 6, 1950): "Gordon Douglas' direction swings the footage through many exciting moments. The bank holdups that follow the personally-inspired raids against the Jameses, the train robberies, the flights through rugged terrain, the more intimate family and romance incidents are all told most acceptably."

Best of the Badmen

(RKO Radio Pictures, August 1951, 84 minutes)

CREDITS: *Director:* William D. Russell; *Producer:* Herman Schlom; *Screenplay:* Robert Hardy Andrews and John Twist.
CAST: Robert Ryan (Jeff Clanton); Claire Trevor (Lily); Jack Buetel (Bob Younger); Robert Preston (Matthew Fowler); Walter Brennan ("Doc" Butcher Ephrim); Bruce Cabot (Cole Younger); John Archer (Curly Ringo); Lawrence Tierney (Jesse James); Barton MacLane (Joad); Tom Tyler (Frank James); Bob Wilke (Jim Younger); John Cliff (John Younger).

Synopsis

Borrowing from Universal's thinking that you can't have too many all-star monsters in a movie (1944's *House of Frankenstein* and 1945's *House of Dracula*), RKO brought all-star outlaws back together for the second "in-name-only" sequel to *Badman's Territory* (1946).

Badman's Territory star Randolph Scott had returned, although he played a different character, in RKO's *Return of the Bad Men* (1948), which put the Younger brothers (but not Frank and Jesse James) and the Daltons together with Billy the Kid, Bill Doolin, et al., led by a quite menacing Sundance Kid (Robert Ryan). In *Best of the Badmen*, Ryan moved up to star billing as a good guy. Well, not that good, especially after being wronged.

In *Best of the Badmen* (1951), Robert Ryan, left, turned outlaw, and planned the heists of Lawrence Tierney, in his second turn as Jesse James.

Months after the end of the Civil War, Union Major Jeff Clanton, formerly a Missouri farmer, tracks down the remaining members of Quantrill's guerrillas and promises them amnesty providing they take the oath of allegiance and can prove they were on the Confederate payroll.

"You're about the only Yank that I'd trust," Captain Cole Younger tells Clanton.

"Maybe I'm about the only Yank that'd trust you," Clanton replies.

Clanton returns the guerrillas to Breckenridge, Missouri, where carpetbagger Matthew Fowler runs a national detective agency (*and* the local law.) Fowler tries to persuade Clanton to turn over the outlaws, at least those with the big rewards on their heads, but Clanton refuses.

As Clanton begins to administer the oath of allegiance, Fowler has his men incite the crowd. In the rush for the guerrillas, Bob Younger is wounded, and Clanton kills one of Fowler's men. Then he finishes the oath, and sends the men out of town.

Fowler isn't one to mess with, however, and he has Clanton arrested. Clanton had been discharged from the military three weeks before, and is therefore convicted of murder and sentenced to hang. In jail, he is visited by Lily, Fowler's estranged wife, who slips him a revolver. Clanton manages to escape, but is wounded in the leg. Now he's wanted dead or alive for murder.

Eventually he is captured by Fowler's men, but saved by the timely arrival of Bob Younger, whose right arm is useless thanks to the gunshot he took in Breckenridge, and horse-stealing guerrilla Doc Butcher. The oath of loyalty the guerrillas took didn't take, thanks to Fowler, because it had been administered by a civilian, so the boys are hiding out in the town of Quinto in the Cimarron sandhills. That's the same Quinto from *Badman's Territory*. "Badman's Territory they called it," Butcher narrates. "Cherokee Strip where they rigged civil law that carpetbaggers couldn't stick their claws in, and the Army wouldn't waste the powder. Plenty of fellas vacationed there. Mostly fast gun-hands who didn't like the smell of rope."

Lily's there, too, singing in the saloon, and Clanton promises to keep her identity a secret. Curly Ringo, maybe the most despicable of Quinto's residents, overhears the conversation.

Clanton hates Fowler with a passion, and he organizes Younger's gunmen to rob banks, trains and stagecoaches. Clanton isn't interested in the money. He's out to ruin Fowler, and he targets organizations the Fowler Detective Agency is contracted to protect. Clanton's method works. Cancellation notices start pouring into Fowler's office, but Clanton also sees the type of men he's working with.

In one bank job, Jesse James cold-bloodedly guns down a teller.

Lily tries to reason with Clanton, but he wants to finish his job — that is, until Cole Younger reveals his scheme to rob a train carrying a fortune in gold. Younger plans to dynamite the train. "What about the passengers?" Clanton asks.

"Who cares?" Cole Younger says, and Jesse adds: "After the explosion, you won't be able to find them?"

(Uh, what about the gold?)

Clanton suggests a less violent way (stopping the train at Yellow Rock). Reluctantly, the outlaws agree.

Bob Younger has a crush on Lily. When he gives her jewelry, Ringo starts a fight with the youngest Younger brother. The fight is stopped, but Ringo reveals Lily's true identity. Clanton whips Ringo in a fight, and runs him out of town, but the other outlaws are skeptical. She comes along with the gang on the train job, but it's a disaster. Ringo has informed on the outlaws to Fowler, and the detective has the train filled with gunmen.

Despite being wounded in the shoulder, Lily manages to save Clanton's hide, and they race back to Quinto. She's accused of a set-up, and Clanton, Bob Younger and Doc Butcher have to leave Quinto with the wounded woman. She's eventually recaptured by her husband and his men — and they take her back to Breckenridge. Clanton, naturally, goes after her, even though he knows it's a trap. Butcher and Bob Younger stick with him.

In the gunfight in Breckenridge, Bob Younger kills Ringo, and Fowler is shot by one of his own men before Bob, Butcher, Clanton and Lily make their getaway.

Safe, Bob Younger says he and Butcher will go to California, where there's gold. Butcher snickers, "There's gold in the mint at Denver, too, and it's a lot closer."

Clanton, with Lily at his side, announces that he plans to turn himself in and clear his name. Considering all the crimes Clanton helped organize or took part in, that's going to take a lot of doing. My bet is he hangs. On the other hand, Frank James was acquitted — twice.

The History

Legend has it that Jesse James was wounded when he tried to surrender in May or June 1865 when he and other guerrillas rode to Lexington, Missouri. Frank James had surrendered at Samuel's Depot, Kentucky, on July 26, 1865, and was paroled with other Quantrill survivors upon General John M. Palmer's orders. Cole Younger was in California at the war's end, and there's no record that he ever surrendered and took the oath of loyalty. Jim Younger took the oath after he was captured and held in an Alton, Illinois, prison. John and Bob Younger were thirteen and twelve years old, respectively, at the war's end, and, having never fought in the war, had no need to take the oath.[76]

The oath of loyalty was certainly controversial in Missouri. Charles D. Drake, a St. Louis lawyer and leader of the Radical Republicans, saw several of his ideas incorporated into the new state constitution — so many, in fact, that the 1865 constitution became known as the Drake Constitution. The new law of the land prohibited former Southern sympathizers from voting, holding any public office, or being employed in any professional position. They couldn't even be a church officer. A partial amnesty was available. Confederate supporters could take the oath of loyalty in which they swore allegiance to the United States and the 1865 Missouri constitution and thus be paroled. On the other hand, no one who served in the Union army or state militia could be prosecuted in civil or criminal court for acts they committed after January 1, 1861. Confederates could be held accountable.[77]

The result of the Drake Constitution, Cole Younger wrote, was that "the state was overrun with 'carpetbag' officeholders, many of whom came from Kansas, and during the war had been freebooters and bushwhackers up and down the Kansas border."[78]

Therefore few could debate the facts stated in the movie's opening scroll: "Months after the tragic war between the States had ended there was still no peace on the Western Frontier."

Doc Butcher and Curly Ringo were fictitious characters. So was Jeff Clanton. It seems the screenwriters turned to Tombstone, Arizona, for some names. Doc, as in Doc Holliday; Curly Ringo, as in Curly Bill Brocious and Johnny Ringo; and Clanton, as in Ike and Billy Clanton.

Bob Younger always had the use of both of his arms. Sure, he was badly wounded before being captured at Hanska Slough in 1876 after the bank robbery — mainly from a bullet in his lung, not arm. He died in the Stillwater, Minnesota, prison on September 16, 1889, at age thirty-four, and was buried in Lee's Summit, Missouri, four days later.[79]

Doc Butcher describes Jesse as "the quick and quiet one who lived and slept with both eyes open. No one ever rightly knew what he was thinking. He was all wrapped up in fire inside of him." Frank, Butcher says, "was just a homesick farmer who traded his plow for a rifle, and always a mite bitter about it." Many historians wouldn't argue with those descriptions.

The cold-blooded murder of an unarmed bank teller could also be traced to history. Inside the Daviess County Savings Association on December 7, 1869, Jesse shot John W. Sheets, the bank owner, in the chest and head. Of course, Jesse thought he was murdering Samuel P. Cox, who had killed Bloody Bill Anderson. On September 7, 1876, in the First National Bank of Northfield, the last bandit to leave the building — probably Frank James — killed Joseph Heywood with a bullet to the head.[80]

The Players

"The bread-and-butter pictures at RKO seem to be those about 'bad men,'" the *Los Angeles Times* reported, pointing out the success of *Badman's Territory* and *Return of the Bad Men*. "The 'bad men' pictures are reported consistent money-makers and the new one will probably return several members of the former casts to duty."[81]

Not quite.

Veteran character actor Tom Tyler was the only actor to appear in all three films, having played Frank James in *Badman's Territory* and Wild Bill Yeager in *Return of the Bad Men*. He repeated his Frank James role in *Best of the Badmen*, and had the same on-screen sibling.

By 1950, Lawrence Tierney, cast again as Jesse James, was seeing his career slide after such a powerful performance in *Dillinger* (1945). RKO had once thought of Tierney, the brother of actor Scott Brady, as a star, and cast him in a string of tough-guy roles. "I resented those pictures they put me in," he said. "I never thought of myself as that kind of guy. I thought of myself as a nice guy who wouldn't do rotten things."[82]

Newspaper headlines painted a different picture. Tierney was constantly making headlines for brawls and drunken incidents. In 1955, a newspaper reported that Tierney had been arrested sixteen times, more than Dillinger.[83]

His movie roles got smaller, but in 1982 he quit drinking after suffering a stroke. "I threw away about seven careers through drink," he said. He would manage something of a comeback in the 1990s, as Elaine Benes' father in a hilarious episode of NBC's hit sitcom *Seinfeld* (1991) and as the gang leader in Quentin Tarantino's *Reservoir Dogs* (1992). He died in Los Angeles on February 26, 2002.[84]

Born Warren Higgens in Dallas, Texas, Jack Buetel was an unknown when Howard Hughes cast the twenty-two-year-old as Billy the Kid in *The Outlaw*. He was a "devilishly handsome, lean but muscular, 'walking streak of sex' with a slight leer and a cocky gait."[85] The movie was finished in 1941, but, mainly due to censorship issues, was not released until 1943. Howard Hawks had considered casting Buetel as Matthew Garth in *Red River* (1948), but went with Montgomery Clift instead. As it was, Buetel — feuding with Hughes — wouldn't be seen again until he landed the role of Bob Younger in *Best of the Badmen*. He wouldn't be seen a whole lot afterward, although he did show up as Frank James in the abysmal *Jesse James' Women* (1954).[86]

Claire Trevor might have had the most inconsistent record of any actress. An Oscar winner for *Key Largo* (1948) and nominee for *Dead End* (1937) and *The High and the Mighty* (1954), she was know as the "queen of the B's" for her roles in low-budget movies who took advantage of her A-movie opportunities. She usually played hard-bitten dames in *noirs* like *Murder, My Sweet* (1944) or prostitutes in Westerns such as *Stagecoach* (1939). But it's hard to see how an actress who was so fantastic in *Key Largo* could be so pathetic in *Best of the Badmen*.[87]

It's difficult to say whether Robert Ryan today is better remembered for his Westerns or film noirs. Likely, his noirs, including *Crossfire* (1947), *Act of Violence* (1948), *The Set-up* (1949) and *On Dangerous Ground* (1952), were on the whole better, but he certainly was well-suited for Westerns.

During the Great Depression, the Chicago-born and Dartmouth-educated Ryan and a friend headed to northern Montana chasing a gold mine, "a sure thing" that wasn't. His father had taught him how to ride a horse, so when Ryan landed in Missoula, Montana, he took a job as a cowpuncher for $8 a week. He later supported himself as a clothes model, bodyguard, and cemetery plot salesman before finding his niche as an actor. He had a few roles before World War II. After the war, he returned to Hollywood to star in *Trail Street* (1947) with Randolph Scott. After a film *noir*, he played the bigot in *Crossfire*, earning an Academy Award nomination for Best Supporting Actor.[88]

"*Best of the Badmen* ignited no critical note," Ryan biographer Franklin Jarlett wrote, "but it appealed to the masses, while its box-office proceeds secured Ryan's knowledge that he could always lean on the Western if all else failed."[89]

He would make nineteen Westerns — nearly a third of his output — including *The Naked Spur* (1953), *The Professionals* (1966), *The Wild Bunch* (1969) and the contemporary Western *Bad Day at Black Rock* (1955) before his death of lung cancer in 1973. The great thing about Robert Ryan was that he never gave a bad performance. Which isn't to say he never made a bad movie.

Case in point: *Best of the Badmen*.

Analysis

Although strikingly filmed in Technicolor and rapidly paced — "In short, the badmen never had it better," the *New York Times* reviewed — *Best of the Badmen* is lame.

It certainly is pleasing to look at. Locations included the Iverson and Juaregui ranches outside of Los Angeles, and Utah's Kanab Canyon, Paria, Duck Creek and Strawberry Valley.[90]

William D. Russell was directing his first Western,[91] and he was saddled with a ridiculous script, although Doc Butcher got some good lines ("I'd sooner be a sensible live quitter than a stubborn dead hero"; "Step back, gents, and reflect on the joys of living"; "Nope, I don't [know what I'm doing]. But my impetuous nature got me into this, so it's going to have to get me out!").

Most of the screenplay is reduced to tired offerings such as Lily's plea to Clanton to see the error of his ways. "Jeff, you're so wrong," Lily wails. "You've got to stop this. You're terrorizing the whole country."

The *New York Times* said the movie was "easy to take,"[92] and it certainly was, but it proved even easier to dismiss and forget.

And for history? Before filming began, the *Los Angeles Times* reported that the movie "will assume semihistorical character."[93]

"Semi" might be stretching things.

* * *

New York Herald-Tribune (August 10, 1951): "An unusually fine cast is thrown into the hopper this time, but it's ground up with a painfully unoriginal story."

Woman They Almost Lynched

(Republic, March 1953, 90 minutes)

CREDITS: *Director-Producer:* Allan Dwan; *Screenplay:* Steve Fisher.
CAST: John Lund (Lance Horton); Brian Donlevy (Quantrill); Audrey Totter (Kate Quantrill); Joan Leslie (Sally Maris); Ben Cooper (Jesse James); Nina

Varela (Mayor Delilah Courtney); Jim Davis (Cole Younger); Reed Hadley ("Bitterroot" Bill Maris); Ann Savage (Glenda); Virginia Christine (Jenny); Marilyn Lindsey (Rose); Nacho Galindo (John Pablo); Ellen Corby (First Woman); Minerva Urecal (Mrs. Stuart); Dick Simmons (Captain); Gordon Jones (Yankee Sergeant); James Brown (Frank James).

Synopsis

"One of the worst titles ever," Ben Cooper says.[94]

During the Civil War, the Western frontier saw law and order disappear, replaced by lynch law. Renegades and raiders were busy, the narrator tells us, "murdering, looting, pillaging, shooting, slashing their way through one of the darkest pages of our history."

Yet peace existed in the Ozark Mountains town of Border City, situated on the Arkansas-Missouri line, half the town in Yankee land (Missouri), half in the Confederacy (Arkansas). The town has declared itself neutral, and Mayor Delilah Courtney is adamant that it stays neutral. Armies on both sides are prohibited from coming closer than five miles to town without permission, and anyone who tries to break that neutrality is lynched.

Beautiful and refined Sally Maris is traveling to Border City by stagecoach to surprise her brother, whom she hasn't seen in years. A Union cavalry patrol escorts the stage toward Border City, but Quantrill's raiders attack, kill the soldiers and stop the stage. One of the raiders has a slight saber cut across the shoulder, so he's put in the stage to ride into Border City. Turns out the young fella is none other than Jesse James.

Quantrill has reason for visiting Border City: He wants lead from Courtney's mine. Quantrill's wife, pants-wearing, pistol-packing Kate, has reason to visit, too. She wants to torment her former beau. Sally, who has spent all her money on the trip, just wants to see her brother. Nothing really works out for any of them.

Sally is repulsed when she learns that her brother, Bitterroot Bill, runs a saloon and is a lecherous, despicable gambler. Courtney won't sell Quantrill any lead, and gives him twenty-four hours to get out of town. Bitterroot Bill also turns out to be Kate Quantrill's beau. Two years earlier, she had been kidnapped by Quantrill, but now seems to enjoy riding and killing with him. Seeing her, plus his sister's unexpected arrival, torments Bitterroot so much that he starts drinking heavily. After Bitterroot tries to kill Kate, the bartender says, "He gets in trouble every time he takes a drink." He won't any more. Courtney's foreman, Lance Horton, intervenes, and is forced to kill Bill in self-defense.

Sally's horrified by the violence, and by Lance Horton — especially when Horton says he must now protect her. She doesn't need any help. She can shoot better than many men. She closes the Lead Dollar Saloon and tries to find respectable work, but the women in town think she's a tramp. She can't sell the saloon, either, because her brother had too many debts. Reluctantly, she reopens the Lead Dollar and starts running it with the help of saloon girls Glenda, Rose and Jenny and the piano player, John Pablo.

When Kate comes back to the Lead Dollar, she tries to start a riot by singing "Dixie." Turns out half the people inside are Northerners, the other half Southerners. Sally has to intervene, and the catfight is on. "This is a better fight than the one between the North and the South," one spectator says. Sally wins the bout and drags Kate out of the saloon, but she's upset with herself. "Brawling like a common hussy," she moans, and has a change of

"I'd rather be hanged than owe my life to Lance Horton," she said.

THE WOMAN THEY ALMOST LYNCHED

By MICHAEL FESSIER

The boys were riled up. They were going to hang someone — and they didn't much care if the victim wore skirts.

ILLUSTRATED BY MELBOURNE BRINDLE

WHEN Grammaw Horton was one hundred years of age the Horton County Chamber of Commerce gave her a testimonial dinner in Hortonsville and all the important citizens of the state, most of whom were Hortons, carefully stuffed their shirts, put on their most pompous, self-satisfied faces and attended. Governor Dunkel, who was distantly related to the Hortons, made a speech in which he insisted that Grammaw Horton and her departed husband, J. Lance Horton, had, between them, practically built the West and had contributed more than any other two persons toward making the United States of America what it is today.

Grammaw Horton, for all her years, sat stiff and straight at the head of the table and listened attentively to what the governor said. She had a crop of fine white hair, and skin that was wrinkled but still alive — the cheeks faintly pink — and eyes that were dark and alert, and could be imperious when she felt in the mood. As the governor droned on about her being the grand old matriarch of the state and listed her many virtues, all of which he contended the younger generation could emulate with profit, she smothered a slight yawn and her eyes began to rove disinterestedly over the table. Finally she caught sight of me, and she grinned impishly and winked.

I grinned and winked back at her. I was the only unimportant person there and I was the only one who had been personally invited by Grammaw. As she grinned at me, I knew that she knew what I was thinking.

I was thinking of how this distinguished company would react if they knew that, at one time, in another state and in another county, Grammaw Horton had gone by the name of "Salt Creek Sal" and that she had once almost been the guest of honor at a lynching bee.

heart regarding her feelings toward Horton. Just about everybody has changes of heart in this movie.

Horton tells Sally that she saved a lot of lives. He also lets her in on a secret: He's actually a Confederate captain. He'll get lead to his soldiers, but not to Quantrill — especially not after the Quantrill-led slaughter at Lawrence, Kansas. If Courtney learns he's a spy, he'll hang. When Horton leaves the saloon, he is disarmed by Jesse and other raiders and taken to Quantrill, who tries to blackmail Horton (Quantrill knows Horton's a Confederate officer) into getting lead for the guerrillas.

Sally has another protector, too, youthful Jesse James. He stops Cole Younger's unwelcome advances toward her, and lets her know that Kate Quantrill plans revenge. He even leaves Sally one of his guns. Kate and Sally meet in a walk-down showdown, but Sally's quicker and more accurate, and wounds the outlaw queen in the arm.

Horton has sent for Confederate troops, and Courtney has asked the Union Army to come to town. Border City is about to explode. When Quantrill tries to leave town with Horton, the powder keg detonates. Cole Younger wants to get a wife — hey, his boss got one that way — and Younger and his brother Jim run into the Lead Dollar to kidnap Sally. That provokes Jesse, who lets Horton take one of his guns and go after the Youngers. Horton wounds Jim Younger, but is wounded himself, the Yankees arrive, and the battle is on.

When Kate Quantrill is thrown from her horse during the battle, Sally helps her inside the saloon. She also gets Horton upstairs. The Union soldiers drive off the guerrillas, then start looking for Kate. Dressed up as a saloon girl, however, Kate fools the soldiers. She also lets Sally know that it's Quantrill that she really hates — for kidnapping her, for ruining the life she might have had with Bitterroot Bill.

Wounded guerrillas reveal Horton's true identity, and Courtney is determined that Horton hang. Sally's resolved to save his life, so she writes a note that identifies Bitterroot Bill as the spy and that she is determined to finish the job. That's enough for Courtney, who orders Sally lynched. She's marched to the gallows tree, but before she can be executed, Kate rides up and tells the truth (by then, Horton is safe with his Confederate troops) and gallops away.

Life returns to normalcy in Border City, until Lance Horton shows up in town wearing the uniform of the Confederacy. Courtney threatens to hang him, but Horton says the war's over. "Who won?" Courtney asks.

"Nobody won. We just quit fighting," Horton tells her.

There's a hot time in the old town as the residents celebrate the end of the war, especially Lance and Sally.

The History

What history?

When Mayor Courtney points out that Arkansas is Confederate and Missouri Union, she's only partly right. Missouri was a border state, claiming no side and trying to remain

Opposite: Melbourne Brindle illustrated Michael Fessier's story "The Woman They Almost Lynched," which appeared in the January 6, 1951, edition of *The Saturday Evening Post.* For the 1953 movie version, screenwriter Steve Fisher added Jesse James to the storyline.

neutral, but in fact it was bitterly divided and extremely violent. Although Arkansas had reluctantly joined the Confederacy on May 5, 1861, by 1863 it too was a state divided. Little Rock was under Union control, and the Confederacy had set up a state in Washington, near the Texas border. By early 1864, there would be two governments, with the Arkansas River basically dividing the North and South.[95]

Upon Horton's return to Border City, he announces that the war ended "yesterday in Richmond, Virginia." Richmond? On April 12, 1865, General Robert E. Lee officially surrendered to General Ulysses S. Grant at Appomattox Court House — not Richmond, which was in Federal hands by April 3, 1865. Joseph E. Johnston surrendered to General William Sherman at Durham Station, North Carolina, on May 3. The last Confederate general to surrender was the Cherokee Stand Watie, who capitulated on June 23, 1865, in Doaksville, Indian Territory (present-day Oklahoma).[96]

While the movie certainly wasn't historically accurate, the wardrobe department, Cooper recalls, tried to create a guerrilla shirt similar to one worn by Jesse James in a photograph. And those two guns Jesse wears? "I don't think he wore two guns the way I did in that one," Cooper says, "but I had to give one of my guns to Joan."[97]

In the scene in which Jesse rides into town with Sally in the stagecoach, he gives his reasons for joining Quantrill: "How'd you like to come home and find your father hanging and your mother all cut up with a broken leg and your older brother gone away — nobody there at all! How would you like it?" Jesse says he tried to join Quantrill, but was told he was too young. "But he took me, finally."

Says Cooper: "I don't know how accurate the writing was. [It wasn't.] I didn't want to get involved in that. I just wanted to play cowboy and have fun."

The Players

Between 1911 and 1961, Allan Dwan directed an astonishing 400-plus movies, his best probably being *Sands of Iwo Jima* (1949). "Allan Dwan had been a really big, famous director," Cooper says, "and this was in his later years."[98]

One can imagine how he felt directing something as corny as *Woman They Almost Lynched*. During the showdown scene between Totter and Leslie, Cooper recalls, Dwan sat in his chair, "giggling and saying, 'This is the funniest thing I've ever seen, the funniest thing I've ever seen.' He knew what he was doing. But he had fun."

Dwan was by no means washed up. After *Woman They Almost Lynched*, he directed two excellent Westerns for RKO, *Silver Lode* (1954) and *Tennessee's Partner* (1955), both starring John Payne.

Screenwriter Steve Fisher adapted Michael Fessier's short story "The Woman They Almost Lynched," which had been published in *The Saturday Evening Post*. The "The" was dropped for the movie title. In the story, there were characters named Sally Maris, Bitterroot Bill and Lance Horton, but the lynching party (over cattle theft) turned into a wedding party. There were no lead mines, no Border City, no Civil War, no Quantrill, and no Jesse James.[99] Those were all Fisher's additions.

Ann Savage had a small role as one of the saloon girls. After several small roles in the mid–1940s, she gave a dynamite performance in the classic film noir *Detour* (1945), but her career went nowhere. *Woman They Almost Lynched* proved to be her last movie role until

Six. The Proliferation of Jesse James, 1950–1960

Fire with Fire (1986). She made a few TV appearances but went into semi-retirement in the late 1950s, and died in 2008, a year after her last film, *My Winnipeg*, was released.[100]

Audrey Totter, best known for *film noirs*, didn't think much of the script. "The funny thing is, Steve Fisher wrote that and he wrote *Lady in the Lake* which is excellent. Very smart dialogue. But I guess that's his forte — not writing westerns. Some of it was just so corny."[101]

Joan Leslie, Totter recalled, thought much of her dialogue was laughable, too. "We used to be just hysterical," Totter said.[102]

Said Leslie: "The movie is dramatic but silly. Actually, it's a pretty fast-moving little movie. It's odd the way Republic brings music into the story [Totter's voice for the songs was dubbed] — it's a scream, it seems out of place!"[103]

Both actresses had certainly seen better parts. A former radio performer, Totter had picked up notice for strong performances in *The Postman Always Rings Twice* (1946), *Lady in the Lake* (1946) and *The Set-up* (1949). By 1954, she would appear predominantly on television. Leslie was signed by Warner Brothers before she had turned eighteen, and landed roles in *High Sierra* (1941) and *Yankee Doodle Dandy* (1942). After her contract expired in 1947, she freelanced and appeared in predominantly B-movies and on television.[104]

Both actresses loved working with Cooper. "He's a very good actor," Leslie said.[105] Totter recalled, "Ben Cooper was the cutest little thing in the world. Real young [nineteen at the time], sweet guy. I never saw anybody drink so much milk. He drank quarts of milk."[106]

The movie was shot at Lone Pine, California, and on the Republic lot. During a break in shooting, Cooper recalls, "a little baldheaded man" arrived on the set and began chatting with him. The man asked how Cooper, from New York, had learned to ride horses, and Cooper told him he had owned his own horse on Long Island and taught himself to ride and jump because he wanted to do Westerns.

"Really? What kind of parts do you like to play?" the man asked. When Cooper said he'd like to play heavies, the man asked him why. Cooper answered, "Because I don't think I look like one, and that way it would be more frightening for the audience if the audience knows I'm a bad guy but every one else thinks I'm a good guy."

Before the man left, they chatted some more. When the stranger had gone, Cooper asked the camera operator, "Whitey, who was that guy?" The answer: Herbert Yates. Cooper then asked, "Oh, who's that?"

The cameraman answered, "He owns us." Yates was head of Republic.

The next day, Cooper got a phone call from his agent, who asked the young actor, "What did you say to Herbert Yates yesterday?"

"I thought, 'Oh, God, trouble,'" Cooper recalls. "'Well, I just answered his questions. Why?' He said, 'Well, he wants to put you under contract.'"

Cooper, who would indeed play heavies, remained at Republic almost to the studio's fall. He left in 1957, and Republic shut down the following year.[107]

Analysis

Undoubtedly the oddest Jesse James movie of the 1950s — and that's including the Bob Hope comedy *Alias Jesse James* — *Woman They Almost Lynched* could have been a rip-roaring comedy. Yet no one seemed to know exactly what they were aiming for.

Leslie played it straight; Totter played it as a farce (Cooper thought Totter "was kinda overdoing it").[108]

Instead, it proved an inconsistent misfire, part cornball horse opera, part comedy, part traditional Western–Civil War yarn — all done on the cheap.

* * *

Hollywood Reporter (March 30, 1953): "[T]he story goes to pieces, submerged by incredible character reversals. Allan Dwan's production is good and his direction is excellent, particularly in his staging of the action scenes which have a realistic quality that is genuinely exciting."

The Great Jesse James Raid
(Lippert, April 1953, 73 minutes)

CREDITS: *Director:* Reginald Le Borg; *Producer:* Robert L. Lippert Jr.; *Screenplay:* Richard Landau.

CAST: Willard Parker (Jesse James); Barbara Payton (Kate); Tom Neal (Arch Clements); Wallace Ford (Elias Hobbs); Jim Bannon (Bob Ford); James Anderson (Johnny Dorette); Richard Cutting (Sam Wells); Barbara Woodell (Zee James).

Synopsis

Just when you thought Jesse James couldn't sink any lower....

Shortly after he awakens from a nightmare in which a Union soldier was whipping him to find out where Frank James was hiding, a bitter, frustrated, older Jesse is visited by gang member Bob Ford and Ford's friend from Creede, Colorado, Sam Wells. The two have a scheme to take $300,000 in gold from a Creede mine, but they need Jesse's help. He can bring in a gunslinger, a teamster and an explosives expert, men who won't talk in case they're caught. For that, Ford and Wells are willing to give Jesse twenty-five percent of the take — enough dough for Jesse to disappear with his wife and son. Jesse's wife begs him not to go with Ford — she doesn't trust him — but Jesse sees this as his big chance. The next morning, Wells and Ford ride back to Colorado, and Jesse heads off to round up his men.

First is the gunslinger Arch Clements. Jesse breaks him out of jail, and Clements cold-bloodedly murders the jailer. Next Jesse and Arch rescue the demo man, Elias Hobbs, from a crooked card game. Finally, they come to a ranch looking for Pat Jorrette, the teamster, but Pat has been lynched, and they find Jorrette's son, Johnny, instead. When the men who murdered Johnny's pa return, Jesse and friends shoot down those bad men and get away. Jesse talks Johnny into joining them.

They meet Bob Ford at his saloon, and Johnny's attracted to Bob's woman, Kate. So is Arch Clements, who'll try to force himself upon her before the movie's over. The next morning, the men ride to Sam Wells's cabin and mine.

The plan is to dynamite and dig their way through an abandoned tunnel to reach the gold shipment, then haul the gold off in a wagon. Bob heads back to town to bring the wagon. He returns with not only the wagon, but Kate.

Six. The Proliferation of Jesse James, 1950–1960

Arch Clements (Tom Neal) guns down the jailer (actor unidentified) after Jesse James (Willard Parker) busted the gunman out of jail in *The Great Jesse James Raid* (1953), one of several Lippert productions about the outlaw in the early 1950s.

He also returns with some men from Creede, leaving them hidden in the hills. They'll kill Jesse (for the $10,000 reward) and his men when they come out of the mine, and leave the $300,000 for Ford and Wells. Make that just Ford. He kills Wells with a shovel, and makes it look like an accident.

Clements, left guarding the mine entrance, gets knifed in the back, but manages to drag himself into the mine to warn the others before dying—"probably the kindest thing he did in his whole life," Hobbs says.

Hobbs tries to blast through the mine tunnel so his colleagues can escape, but he drowns when the explosion rips open an underground river. Jesse, Ford, Johnny and Kate rush to the entrance and try to escape in a wagon driven by Johnny. When one of the ambushers throws a dynamite stick, Ford and Jesse leap from the wagon. The explosion kills Johnny and Kate, but Jesse guns down the other bad men.

There's nothing left for Ford and Jesse to do but return to Missouri. Jesse's resigned to his fate. "Someday," he tells Ford, "one of us will pick up a paper and read about how someone put a bullet in the back of one of our heads." He rides off to St. Joseph, and Ford heads to his brother Charlie's place. On the way, Ford sees a reward poster for Jesse. He lights a cigar, burns the poster, and rides on.

The History

When Bob Ford and Sam Wells arrive at Jesse's St. Joseph home, the address is 18 Lafayette Street. Close. Jesse lived at 1318 Lafayette Street, having moved his family there on Christmas Eve, 1881.[109] Bob says he learned where Jesse was living from his brother Charlie, who had run into Cole Younger. Where? At the Stillwater, Minnesota, prison—Younger's home since pleading guilty to the Northfield bank robbery in 1876?[110]

Jesse says he hasn't seen Ford since the Blue Cut robbery (September 7, 1881). According to Dick Liddil's confession, Bob Ford didn't take part in the raid.[111] Ford says he owns a saloon in Creede, which he *did*, but not in 1881 or 1882, but years after he killed Jesse.[112] Lippert seemed to be fascinated with the town Creede. Of the four Lippert films about Jesse (*I Shot Jesse James, Gunfire, The Return of Jesse James* and *The Great Jesse James Raid*), three are at least partially set in Creede, which wasn't founded until the 1890s. And that $300,000 in gold? Silver was king in Creede.[113]

When Jesse and Hobbs are trying to figure out who they can get to as a teamster, Johnny Reno's name is brought up. Reno was one of the Reno brothers, whose high-profile gang robbed trains in the post–Civil War Midwest. Convicted in 1868, Reno was sentenced to twenty-five years in the Missouri State Penitentiary, but paroled in February 1878, though he'd return to prison, for counterfeiting, in the 1880s. There is no documentation that Reno and Jesse ever met.[114]

Clell Miller's name is suggested, but Hobbs says Miller has gotten married. Actually, Miller had gotten killed, shot dead in the Northfield holdup, although rumors later suggested that Miller actually escaped and died of natural causes in Murray, Arkansas.[115]

No such stories about Arch Clement/Clements. Little Arch met his end by gunfire in 1866 in Lexington, Missouri.[116]

Sam Wells was also a name out of James-Younger history. Sam Wells was an alias of Charlie Pitts, or Charlie Pitts was an alias used by Sam Wells. Pitts-Wells, however, wasn't killed in a Creede, Colorado, mine, but died "game" during the Hanksa Slough gunfight in Minnesota that left the Younger boys badly wounded.[117]

What does the script get right? Very little. Jesse was called "Dingus,"[118] and there's one scene that rings true when Jesse says he doesn't give orders: "I never tell my men what to do. If they like the set-up, they go. If they don't, they forget about it."

The Players

Robert L. Lippert Jr., son of Lippert Pictures founder Robert L. Lippert, entered independent film production with *The Great Jesse James Raid* in the spring of 1953.[119] He assembled a has-been cast perhaps familiar to B-movie fans.

Willard Parker, born Worster Von Eps in New York, was a meter reader-turned pro tennis player who turned to acting at age twenty-five, changing his name for his first role in the Dick Foran Western *The Devil's Saddle Legion* (1937). He was signed by Columbia in the 1940s, but didn't get much attention after a series of B-leads and co-leads. That changed, slightly, after *The Great Jesse James Raid*. Producer Jack Cummings and director George Sidney picked Parker to play Tex Callaway, the wealthy cattle baron, in *Kiss Me Kate* (1953), a musical starring Kathryn Grayson and Howard Keel. Parker was the only star who didn't sing and dance. Parker's most remembered role was likely that of Ranger Jace Pearson in television's *Tales of the Texas Rangers* (1955–59). He gave up acting and sold real estate, dying of heart failure in 1996 at age 84.[120]

Wallace Ford's career was also in decline. After making his Broadway debut in 1921, he had signed with MGM in 1932. He was third-billed, behind Victor McLaglen and Boris Karloff, in *The Lost Patrol* (1934), directed by John Ford, who also cast Ford in the Academy Award–winning classic *The Informer* (1935). By the 1940s, he was doing character roles in films like *T-Men* (1947) and *The Set-up* (1949), and from the 1950s most of his movies were Westerns. Some good—*The Man from Laramie* (1955), *Warlock* (1959). Many mediocre, if that—*Warpath* (1951), *The Spoilers* (1955). He died in 1966.

Maybe the best example of fading star was the beautiful Barbara Payton. Signed by Universal when she was in her twenties and later signed by Warner Brothers, she worked with James Cagney in *Kiss Tomorrow Goodbye* (1950), Gary Cooper in *Dallas* (1950) and Gregory Peck in the terrible *Only the Valiant* (1951). She was more known for her relationships. Warner Brothers had dropped her because of her "scandalous sexual adventures."[121]

After Franchot Tone and bodybuilding actor Tom Neal brawled over her on September 13, 1951, Tone wound up in the hospital for two weeks. Payton married Tone. In less than a year they were divorced, and she went back to Neal, though they never married. Tone played Arch Clements in *The Great Jesse James* pretty much as he played Payton's lover: abusively, although Payton denied that, writing, "There were all kinds of rumors about him but the fact is he was a gentle, even though physical man."[122]

Neal wasn't so gentle. His career faded, too, and he was a landscape gardener in Palm Springs when he was accused of murdering his estranged wife in 1965. He was convicted of involuntary manslaughter—prosecutors had sought the death penalty—and handed a one- to ten-year sentence at Soledad State Prison. Released in 1971, he died of a heart attack on August 7, 1972.[123]

Payton describes her slide, and *The Great Jesse James Raid*, in her memoir, *I Am Not Ashamed*: "Then all of a sudden you find yourself doing a western. A western with *Jesse James* in the title. I did one, *The Great Jesse James Raid* with Willard Parker. It was no disgrace but it didn't mark a step up."[124]

Scripts were becoming fewer. Self-destruction set in. "You drink a little bit more. You get on that sorry-for-yourself kick. If you're like me you need more affection and sex because you have to prove there's one area of living you can still score in."[125]

Drugs and alcohol took their toll. She wound up a prostitute, "high-class" at first, then "selling her body for just $5 a trick."[126] She died in the bathroom at the home of her parents in San Diego in 1967. She was thirty-nine.[127]

Analysis

Lippert pictures were always B's, but *The Great Jesse James Raid* takes the low budget to the extreme. Backlot scenes are often devoid of any extras. Movie advertisements heralded the movie's new Ansco color process (Lippert's three previous Jesse James movies were all black-and-white). However, "Ansco color negatives lacked the resolution and sharpness of Kodak color negatives."[128]

Given the Neal-Payton relationship, the scene in which he attempts to rape her is even more difficult to watch.

This is a bad movie. Poor history, badly acted — Barbara Woodell is wasted again in her fourth James spouse role — terribly directed, and saddled with an idiotic script. It seems that Jesse James was thrown in just to exploit the outlaw's name.

* * *

Brian Garfield, *Western Films* (1982): "The typical Lippert mixture of history, fiction and 'B' action is a notch below normal, mainly because the cast is humdrum."

Jesse James vs. the Daltons
(Columbia, April 1954, 65 minutes)

CREDITS: *Director:* William Castle; *Producer:* Sam Katzman; *Screenplay:* Robert E. Kent.

CAST: Brent King (Joe Branch, aka Jesse James Jr.); Barbara Lawrence (Kate Manning); James Griffith (Bob Dalton); William Phipps (Bill Dalton); John Cliff (Grat Dalton); Rory Mallinson (Bob Ford); William Tannen (Emmett Dalton); Richard Garland (Gilke); Nelson Leigh (Father Kerrigan).

Synopsis

Jesse James rides in 3-D against the Daltons!

Well, not really. Actually, Joe Branch rides into Coffeyville, Kansas, and quickly rescues Kate Manning — a woman almost lynched — from a mob about to stretch her neck. It seems that Kate killed the son of wealthy rancher Corey Bayliss, who runs Coffeyville. She claims self-defense. The mob wanted to please Bayliss.

Branch didn't rescue Kate because he's a nice guy. He isn't. When Bayliss's foreman takes a shot at Kate, Branch guns him down. Ruthlessly. "Jesse James could kill like that," Kate tells Branch.

The fact is, Branch needs Kate. Most people think Jesse James was Branch's father, and Branch has to know for sure. He's tired of carrying that baggage, being told to "drift" by every lawman in every town. It's not easy being Jesse James's son.

"I've heard there was some good in Jesse James," Kate says. "Can't you remember that, too?"

Kate's father used to ride with Jesse James, and Branch has heard there's $100,000 stashed away in the outlaw's old hideout. He also has heard that Jesse James wasn't killed ten years earlier, and that money might bring Jesse out of hiding. If so, Branch can confront him and learn the truth. Kate agrees to help. Before long, they'll fall in love. It's what people do in B-Westerns.

But how can they find Jesse's hideout? Kate went there once, but she was too young to remember much about it. An even bigger question is how can they get in touch with Jesse — if he, indeed, is alive? The answer's obvious. "The Daltons would know," Branch says. How? That part's never explained.

When Branch and Kate learn about an Army payroll being shipped by railroad, Branch concocts an idea. Knowing the Daltons are sure to rob the train, Branch beats them to it. He warns the law about the Daltons, and volunteers to help guard the payroll. Most of the

Six. The Proliferation of Jesse James, 1950–1960

Jesse James vs. the Daltons, a 1954 Columbia 3-D release, had a misleading title. Brett King didn't play Jesse, but a man suspected of being the outlaw's son.

lawmen are in the rear cars of the train, but Branch finagles a way to get closer to the express car. Then, he uncouples the cars carrying most of the lawmen, and the locomotive and express car travel on to Adair, Oklahoma. Apparently, the engineer and fireman didn't notice they were leaving several cars behind. Next, Branch gets the drop on the guards in the express car and gets away with the $50,000. (By the way, when the locomotive leaves the station, it's engine No. 8. When it arrives in Adair, where the Daltons are waiting, it's engine No. 11.)

Branch isn't really a thief. With the help of a Coffeyville priest, Branch arranges a meeting with the head of the railroad and returns all but $10,000. He asks the railroad man to have reward posters printed for Branch's capture, and not to let anyone know that most of the money has been returned. That should bring the Daltons after him. The railroad executive agrees. Go figure.

Branch and Kate ride to Bartlesville, knowing the Daltons will come after them. Sure enough, Bob and Grat Dalton find out where Branch is staying, and try to retrieve the money that rightfully should belong to them, but Branch gets the drop on them. He introduces Kate as his wife — mainly to keep Grat away from her — and tells Bob that if they will help him find Jesse James, he'll split the $100,000 from the old Jesse job and the $50,000 from the railroad robbery with them. To show he's sincere, he gives Bob the $10,000.

Grat's not in favor of the idea. He wants to rob the bank in Coffeyville, but Bob opts for Branch's plan. The Daltons are the only ones who know where Frank James is. (Why? That's another unresolved question!) So they send a rider to tell Frank what's going on. "If Jesse's alive," Bob says, "Frank will know how to reach him." Then the outlaws take Branch and Kate to Jesse's old hideout.

In the mountain hideout, Grat attacks Kate, but Branch arrives, and the two men go at each other with axes on the lake front, then go into the lake. Kate stops Branch from drowning the vile Dalton. A short while later, a stranger arrives. It's Bob Ford. Frank James sent him! The Daltons ask about the money, and Ford says it's only right they should have it. He shows them where it is, and the Daltons are disgusted to find it's worthless Confederate currency. The Daltons are so angry, they knock out Ford and Branch, and decide to rob not one but *two* Coffeyville banks. They bring Kate along because she can tell them about Coffeyville.

When Branch and Ford regain consciousness, Ford tells Branch the truth: Jesse isn't Joe's father. Jesse found Branch as an infant after Quantrill's men killed the boy's mother and father, and it was Jesse who brought the baby to the Branch household and left a note asking them to bring up the boy. Then Ford lays another load on Branch. "Joe, I've been taking a beating for over ten years — because Jesse is my friend."

Wait. Did he say *is*? Not *was*?

That's right. Ford didn't kill Jesse. Somebody else is lying in Jesse's grave.

Well, enough about that. Branch has to stop a bank robbery, and Ford asks to come along. They hop a train and beat the Daltons to Coffeyville, alert the law, and the town's waiting to ambush the Daltons.

The Daltons hit two banks, but are shot to pieces when they come out. When Grat tries to use Kate as a shield, Branch kills him. The Daltons are wiped out, and Bayliss, who was wounded in the shootout, clears Kate of the murder charge. She and Branch hurry to the church to be married.

The History

Certainly there have been stories that Jesse James faked his death, that Bob Ford didn't kill him, that somebody else was buried in Jesse's grave.

In 1995, the remains from the body in Jesse's grave were exhumed for DNA testing. On February 22, 1996, Professor James Starrs of George Washington University's forensic science department announced his findings at a news conference in Nashville, Tennessee. A tooth from the grave matched the mitochondrial DNA pattern for the remains and descendants of Jesse's sister, Susan James Parmer. "I will go out on the deep end," Starrs said, "and say I feel with a reasonable degree of scientific certainty that we have the remains of Jesse James."[129] That silenced some, but not all, of the Jesse conspiracy theorists.

Frank James is apparently in hiding in the movie. Why? He had been a free man since 1885 after the state of Missouri's case against him for the Otterville train robbery was dropped.[130]

In the movie, the Daltons try to rob the Cattlemen's Bank and the Farmers Bank. The actual names of the banks were Condon Bank and the First National Bank of Coffeyville. Nor would the Daltons have need of Kate to give them the lay of the land; the Daltons had settled not far from Coffeyville and, despite trying to disguise themselves, possibly with theatrical facial hair, might have been recognized by townspeople when they rode into town.[131]

Scores of outlaws and townsmen are killed on-screen in the furious 3-D gunfight. In reality, four defenders were killed along with four outlaws; Emmett Dalton, though badly wounded, survived and spent fifteen years in prison. Nor did the outlaws hitch their horses in front of the two banks. Eighth Street was being repaired, and the hitching posts had been removed, so the gang tied their horses by a wooden fence in an alley about a half block from their targets. Most of the outlaws were killed in the alley, which became known as "Death Alley."[132]

Lastly, it would have been hard for Bob Ford to make an appearance during the Coffeyville raid. The robbery took place in October 1982. Ford had been killed in Creede, Colorado, in June of that year.[133]

The Players

Brett King made some pretty good movies—*Battleground* (1949), *Side Street* (1950), *The Racket* (1951)—but they weren't good because of him. That's not slighting his acting ability, but King was a supporting or bit player. *Jesse James vs. the Daltons* was his first starring role. It was also his last. After this movie, he acted primarily in guest spots on television series, often Westerns. His last TV appearance came in a two-part episode of *The Green Hornet* in 1967. He died in 1999.[134]

Likewise, Barbara Lawrence was primarily a supporting actress. She had appeared in *Her Twelve Men* (1954), Greer Garson's last film at MGM, and a year after *Jesse James vs. the Daltons*, reprised her stage role as Gertie Cummings in the musical *Oklahoma!* She was, after all, an Oklahoma native (born in 1928 in Carnegie), though she grew up in Kansas City. She retired from acting in 1962 and moved into real estate.[135]

The best performance likely came from James Griffith, a former musician—he had played in Spike Jones's band—who moved into acting in the 1930s and made his first movie, *Blonde Ice*, in 1948. He would have a steady career as a character actor in films, often Westerns, and on television. He died in 1993.[136]

The best thing about *Jesse James vs. the Daltons*, however, is the direction. "William Castle's megging is vigorous," *Variety* reported, "the action scenes being forcefully handled."[137]

Castle (best-known for his low-low-budget horror films such as *Macabre* [1957], *House on Haunted Hill* [1958] and *The Tingler* [1959]) milked the 3-D process for all he could. Battering rams ... pots falling ... bodies falling ... fists flying ... wine gushing out of a bullet hole—straight at the lens, and audience.

"The films themselves are cheap and cheerful; but at least Castle made something of them," David Quinlan writes, "and they never stop coming at you."[138]

The same can be said for *Jesse James vs. the Daltons*.

Analysis

The misleading and preposterous title aside, *Jesse James vs. the Daltons* starts with an interesting premise. It just doesn't get anywhere, despite moving at a brisk pace over a terse 65 minutes.

Although watchable (even somewhat enjoyable, in the right frame of mind), the meandering story requires some giant leaps of faith, and the plot has more holes than the town of Coffeyville at the movie's end.

* * *

Hollywood Reporter (January 22, 1954): "The combination of lively action and the kind of sharp shooting that oater fans like goes a long way toward covering a vague story with hazy motivations that consistently leave the viewer wondering what is going on."

Jesse James' Women

(United Artists, September 1954, 83 minutes)

CREDITS: *Director:* Donald Barry; *Producers:* Lloyd Royal, T.V. Garraway; *Screenplay:* D.D. Beauchamp.

CAST: Donald Barry (Jesse James); Jack Buetel (Frank James); Peggie Castle (Waco); Lita Baron (Delta); Joyce Rhed (Caprice Clark); Betty Brueck (Cattle Kate Kennedy); Laura Lee (Angel Botts); Sam Keller (Cole Younger); Jimmie Hammons (Sheriff Botts); Michael Carr (Bob Ford); James Clayton, billed as Cully Abrell (Cameo Kane).

Don Barry, center, played Jesse James as a seducer and thief stuck in a tiny Mississippi town in *Jesse James' Women* (1954).

Six. The Proliferation of Jesse James, 1950–1960

Synopsis

The exploitation of Jesse James's name in the 1950s hits an all-time low as Jesse is turned into a Casanova.

Jesse and Frank James, Cole Younger, and some other gang members, including Bob Ford, are hiding out in Silver Creek, Mississippi, hoping to earn enough money to get them back to Missouri. Jesse's posing as a cattleman, Jay Woodsen, and is secretly charming and manipulating several women to get his way, and money.

His first victim is Caprice, the banker's daughter, whom he uses to get her father's key to the bank. He steals $10,000—apparently not enough dough to get the gang back to Missouri.

Then there's saloon owner Waco. She believes that her partner, shiftless gambler Cameo Kane, is about to make off with all their money, and Jesse sees another opportunity. He talks Cole and Frank into playing in a poker game with the gambler, and lose. When Kane wins a final hand, Jesse's there to call him a cheat. But Kane has two men backing his play, and the three of them lope out of town with the loot.

Just as Jesse wanted. With Cole and Frank, Jesse goes after them, killing Kane's two henchmen and capturing the thieving gambler. Jesse beats the location of the money out of Kane—it's on one of the dead men—and Jesse lets the gambler go. He collects the money and tells the sheriff and Waco that Kane had too much horse and got away.

Meanwhile, Bob Ford has stirred up trouble by leading the other boys off to rob a stagecoach. The robbery didn't turn out well, and Bob had to take a woman hostage. When Jesse hears about this, he rides off and saves the woman, a new saloon singer named Delta, from Bob's unwelcome advances.

Delta, however, is about as mercenary as Jesse. She keeps Bob Ford's identity a secret, and starts to bleed Jesse dry. That's too much for Jesse—after romancing her, of course—and he sends his gang members, with the exception of Frank and Cole, off on their own. Bob's angry to be shipped off, and mails a photograph he has taken of Jesse, Frank and Cole to the Silver City sheriff.

There's another girl in Jesse's life, the sweet, innocent daughter of Sheriff Botts, Angel. She's enamored with Jesse James, even though the man she knows as Jay Woodsen keeps telling her she needs to find herself a new hero. When she sees the photograph, Angel realizes that Jay Woodsen is none other than the outlaw. She keeps the letter from her father, and tells Jesse about it, promising to keep his identity a secret and be on the lookout for any more letters from Bob Ford.

Meanwhile, Cattle Kate Kennedy, whom Jesse once robbed in Montana, arrives in town with a herd of cattle. The banker needs more time to round up the money to pay for the herd.

Jesse's women wind up at Waco's saloon, where Delta sings a lovely song to Jesse. That enrages Waco, who decks Delta and fires her. When Cattle Kate shows up, Waco decks her, too, and the bar fight between the two women is on. "This is the greatest fight since the Battle of Bull Run!" a Civil War veteran says. The fight ends when Jesse pours a bucket of beer on the two women's heads, and sends them away, but Kate has vowed to kill Waco.

Jesse tries to send Delta out of his life, but she hooks up with a traveling boxer who offers $1,000 to anyone who can stay in the ring with him for three rounds. Delta cons Jesse into trying his hand in the ring, even though he's a lover and not a fighter, and bets are taken. Delta promises to slip the boxer, O'Toole, a mickey that will allow Jesse to win, but she double-crosses him. Jesse gets pummeled and is knocked out in the second round.

Waco has bet heavily on Jesse to win. So have Jesse, Cole and Frank, but that's all right. The boxer, his doctor-manager and Delta leave Silver Creek, and Jesse, Frank and Cole ride them down. Frank buffalos the boxer with his six-shooter. They get their money back, and ride to steal Cattle Kate's herd.

Informed that Cattle Kate has ridden to Silver Creek to kill Waco, Jesse sends Cole and Frank off with the herd, then gallops back to town to save the day and get more money.

By then, the banker has paid Kate her money for the cattle, and the banker's daughter is threatening to expose Jesse as the real bank robber. Yep, it's time to leave town.

Cattle Kate and Waco meet on the streets in a face-down gunfight — reminiscent of *Woman They Almost Lynched*— but Jesse shoots the guns out of both of their hands, and has the sheriff lock them up. Then Jesse graciously agrees to take Cattle Kate's money belt to the bank (*sure* he will) warning Sheriff Botts that Kate is prone to "spells" and sometimes calls him Jesse James. He also suggests to Botts that Caprice, the banker's daughter, had access to the bank key and could have pulled off that robbery. After all, the sheriff always has thought it was an inside job.

Before leaving town, Jesse again informs Angel Botts that she needs a new hero, giving her money so that she and her father can buy a ranch. He also gives money to the preacher so he can fix up his church. Then he rides off to join Frank and Cole on the cattle drive.

A newspaper headline flashes that Jesse James has been killed by Bob Ford, and the final scene shows Angel Botts walking with others to the new church in Silver Creek.

The History

Mississippi? The Jameses and Youngers hid out in several states other than Missouri: California, Texas, Tennessee, Kentucky, Virginia, Maryland. There's no documentation, however, that they ever hid out in Mississippi. Although they have been accused of robbing the Tishomingo Savings Bank in Corinth, Mississippi, on December 7, 1874, that would have been next to impossible since they robbed a train in Muncie, Kansas, the very next day.[139]

Nor is there any documentation that Bob Ford was an amateur or professional photographer, or his wardrobe was that of a Civil War cavalry soldier. As has been previously pointed out, Ford was much too young to have served in that conflict.

"There never has been a picture of the James boys," Jesse admonished Bob Ford early in the movie, "and there never will be."

Well, certainly there never was a photo of the James-Younger Gang like there was of Butch Cassidy, the Sundance Kid and their cohorts — which helped lead to the end of that outlaw gang — but Jesse wasn't exactly camera-shy. Historians Phillip W. Steele and George Warfel note that the earliest documented photograph of Jesse was made in Kansas City in 1862 and that "Jesse James obviously enjoyed having his photo taken...."[140]

A drunken Cole Younger related how the gang "invented train robbery" with the July 1873 job at Adair, Iowa. As has been previously shown, the James and Younger brothers weren't the first outlaws to rob a train, and the derailment of the train near Adair did not become the M.O. for the gang's future train heists.

The Players

A.L. Royal, who owned a group of movie theaters based in Meridian and Prentiss, Mississippi, and businessman Tom Gallaway formed Panorama Pictures Corp. with the idea of filming productions in the state and turning Mississippi into "Hollywood of the South."[141]

Jesse James' Women was filmed predominantly in Silver Creek, Mississippi, in twenty-one days. Producers brought in a mix of established Hollywood stars (Donald Barry, Peggie Castle, Jack Buetel, Lita Baron) to appear opposite local talent. Joyce Rhed Barrett of Gulfport and Betty Brueck of Brookhaven had won a statewide beauty contest and were cast as two of Jesse's conquests. Seventeen-year-old Laura Lee of Louisiana landed the role of Angel Botts. L.L. McAllister, a Meridian city councilman, and Sam Weller, a Meridian police officer, also got parts in the movie.[142]

Other locals cast included Curtis Dessel (or Dossett) of Hattiesburg (as banker Clark); Jimmie Hammons of McComb (as Sheriff Clem Botts); Frank Cunningham of Moss Point (as Pete); and Al Hillman of Monticello (as Champ O'Toole). Hammons was invited to Hollywood for screen tests at MGM.[143]

The producers found distribution through United Artists,[144] but had to overcome objections from censors who saw the film as a glorification of a "robber and seducer." To get clearance, Barry added the newspaper headline at the film's end revealing Jesse's death. The PCA reluctantly agreed, but required some trims as well.[145]

Filmed in Technicolor, *Jesse James' Women* opened across the state on Friday, September 3, 1954. Barrett, Hammons, Cunningham and Swan were on hand in Meridian for the premiere. Newspaper advertisements billed the picture as "Mississippi's own exciting production" and "Filmed at Silver Creek, Miss. with a Hollywood, Mississippi and Hattiesburg cast!"[146] In Jackson, Governor Hugh White proclaimed Thursday, September 2, "*Jesse James' Women* Day" in ceremonies attended by state and city officials and local business leaders.[147]

Jesse James' Women attracted long lines when it premiered in Mississippi,[148] but elsewhere the movie was less revered. That said, the movie was made for $138,000 or $160,000, and Barry claimed it grossed $2.6 million.[149]

The producers' dreams of turning Mississippi into "Hollywood of the South" and turning out more state-made movies, several with scripts written by Mississippians, never panned out, either. Garraway produced no other movies, and Royal produced only two more, *Frontier Woman* (1956) and *Natchez Trace* (1960).

A talent scout discovered Peggie Castle while she was dining at a Beverly Hills restaurant. That sounds like a Hollywood story, but Castle's life didn't have a Hollywood ending. The green-eyed blonde began her career in the late 1940s and appeared in mostly B-movies with titles like *Harem Girl* (1952); she occasionally interacted with major stars in pictures such as *Payment on Demand* (1951) with Bette Davis; *99 River Street* (1953) with John Payne and *Miracle in the Rain* (1956) with Jane Wyman. She was probably best known as the dance hall girl (and the marshal's love interest) in television's *Lawman*, which ran from 1958 to 1962. When *Lawman* ceased production, she left acting. In 1973, one of Castle's ex-husbands found her body in her Hollywood apartment. She had died, the coroner reported, of cirrhosis of the liver and a heart condition. She was forty-five.[150]

Barry's end was also tragic. With the really low-budget Westerns losing their audience to television, Barry was seeing his career fade, and with his huge ego he had never been an easy actor to work with. "He had such a temper!" recalled Vivian Austin, Barry's co-star from his star-making *Adventures of Red Ryder* serial. "[H]e wasn't a very nice fellow when we worked together."[151]

He had a reputation as a ladies' man, as a brawler, and as an egomaniac, turning off directors, producers and co-stars. *Jesse James' Women* was one of his last starring roles; he continued to act in mostly supporting roles on the big screen and on television.[152]

On July 17, 1980, Barry quarreled with his wife Barbara at their North Hollywood home. Police were called to the scene, and Barbara and ten-year-old daughter Deborah left the house. Police officers were re-entering their car when Barry came outside with a .38 revolver. The officers told him to put the gun down. Instead, Barry shot himself in the head. He was pronounced dead on arrival at Riverside Hospital.[153]

Analysis

With no historical basis, and not much of a plot, *Jesse James' Women* is sexist, cheaply produced, badly directed and filled with amateur actors.

Most people remember it, if they remember it at all, for the cat-fight scene with Castle and Barrett. Even that's insignificant and forgettable, though it might have entertained male viewers in 1954.

It's probably not the worst Jesse James movie, but it's right up there with the truly awful ones.

* * *

New York Times (September 29, 1954): "Perhaps this cheap caricature of a picture will become aware of its grubbiness and will quietly go away."

Outlaw Treasure

(American Releasing Corp., May 1955, 65 minutes)

CREDITS: *Director:* Oliver Drake; *Producer-Screenplay:* John Carpenter.
CAST: John Carpenter, billed as John Forbes (John Parker/Dan Parker); Adele Jergens (Rita Starr); Glenn Langan (Sam Casey/Black Bart); Hal Baylor (Ace Harkey); Frank "Red" Carpenter (Red); Michael Whalen (Major Cooper); Frank Jenks (Sergeant); Robert Hinkle (Frank James).

Synopsis

By 1955, B programmers certainly weren't what they used to be.

Army troubleshooter Dan Parker, with only two days to go before his contract expires, is ready to join his father at a ranch near Central City, California, in the spring of 1868. He decides, however, to go after Black Jack, the leader of a rustling gang that has been stealing cavalry remounts. He catches Black Jack and four other horse thieves, before other gang members try to free them in a violent, smoky, ridiculously staged showdown. Once the bad

Six. *The Proliferation of Jesse James, 1950–1960* 155

John Carpenter, center, billed himself as John Forbes in *Outlaw Treasure*, a 1955 programmer that found him on the trail of bad guys who were using the James brothers to help them steal.

guys are driven off and Parker goes after them, Lieutenant Burke, who is in cahoots with Black Jack, frees the outlaw chief and tries to ambush Parker.

Parker's missing, so Major Cooper orders Burke to go to Central City and work with undercover operatives who suspect that Frank and Jesse James are robbing stagecoaches transporting federal gold shipments. When Parker shows up after having his horse shot from under him, Cooper sends Parker to California, too. By then, of course, Parker is no longer employed by the Army — but no one (director, screenwriter) seems to remember that.

In Central City, Black Jack, who goes by the name Ben Casey, has hired the James boys to pull those stagecoach jobs. He doesn't care much for Jesse or Frank, telling them: "You're not in Missouri. Out here, we shoot back," and, "You and Frank'll never amount to anything. All you think of is splitting and running."

The stolen gold is buried on land where Casey has filed for homestead rights. Or so he thinks. Actually, Casey learns that the gold's actually on the ranch of John Parker, Dan's father. Casey and henchman Ace Harkey head to the ranch to try to buy the land, but old Parker won't sell.

Back in town, Casey orders John Parker's death, and the murder of those undercover agents. His secretary Rita overhears the plot and warns the sheriff before heading to the Parker ranch. Jesse, however, guns down the sheriff, and Rita's too late to save John Parker. Ace Harkey shows up and chokes him to death, then stops to pet Parker's dog before leaving (the one interesting scene in the entire movie).

Dan Parker arrives to find his father's grave, and Rita and two orphan boys John had been rearing. Parker identifies himself, but Rita doesn't trust him, saying, "You look like any of the other border bums." (It's odd that she wouldn't detect a family resemblance, since John Carpenter was playing dual roles as Dan and John Parker.) She rides off to verify Parker's identity, but is roped from her horse by Harkey. When Parker finds her, Harkey gets the drop on him, but decides to beat Parker to death with his own hands.

You'd think Harkey could take Parker in a fistfight. After all, actor Hal Baylor was a Marine combat veteran and former amateur and pro boxer who had certainly given Robert Ryan a run for his money in the ring in *The Set-up* (1949). Instead, Ace Harkey gets the worst of it, and when he goes for his gun, Parker guns him down.[154]

By now, Casey has decided that maybe Frank and Jesse are right, and it's time to split and run and get his $500,000 out of California. The gold is loaded in a wagon, but the operatives are watching. Casey tries to talk Burke into getting behind them, as they wouldn't suspect he's actually working for Casey, and gun them down. Burke has some scruples. He won't shoot men in the back. Casey has none. He knocks out Burke, and he and Frank head to the wagon.

Burke wakes up, staggers out to warn the agents, and is shot dead by Frank and Casey. That starts the ball. In the ensuing, idiotic gun battle, the outlaws are defeated, Parker arrives in time to kill Casey, and Jesse arrives in time to save Frank's hide. They gallop off, and are not pursued. Parker tells his colleagues, "They can go back to Missouri and discourage others from trying the same thing."

Parker's free to marry Rita, and help rear the two twins on the ranch.

The History

Frank and Jesse were likely in California in 1868. They went to Hangtown in search of their father's grave, and later traveled south to Paso Robles, where an uncle owned a hotel and spa. There's no documentation that they were ever suspected of any stagecoach robberies, and they were back in Missouri by 1869, robbing the Daviess County Savings Association in Gallatin on December 7.[155]

There was a stagecoach robber in California named Black Bart, but he wasn't as violent as Sam Casey, and took only $18,000 in twenty-eight or twenty-nine robberies in the mid–1870s. He called himself the "PO8," and left behind rhymes with his crimes. One example:

> *I've labored long and hard for bread*
> *for honor and for riches*
> *But on my corns too long youve* [sic] *tred*
> *You fine haired Sons of Bitches.*

He was eventually caught and pled guilty to one count of armed robbery. Black Bart, actually Charles E. Boles, earned a six-year stay at San Quentin.[156]

Major Cooper says that in Missouri, Governor Crittenden had posted a $5,000 reward for the capture of the James boys, which might have driven the outlaws to California. It wouldn't have happened in 1868, however; Crittenden wasn't elected until 1880, campaigning on promises to end the James gang's banditry.[157]

The Players

Oliver Drake spent most of his directing career in cheap productions, including his Yucca Productions' series of 16mm Sunset Carson B-Westerns in 1948–49. He eventually moved to television. He did direct another movie about Frank James, the 1969 sexploitation film *Ride a Wild Stud* (Drake used the backwards name Revilo Ekard). In the movie, William Quantrill enslaves women in his House of Pleasure. I don't include that movie in this book, not because it's repulsive (women being raped begin to enjoy it) but because Jesse isn't mentioned.[158]

Drake's direction of *Outlaw Treasure* is juvenile. "[S]ome of the choreography in Carpenter's gunfight scenes is astonishing," Brian Garfield writes, "and the grimacing and grunting seems inspired by the war games of nine-year-olds."[159]

In a long career as producer, director and writer, Drake's most famous contribution to cinema might have been on the Republic serial *The Lone Ranger* (1938). Drake is credited with coming up with the idea of the Lone Ranger's origination: sole survivor of an ambush, nursed back to health by an Indian, and deciding to mask his face to keep his true identity a secret. The idea was later adapted by radio and television writers and "became the basis of the Lone Ranger's legend."[160]

"New York's No. 1 Showgirl" and a former Radio City Music Hall Rockette, Adele Jergens had a crazy Hollywood career, appearing as Marilyn Monroe's mother (Jergens was only nine years older) in *Ladies of the Chorus* (1948), and playing opposite the likes of the Bowery Boys, Abbott & Costello and Red Skelton. She had excellent turns in the *films noir Side Street* and *Armored Car Robbery* (both 1950), but by the mid-1950s the parts were drying up, and she was appearing in trivial films like *Outlaw Treasure*. She disappeared from the screen after 1956 and died in 2002.[161]

John Carpenter (born Jasper Carpenter, also known as Johnny or Johny Carpenter, and no relation to future writer-director John Carpenter) had seen his dreams of playing major-league baseball end in a hit-and-run accident in 1936 when he was in spring training with the Chicago White Sox. He and his brother Frank moved to Los Angeles in the 1940s, and John Carpenter gained notice with his horseback skills (he rode a horse in the Grand National race in 1944's *National Velvet*). He moved up to bit parts before becoming a B-Western star himself.[162]

"He was the last guy to independently turn these little B-western pictures out," *Western Clippings* publisher Boyd Magers told the *Los Angeles Times*. "Had he come along a little earlier and been with a decent studio, he could have been a lot bigger."[163] Film historian Brian Garfield noted that "most of his ten-cent movies were independent releases that rarely turned up anywhere except at the bottom of quadruple bills in drive-in cinemas...."[164]

For some reason, in *Outlaw Treasure* and *I Killed Wild Bill Hickok*, Carpenter billed himself in the acting credits as John Forbes, but used John Carpenter on the credits as writer and producer.

Carpenter's biggest contributions, however, came off-screen. In the mid-1940s, Carpenter taught a group of blind musicians to ride and eventually to jump horses at a ranch in Griffith Park. More people with disabilities began coming to him, wanting to learn how to ride, and in 1969, Carpenter leased 4½ acres in Lake View Terrace, dubbing the spread Heaven on Earth Ranch. Volunteers helped him build an Old West town replica, and thousands of children with disabilities were able to visit the ranch for free. In 1993, Carpenter had to relocate his ranch because the owner wanted to sell or subdivide the property. He moved Heaven on Earth to various locations before closing it down for good in 1996. "I've gotten more satisfaction out of this ranch than anything else I've ever done," he said.[165]

Carpenter died of cancer on February 27, 2003, in a Burbank, California nursing home. He was eighty-eight.[166]

Analysis

Brian Garfield calls Carpenter's films "often hysterical" and "pretty awful." *Outlaw Treasure* certainly is.

The acting's amateurish, the script preposterous, the history nonexistent and the action scenes poorly staged. Television was about to kill off the cheapie B's. Good riddance. Watching *Outlaw Treasure* makes one realize just how good *Days of Jesse James* and *Jesse James at Bay* really were.

* * *

Brian Garfield, *Western Films* (1982): "This serves up an army troubleshooter and the James brothers looking for a lost federal gold shipment — a familiar mixture, badly stirred."

The True Story of Jesse James

(20th Century–Fox, February 1957, 92 minutes)

CREDITS: *Director:* Nicholas Ray; *Producer:* Herbert B. Swope Jr.; *Screenplay:* Walter Newman; *Earlier Screenplay:* Nunnally Johnson.

CAST: Robert Wagner (Jesse James); Jeffrey Hunter (Frank James); Hope Lange (Zee); Agnes Moorehead (Mrs. Samuel); Alan Hale Jr. (Cole Younger); Alan Baxter (Remington); John Carradine (Reverend Jethro Bailey); Rachel Stephens (Anne James); Barney Phillips (Dr. Samuel); Biff Elliott (Jim Younger); Frank Overton (Major Rufus Cobb); Barry Atwater (Attorney Walker); Marian Seldes (Rowena Cobb); Chubby Johnson (Arkew); Frank Gorshin (Charley Ford); Carl Thayler (Robby Ford); John Doucette (Sheriff Hillstrom); Mark Hickman (Sam Wells); Clegg Hoyt (Tucker).

Synopsis

September 7, 1876. Not a good day for the James and Younger brothers.

Their plan to make a fortune gets shot to pieces — and so do a lot of gang members — and the outlaws ride out of Northfield as the local lawman, Hillstrom, organizes a massive manhunt.

Using dynamite, the posse blows gang member Sam Wells out of a cave, then riddles the Younger brothers — Cole, Bob and Jim — with bullets. Jesse and Frank escape, diving their horses off a cliff and into a lake, then hiding out with another gang member, Tucker, in a cave.

Back in Clay County, Missouri, Jesse's mother, stepfather and wife have gathered in Jesse's boyhood home, worrying and fretting over their loved ones. Thus begins a series of

Six. The Proliferation of Jesse James, 1950–1960

Jesse's mother (Agnes Moorehead) pleads with her son (Robert Wagner) in a scene from *The True Story of Jesse James* (1957), which wasn't entirely factual.

flashbacks — "as seen through the eyes and hearts of the people who loved him," the movie's trailer says — from the viewpoints of Jesse's mother, wife and brother, telling how Jesse James became a notorious outlaw.

It started during the Civil War, when Union sympathizers, including neighbor Arkew, try to learn of Frank James's whereabouts. Frank is riding with Quantrill, and the Jayhawkers have Arkew try to whip the information out of Jesse, but all that does is lead Jesse and farmhand Hughie to ride out and join Quantrill.

After the war, an unarmed Jesse is badly wounded by Union soldiers while trying to surrender. Frank and their mother bring him to the farm of Major Rufus Cobb (not the newspaper editor of 1939's *Jesse James*), and Jesse falls in love with his nurse, Cobb's niece, Zee. He proposes, and wants to return to a life of peace, but Northern sympathizers won't allow that. They raid the farm, kill Hughie, and warn that Frank and Jesse will be next.

That propels Jesse to a life of crime. The Younger brothers and other Southern sympathizers join him. They plan to rob Yankee-run banks for a grubstake so they can start a new life. Only a few jobs. Then they'll return to farming. But that doesn't happen. Years pass. The reward for Jesse increases. Finally, Jesse returns to the Cobb farm and rides away with Zee.

The newlyweds settle in St. Joe, living in a rented house under the name Howard. Jesse tells his landlord he's in "railroads and banks." Zee's happiness is short-lived, because Jesse is soon called out on another job. Eventually the outlaws turn to robbing trains. "That's when our luck started to turn bad," Frank laments. That also brings in the Remington Detective Agency to pursue the outlaws.

Bill Ryan is arrested, tried and becomes the first James-Younger Gang member convicted. Jesse, Frank and their wives watch the trial from the balcony, and take the train to visit their mother. The train makes an unscheduled stop near the Samuel farm, and Frank and Jesse suspect trouble. They reach their home too late. The lawmen have thrown a bomb into the house, killing the James brothers' young stepbrother and badly wounding their mother. That riles their neighbors, who try to get the government to grant amnesty to the brothers. All hopes of that happening is killed when Jesse murders Askew, who had taken part in the raid.

After that, Jesse leads the gang to Northfield, but things go wrong after Tucker fails to cut the telegraph wires, allowing the law to alert authorities across the state. Jesse and Frank argue. Jesse isn't raiding banks and trains for vengeance any more. "We're doing this for you," Frank tells him, and leaves him.

Tucker tries to kill Jesse for the reward, but Jesse guns him down and plants his watch on the corpse. Tucker's body is mistaken for Jesse's, and that allows Jesse to stumble back inside his mother's home, and into Zee's arms.

As Jesse recovers, he and Frank reconcile, and Jesse decides it's time to quit being an outlaw. He knows of a pretty farm in Nebraska, and plans to take his wife and their two children there.

As they are packing their belongings in St. Joe, Robby and Charley Ford arrive. Jesse gives his guns to the brothers, and tells them how being an outlaw isn't all it's cut out to be. People he didn't trust would be willing to kill him for the $30,000 on his head. While removing a sampler hanging on the wall, Jesse is shot in the back by Robby Ford, who runs down the streets, exclaiming that he has killed Jesse James.

By then, Frank has arrived with his mother. They enter the house and find Jesse dead. Numbly, Frank walks away. When asked if Frank has been captured, Frank says, "No, but I expect that he'll give himself up now."

The History

"Much that you will see here is fact," a scroll informs the viewer after the opening credits, "and much is as close to what actually happened as any man can testify."

Even before the movie's release, skeptics were questioning the truth of the script. Director Nicholas Ray tried to explain: "In the first place," he told the *Los Angeles Times*, "ours isn't the 'true' story of Jesse. But it's as true as anyone living these days, and possessed of our insight, can make it."[167]

Really? How about that teller in Northfield who's killed by Jesse James during the bank robbery? His name in the movie is Burnside. When three bandits entered the First National Bank on the afternoon of September 7, 1876, the bank employees working that day were teller Alonzo E. Bunker, assistant bookkeeper Frank J. Wilcox, and bookkeeper Joseph Lee Heywood, the acting cashier. Heywood was killed, and Bunker wounded.[168]

Said Ray: "Asked on his deathbed who killed the cashier of the bank at Northfield, Minnesota, Cole Younger replied, 'The one who rode the dun horse.' But it has never been established who rode the dun horse."[169]

That's true, and historians remain divided, with some pointing to Jesse, and others, including me, naming Frank. (Cole Younger had previously named Charlie Pitts, probably because Younger and Frank were great friends.) The movie has Jesse firing in self-defense as the cashier goes for a pistol. Although Cole Younger insisted that was the case, it most certainly wasn't — Younger wasn't even inside the bank at the time. Joe Heywood's assailant might have thought the cashier was going for a gun, or he might have just killed him out of spite.[170]

In the movie, Jesse's mother tells the Jayhawkers that the family is loyal to the South but does not own slaves. The real family, however, did own slaves.[171]

Nor was the sheriff of Rice County named Hillstrom. His real name was Ara Barton, and he took no part in the capture of the Younger brothers at Hanska Slough near Madelia. That posse was led by William Wallace Murphy and Watonwan County Sheriff James Glispin.[172]

A minor character in the movie, Sam Wells, aka Charlie Pitts, wasn't blown out of a cave by the posse, nor did he survive. He was killed in the gunfight at Hanska Slough.[173]

What the movie did get right was the giant manhunt for the Jameses and Youngers that began immediately after Northfield. "Before Thursday night two hundred men were in the field, and on Friday five hundred," historian George Huntington wrote in 1895. "Other hundreds still joined the chase later on, swelling the number at one time to at least a thousand."[174] It was the largest manhunt in Minnesota history.[175]

Yet the posse that took part in the actual capture of Cole, Jim and Bob Younger and the killing of Wells-Pitt was much smaller, totaling only sixteen. Of those, Glispin had to ask for volunteers to enter the thickets of Hanska Slough, and only six men joined him.[176]

On the outlaws' side of things, the movie probably has Jesse make an accurate assessment of what went wrong in Northfield. "Stiles, the only man who could lead us out of this state, had to go and get himself killed right off the bat."

A Minnesotan, Stiles, alias Bill Chadwell, had staked out Minnesota two months before the robbery. During the robbery, however, Anselm Manning sent a bullet through the outlaw's heart, dropping him dead from the saddle.[177]

Cole Younger (Alan Hale Jr.) makes a point during a hold-up in *The True Story of Jesse James* (1957).

Posse members have found their man, but it isn't Jesse, in *The True Story of Jesse James* (1957).

The movie also puts outlaws in Northfield who weren't there. Dick Liddil and Tucker Bassham, neither of whom had fought as Confederate guerrillas during the Civil War, did not join up with Jesse James until perhaps three years after the botched Minnesota raid.[178]

Bassham wasn't killed by Jesse James, either. Arrested in July 1880, he pleaded guilty to taking part in the Glendale train robbery, then agreed to testify against Bill Ryan in the 1881 trial. His betrayal of Jesse wasn't popular. When he testified, a mob burned his house, and Ryan threatened to "perforate Bassham's liver pad with so many bullets it could never be used again."[179] Bassham got the message. After the trial, he moved away, and left no forwarding address. He pretty much disappeared from history.[180]

Ryan was tried in September 1881 in what historian William A. Settle called "the first real test of efforts to break up the band of outlaws."[181] The jury needed only five minutes to find Ryan guilty.[182]

That was a big coup for prosecutor William H. Wallace — not Walker, as he's named in the movie. Nor was Wallace Jesse's neighbor in St. Joseph. He couldn't have been. St. Joseph is in Buchanan County, and Wallace was prosecutor for Jackson County. Besides, Jesse didn't move to St. Joseph until November 1881.[183]

Most certainly, Frank and Jesse weren't in the courthouse to watch Ryan's trial. In the movie, after the trial, detective Remington and Walker lead the raid on the Samuel farm. Actually, the raid took place more than six years before Ryan's trial. A James neighbor named

Six. The Proliferation of Jesse James, 1950–1960

Northfield residents examine the body of a dead member of the James-Younger Gang in *The True Story of Jesse James* (1957).

Daniel Askew (not Arkew), suspected of helping the Pinkerton detectives on the raid, was shot down, not on a road, but on his doorstep on the night of April 12, 1875. No one was ever brought to trial, but the James boys were definitely suspects.[184]

By most accounts, Frank did not leave Jesse behind after the Northfield robbery. The movie has Jesse stumbling into the family farm, recovering, then deciding to plan a life of peace on a Nebraska farm. It's true that, a month before his death, Jesse wrote D.H. Calhoun in Lincoln, Nebraska, about a 160-acre farm he had advertised for sale in the *Lincoln Journal*.[185] But that was almost six years after Northfield. The movie skips those years of crimes.

In the movie, Jesse's killed by Robby Ford. Robby? Robert or Bob, yes, but I've never read of or heard him called Robby. Frank hadn't gone to Clay County to fetch their mother, and Frank certainly never saw Jesse's dead body. He was in Lynchburg, Virginia, when he learned of Jesse's death. His mother was brought to St. Joseph for the inquest, and identified the dead man as her son, lamenting, "Would to God that it were not!"[186] And Jesse's reward never reached $30,000.

The True Story of Jesse James might be the first movie to depict the legendary myth of Jesse saving the widow from the banker. According to legend, Jesse and his gang stop at the farm home of a widow for a meal. While she feeds them, she tells them that a banker is coming later that day to foreclose on her home. In the movie, she owes $600. Tales depict the amount anywhere from $300 to $3,000. Jesse hands the weeping woman the money, tells her to get a receipt, and they leave. The banker arrives, surprised to find the widow able to pay off the note, gives her a receipt, and departs. Jesse then robs the banker of the money. Most historians dismiss that story as hogwash, but some people believe it's true.[187] Then again, I once heard a similar story, only the outlaw was Butch Cassidy, and the person telling me the story, which he said came down from one of his grandparents, swore it was true.

The Players

"The first question, naturally, is what in thunderation can be said about old Jesse that hasn't been said before," the *New York Times* opined in its favorable review of *The True Story of Jesse James*.[188]

The movie tried to strike a cord with the younger generation, so, in theory at least, maybe it did have something new to say. It certainly had many throwbacks, and scenes, from screenwriter Nunnally Johnson's original. Both movies even had John Carradine. The actor who played Bob Ford in the 1939 movie returned as the preacher who baptized Jesse in the 1957 film.

"*The True Story of Jesse James* is less of a sympathetic interpretation than the previous films," historian R. Philip Loy writes, adding that although Wagner's Jesse "is less of a populist hero ... he is not much less of a sympathetic figure."[189]

While previous movie versions pictured Jesse as a good-man-turned-bad while fighting the system, the 1950s stressed "juvenile rebelliousness."[190]

It wasn't just *The True Story of Jesse James*. In 1956, future *West Side Story* and *Peyton Place* star Russ Tamblyn was trying to escape being the son of a hanged outlaw in *The Young Guns*, which film historians George N. Fenin and William K. Everson call "an obvious attempt to transport *Blackboard Jungle* [1955] to the West."[191] In 1958, director Arthur Penn, screenwriter Leslie Stevens and actor Paul Newman transformed Billy the Kid from heroic youth into juvenile punk in *The Left Handed Gun*. In 1960, in a sort of Westernized version of *The Wild One* (1953), young Ray Stricklyn, John Saxon and friends tried to take over a Kansas cowtown in *The Plunderers*.

For this youthful variation on an old story, 20th Century–Fox assigned the project to director Nicholas Ray. After all, Ray had written and directed the 1950s standard of teen angst and rebellion, *Rebel Without a Cause* (1955), earning an Academy Award nomination for his screenplay. The star of *Rebel*, James Dean, was reportedly Ray's choice to play Jesse, but Dean was killed in a car crash in California on September 30, 1955, at age twenty-four.[192] Ray was also interested in casting Elvis Presley as Jesse, who had scored a hit in his first movie, *Love Me Tender* (1956).[193]

Instead, Ray wound up with straight-laced Robert Wagner, a twenty-six-year-old, Detroit-born actor who had appeared in the Westerns *The Silver Whip* (1953), *Broken Lance* (1954) and *White Feather* (1955) and had shown his acting chops in director Greg Oswald's B film noir *A Kiss Before Dying* (1956). The latter movie co-starred Jeffrey Hunter, another young actor who had garnered notice mostly for playing second leads to major stars such as John Wayne in *The Searchers* (1956) and Robert Ryan in *The Proud Ones* (1956). Hunter landed the part of Frank James.

Outlaws try to make their escape — and this time it's not stock footage from 20th Century–Fox's *Jesse James* (1939) — in *The True Story of Jesse James* (1957).

"They are impressively coiffed — hair combed scrupulously back at the sides, but with a lock or two flopped broodingly over the forehead — and they do not always wear shirts," the *New York Times* remarked.[194]

For the love interest, Hope Lange was cast as Zee. At 11, Lange had debuted on Broadway in *The Patriots*, but at age 25, *The True Story of Jesse James* was only her second movie. Her first had been *Bus Stop* with Don Murray, whom Lange married in 1956 (they divorced five years later), and Marilyn Monroe, who reportedly disliked appearing in a movie with a younger, attractive blonde. Shortly after the release of *The True Story of Jesse James*, Lange began production on the movie that made her a star: she received an Oscar nomination for her supporting role as Selena Cross, who murders her rapist stepfather, in *Peyton Place*. She went on to win Emmy Awards in 1969 and 1970 for *The Ghost and Mrs. Muir*, and died in 2003.[195]

Wagner recalled that he was looking forward to making a movie with Ray, but found him to be "a very strange man" and "a very confused and convoluted personality, even for a director...."[196]

Ray had a serious drug addiction and alcohol problem. Before starting the movie, he fell down some steps while drunk, and required a cane for several weeks.[197] Gavin Lambert, Ray's friend who helped on the script (without credit), said that Ray had hoped to parallel the adolescent bandit of the post–Civil War West with today's young delinquents. He also hoped to film the movie "as a ballad," shooting everything on a stage.[198] "It was all about emotions," Wagner wrote, "and that's what he tried to put into the movie."[199]

That wasn't, however, what the studio wanted, and Ray constantly clashed with Fox executives.[200] Ray did get to work with his son Tony, who was cast as Bob Younger,[201] but wound up dismissing the movie. Wagner thought the film "turned out okay"[202]; Nicholas Ray called it "f—ing god-awful."[203]

Analysis

It's hardly the truth, and it's not very entertaining.

Aside from the miscasting of Wagner, the most troubling aspects of *The True Story of Jesse James* might be the stock footage from Fox's 1939 hit *Jesse James*, shamelessly used in this movie.

Among the Technicolor shots from the 1939 classic inserted into the 1957 CinemaScope production include Frank and Jesse's death-defying jumps on horseback into Lake of the Pines; Jesse's leap from the saddle onto the St. Louis Midland Railroad train, and his nighttime dash across the top of the cars to the locomotive; and the famous flight from Northfield in which Frank and Jesse ride their horses through a plate-glass window and across the store.

As far as depicting angst and rebellion in the Wild West, *The Plunderers* would do a much better job.

Granted, *The True Story of Jesse James* was slightly—*slightly*—more factual than the 1939 original—but it was nowhere near as entertaining.

* * *

Christian Science Monitor (March 1, 1957): "If truth can be stranger than fiction, as the saying goes, there are also times when truth can be duller."

Hell's Crossroads

(Republic, March 1957, 73 minutes)

CREDITS: *Director:* Franklin Adreon; *Producer:* Rudy Ralston; *Screenplay:* John K. Butler.

CAST: Stephen McNally (Victor "Vic" Rodell); Peggie Castle (Paula Collins); Robert Vaughn (Bob Ford); Barton MacLane (Pinkerton Agent Clyde O'Connell); Harry Shannon (Clay Ford); Henry Brandon (Jesse James); Douglas Kennedy (Frank James); Grant Withers (Sheriff Steve Oliver); Myron Healey (Cole Younger); Frank Wilcox (Governor Crittenden); Jean Howell (Mrs. Jesse James); Morris Ankrum (Wheeler).

Synopsis

Here's a movie that makes Henry King's *Jesse James* (1939) look like a documentary.

On a quiet Sunday morning, Jesse James and gang member Vic Rodell stop a Muncie, Kansas, express agent on his way to church and take him to his office, where they and four other outlaws force him to open the safe.

Unfortunately for the outlaws, the hardware store owner sees them, runs out the back door, and spreads the warning. When Jesse, Vic and the others come out, the Kansans are ready for them.

One outlaw is killed, two citizens are gunned down, and Vic is shot in the leg. Jesse won't leave one of his men behind, so he gallops back and rescues Vic. After they've lost their pursuers, Jesse doctors Vic's leg and has the gang disperse. Vic is sent home with Bob Ford. Vic's reluctant to go. Years ago, he wanted to marry Bob's sister Paula.

Vic's a bit too thoughtful. As Jesse tells him, "A man in our line of work has to keep on the go. You stop and think, and you're liable to wake up dead."

Young Bob, in his first raid with the James-Younger Gang, brings Vic back to the farm near Rayville, Missouri. Paula, a widow, is living there now. Her husband, a bank cashier, was killed by Jesse James, but she still loves Vic. Paula and Bob's father, however, despises him. He once threw Vic out of the house, saying he wasn't good enough to marry Paula, and that certainly hasn't changed. Especially now that the law's after Vic for shooting up Muncie, Kansas. He has half a mind to tell the local sheriff, but Bob stops that by confessing that he was in that robbery, too.

Bob rides off to get fresh horses, and during his two-week absence, Paula and Vic renew their relationship. Yet Vic knows Paula's father is right. He has seen how Jesse lives

Hell's Crossroads (1957) cast Stephen McNally as a gang member hoping to go straight during the last years of Jesse James' life.

with his wife and children, under assumed names, moving from town to town. "I'd never ask a wife of mine to live that way," he says, and admits that he has been thinking about turning himself in to Governor Crittenden. Paula says she'll wait for him.

But not so fast. A Pinkerton agent has traced down Bob Ford. The young outlaw dropped his Winchester in the Muncie raid, and the Pinkerton operative traced the serial number to Rayville, and Bob Ford. He enlists the help of the local sheriff and they ride out to see the Fords. It just so happens that that's the day Bob Ford returns with new horses.

Vic warns Bob off, but the lawmen catch the young outlaw and take him to the Rayville jail. The mood in Rayville is ugly. Townsmen think anybody who rode with Jesse ought to be strung up. There's going to be a lynching, and that prompts Bob's father to plead with Vic to help save his son. So much for turning himself in.

Instead, Vic rides to St. Joseph and Jesse James. Jesse, Vic, Frank James and Cole Younger return to Rayville, stop the lynch mob, and save Bob Ford.

Vic hides out in Jefferson City, and Paula pleads with the governor on Vic's and her brother's behalf, but there's nothing Crittenden can do. The amnesty bill that would have freed Vic or Bob has been declared out of order. There is, however, one thing Bob or Vic can do, Crittenden suggests: Bring in Jesse. Dead or alive.

When Paula delivers the governor's message to Vic, he won't do it. He rode in the war with Jesse. They grew up together. Jesse saved his life.

But Vic also knows he can't ride with Jesse any more. He travels to St. Joe to tell Jesse he's through. That's too bad. Jesse, Frank and Cole Younger are planning the Northfield raid and could use a man like Vic. But Vic wants to lay low for a year and see if the amnesty bill will be passed in the next session.

Northfield doesn't work out too well for the James-Younger Gang, but Paula gets her brother to see Crittenden. Bob's ready to deal. Paula thinks he means to bring Jesse in alive, but Bob has no such intentions. He tells the governor he knows where he can find Jesse on Christmas, and heads to St. Joe.

While Jesse is putting the star on top of the Christmas tree in his home, Bob Ford guns him down. In the back. That ticks Vic off. Paula swears she had nothing to do with Bob's treachery, but Vic tells her their future is over. Jesse has friends, and they'll be gunning for him and Bob. "I'm more hunted now than I ever was."

Sure enough, as soon as he leaves the farm, he's warned by Mr. Ford that Cole Younger, Frank James and another bad guy have been seen around Rayville. Just like that, the outlaws appear. They plan to kill him, but Vic manages to get behind some rocks, and the gunfight begins.

Mr. Ford races to the farm, gets his gun, and pleads with Bob Ford to come help save Vic. Bob won't do it. He's looking out for No. 1.

"You dirty little coward!" his father roars. "When you leave here, you're leaving for good. Don't you ever come back."

Mr. Ford heads back to save Vic, and Bob starts to ride off, but he just can't do it. He joins the gunfight. So does the sheriff and the Pinkerton agent. Vic's badly wounded, but Cole Younger and the other gunman are killed.

When Vic regains consciousness in the Ford farm, everything's fine. Cole Younger's dead, Frank James has turned himself in, and Bob Ford is meeting with Governor Crittenden to pick up pardons—for himself and Vic Rodell.

Six. The Proliferation of Jesse James, 1950–1960   169

The History

On December 8, 1874, the James-Younger Gang did pull a job in Muncie, Kansas, only it wasn't an express agent they robbed. Jesse, Cole Younger and three other bandits stopped the Kansas and Pacific Railroad train. After uncoupling the other cars from the express car and locomotive, they ordered the express agent to unlock the safe.[204]

In about twenty minutes, the outlaws had made off with $30,000. There was no furious gun battle. As the outlaws rode away, they waved to the train crew, shouting, "Good-bye boys, no hard feelings."[205]

Crittenden, as previously pointed out, was not governor of Missouri in 1874, and Bob Ford, going on thirteen years old, certainly wasn't riding with the Jameses and Youngers that year.[206]

Bob Ford's father is called "Clay" in *Hell's Crossroads*; his name was James Thomas, but he was commonly called J.T. He and his wife Mary Ann had a large family, but no daughter named Paula. In addition to Bob, their children were named John, Elias, Martha, Amanda, Wilber and Charles, of course.[207] What happened to Charlie in *Hell's Crossroads*?

When Crittenden proposes to Paula that either Vic or her brother capture Jesse, she mentions that the last person who sought to take Jesse, John Whicher, tried to shoot Jesse in the back but was killed by Jesse before ever firing a shot.

We'll never know exactly what happened to undercover Pinkerton operative Joseph — not John — W. Whicher, but it undoubtedly didn't happen that way. Whicher arrived at the James farm on the afternoon of March 10, 1874. Around 3 o'clock on the morning of March 11, riders called for a ferryman to take them across the Missouri River. One man's hands were bound and his ankles tied together underneath his horse's belly. One of the other three riders — later identified, based on descriptions, as Jesse, Jim Anderson (Bloody Bill's brother) and gang member Arthur McCoy — told the ferry operator that he was Clay County sheriff's deputy Jim Baxter and that his prisoner was a horse thief. They were going into Jackson County to catch another thief. The ferry took the riders across the river, and they rode on. The "horse thief" was found dead later that morning four miles east of Independence, shot in the temple, neck and shoulder. Reportedly, a note was pinned to the corpse: "This to all detectives."[208]

About as close to history as the movie gets regards the amnesty bill. Surprising as it might sound, a proposed amnesty bill made the rounds through Jefferson City in 1874 and 1875. It would not have pardoned gang members for turning in the Jameses or Youngers. Instead, the bill was aimed at granting amnesty to the James and Younger brothers themselves for wartime crimes and would guarantee them a fair trial for any crime committed after the war. "[A]s a political document," Jesse James biographer T.J. Stiles writes, "it was outstanding."[209]

It was created by journalist John Newman Edwards and introduced by Representative Jefferson Jones. When public opinion was turning pro–James-Younger Gang after the Pinkerton raid on the James family farm in early 1875, the measure was declared unconstitutional by the attorney general. Rewritten and reintroduced, the resolution was kept from passing by a 58–39 vote. Crittenden, however, was not governor. That office was held by Charles H. Hardin.[210]

Bob Ford promises Crittenden, "I'll give you Jesse James for a Christmas present," and guns him down a day or two before Christmas. The real Jesse, however, was killed on April 3.

Cole Younger takes a bullet in his back while trying to flee the failed ambush on Vic Rodell. First of all, the real Cole Younger was in the state pen in Stillwater, Minnesota, when Jesse James got killed. Cole was not shot dead in Ray County, Missouri, in 1882, but rather outlived his outlaw brothers and outlaw comrades Frank and Jesse James, dying on March 21, 1916, at age seventy-two.[211]

The Players

Originally named Horace, New York City–born Stephen McNally graduated from Fordham Law School and was a practicing attorney before turning to acting. He started out on stage in New York before moving to Hollywood in 1942. He was usually cast as a villain, and was much more convincing in supporting bad-guy roles — the rapist in *Johnny Belinda* (1948), James Stewart's vicious brother in *Winchester '73*— than as a leading man — *The Duel at Silver Creek* (1952), *The Stand at Apache River* (1953). He continued acting in film and on television until 1980, and died of heart failure in 1994 at age eighty-two.[212]

Robert Vaughn was born into New York City show business, the son of a radio actor and stage actress. He had made a few television appearances, but *Hell's Crossroads* marked his "first role in a picture where I received star billing."[213] Two years later, he played another young punk in another B-Western, the Fred MacMurray vehicle *Good Day for a Hanging*, but that same year he made his mark as Chet Gwynn in *The Young Philadelphians*, for which he earned an Academy Award nomination for Best Supporting Actor. He went on to act in the popular television series *The Man from U.N.C.L.E.* (1964–68), and in film hits such as *The Magnificent Seven* (1960), *Bullitt* (1968) and *The Towering Inferno* (1974). He continues to act today.[214]

Although he brings a quiet dignity and authority to the role, Henry Brandon's casting as Jesse James might be one of the oddest choices. Born Heinrich von Kleinbach in Berlin, Germany, in 1912, he emigrated to the United States shortly after his birth, and studied acting at Pasadena Community Playhouse. He was the villainous Barnaby in Laurel and Hardy's *Babes in Toyland* (1934), and found a career playing bad men, with a few good-guy turns (1937's *Black Legion*, for instance). On the other hand, Jesse James might not be his strangest role. Despite a pair of brilliant blue eyes, Brandon had a steady diet as Indians: Chief Maygro in *War Arrow* (1953), Black Cloud in *Comanche* (1956), Scar in *The Searchers* (1956) and Quanah Parker in *Two Rode Together* (1961). He died of a heart attack in 1990.[215]

By 1957, Republic Studios was struggling. A studio that had produced fifty to sixty movies a year, it would release only twenty-six in 1957, and only seventeen the following year. The studio reported a loss of $1,362,420 in 1957. Later that year, Republic resigned from the Motion Picture Association and the Motion Picture Export Association. Herbert Yates announced at the annual stockholders meeting, "We have one problem — getting out of the motion picture business." On July 1, 1959, Yates relinquished control of the studio to a California banker and real estate operator, and Republic Studios, for all intents and purposes, was dead.[216]

Analysis

Hell's Crossroads is an uninspired movie with disaffected actors, tired direction and lousy history. Movies like this led to Republic's demise. "Republic just did not adapt," historian Richard Maurice Hurst noted.[217]

Hell's Crossroads was the tenth original movie about Jesse James to hit the theaters in the 1950s, and it seemed there was nothing left to say. And there wasn't, until Bob Hope came along with another take on the Missouri outlaw.

* * *

Variety (May 16, 1957): "The basic storyline holds little interest ... so it all shapes up as a below-par programmer.... Acting runs along acceptable lines, newcomer Robert Vaughn making the best impression. Showing up well, too, as Jesse James, is Henry Brandon."

Alias Jesse James

(United Artists, March 1959, 93 minutes)

CREDITS: *Director:* Norman McLeod; *Producer:* Jack Hope; *Screenplay:* William Bowers, D. D. Beauchamp.
CAST: Bob Hope (Milford Farnsworth); Rhonda Fleming (Cora Lee Collins); Wendell Corey (Jesse James); Gloria Talbott (Princess Irawanie); Jim Davis (Frank James); Will Wright (Titus Queasley); Mary Young (Ma James); Mickey Finn (Tough #2 in Dirty Dog Saloon); Bob Gunderson, Fred Kohler Jr., Ethan Laidlaw, Glenn Strange (James Gang members).

Synopsis

Milford Farnsworth, inept insurance salesman for the Plymouth Rock Insurance Company, meets up with T.J. James at a New York City saloon in the early 1880s and sells him a $100,000 life insurance policy. Mr. James pays the full premium, more than $30,000, in cash. Farnsworth doesn't know much about Mr. James, but tells the company president, Titus Queasley, "I gather from him that he's well known in railroading and banking circles."

He most certainly is, and Queasley blows a gasket when he reads in a newspaper that T.J. James, who has returned to Missouri, is none other than the notorious outlaw Jesse James. Queasley charges Farnsworth to head west and buy back the policy, and keep Jesse James alive. If Jesse's killed, paying off the policy will bankrupt the insurance company. "Lay down your life to protect his," Queasley tells Farnsworth.

The paleface takes the first train west to Angel's Rest, Missouri. Jesse and his gang hold up the train and relieve Farnsworth of his gold watch and all the money. When Farnsworth arrives in Angel's Rest, he sends a wire to Queasley asking for more money, and looks for Jesse in the Dirty Dog Saloon. It's a tough crowd. "Killin' will get you 90 days," Frank James informs Farnsworth at a poker table. "Cheatin' will get you shot."

The boys have some fun with Farnsworth, stripping him to his long johns. The insurance rep flees upstairs into the room of Cora Lee Collins, whom Jesse intends to marry and has left as his beneficiary. When Farnsworth is put on the eastbound train, Jesse is given the telegram he has sent, and Jesse decides to keep Farnsworth around. Jesse stops the train, but this time takes only Farnsworth, and they head to the family ranch in time for a party. That has to mean a song and, sure as shooting, Farnsworth and Cora Lee perform a duet.

Jesse sees a way to get free of the law — *and* collect $100,000. Farnsworth just has to

Bob Hope, with help from Rhonda Fleming, shoots it out with the James Gang in *Alias Jesse James* (1959).

get killed. Jesse takes Farnsworth on another train robbery — relieving Queasley of all his cash — and then tries to shoot down Farnsworth. When the insurance salesman topples off his horse, Frank and Jesse ride triumphantly away. In Cora Lee's room, Jesse tells her about an accident at the train robbery. "I got killed," he says, and takes her to the ranch.

Lo and behold, Farnsworth arrives later that night, shocking Ma James and Jesse, but relieving Cora Lee. Seems Farnsworth borrowed a suit of armor, which he wore underneath his clothes, and this makeshift bulletproof vest saved his life. Jesse's not finished, though. He sends Farnsworth to town the next morning ... into an ambush.

Yet Cora Lee sends an Indian princess after Farnsworth, and she saves his life. When Farnsworth realizes that Jesse plans on marrying Cora Lee that day, he knows he must stop the wedding because Cora Lee's in love with him, and he loves her. He kayoes the justice of the peace, assumes his identity and heads to the ranch. There, he stops the wedding and grabs Jesse's insurance policy. Farnsworth and Cora Lee escape in a buckboard, but the James Gang is hot on their trail. They miss the train, and the sheriff's office is deserted, so Farnsworth must shoot it out with the bad guys.

Queasley has sent a telegram to all peace officers, informing them that if they want to capture Jesse James, they should come to Angel's Rest. Farnsworth thinks he's acting alone, with Cora Lee loading his weapons, but he's not. The best gag of the movie has several television and movie stars assisting Farnsworth in the gunfight: Hugh O'Brian as Wyatt Earp from ABC's *The Life and Legend of Wyatt Earp* ... Ward Bond as Major Seth Adams from NBC's *Wagon Train* ... James Arness as Marshal Matt Dillon from CBS's *Gunsmoke* ... Roy Rogers from NBC's *The Roy Rogers Show*, who says after dropping a bad guy, "Happy trails to you!"... Fess Parker as Davy Crockett from NBC's mega-hit "Davy Crockett" episodes ... Gail Davis as Annie Oakley from the syndicated series *Annie Oakley* ... Academy Award–winning actor Gary Cooper of *High Noon* and *The Westerner* fame ... Jay Silverheels as Tonto from ABC's *The Lone Ranger* ... and Hope's longtime friend and co-star Bing Crosby, who shoots the gun out of Jesse's hand, saying, "This fella needs all the help he can get."[218]

Jesse and the bad guys surrender, and all ends well.

The History

Jesse James reportedly did visit New York. That much history *Alias Jesse James* got right.

In the late 1860s, Jesse is believed to have left New York City on a ship bound for California, via Panama, to visit his uncle, Drury Woodson James. Frank may have went with him, or may have traveled overland.[219]

Since the movie is set in 1880, Jesse could not have been trying to marry a saloon girl named Cora Lee — unless he wanted to add bigamy to his crimes. He had married Zerelda Mimms on April 24, 1874, and by 1880 he had two children, Jesse Edwards (born August 31, 1875) and Mary (born June 17, 1879).[220]

Nor did Jesse ever buy a life insurance policy. His family certainly could have used one. After his death, many of the family's household items were auctioned off. Newspaper editor John Newman Edwards raised donations of several hundred dollars for Jesse's widow, who lived in poverty until her death in 1900.[221]

But this was a comedy, which means all fact-checking should be left at the door before you enter.

The Players

"For the sake of argument that doesn't call for six-guns on a dusty cow-town street," the *New York Times* opined in its review of *Alias Jesse James*, "it can safely be stated now that Bob Hope is crazy about the Old West."[222]

Hope had certainly scored some comic hits in Old West settings with his films *The Paleface* (1948), *Fancy Pants* (1950) and *Son of Paleface* (1952), yet he assembled a crew and cast not known for laughs. Hope explained, "We couldn't touch the high priced comedians for less than $200,000 a head. So we made comedians out of great actors — people like Wendell Corey, Rhonda Fleming, Jim Davis, Gloria Talbott, Mary Young and Mickey Finn. That bunch gave Norman McLeod everything he asked for."[223]

Corey, who played Frank James in *The Great Missouri Raid*, gave a wooden performance. Comedy definitely wasn't his strong suit.

Screenwriter William Bowers started out with comedies and musicals, and certainly knew the west, having penned Oscar-nominated scripts for *The Gunfighter* (1950) and *The Sheepman* (1958) as well as *The Law and Jake Wade* (1958). He went on to write one of the best comic Westerns, *Support Your Local Sheriff!* (1969). D.D. Beauchamp also knew the Western genre with screenplays including *The Man from the Alamo* (1953), *Rails into Laramie* (1954), *Tennessee's Partner* (1955), and *Man Without a Star* (1955). He also wrote comedy, including, if you found it funny, *Jesse James' Women* (1954). The two writers had often teamed together on screenplays including *River Lady* (1948) and *She Couldn't Say No* (1954).[224]

One of the best gags was actually an improvisation. A few minutes before the party scene was shot, Hope and the writers began discussing a gag and coached nine-year-old Dana Fields on two words of dialogue. Fields was put at a piano, and a pair of gold-rimmed eyeglasses were put on him. When Hope walked past him, he asked, "And what's your name, young man?"

Fields replied, "Harry Truman."

"Keep playing, Harry," Hope said. "You'll help the party."

The writers and crew reasoned that the scene would fit in logically. After all, Truman was born in Lamar and grew up and still lived in Independence. "He was just about that age at the time Jesse James operated in western Missouri," the movie's pressbook noted.[225] Well, not quite. Truman was born in 1884, two years after Jesse James was killed.[226]

Gorgeous Rhonda Fleming had moved well from films noir — *Out of the Past* (1947) and *Cry Danger* (1951) — and Westerns — *Abilene Town* (1946) and *Gunfight at the O.K. Corral* (1957) — but never really became a major star, despite her beauty, a fine singing voice and talent. She enjoyed her work on *Alias Jesse James*, saying it was "more fun and shootin' than anything I've ever been in. Bob Hope's a circus to work with."[227]

McLeod had a great reputation as a director of comedies, having worked with the Marx Brothers in *Monkey Business* (1931) and *Horse Feathers* (1932), W.C. Fields in *It's a Gift* (1934), Cary Grant in *Topper* (1937) and Danny Kaye in *The Secret Life of Walter Mitty* (1947). He had first teamed with Bob Hope on *Road to Rio* (1947), and they had subsequently worked on *The Paleface* (1948) and *My Favorite Spy* (1951). "Each time Hope's career looked like [it was] sagging a bit, a McLeod film revived it," David Quinlan writes.[228] Maybe that's why Hope turned to McLeod again. *The Seven Little Foys* (1955) and *Beau James* (1957), a rare dramatic turn for Hope, had been hits, but *Paris Holiday* (1958) was less successful. Hope's film career was fading, and McLeod was a pro. "I learned many years ago not to stick exclusively to my own sense of humor," he told the *Los Angeles Times*. "Personally, I like subtlety, satire; but you've got to be careful of those things. In the end your experience tells you what to eliminate ... the bad comedy."[229]

Alias Jesse James, if not bad comedy, wasn't very funny. It didn't help either Hope or McLeod. It was McLeod's last movie as a director; he directed a few television episodes through 1961 before his death in 1964.[230]

"This last Hope film of the '50s became a miss," Donald McCaffrey writes in *The Road to Comedy: The Films of Bob Hope*. "Some works in the '60s had merit, but the golden years of the film comedian were evaporating into a decline. Few great stars knew when it was time to retire, but Bob Hope would struggle through the '60s and score some hits when he moved to television. Audiences still loved this personable, adroit actor who conquered all the media."[231]

Analysis

Aside from the classic gunfight scene, there really isn't much to say about *Alias Jesse James*. It certainly had no historical basis, and there wasn't much humorous about it, either, although the *Los Angeles Times* called it "very funny" and found a comedy "at least a novelty in these days of psychological soul-searching."[232]

Most reviewers found it nowhere near as funny as Hope's earlier comedies. Perhaps A.H. Weiler put it best in his *New York Times* review when he noted that the movie's failure "indicates that our once indefatigable hero or, perhaps, his gag men, are tiring fast."[233]

That's too bad. After a string of dreadful Jesse James movies like *The Great Jesse James Raid, Jesse James' Women* and *Hell's Crossroads,* the Missouri border bandit certainly needed a cinematic lift. So did Bob Hope. *Alias Jesse James,* Hope's last period comedy, was simply a misfire.

The 1950s had not been kind to Jesse James. The 1960s, however, would prove even worse.

* * *

New York Times (May 18, 1959): "The Old West, it would appear from this uneven excursion, is occasionally funny but not an uproarious place to visit.... *Alias Jesse James* ... is somewhat slow in getting to the point and it is only about half-way through these sporadic goings-on that the gags and quips fly with any regularity and effect."

Young Jesse James

(20th Century–Fox, August 1960, 93 minutes)

CREDITS: *Director:* William F. Claxton; *Producer:* Jack Leewood; *Screenplay:* Orville H. Hampton, Jerry Sackheim.

Cast: Ray Stricklyn (Jesse James); Willard Parker (Cole Younger); Merry Anders (Belle Starr); Robert Dix (Frank James); Emile Meyer (Charlie Quantrill); Jacklyn O'Donnell (Zerelda "Zee" Mimms); Rayford Barnes (Pitts); Rex Holman (Zack); Robert Palmer (Bob Younger); Sheila Bromley (Mrs. Samuels); John O'Neill (Jim Younger); Leslie Bradley (Major Turnbull); Norman Leavitt (Folsom); Lee Kendall (Jennison); Tyler McVey (Banker); Britt Lomond (Yankee Officer); Ollie O'Toole (Sheriff); Howard Wright (Storekeeper Jenson); Richard Cowl (Neely).

Synopsis

After 20th Century–Fox's *The True Story of Jesse James* (1957), the studio again aimed at the youth movement with another retelling of the Jesse James story, this time in a low-budget Western.

After watching Kansas Redlegs hang his father, young Jesse James leaves his farm, and girlfriend Zerelda "Zee" Mimms to join his brother Frank and ride with Major Charlie Quantrill's Confederate guerrillas.

Almost laughed out of Quantrill's camp for being so young, Jesse makes an enemy in a young punk named Zack, and is dismissed by Quantrill. "I don't need hotheads," Quantrill tells him. "I need men.... When you've grown into a fighting man, maybe I'll need you." Quantrill changes Quantrill's mind, however, when Jesse shows his prowess with a revolver by shooting a dipper out of the hand of his friend and cousin, Cole Younger.

Jesse's first assignment has him dressed as a woman to get some valuable information

Zack (Rex Holman) will soon learn a guerrilla should never try to rape Jesse James's true love (Jacklyn O'Donnell) in *Young Jesse James* (1960).

from a printer and Rebel spy in a Union-controlled town. A Federal officer notices Jesse's boots and is about to arrest him when Cole and Frank barge in. Cole kills the officer with a bullet through the head, which sickens Jesse. Pretty soon, however, Jesse becomes used to such savage violence.

When the Union soldier who lynched Jesse's father is captured, Jesse ruthlessly guns him down. His taste for vengeance slaked, he quits Quantrill and heads home. "He'll be back," Cole says.

Yep, the homecoming is bittersweet and brief. He tells Zee that the war has changed him, and he's struggling with his emotions, knowing he is drawn to violence. Sadly, he leaves his mother and sweetheart and rejoins Quantrill, becoming as cold-blooded as Quantrill. That troubles Cole, who has become disillusioned with the war.

When Jesse and Cole ride into Indian territory, Jesse breaks his ankle, forcing Cole to take him to the cabin of Belle Starr, who's in love with Cole. There, Jesse tries to seduce Belle, who slaps him and says, "You ain't even man enough to hold Cole Younger's horse."

Cole announces to Jesse that he's quitting Quantrill and plans to join Jo Shelby and a real Confederate army in Louisiana. After Jesse returns to Quantrill's camp, Zee arrives looking for Jesse. When Zack tries to rape her, Jesse guns him down and takes Zee home.

Yankees have burned the farm, and Jesse's mother has lost her arm, fueling Jesse's hatred of the Union even more. News comes, however, that General Robert E. Lee has surrendered. "There's lots of scores to settle," Jesse tells Zee, "lots of fighting left, war or no war." Zee, however, persuades Jesse to surrender, promising to marry him if he will quit fighting and try to live in peace.

As Jesse rides into town under a flag of truce, a Union soldier panics and, fearing "another one of Quantrill's tricks," shoots Jesse in the chest. After recovering, Jesse marries Zee and tries to live the life of a Missouri farmer.

Farmers need money, however, and Jesse and Frank can't get any credit from banks or stores because of their reputation. Cole Younger returns with his brothers; they've turned outlaw, and want Frank to join them. Frank reluctantly agrees, but only if Jesse can ride with them, too. Cole doesn't like it, but he has no choice.

Jesse suggests they start with the Liberty bank. The banker had denied the James brothers a loan, and then offered to buy the farm at a fraction of its worth.

Liberty's full of former Union soldiers, so Cole insists that the bank robbery be committed without violence. Jesse has other ideas. He murders the banker, and the town is alerted. Townsmen and outlaws are shot down, but the Youngers, the Jameses and a few others escape.

Jesse thinks the bank money will change Zee's mood; he doesn't care about the dead friends they left behind in Liberty. Cole, desperately trying to stop the bleeding from a bullet hole in Jim Younger, asks for the money bag to use as a bandage; Jesse refuses. Frank draws his gun and points it at Jesse's back, making Jesse relent.

After threatening to kill Frank if he ever pulls a gun on him again, Jesse takes his share of the money and rides away. Frank's torn, wishing he had done more to stop Jesse's slide from farm boy to ruthless killer. Still, he knows he has to ride with Jesse.

"I understand," Cole says. "He's your brother."

The History

Jesse's father died in California during the Gold Rush in 1850, and it was his stepfather, Dr. Rueben Samuel, who was hanged by Union militia when Jesse was fifteen. Samuel wasn't killed, however, but jerked off his feet four times. The legend said that Samuel remained quiet, and that his wife cut him down after the soldiers left him hanging there. The truth was that Samuel broke, talked and even led the militia to the guerrilla camp near the house.[234]

In this movie, William Clarke Quantrill is called Charlie Quantrill — "Charley Hart" was one of his nicknames — and promoted to the rank of major. In actuality, his rank was captain.[235]

When Cole Younger quits Quantrill, he says he's riding to Louisiana to join Jo Shelby. Joseph Orville Shelby fought in Missouri, Arkansas and Kansas. Younger was actually on a Confederate mission in California when the war ended.[236]

In the movie, when Cole arrives at Belle Starr's cabin, he asks about Belle's husband Sam, only to learn he has been killed. That's jumping the gun by more than a decade. Belle married Sam Starr, her third husband, some time after 1880. Sam was killed in 1886.[237]

Also out of time sequence is the loss of Jesse's mother's arm. That happened in 1875 during a Pinkerton raid on the family farm, ten years later than as depicted in the movie.

Cole Younger is given credit in the movie for having robbed a couple of banks in Kentucky and another one in Gallatin, Missouri. The Nimrod L. Long & Co. bank in Russellville, Kentucky, was robbed — perhaps by the James-Younger Gang — on March 20, 1868. Another Kentucky bank job attributed to the James-Younger Gang happened at the Bank of Columbia in 1872. And Gallatin? That bank heist was pulled off on December 7, 1869.[238]

All of those happened *after* the robbery of the Clay County Savings Bank in Liberty on February 13, 1866, the first daylight bank heist pulled off in the United States that wasn't an act of war. Nor was the robbery as violent as depicted in *Young Jesse James*. Jesse didn't kill a banker — many historians even doubt that Jesse was there. The two bank employees, Greenup Bird and his son William, were put in the vault, although the lock failed to catch. As the outlaws, numbering from ten to thirteen, rode out of town, firing wildly, George Wymore, a student at William Jewell College, became the one casualty.[239]

The Players

After playing Jesse James in *The Great Jesse James Raid*, Willard Parker here got the role of Cole Younger. Robert Dix, whose father, actor Richard Dix, had been wounded in a shootout with Jesse James in *The Kansan* (1943), took on the role of Frank James. Emile Meyer, best remembered as evil rancher Rufus Ryker in *Shane* (1953), added meat to the role of Quantrill.[240]

Among the actresses, Merry Anders, who had been discovered by a Fox talent scout while acting at the Ben Bard Playhouse, knew about outlaws, having played Holly Dalton in *The Dalton Girls* (1957). Movies like that pretty much defined her career. She did better than Jacklyn O'Donnell, who was making her big-screen debut after a few television appearances. "Jacklyn O'Donnell is drab as the farm girl who fails to satisfy," the *New York Times* opined.[241]

The *Times* was kinder to Ray Stricklyn, calling him "a likely young actor" who "makes an acceptably neurotic Jesse...."[242] An incredibly talented actor, though likely better on stage than on screen, the Houston-born Stricklyn had won a Golden Globe as most promising new actor for playing Gary Cooper's son in *Ten North Frederick* (1958), and columnist Louella Parsons labeled him "the next Montgomery Clift."[243]

He was thirty-two when shooting began on *Young Jesse James* in November 1959, but that was all right. "When I was 27, I still looked 16, but there was a whole crop of boys coming up who really were that age," Stricklyn said. "Before, I'd thought my career was going straight up. So, like a lot of foolish young actors, I started living beyond my means. Once you think you're going to be a star, then you're not — it's a rude awakening."[244]

Fox declined to renew his contract after *The Remarkable Mr. Pennypacker* (1959), but the studio shocked him by inviting him to star in *Young Jesse James* in his first lead role.[245]

"I was in almost every scene in the picture," he said. "Fortunately, I'd taken a few horseback-riding sessions in the meantime, though I wasn't going to give John Wayne any competition."[246]

After *Young Jesse James*, Stricklyn followed with another Western, as another troubled young kid, in *The Plunderers* (1960), earning him a Golden Globe nomination for best supporting actor. Life looked good on the professional front — though his film career quickly faded — but things weren't so pleasant on the personal level.[247]

His father, suffering from a mental disability, had become more violent toward his

Six. The Proliferation of Jesse James, 1950–1960

Zack (Rex Holman) and young Jesse James himself (Ray Stricklyn), left, take part in a guerrilla raid in this 1960 20th Century–Fox release.

mother, and the family decided to commit him to a hospital. Stricklyn returned to Houston. While he was signing the papers, his father began screaming. A nurse finally entered the office and told the young actor, "Mr. Stricklyn, we've given your father a sedative. But I'm afraid he's much more disturbed that we'd realized."

"Oh?" Stricklyn said.

"Yes," said the nurse, "he kept screaming that his son was Jesse James!"

Feeling his hatred for his father turn into compassion, Stricklyn told the nurse: "I *am* Jesse James!"[248]

Stricklyn died in 2002.

Analysis

Ray Stricklyn did his best to lift *Young Jesse James* above the routine horse opera, bringing a complexity to the role of Jesse.

Yet the movie just didn't work. Its history was skewed, the direction lackluster, the plot meandering, and none of the other actors could match Stricklyn's intensity.

Maybe the problem, however, was that Jesse's story had been oversaturated, especially in the previous decade. As the *New York Times* noted: "Aside from its original motivational implications, the Twentieth Century–Fox release does offer one dubious claim to distinction. For the record, it is the first feature about the life of the notorious outlaw to arrive on local screens this year."[249]

Hollywood might have taken the hint. Only two more movies about Jesse James were released during the 1960s. (Another, *A Time for Dying*, was filmed in 1969 but not released until years later.)

Jesse James, it seemed, was firing his last shots on the big screen.

* * *

Variety (August 10, 1960): "Mrs. James' son, Jesse, has, through overexposure, become a caricature of himself. It is an easy matter now for an educated audience to anticipate his reactions — an element of familiarity that ought to curb future filmland inclinations to tackle the hackneyed story."

CHAPTER SEVEN

Oddball Jesse (1965–1969)

Jesse James's screen appearances began fading quickly after *Young Jesse James* (1960), with the outlaw relegated in the 1960s to a Three Stooges comedy and B-movie pitting him against Frankenstein's granddaughter. Another movie, *A Time for Dying*, would be filmed in 1969 but not released until the '70s. Those three movies are covered in this chapter.

Not covered are two Italian Westerns, *Two Gangsters in the Wild West* (1964) and *Son of Jesse James* (1965), and a sexploitation movie, *Ride a Wild Stud* (1969). The first two are covered in Chapter Nine, which examines Jesse's appearances in European movies. *Ride a Wild Stud* isn't included in this book because although that movie has William Quantrill and Frank James as characters, Jesse is never mentioned.

The Outlaws IS Coming!

(Columbia, January 1965, 88 minutes)

CREDITS: *Director-Producer:* Norman Maurer; *Screenplay:* Elwood Ullman.

CAST: Joe DeRita (Curly-Joe); Larry Fine (Larry); Moe Howard (Moe); Adam West (Kenneth Cabot); Nancy Kovack (Annie Oakley); Mort Mills (Trigger Mortis); Don Lamond (Rance Roden); Rex Holman (Sunstroke Kid); Emil Sitka (Mr. Abernathy/Witch Doctor/Cavalry Colonel); Henry Gibson (Charlie Horse); Murray Alper (Crazy Horse); Tiny Brauer (Bartender); Sidney Marion (Hammond); Jeffrey Scott, billed as Jeffrey Alan (Kid); Marilyn Fox (Girl No. 1); Audrey Betz (Fat Squaw); Lloyd Kino (Japanese Moe); Joe Bolton (Rob Dalton); Bill Camfield (Wyatt Earp); Hal Fryar (Johnny Ringo); Johnny Ginger (Billy the Kid); Wayne Mack (Jesse James); Ed T. McDonnell (Bat Masterson); Bruce Sedley (Cole Younger); Paul Shannon (Wild Bill Hickok); Sally Starr (Belle Starr).

Synopsis

Rance Roden, an Old West version of a syndicate crime boss, has rounded up the toughest guns in the West, aiming at taking over all of the Western territories by having the Indians rise up against white settlement. What's the best way to do that? Slaughter the buffalo, of course.

Only a bunch of idiots would try to stop Roden and his cadre of gunfighters, which includes Jesse James.

Did somebody say "idiots"? Why, curse the luck, the publisher of Boston-based *Society for the Preservation of Wildlife* magazine orders editor Kenneth Cabot to Casper, Wyoming Territory, to find out what's going on with the buffalo. He sends Cabot's assistants, the Three Stooges, to accompany the editor. "You can take them out West with you ... but don't bring them back!"

Cabot's about as incompetent as the Stooges, but he's wooed, and smitten, by Annie Oakley, whose quick trigger and keen eye save him a few times from the bad guys.

With help from the Stooges, and Annie, Cabot wins over the gunfighters, who swear to fight for law and order from now on. The real bad guys, Roden and his henchman Trigger Mortis, are whipped by Cabot, who finds his courage. An Indian uprising is thwarted, the buffalo are saved, and Cabot marries Annie. The newlyweds get to ride off in the sunset with the Stooges. Or would have ... if not for a sudden torrential downpour.

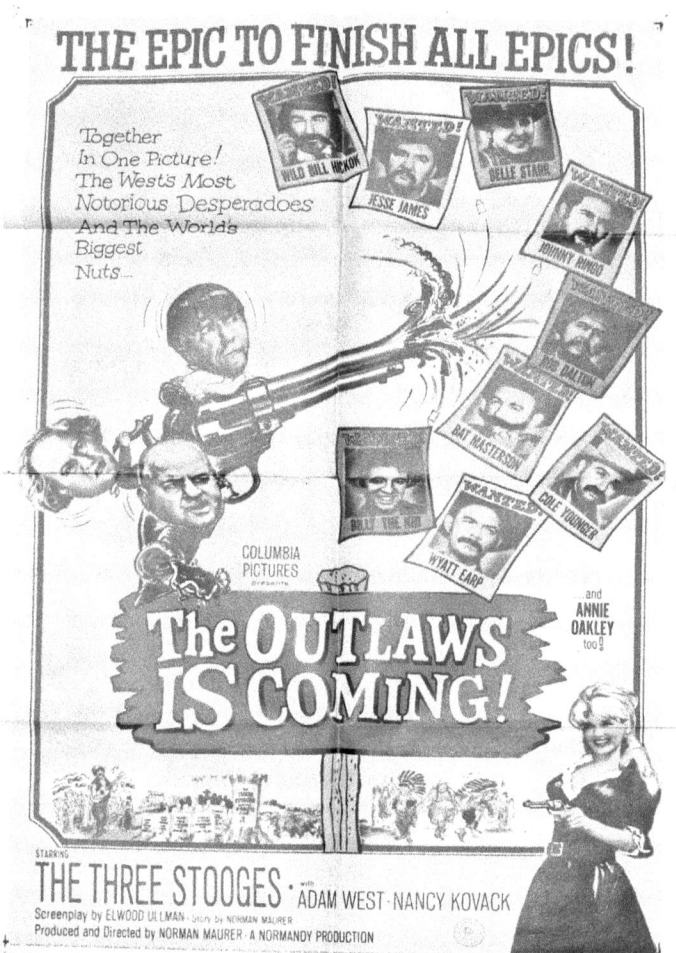

The last feature film of the Three Stooges, *The Outlaws IS Coming!* (1965), put the bumbling nuts up against some of the West's top villains.

The History

History? In a Three Stooges film? I think we can skip any history this go-round.

The Players

Making *The Outlaws IS Coming!* was pretty much a family affair for the Three Stooges.

Don Lamond, playing Rance Roden, was Larry Fine's son-in-law. Jeffrey Scott, playing Kid, was Moe Howard's grandson. Scott's father and Howard's son-in-law, Norman Maurer, was hired to direct.[1]

"Norman was a very nice guy," said Edward Bernds, a writer-director probably best known for his collaboration with the Three Stooges, "but his ideas about comedy were a little peculiar."[2]

Howard, born Moses Horwitz, and Ted Healy had formed a vaudeville act in 1922 that became the Three Stooges, which eventually included Howard's brothers Jerome and Shemp. Moe Howard's sixty-six-year career included more than 250 films, including some 190 Three Stooges shorts. When Howard died in 1975, the Stooges act was over.[3]

By 1964, when filming began on *The Outlaws IS Coming!*, the trio had undergone several changes. High-voiced, bald Jerome "Curly" Howard, who had joined the group in 1932, was forced to retire after suffering a massive stroke during the filming of *Half-Wits Holiday* (1947), and died in 1952 at age forty-eight. His replacement, Shemp Howard, died in 1955 of a heart attack. Joe Besser, who had appeared in several Abbott and Costello films, joined the Stooges in 1956 but quit two years later. He was replaced that year by Joe DeRita, who became the trio's Curly-Joe. After Moe's death, DeRita retired, and died in 1993.[4]

The other Stooge was Larry Fine, a former violinist, singer and boxer, who started in vaudeville in the early 1920s. Fine joined Healy and Howard as a Stooge in 1925. A stroke while filming the television pilot *Kook's Tour* (1970) forced him to retire in 1970, and he died in 1975.[5]

Stooges regular Emil Sitka, who appeared in thirty-five shorts, took on three parts in *The Outlaws IS Coming!* The only actor to appear with all six Stooges, he would even replace Fine and become a Stooge himself after Fine's retirement. Sitka died in 1998.[6]

Although he had appeared in several television shows and movies by 1965, Walla Walla, Washington-born Adam West was a relative unknown. That would change in 1966 when he landed the role of Bruce Wayne–Batman in ABC's campy hit *Batman*, which ran until 1968.

For the outlaws, the Stooges decided to invite selected hosts of kiddie shows. "The Stooges felt that this was not only a way of thanking the hosts for promoting their comedy films over the years and welcoming them in their respective cities, but they were certain it would result in an excellent publicity scheme to promote the film."[7] It worked. On top of Columbia's national campaign and the Stooges' personal appearances, newspapers ran articles about the local television hosts starring in the movie.[8]

"Officer Joe" Bolton (New York City) played Rob Dalton. Bill "Icky Twerp" Camfield (Dallas–Fort Worth) played Wyatt Earp. Hal "Harlow Hickenlooper" Fryar (Indianapolis) played Johnny Ringo. Johnny Ginger (Detroit) was Billy the Kid. Ed "Major Mudd" McDonnell (Boston) played Bat Masterson. Bruce Sedley (San Francisco) was Cole Younger. Paul Shannon (Pittsburgh) was Wild Bill Hickok. Sally Starr (Philadelphia) played Belle Starr. Harry "Captain 11" Fender (St. Louis) was scheduled to play Doc Holliday, but a scheduling conflict forced him to bow out.[9]

The role of Jesse James went to Wayne "The Great McNutt" Mack of New Orleans. Born Wayne McGlinn, he was a longtime Crescent City sportscaster who had started his kiddie show, *The Great MacNutt*, around 1960. Later, he was an on-field announcer for the National Football League's New Orleans Saints. He died in 1993.[10]

The movie was originally titled *The Three Stooges Meet the Gunslingers; Or How the Stooges Won the Wild, Wild, Wild West*. It was changed to *The Outlaws IS Coming!* to parody the advertising slogan for director Alfred Hitchcock's *The Birds* (1963): "*The Birds* Is Coming."[11]

The Outlaws IS Coming! would mark the Stooges' last completed film together. A travelogue television pilot, *Kook's Tour*, was being filmed, directed by Maurer, when Fine suffered his stroke on January 9, 1970. Scenes were scrapped, others were shot with a double for

Fine, and the movie was completed, but never sold for television broadcast. "There was a reason for that," Fine's biographers Stephen Cox and Jim Terry write. "It was unfunny and, at times, pathetic. It was a sad swan song for this legendary team."[12] Eventually, Maurer had it released on the Super 8 home movie market in the 1970s, and it later appeared on video.[13]

Analysis

My then eight-year-old son got a kick out of this when I screened a video while writing this book, so I guess the Three Stooges still have fans — mostly young boys, or older men who just never grew up.

You can also see some of the deadpan humor that actor Adam West would pretty much trademark in *Batman*. The real stars of the movie, however, might have been the buffalo, courtesy of the B-Bar-B Buffalo Ranch in Gillette, Wyoming, where the film was partially shot.

Three Stooges fans will probably find something to like — after all, pies are thrown!— but Jesse James buffs can pretty much skip this one.

* * *

Hollywood Reporter (January 8, 1965): "[This] will undoubtedly find great response with audiences composed of extremely unsophisticated 12-year-olds and under. If anything, the picture is quite above the usual cut of Stooges' antics, an attempt having been made to give the trio more of a story line to follow, which they do to the accompaniment of their usual sight gags."

Jesse James Meets Frankenstein's Daughter

(Embassy, March 1966, 82 minutes)

CREDITS: *Director:* William Beaudine; *Producer:* Carroll Case; *Screenplay:* Carl Hittleman.

CAST: John Lupton (Jesse James); Narda Onyx (Maria Frankenstein); Felipe Turich (Mañuel); Estelita Rodriguez (Juanita); Cal Bolder (Hank Tracy/Igor); Steven Geray (Rudolph Frankenstein); Rosa Turich (Nina); Jim Davis (Marshal McFee); Rayford Barnes (Lonny Curry); William Fawcett (Jensen the Pharmacist); Nestor Paiva (Saloon Owner); Roger Creed (Butch Curry); Fred Stromsoe (Stacy); Dan White (Pete Ketchum); Page Slattery (Deputy Andy).

Synopsis

"Just what the title implies," Brian Garfield writes in *Western Films*.[14]

Well, not quite. After all, it's actually the baron's granddaughter, Maria Frankenstein, who is conducting unholy experiments with her brother Rudolph in an old monastery (that looks more like a painting) on a hill overlooking a Southwestern desert town.

Jesse James is erroneously rumored to be dead, after much of his gang was wiped out

Seven. Oddball Jesse (1965–1969)

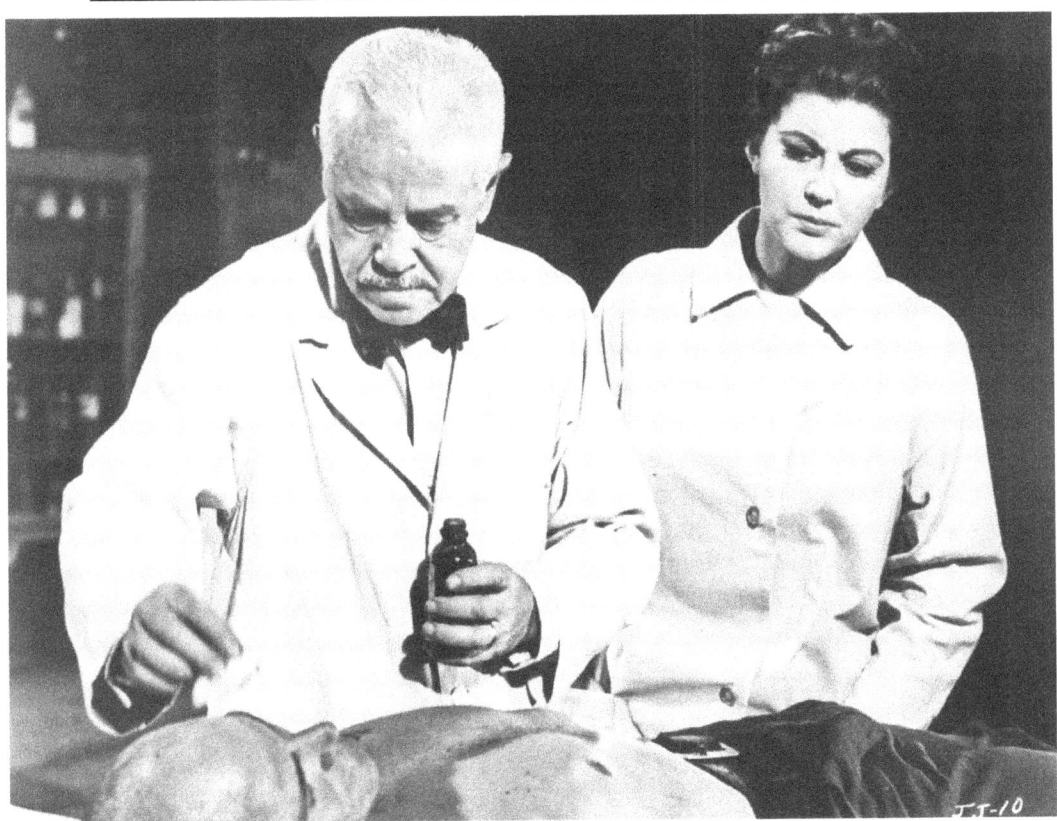

Rudolph Frankenstein (Steven Geray) prepares to put a new brain in Hank Tracy (Cal Bolder) while Maria Frankenstein (Narda Onyx) watches in *Jesse James Meets Frankenstein's Daughter* (1966).

at Northridge. Jesse and his dimwitted but loyal giant friend Hank Tracy team up with the remnants of the Wild Bunch, led by Butch Curry, to rob a payroll. Tempted by the $10,000 reward on Jesse's head, Curry's brother Lonny double-crosses the outlaws by alerting the local marshal, McFee. An ambush is arranged.

"That's the end of the Wild Bunch," a posse member tells McFee after the shootout leaves Butch Curry and another gang member dead. But not the James Gang. Jesse and Hank get away after Hank saves Jesse's life by taking a bullet in the shoulder fired by Lonny. Hank's fading fast, however. He needs a doctor.

When the two outlaws stumble onto the camp of Juanita and her parents, Juanita agrees to lead Jesse and Hank to the nearest doctors, the Frankensteins. Yikes!

Along the way, Jesse saves Juanita from an Indian, killing the brave with a knife. Then a whole party of Indian raiders gallops by. They must have been on their way to another movie, because they never appear again in this one. Jesse and Juanita fall in love.

Maria Frankenstein is glad to see Jesse and (especially) Hank. She can try a brain-transplant experiment on the wounded outlaw, once he has recovered. Juanita helps nurse the gentle giant back to health, and Hank falls in love with Juanita too. Meanwhile, Maria tries to seduce Jesse, especially after Hank lets Jesse's true identity slip out—but Jesse's no two-timer. He shuns her advances.

That enrages Maria, who sends Jesse off to town allegedly to get needed drugs for Hank. (Hmmmm. Earlier in the movie, Juanita's parents had lamented that they were the only ones left in town. The residents must have come back.) The envelope Maria gives Jesse contains not a prescription, but a note alerting authorities that the bearer is the notorious outlaw. Luckily, McFee and the sheriff are out of town. Lonny Curry tries to collect that reward; Lonny's no match for Jesse and is shot dead.

While Jesse's gone, Maria conducts her evil experiment on Hank, and it works. Hank becomes Igor, whom Maria can control. First, she has Igor dispatch her conscience-stricken brother Rudolph, whom she learns has been sabotaging her earlier experiments. By then, Jesse's back, and Maria has Igor knock him out.

Juanita, who has witnessed Maria's experiment on Hank, alerts Marshal McFee, and they return to the monastery before Maria can transform Jesse into a zombie. Igor knocks out McFee, but when Maria orders him to kill Juanita, he can't do it. He turns on Maria, choking her to death instead. Then Hank — I mean, Igor — tries to kill Jesse, forcing Juanita to shoot him down.

Juanita promises to wait for Jesse, but Jesse won't hear that, telling her that a rope's waiting for him. They kiss, then Jesse rides off with Marshal McFee.

The History

Northridge? Shouldn't that be Northfield? And who was that Butch Curry leading the Wild Bunch? *Butch* Cassidy and Harvey Logan, alias Kid *Curry*, were members of the Wild Bunch, but they didn't begin their crime spree until after Jesse James's death.[15]

Well, maybe film historian Robert Nott put it best: "Jesse James never met Frankenstein's daughter. Nor is there any documentation to suggest that Billy the Kid met Dracula."[16]

The Players

In June 1965, Embassy Pictures signed with Circle Productions to film two movies to be shown as a double-feature: *Jesse James Meets Frankenstein's Daughter* and *Billy the Kid Versus Dracula*.[17] The twin bill was dubbed "Shockorama" and "The NeWest in Terror-tainment!"[18] Both movies were produced by Carroll Case, written by Carl K. Hittleman (who had gotten a story credit for 1950's *The Return of Jesse James*), and directed by William Beaudine.

Born in 1892, Beaudine had been in movies since he joined the Biography Company "in the halcyon days of the silent screen." As an actor, he had appeared with Mark Pickford and D.W. Griffith, but moved to directing, first as an assistant, in 1911. He spent most of his career directing programmers for Poverty Row studios and was known as "One-Shot Beaudine." One oft-quoted anecdote shows his disdain for most of his movies. When told that an East Side Kids quickie he was making for Monogram had fallen behind schedule, Beaudine said, "You mean someone out there is actually waiting to see this shit?" After the "Shockorama" movies, Beaudine spent the rest of his career filming television shows before his death in 1970.[19]

Both Shockorama features were filmed at California's Red Rock Canyon and Corrigan Ranch, two famous movie locations. Cast members weren't quite as famous.

A "Shockorama" double feature of two terrible movies, 1966's *Billy the Kid versus Dracula* and *Jesse James Meets Frankenstein's Daughter* (actually, his granddaughter).

Playing Hank, Cal Bolder was born Earl C. Craver. The movie's pressbook said he had been a professional football player before turning to acting. Obituaries never mentioned any pro career, but did point out he had played at Wichita State University in his native Kansas, served as a Marine during the Korean War, and spent fourteen years as a Los Angeles police officer. "I had a 32-inch waist, a 52-inch chest, and 22-inch arms," Bolder said. Which pretty much got him the part of Hank/Igor. Bolder got his break in the movies after he stopped agent Robert Raison for speeding. Raison recommended the police officer to agent Henry Willson, who changed the aspiring actor's name, "Cal" being short for "California" and "Bolder" meaning "big rock" or "fearless," depending on the spelling. Bolder soon gave up acting and moved to Washington state, wrote at least one novel, *The Last Reunion*, and died in 2005.[20]

Narda Onyx, playing Maria Frankenstein, was a child actress in Estonia who had escaped Nazis and Russians with family members during World War II by fleeing to Sweden. In 1948, she came to England, becoming a member of London's Old Vic theater company. She moved to Toronto at age nineteen and in 1956, when her U.S. residency permit came through, she went to Hollywood. She appeared mostly on television during the late 1950s and early 1960s. She also wrote a biography of Tarzan portrayer Johnny Weissmuller titled *Water, World and Weissmuller*, published in 1964. *Jesse James Meets Frankenstein's Daughter* was her last movie. She died in 1991.[21]

This was also the last movie of Cuban Estelita Rodriguez, who often billed herself only as Estelita. Often paired with Roy Rogers as a *señorita* in Republic programmers of the 1940s, she also played Consuela, the feisty wife of the hotel owner in the classic Western *Rio Bravo* (1959). She died, reportedly of influenza, on March 12, 1966, but considering her death occurred about the same time as the release of *Jesse James Meets Frankenstein's Daughter*, she might have died of fright, or shame.[22]

John Lupton, as Jesse, was a Shakespearean-trained actor who had appeared with Katharine Hepburn in a traveling production of *As You Like It* in 1950. He had many (mostly minor) film roles, and is likely best remembered as Tom Jeffords in the TV series *Broken Arrow* (1956–58) or as Tommy Horton Jr. on the soap opera *Days of Our Lives* (1967–72, 1975–79). The latter teamed him with another Jesse James star, Macdonald Carey (Tom Horton), who played the outlaw in *The Great Missouri Raid* (1950). Lupton died in 1993.[23]

The movie's biggest name was veteran character actor Jim Davis, who had been acting since the 1940s. No stranger to Jesse James, Davis had played Cole Younger in *Woman They Almost Lynched* (1953) and Frank James in *Alias Jesse James* (1959) and had pursued Jesse James in an episode of the syndicated television series *Stories of the Century* (1954).[24] ("Jim Davis ... had been around Hollywood for about 20 years and I managed to get billing above him," Bolder told Michael Barnum in an interview with *Horror-Wood* webzine, "and nobody had ever heard of me! Including Jim Davis."[25]) Davis died in 1981.

Analysis

Like *Billy the Kid Versus Dracula*, *Jesse James Meets Frankenstein's Daughter* has enjoyed some success as a cult film. Some movies are so terribly acted, so ridiculous, so cheaply produced, they become unintentionally hilarious. *Jesse James Meets Frankenstein's Daughter* ranks right up — or, rather, down — there with *The Brain from Planet Arous* (1957), *Plan 9 from Outer Space* (1959) and (of course) *Billy the Kid Versus Dracula*.

It's too bad the actors and director didn't turn *Jesse James Meets Frankenstein's Daughter* into a comedy rather than playing it straight. After a couple of beers, *Jesse James Meets Frankenstein's Daughter* might come across as funnier than *Alias Jesse James*.

* * *

Brian Garfield, *Western Films* (1982): "This was the last of Beaudine's approximately 250 directorial jobs on 'B' movies — it also was just possibly the very worst. Did they really have red plastic helmets in Jesse's day?"

A Time for Dying

(FIPCO Productions; November 1971 European release;
June 1982 U.S. release; 67 minutes)

CREDITS: *Director-Screenplay:* Budd Boetticher; *Producer:* Audie Murphy.
CAST: Richard Lapp (Cass Dunning); Anne Randall (Nellie Winters); Robert Random (Billy Pimple); Victor Jory (Judge Roy Bean); Audie Murphy (Jesse James); Beatrice Kay (Mamie); Peter Brocco (Seth); Burt Mustin (Ed); Ron Masak (Sam — Bartender); Terry Murphy (Sonny); Randy Shields (Cauliflower); Bob Herron (Rankin); Willard Willingham (Frank James); J.N. Roberts (Frank James); William Bassett (Southerner); Casey Tibbs (Sidekick).

Synopsis

Young farmer Cass Dunning makes his way to Silver City, where most of the town is drunk and awaiting the arrival of a new girl at Mamie's brothel. The man responsible for the inebriation of the town is outlaw Billy Pimple (Cass met him and two cronies on his way to town), who, the bartender says, "ain't quite Billy the Kid, but he's sure workin' on it." Cass shows his prowess with a Colt by shooting Billy Pimple's wanted poster off the saloon wall.

When the new girl, Nellie Winters, arrives on a stagecoach, Cass realizes she is quickly learning that she has been hired as a prostitute. He rescues her, and the two ride off out of town.

They have no idea where they're going, but eventually check into the hotel in the West Texas town of Vinegaroon. Decent Cass, naturally, sleeps in a chair outside the door to the room. But that doesn't stop the local law, Judge Roy Bean, from having his deputies bring the couple into his makeshift court for trial. There are decency laws in Vinegaroon, you know.

First, Bean sentences a suspected horse thief to hang. The next case — after a brief whiskey break — is Cass and Nellie's. Bean gives the couple a wedding ring and marries them. "Stick the ring on the finger, boy, and kiss her," Bean instructs Cass. "May God have mercy on your souls." Naturally, Bean asks for the ring back, and charges Cass five dollars for the ceremony.

Without horse, rifle or Colts — confiscated by Bean and his deputies — Cass and Nellie take a walk up the hill, where Bean joins them. When the judge learns that Cass's father has actually seen the love of Bean's life, actress Lillie Langtry, he softens, and returns Cass's guns and horse. He even makes a present to Nellie of the horse of the man he just hanged.

There's a wild celebration in town, and the next morning the newlyweds continue their journey. Cass plans on dropping off his bride at his father's farm, explaining to his new

A French poster for Audie Murphy's final film, *A Time for Dying*, made in 1969. Audie got top billing, but he had only a cameo.

bride that he has something he has to do, and that's become a bounty hunter. Nellie is amazed at his shooting prowess, but they have an argument over Cass's ambitions. That's when Jesse James arrives. He gives Cass some important instructions about gunfighting, tells Nellie that "you make Belle Starr look like a nun," then rides off with his brother Frank and "cousin" Bob Ford, telling Cass, "When you get tired of being a farmer, look me up." He warns them to stay clear of Silver City, but Cass, ever stubborn, doesn't listen.

A short while later, a gang, presumably of Jesse's outlaws, led by a Southerner, takes Nellie hostage and returns to Silver City, to rob the bank. Cass catches up, kills two of the bandits and rescues Nellie. Now he's a hero, but there's no happy ending for the newlyweds because Billy Pimple is back in town and calls out Cass.

Nellie tries to save her husband, but in the end, it's a showdown between Cass and Billy. Cass is nervous, his palms are sweaty — Jesse had warned him about that — and the guns slip out of his hands. He's promptly shot down by Billy. Mamie carries the grief-stricken widow to her brothel. Later that night, another "new" girl arrives in Silver City. The cycle, it seems, is about to begin again.

The History

Cass and Nellie run into a couple of legendary Westerners (Cass's pa even met gunman John Wesley Hardin), but Budd Boetticher's script has a few calendar problems. Roy Bean, who became known as the "Law West of the Pecos," was appointed justice of the peace of Pecos County, Texas, in August 2, 1882[26] — four months after Jesse James was killed in St. Joseph, Missouri. Plus, Bob Ford is mistaken for Jesse's cousin again.

I'm a little confused about the location of Silver City, too. Is it Silver City, New Mexico? (The movie was shot at Apache Junction, Arizona, in the spring of 1969.) Maybe it's Silver City, Texas, a farming community in Navarro County, Texas, that was founded before the Civil War.[27] Then again, it's hard to imagine Cass and Nellie riding roughly 500 miles from Silver City, Texas, on that one horse. Or 450 miles from Silver City, New Mexico.

There are three other places called Silver City in Texas, in Fannin County (500 miles from Vinegaroon); Milam County (300 miles); and Red River County (550 miles). But only the Navarro County location was around in Jesse's day.

The Players

FIPCO Productions Inc. was founded by Audie Murphy in the spring of 1969. Murphy was president. Other officers included chairman of the board J.C. Spellman, president of the First Investment Planning Co. of Washington, D.C., and executive vice-president R.C. Clinton, president of Clinton Oil Company of Wichita, Kansas.[28] *A Time for Dying* would be the company's only movie.

The film was hoped to be a bit of a comeback for both Murphy and Boetticher. Murphy's last film had been *40 Guns to Apache Pass*, released in May 1967.[29] Boetticher had left Hollywood for Mexico in 1960 to make his biopic of bullfighter Carlos Arruza, but had run into a score of devastating setbacks: Arruza was killed in an automobile accident in 1966, and Boetticher's marriage to actress Debra Paget ended, he went bankrupt, almost died of pneumonia, stayed in prison a week for not paying a hotel bill, and, after a drinking binge, spent a week in a mental institution. His movie, *Arruza*, would not premiere until 1971.[30]

Murphy, whom Boetticher had directed in *The Cimarron Kid* (1951), had helped Boetticher in Mexico. When Murphy learned Boetticher's situation, he came to Mexico, visited Boetticher in the hospital, and gave him a cashier's check for $5,500. All he said he wanted in return was maybe a 16mm print, though he also mentioned he would like to produce movies one day and that maybe Boetticher would direct one.[31]

That time came in 1969. Murphy had run up gambling debts, according to Boetticher and other sources, and he also owed the Internal Revenue Service money for back taxes.[32] Boetticher said, "Audie got in real trouble with some people in Las Vegas, and he needed a director to make a picture, and he would be the producer. He was a friend, and he was in trouble; so I made the picture for him."[33]

Murphy "didn't really like things when they was [sic] going good," said his friend, rodeo star Casey Tibbs.[34]

The movie was a way to bail Murphy out. Boetticher had written *A Time for Dying*, and planned to make it with Peter Fonda in the role of Cass. That wouldn't help Audie, but "Audie was one hell of a lot more important to me than the budget of my proposed picture," Boetticher said, "so we worked out a deal to his satisfaction in less than five minutes over the phone."[35] Fonda was out; Murphy was in.

Boetticher and Murphy might have dreamed of recreating the magic of Boetticher's pairing with Randolph Scott in a string of outstanding Western films from 1955 to 1960. After *A Time for Dying*, they planned to film another Boetticher script, *When There's Sumpthin' to Do*, in northeastern Mexico, and then *A Horse for Mr. Barnum*, from another Boetticher script, in Spain in April 1970.[36]

Murphy's two teenage sons got speaking roles in the film, and Tibbs landed the role of Sidekick, one of the bad guys who try to rob the Silver City bank. Actor Ron Masak recalled the scene in which Tibbs was to ride a bucking horse: "When Casey asked Budd where he would like him to try to fall for the camera, Budd said, 'Casey, you're the greatest bucking-horse rider in history. Don't fall off— ride him out of town.' Casey did just that."[37]

Lucien Ballard was hired as director of photography. An Academy Award nominee for *The Caretakers* (1963), Ballard is remembered mostly for his films with Sam Peckinpah, but had worked with Boetticher on *The Magnificent Matador* (1955), *The Killer Is Loose* (1956), *Buchanan Rides Alone* (1958), *The Rise and Fall of Legs Diamond* (1960) and *Arruza*. He had done quite well in Westerns, having made *The Sons of Katie Elder* (1965), *Nevada Smith* (1966), *Hour of the Gun* (1967) and *Will Penny* (1968), and was coming off working on Peckinpah's *The Wild Bunch* (1969) and director Henry Hathaway's *True Grit* (1969) when filming began on *A Time for Dying* in late April 1969.[38]

Boetticher had filmed most of his Randolph Scott Westerns at Lone Pine, California, but turned to Arizona this time. It was shot at Apacheland, a town set in Apache Junction. (Elvis Presley had filmed his last movie, *Charro!* [1969], there the previous summer. Murphy had also filmed *Arizona Raiders* [1965] there.) About a week after filming of *A Time for Dying*, much of the set, conceived as a tourist destination and film site in 1959 (à la Tucson's Old Tucson Studios), was destroyed in a fire. After another fire in 2004, the set's chapel and barn were moved to Superstition Mountain Museum in Apache Junction.[39]

"Although the landscape here is Arizona ridge and cactus rather than California's Lone Pine rock formations, the interplay of barren open range and pastoral forest faithfully evokes Boetticher's world of the morality play," Jim Kitzes observed.[40]

Murphy played Jesse James in a four-minute cameo "for box office insurance,"[41] but also had an important off-screen role in the opening scene in which Cass Dunning saves a rabbit by blowing the head off a rattlesnake. Artist Walt LaRue, who provided the opening title credit paintings, recalled that "they had four or five different snakes ... and Audie shot all their heads off. [*Chuckles*] He was probably ten yards away. A snake moves his head around pretty rapidly, but he was a hell of a shot."[42]

Boetticher was initially excited about the project, but soon grew less so. He loathed Lapp. On the last day of the shoot, Lapp protested his death scene. Boetticher fired back: "Richard, let me tell you something. I've put up with you for eighteen days, and I said, you're gonna do it this way if I have to stay here all night, and one more word out of you, the minute we say wrap, I'm gonna beat your fucking brains out." Cast and crew applauded.[43] Eventually, Boetticher would disavow the movie, calling it "crap,"[44] and saying, "It's never been seen again and it never will."[45] (He was almost right.)

Murphy struggled to furnish the money. Tibbs recalled telling him, "'Hey, I got too much money when I took the job. I don't need nothing.' He appreciated something like that. Not too many people really tried to do it; they all tried to stick it in him."[46]

When money finally dried up, the movie was several minutes short, and Murphy spent another eighteen months trying to raise more capital so *A Time for Dying* could be completed and distributed. The movie wasn't shown until 1971, when it premiered in France; it finally made the rounds in a few American cinemas in 1982. The movie received a limited video release in the 1990s; bootleg copies are now easy to find.[47]

In addition to planning to star in the other Boetticher Westerns, Murphy had agreed to play the deranged sniper in director Don Siegel's *Dirty Harry*, but none was meant to be. A month shy of his forty-sixth birthday, Murphy was killed in a plane crash near Roanoke, Virginia, on May 28, 1971.[48]

"I'll bet that Audie knew, with no regrets just before that plane hit the ground, that his own *Time for Dying* had arrived," Boetticher said.[49]

With the exception of the 1985 documentary *My Kingdom For...*, Boetticher would not make another movie either. He died on November 29, 2001, of multiple organ failure. He was eighty-five.[50]

Analysis

"I had one hangup as an actor," Murphy told the *Los Angeles Times*. "I had no talent."[51]

Actually, compared to the rest of the cast (with the exception of Victor Jory, who has a ball hamming it up as Judge Roy Bean), Murphy seems like a Spencer Tracy or Henry Fonda in *A Time for Dying*.

Film historian Robert Nott called Lapp "unknown (and untalented),"[52] while, in *The Films of Audie Murphy,* Bob Larkins and Boyd Magers said that Anne Randall, the *Playboy* centerfold for May 1967, and Lapp "were quite bland, and the film did nothing to further their careers."

They are definitely the weakest part in a movie, hailed by some critics, rebuked by many others. It actually falls somewhere between, definitely below Boetticher's masterful Westerns with Randolph Scott, but far above Murphy's weak Westerns such as *The Duel at Silver Creek* (1952) and *The Texican* (1966).

It's not much of a Jesse James movie — Roy Bean has a larger, funnier part — but Murphy, older, fatter and sporting a rough mustache and beard, gives an engaging performance as the wary outlaw. Murphy is too easily dismissed by most critics, but *A Time for Dying* shows that when under the guidance of a great director (John Huston in 1960's *The Unforgiven*, for example), he had no hangups as an actor, and, indeed, could act very well.

* * *

Boston Globe (June 17, 1987): "The film ... stands the western genre on its head in several respects, demythifying it by denying its violence even the smallest shred of nobility. In the truest sense, it's an absurdist western, with bullets fired and lives lost for no good reason at all."

CHAPTER EIGHT

Revisionist Jesse, 1972–2010

By the end of the 1960s, Western movies were fading into the movie-theater sunset. The early 1970s, however, ushered in a movement toward revisionism, and the result has been a mostly interesting display of new looks at Jesse James.

Two exceptions are *American Outlaws* (2001), and *American Bandits: Frank and Jesse James* (2010), neither historically based nor entertaining.

The Great Northfield Minnesota Raid
(Universal, April 1972, 91 minutes)

CREDITS: *Director-Screenplay:* Philip Kaufman; *Producer:* Jennings Lang.
CAST: Cliff Robertson (Cole Younger); Robert Duvall (Jesse James); Luke Askew (Jim Younger); R.G. Armstrong (Clell Miller); Dana Elcar (Allen); Donald Moffat (Manning); John Pearce (Frank James); Matt Clark (Bob Younger); Wayne Sutherlin (Charley Pitts); Robert H. Harris (Wilcox); Jack Manning (Heywood/Landlord); Elisha Cook Jr. (Banker); Royal Dano (Gustavson); Mary Robin Redd (Kate); Bill Calloway (Calliopist); Arthur Peterson (Jefferson Jones); Craig Curtis (Chadwell); Barry Brown (Henry Wheeler); Nellie Burt (Doll Woman); Liam Dunn (Drummer); Madeleine Taylor Holmes (Granny Woman); Herbert Nelson (Chief Detective); Erik Holland (Sheriff); Anna Barton (Clell's Wife); Marjorie Durant (Maybelle); Inger Stratton (Singing Whore); Velda J. Hansen (Nude Girl); William Challee (Old Timer); Robert Gravage (Farmer).

Synopsis

It might not be the greatest Jesse James movie, but this has to be the quirkiest.

In 1876, the James and Younger brothers are trying to live in peace, waiting for the Missouri state legislature to award them amnesty. After all, railroad barons are the real bandits, driving poor families from their farms, and the railroad is ruthless, having hired Allan Pinkerton to kill those outlaws before they are given amnesty. The boys can enjoy their amnesty, Pinkerton says, "in the hereafter."

Cole Younger is holding court, showing off his bulletproof vest. "Ain't bad," he tells an admiring youth. "Helps you sit up straight." That vest comes in handy moments later when Pinkerton's men ambush Cole, Jim and Bob Younger. His brothers kill the detectives but Cole's badly wounded.

Cole Younger (Cliff Robertson), bloodied and captured at the end of *The Great Northfield Minnesota Raid* (1972).

While Cole is recovering, Jesse has a "vision"—a vision helped mightily after he discovered newspaper clippings about a bank in Northfield, "the largest bank West of the Mississippi," while sitting in the privy with Frank. His inspirational, tent-revival style "vision" whips Frank, Bob Younger and Chadwell into a frenzy, and they take off 480 miles north, behind enemy lines, to Northfield.

When Cole recovers and learns that Jesse is leading another raid, he takes Jim Younger, Charley Pitts and Clell Miller to Minnesota to stop Jesse from ruining their chances at getting amnesty. On the train ride north, however, they learn that the railroad has bribed the speaker of the house into killing the amnesty bill. So they might as well rob that Northfield bank. They can use that $60,000, Cole thinks, to bribe the legislature into giving them amnesty after all.

One problem: That allegedly rich bank is practically insolvent. People just aren't depositing money since the Panic of '73, Cole is told after reaching the city. So Cole concocts a plan with bank president Wilcox and bank employee Bunker to con the residents of Northfield into depositing all their money. He also teaches young Henry Wheeler how to fire a rifle.

Meanwhile, Jesse and the boys stop at the home of a widow in Hanska Slough. She's about to be evicted, so Jesse gives her $80 to pay her landlord. This is an interesting take on the Jesse-and-the-landlord/banker myth. The widow pays the landlord, and Jesse kills him. He's a Yankee, after all. Then he frames the widow for the crime. "She's a Yankee, too," he says.

The gang is reunited in Northfield, visit a spa, then a cathouse, and the next rainy morning, the boys ride to Northfield to make a withdrawal. Heywood, Wilcox's accountant, believes the robbery is staged and that Wilcox is in on it with the robbers. He refuses to open the safe, saying it can't be opened because it's on a time lock. Nice try, Cole tells him. The vault isn't even locked, and Chadwell goes inside to load up on money.

Outside, however, an old man named Gustavson, driven insane after his son marched off to war and never returned, hounds Bob Younger, who shoots down the man. He falls on a calliope, which Wilcox had put outside the bank to bring in business. The noise alerts the townsmen and frays the outlaws' nerves.

Heywood locks Chadwell in the vault, and is murdered by Jesse. Bunker makes a break for it, and is shot, then knocked out, and lands in the mud. Drawing from the lessons he received from Younger, Henry Wheeler kills Miller. Bob Younger is badly wounded, but saved by Cole. The outlaws make a hasty retreat.

Jesse James (Robert Duvall) and his cohorts try to make a bank withdrawal in *The Great Northfield Minnesota Raid* (1972).

While Northfield citizens are forming a posse and alerting every lawman in the state, the vault is opened, and Chadwell is shot full of holes.

Jesse brings the outlaws to the widow's home, and Cole decides it's best to stay there since Bob is too hurt to travel. After the widow says she can bring a doctor, Jesse and Frank decide they'll go with her. Apparently, they kill the old woman, and with Jesse disguised in her clothes — "Better cover up them bloodstains," Frank tells him — take her buggy back to Missouri, where Jesse dreams of forming a better gang. "What's that good-looking kid's name? Bob Ford?" Jesse tells Frank. "I think he'd fit in just right."

The Northfield posse discovers the body of the landlord, which leads them to the widow's house. There, Charley Pitts is killed, and the Younger brothers shot to pieces.

Pinkerton's detectives arrive too late, because now the posse is bringing in the Youngers. Cole, hit eleven times in the shootout, somehow manages to get to his feet, and the crowd cheers him. "Ain't that a wonderment," he says.

A narrator tells us that Cole spent twenty-five years in Stillwater penitentiary and died in 1916. "He saw a whole new era come into being, but at Northfield his outlaw days had ended."

The History

Philip Kaufman obviously did a lot of homework when writing the screenplay for *The Great Northfield Minnesota Raid*. "It was a dumb time," he said.[1] He did, however, play loose with the facts.

The movie has "Silent Jim" Younger unable to talk after being shot in the mouth. Yes, Jim Younger was shot — a bullet hit his upper jaw and tore out his upper teeth — but not until the shootout at Hanska Slough. That gunfight, by the way, was in the brush, and not a widow's house.[2]

In 1875, there was a campaign to grant the Youngers and James brothers amnesty in Missouri's General Assembly, but that was barely defeated on March 20 by Unionists — not railroads — 58–39. A two-thirds majority was needed for passage.[3]

Even a Keystone Cops–like comedy scene involving a Northfield baseball game has historic grounding. Before arriving in Northfield, the outlaws hid out in Minneapolis and St. Paul. On August 31, some of them made it to a ballgame between the Winona Clippers and the St. Paul Red Caps. Bob Younger was said to have become a fan of the sport. The boys also spent time in a brothel but St. Paul.[4]

Northfield's First National Bank was not the largest bank west of the Mississippi, but the bankers didn't need to con residents into making deposits there. On September 7, 1876, the bank had $15,455.70 in its drawers and safe. Besides, there is evidence that suggests that Northfield wasn't even the first target of the James-Younger Gang. On September 4 — three days before the Northfield robbery — the outlaws might have considered robbing the First National Bank in Mankato, Minnesota, but, fearing they had been discovered, quickly departed town without entering the bank.[5]

Henry Wheeler was studying to be a doctor — he would graduate from the University of Michigan's medical school in 1877 — and his shot did kill Clell Miller. Cole Younger didn't teach him how to shoot, however. "I knew how to handle a rifle," Wheeler said. "I had done a considerable amount of hunting, from fourteen on."[6]

Bill Chadwell, aka Bill Stiles, wasn't left behind in the vault, but was shot out of the saddle and killed by Anselm Manning during the robbery.[7]

There's an interesting side note to Wheeler and the two dead outlaws. Cadavers were hard to come by for medical schools, so Wheeler either helped dig up or arranged the removal of the bodies of Chadwell and Miller. The corpses were shipped to Ann Arbor, Michigan, in barrels marked "paint." The *Ann Arbor Courier* ran an account of Wheeler's coup — next to, of all things, a sarsaparilla advertisement — noting, "The students of the medical department will this winter have the pleasure of carving up two genuine robbers, being members of the Northfield, Minnesota, gang." When a friend asked Wheeler how he managed to procure such a healthy specimen, Wheeler replied, "I shot him."[8]

Nicholas Gustafsun (spelled Gustavson here) wasn't crazy, and apparently had no children. A thirty-year-old immigrant from Fiddekulla, Sweden, he had arrived in Minnesota that spring with his eleven-year-old nephew. Gustavson spoke little or no English, and when the shooting started, a bullet struck him in the head. He died a few days later.[9]

One wonders, however, about how Northfield residents reacted to the film's portrayal of its bank employees. Frank J. Wilcox was not the bank president, but an assistant bookkeeper at the time of the robbery. Born in 1848, the Baptist minister was working in the bank that afternoon when three men startled him, and he found himself staring down the barrels of their revolvers. Wilcox later said that liquor was strong on the breath of the three men, whom he identified as Pitts, Bob Younger and probably Frank James. Wilcox was soon forced onto his knees. He remained in the bank during the entire robbery.[10]

Twenty-seven-year-old Alonzo Bunker, a bank employee since 1873, at first thought friends were playing a joke on him when the three outlaws entered the bank. Forced to his knees, the teller thought about trying for a .32-caliber Smith & Wesson on the shelf, but Pitts saw the weapon and shoved it in his pocket. "You needn't try to get hold of that," Pitts told Bunker. "You couldn't do anything with that little derringer anyway." After Bob Younger demanded the money outside the safe, Bunker pointed to a box containing change. He never mentioned a drawer underneath the counter, which held $3,000, and the outlaws never found it.[11]

With the banker's attention elsewhere, Bunker made a dash for the rear door. Pitts fired once, missing, then gave chase. Outside, Pitts fired again, from a distance of twenty feet, and the bullet went through Bunker's shoulder. Dazed, but still on his feet, Bunker ran straight for a doctor's office. By then, the town had been alerted, and Pitts returned to the bank. Outside, Cole Younger was yelling at those robbers inside the bank that the boys were getting shot up outside.[12]

In the movie, Wilcox calls Joseph Heywood a hero who had saved the townspeople's money. In the movie, Wilcox is trying to protect his own hide, but the truth is that Heywood indeed was a hero, and is still treated as one today.

Born in New Hampshire in 1837, Heywood was a Civil War veteran who moved to Northfield in 1867. He became bookkeeper at the First National Bank in 1872, but on September 7, 1876, he was working as "acting cashier" because cashier George M. Phillips and bank president J.C. Nutting were attending the Centennial Exposition in Philadelphia, Pennsylvania.[13]

Heywood refused to open the safe — according to one account, he claimed the safe was on a time lock and *couldn't* be opened. When Charlie Pitts stepped into the open vault, Heywood tried to slam the vault door on the outlaw. The robbers quickly subdued him and dragged him away. "Let's cut his throat," said one of the bandits, drawing a knife across Heywood's throat, leaving a scratch. Another fired a gun over Heywood's head.[14]

As the robbers manhandled Heywood, he began crying out, "Murder! Murder! Murder!" The third outlaw, presumably Frank James, brained him with a pistol. By then, with gunfire booming outside, the bandits knew they had to get out of town. The last one out the door put a bullet through Heywood's brain. Joseph Heywood left behind a widow and his five-year-old daughter.[15]

The door to the safe was closed but unlocked. The robbers never tried to open it. Out of more than $15,000 inside the bank, the James-Younger Gang left with $26.70.[16]

The Players

Philip Kaufman had written and directed two independent films in his native Chicago — *Goldstein* (1965) and *Fearless Frank*, or *Frank's Greatest Adventure* (1967) — but *The Great Northfield Minnesota Raid* was his first commercial film. "Kaufman is not an angry revisionist," the *Los Angeles Times* wrote. "He seems to be trying to tell it like it must have been, with an amused detachment, which sees the events as something close to an absurd spectacle."[17]

Philip Kaufman, left, directs Robert Duvall, playing Jesse James in *The Great Northfield Minnesota Raid* (1972).

Kaufman had majored in history at the University of Chicago, later attended Harvard Law School, and considered himself a James Gang authority. As a screenwriter, he went on to pen *The Outlaw Josey Wales* (1976), *The Wanderers* (1979), *The Right Stuff* (1983) and *The Unbearable Lightness of Being* (1988), for which he earned an Academy Award nomination. He also got a story credit for the smash hit *Raiders of the Lost Ark* (1981).[18]

The movie was filmed in Jacksonville, in southern Oregon, during the winter of 1970–71. The town welcomed the production, even hanging signs in businesses — including a bank — that said "Welcome Cole Younger and Jesse James!"[19]

Kaufman aimed to make things look realistic, borrowing a steam-powered tractor, a horse-drawn hearse, a high-wheeled log loader, and various "velocipedes" from a Jacksonville pioneer museum to use in the movie. "[I]t is as crammed with the artifacts of 19th-century America — everything from dolls to a working calliope — as an especially splendid Third Avenue Shop," the *New York Times* noted.[20]

Kaufman even used Northfield's St. Olaf College Choir to sing in the scene in which Jesse James rides by a church. Of course, Northfield doesn't exactly resemble Jacksonville, Oregon. As one Northfield resident said: "That's when the James gang rode across Northfield and I learned we had mountains down here."[21]

With Jacksonville a short distance from Ashland, Kaufman was also able to cast bit parts with actors from that city's famed Shakespeare repertory group. "First time we've been able to round up players capable of saying 'they went thataway' in such pear-shaped tones," Kaufman quipped.[22]

Veteran actors, however, comprised most of the cast. Kaufman liked Cincinnati-born Jack Manning's acting so well, he cast him in two roles — the landlord and Joseph Heywood — both of whom get killed by Jesse James. "Even a single death scene," Manning said, "is considered the answer to an actor's dream; has any player even dared to hope for two?"[23]

Kaufman also admired the work of veteran character actor Elisha Cook Jr., who had been in movies since the early 1930s including *The Maltese Falcon* (1941), *The Big Sleep* (1946) and *Shane* (1953). During the scene in which Cook sounded the alarm and was knocked out, Kaufman wanted Cook to fall back in the mud. "But Cookie said, 'I fell back in the mud in *Shane*,'" Kaufman recalled. "'I think I should fall forward this time.'" That's the way it was filmed, too. Cook also refused a stand-in, Kaufman said, and remained in the mud while horse thundered past.[24]

Robert Duvall's performance insinuated that Jesse James was homosexual,[25] the first such implication since *I Shot Jesse James* (1949). When it's brought up in the brothel that Jesse avoids women, Bob Younger comes to his defense by mentioning Zerelda Mimms (Jesse's wife). Cole Younger quips, "Even a blind chicken will pick up some corn."

The *Los Angeles Times* said Duvall played Jesse "with menacing intensity.... He is a cold-blooded killer, clever but not very bright, deeply neurotic with strong intimations of homosexuality, rationalizing his killings with a spew of Bible citations and hallucinatory shoutings."[26]

Duvall, who had made an impression as Boo Radley in *To Kill a Mockingbird* (1962), was finding a rhythm as an actor, and coming off a good run of films such as *Bullitt* (1968), *True Grit* (1969) and *MASH* (1970). *The Godfather* would also be released in 1972. Duvall gave Jesse an evangelistic touch, which might have served the actor well in *The Apostle* (1997), which he wrote, starred in and executive-produced. He was nominated for a Best Actor Oscar for his performance of the hotheaded evangelist hiding from the law.

A versatile actor of tremendous range — six acting nominations, and winning for Best Actor in *Tender Mercies* (1983)— Duvall always looked comfortable in Westerns, although he pretty much played the same role as the witty, grizzled, old-time cowboy in CBS's *Lonesome Dove* (1989), American Movie Classics' *Broken Trail* (2006) and the big-screen *Open Range* (2003).

Surprisingly, Academy Award–winning actor (for 1968's *Charly*) Cliff Robertson had never been in a big-screen Western with the exception of *J.W. Coop*, a rodeo movie released earlier in 1972. He took the role to heart, spending a year getting into character after reading Kaufman's script. "Most earlier films about the outlaw paint him in but a single color ... black," Robertson said. "There's no denying he made deadly use of the gun and terrorized the countryside.

"But there was far more to the man than his killings. He was as much sinned against as sinning. He was a peaceful farmer until powerful interests took away his land. He fought back the only way he knew."[27]

Robertson certainly filled the screen with an earnest, powerful and ultimately human portrayal of Cole Younger. Even more surprising might be the fact that Robertson has never been in a Western since *The Great Northfield Minnesota Raid*.

Analysis

Many critics and film historians say the Western genre died with *The Wild Bunch* (1969), but movies like *The Hired Hand* (1971), *McCabe and Mrs. Miller* (1971), *Ulzana's Raid* (1972), *The Culpepper Cattle Company* (1972), *Bad Company* (1972) and this one showed that filmmakers had plenty of new things to say about the Old West.

The Great Northfield Minnesota Raid starts off as a pure delight, but somehow goes astray. The subplot involving Pinkerton's pursuit of the boys isn't funny, and doesn't work, and the idea of having Younger and Wilcox con the residents into putting their money in the bank is juvenile and idiotic.

The gunfights seem mishandled, and Kaufman throws too much at the viewer — mountain witchcraft, betrayal, baseball, a lynching and a bunch of really crazy people.

An odd little movie — with disparate performances by Duvall and Robertson — it is still interesting to watch. It could have been, perhaps *should* have been a classic, but somehow lost its way.

* * *

New York Times (June 15, 1972): "The film ... is funny and cruel and, in a couple of instances, technically awkward. Kaufman is not the world's greatest stager of crowd scenes and gun fights. But the places and people look right and the talk is not the slave of melodrama. It is full of quiet surprises, like the moment in the whorehouse when one of the bandits, feeling very guilty and low, says: 'I'd rather gone frog-gigging.'"

The Long Riders

(United Artists, May 1980, 99 minutes)

CREDITS: *Director:* Walter Hill; *Producer:* Tim Zinnemann; *Screenplay:* Bill Bryden, Steven Phillip Smith, Stacy Keach, James Keach.

Eight. Revisionist Jesse, 1972–2007

CAST: David Carradine (Cole Younger); Keith Carradine (Jim Younger); Robert Carradine (Bob Younger); James Keach (Jesse James); Stacy Keach (Frank James); Dennis Quaid (Ed Miller); Randy Quaid (Clell Miller); Kevin Brophy (John Younger); Harry Carey Jr. (George Arthur); Christopher Guest (Charlie Ford); Nicholas Guest (Bob Ford); Shelby Leverington (Annie Ralston); Felice Orlandi (Mr. Reddick); Pamela Reed (Belle Starr); James Remar (Sam Starr); Fran Ryan (Mrs. Samuel); Savannah Smith (Zee); Amy Stryker (Beth); James Whitmore Jr. (Mr. Rixley); John Bottoms (Mortician); West Buchanan (McCorkindale); Edward Bunker (Chadwell); Martina Deignan (Shirley Biggs); Tim Rossovich (Charlie Pitts).

Synopsis

In what many consider the best Jesse James movie, director Walter Hill fashions a series of vignettes to illustrate the outlaw's post–Civil War career, focusing more on the relationships between the outlaws than on their crimes.

The James, Younger and Miller (Clell and Ed) brothers are robbing the First Federal Bank in Missouri when things go to hell. Ed murders the teller, starting a gunfight that

Jesse and Frank James (James and Stacy Keach) try to find the best way out of Northfield in *The Long Riders* (1980).

leaves Jesse with a bullet in his arm. After the outlaws get away, Jesse whips the tar out of Ed and kicks him out of the gang. Even Clell tells his brother, "I ain't sidin' with you."

Jesse is sent to the Mimms household in Nebraska to recover. There he proposes to Zee, who remembers his proposal "during the war about seven years ago." This time's different.

Apparently, however, business comes first. Or maybe Jesse needs some money to pay for the wedding. The gang robs a stagecoach, but Bob Younger shakes the hand of an ex–Confederate soldier who served with Jo Shelby. A young coward also claims to have ridden with Shelby, but when asked where he fought, he replies, "Cold Harbor." The Missourian Shelby never fought at Cold Harbor, Virginia, so the outlaws rob the man of everything but his underwear.

Afterward, the boys visit a brothel where Cole Younger romances Belle Shirley, a prostitute who charges $15 but wants to be respectable. "You'll never be respectable, Belle," Cole tells her. "You're a whore. You'll always be a whore. That's why I like you."

During Jesse's wedding, nerdy Bob and Charlie Ford try to join the gang, but Frank and Cole ignore them. There is a lot of romancing going on. Frank's pursuing Ann Ralston, and Jim Younger's after Beth Mimms, although she is now betrothed to Ed Miller. That romance will be broken up before long. Cole is always chasing Belle. Sitting in her buggy, Belle asks Cole why she wasn't invited. "Because you're a whore," Cole tells her. Before Belle drives off, she says, "Well, at least I ain't a cheap one."

After the boys rob a Chicago, Rock Island and Pacific train, the Pinkerton detective agency begins a full-fledged pursuit of the brothers. That leads to the death of John Younger (Cole, Jim and Bob's cousin), and a raid on the James farm in which a "smoker" explodes, maiming the boys' mother and killing their simple-minded fifteen-year-old stepbrother.

The boys exact bloody revenge, then split up across five states while things cool down. Cole, naturally, heads down to Texas where Belle has married a rather jealous Sam Starr, which leads to a fight. "Boys," Belle tells them, "there's no need to fight over little ol' me, but if you've got to, you make it man-to-man, hand-to-hand." With big knives. And holding a black bandanna in their teeth. A scene straight from the knife duel between Audie Murphy's Jesse and David Wolfe's Rudolph Tate in *Kansas Raiders* (1950). Sam Starr ends up with a knife in his thigh, and Cole rides back to Missouri—and just in time, as Jesse's planning the Northfield raid. Jesse has even brought in a couple of newcomers to the gang, Bill Chadwell and Charlie Pitts. "Good men," Jesse says. "Who says?" asks Cole. "I do," Jesse answers.

Bad career move for the boys.

"The Pinkertons told us you might be coming," bank teller Heywood informs the outlaws before Clell blows him away. Sure enough, Pinkertons and townsmen are waiting for the boys outside, and the gang is shot up. Two men—Chadwell and Pitts—are left dead on the streets.

With Clell dying of a stomach wound, Bob Younger badly wounded, and the other Younger brothers too injured to ride, Jesse decides that he and Frank must leave. Cole is perturbed that Frank is also going to ride away, but Frank tells his friend, "I got to stick with my brother, Cole."

Cole draws a revolver, then decides against shooting. "I like it better this way, Jesse," he says. "I get to see you run."

Jesse and Frank return to Missouri—"We never should have left," Frank says—and

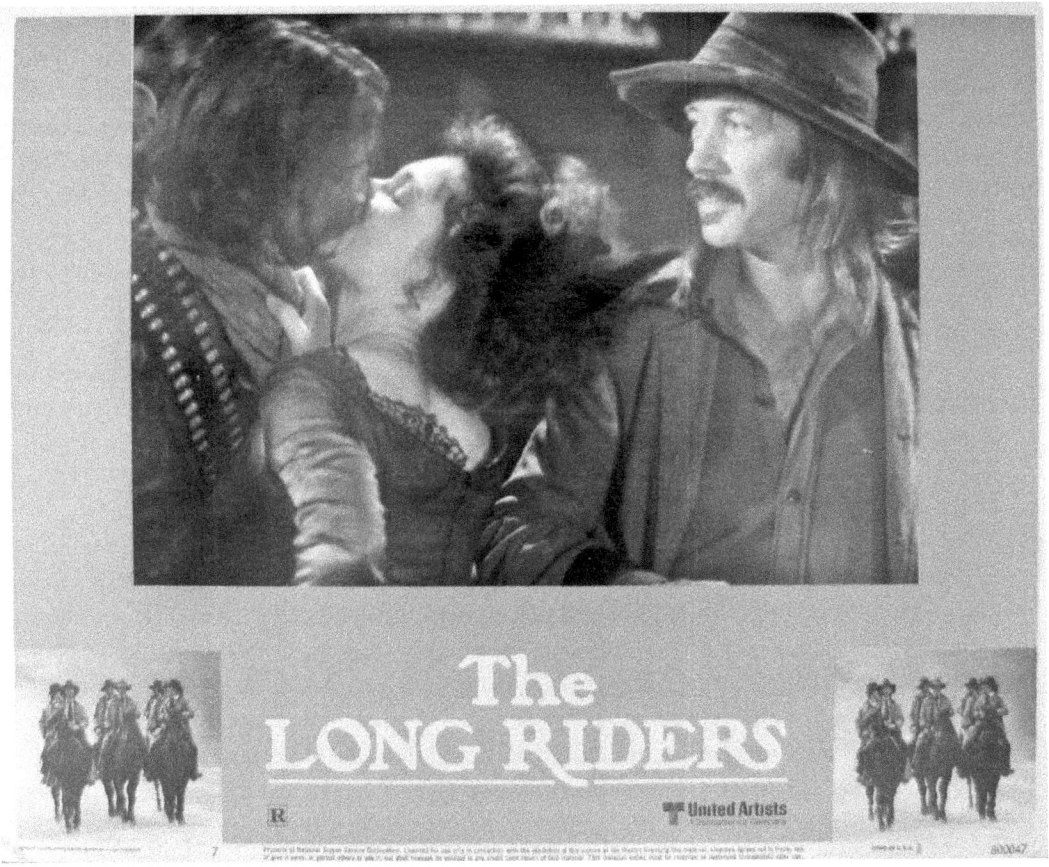

Director Walter Hill's *The Long Riders* (1980) had Cole Younger (David Carradine), right, in an odd relationship with Belle Starr (Pamela Reed).

Jesse vows to form an even better gang. That means bringing in Bob and Charlie Ford. The Fords, however, are working with the Pinkerton agent, who agrees to pay the brothers $15,000 if they can capture or kill Jesse.

At Jesse's home, Jesse is talking to the Fords when he notices a sampler, a wedding-day present from his mother, hanging crooked on the wall. He goes to straighten it, and while his back is turned, Bob Ford draws his revolver, says, "I shot Jesse James," with a grin, and kills the outlaw.

Frank James surrenders to the Pinkerton agent, asking for one thing: He gets to bury his brother ... or he'll kill the detective. Handcuffed, riding in a box car with a coffin and the Pinkerton agent, Frank James rides the rails to Kearney to his brother's funeral.

The History

Although *The Long Riders* apparently takes place over a period of eleven years, there really is no sense of the passage of time other than the fact that Jesse grows a beard on one of his long absences from his wife. (In actuality, Jesse usually left his family only when he was conducting, ahem, business.)

Clell Miller was a part of the gang as early as the robbery of the Obocock Brothers Bank in Corydon, Iowa, on June 3, 1871. Yet only four bandits — presumably the James brothers, Cole Younger and Clell Miller — pulled that job.[28]

Ed Miller didn't join up with Jesse until, apparently, the Glendale, Missouri, train robbery of October 8, 1879 — well after the Northfield fiasco. He definitely knew the brothers before then, however, and had been arrested in August 1874 and questioned, though he did not cooperate (as depicted in the movie). Of course, Jesse's mother had encouraged Miller and the other men arrested to clam up: "They're just taking you down there to pump you; keep your mouths shut and don't tell anything you don't know," she told Miller and the others.[29]

The script accurately captures Jesse's contempt for Ed Miller, although it misses out on a potentially great scene by having Jesse murder Miller, which he apparently did in the summer of 1881.[30] Jesse beats Miller in the movie for shooting innocent people, but the real Jesse had no qualms about murder. "Along their way," historian Robert Barr Smith writes of the James-Younger Gang, "they left some twelve or fifteen dead men behind them."[31]

Did Cole Younger and Belle Starr love each other? Belle said so. Born Myra Maibelle Shirley in Carthage, Missouri, in 1848, Belle married Jim Reed, a former Confederate guerrilla, in 1866. Reed was killed in 1874 by a peace officer near Paris, Texas, and Belle romanced Cole's uncle, Bruce, and married him. That didn't take, she wound up with Sam Starr, and they ran a horse-theft ring and spent some time in prison. Sam was killed in 1886. Reportedly, Sam killed two of Belle's suitors, outlaws named John Middleton and Blue Duck. After Starr's death, Belle romanced an Indian named Jimmy July. All of those romances, but Belle told her daughter Pearl that Cole Younger was the "love" of her life. Pearl wound up running whorehouses; Belle was pretty much a horse thief before she was shot and killed in 1889.[32]

In the movie, Frank and Jesse's mother gives an interview in which she says her first husband died in California, which is true. She says she then married Reuben Samuel. She left out another husband. After Robert James's death in 1850, Zerelda married Benjamin Simms on September 30, 1852. Frank and Jesse didn't care much for him, and after a while their mother didn't care much for him either. Undoubtedly, neither Zerelda nor her sons were sorry to see him killed, by one account, in a horse accident on January 2, 1854. She married Samuel in 1855.[33]

It's difficult to say for certain when Bob and Jim Younger joined their brother and the James boys in a robbery — possibly in 1872 — but John Younger probably took part in the May 27, 1873, robbery of the Ste. Genevieve Savings Bank.[34]

Actor David Carradine said he researched Cole Younger and found that he "really wasn't cut out to be an outlaw. The times and peer pressure forced it onto him. I believe he was a reluctant member of the gang."[35] Maybe, but "reluctant" is probably a better description of Jim Younger. When Bob Younger was determined to join Jesse James on the Northfield raid, Cole Younger had telegraphed Jim in California: "Come home. Bob needs you." As historian John J. Koblas writes: "Jim Younger could always be counted upon to respond to his family's needs."[36]

The movie, however, depicts John Younger as frustrated because he never has been asked to ride with the gang. The movie also calls him a "cousin" to Cole, Jim and Bob (perhaps because there were only three Carradine brothers). In fact, John was their brother, the eleventh of Henry and Bursheba's fourteen children.[37]

The movie depicts a modestly accurate recreation of John Younger's death. On March 17, 1874, Jim and John Younger intercepted Pinkerton Captain Louis J. Lull and detective James Wright, who had been sent to Missouri after the Gads Hill train robbery, and Ed Daniels, the son of a Union veteran from Boston whose family had settled in Osceola, Missouri, after the war. The Youngers had been eating lunch at the home of the Snuffer family in St. Clair County, when the detectives and Wright rode up and asked for directions, saying they were cattle buyers.

The Youngers had hidden and watched; after the men left, John Younger wanted to go after them, saying the men were too well-armed and acted too suspicious to be cattlemen. Reluctantly, Jim Younger agreed.

Instead of the two parties by chance meeting each other as happens in the movie, the Youngers galloped after the three men. Wright saw them coming and spurred his horse into a gallop to flee the scene. Jim Younger yelled at him to stop. Wright didn't. A shot took off Wright's hat, but he didn't slow down.

Lull and Daniels, however, stopped. Bad mistake.

Pointing a shotgun at the two men, John Younger asked if they were detectives, and, if not, why they were armed so heavily. Focusing on Daniels, the two brothers didn't notice Lull draw a Smith & Wesson pistol. The detective shot John Younger in the neck, and spurred his horse down the road. John Younger managed to wound Lull in the arm and shoulder. When Daniels tried to escape, Jim Younger dropped him from the saddle with a bullet through the neck.

A low branch knocked Lull from the saddle, and when John Younger, still alive and still mounted, caught up with him, he put a bullet in the detective's chest. Before he could ride back to Jim, he fell off the horse, dead.

Daniels was also dead. Jim Younger presumed that Lull was dead, but, in fact, he wasn't. Eventually, Lull was transported to the Roscoe House, where a doctor said the detective would live. Instead, Lull died a few days later.[38]

Another fairly accurate depiction is the January 15, 1874, robbery of the stagecoach on the road between Malvern and Hot Springs, Arkansas. Five men — possibly Frank, Jesse, Cole, one of Cole's brothers and gang member Arthur McCoy — stopped the stagecoach at roughly 3:30 P.M. The passengers were told to get out with their hands up, and the leader of the gang took their money, jewelry and watches. One of the passengers was T.A. Burbank, a former governor of Dakota Territory. He handed over a gold watch, a diamond pin and $840. Another passenger was G.R. Crump (not the movie's George Arthur) of Memphis, Tennessee. He gave up his watch and $40 to $45.

One of the outlaws, believed to have been Cole Younger, then asked if any of the passengers had served in the Confederate army. When Crump said he had, the outlaw returned his money and watch, telling him that "they didn't want to rob Confederate soldiers; that the northern men had driven them to outlawry and they intended to make them pay for it." Another passenger, suffering from rheumatism, could not leave the stagecoach and was not bothered.

Other passengers didn't fare so well. When Burbank asked for his private papers to be returned, the leader of the gang said, "Boys, I believe he is a detective — shoot him!" Three pistols were immediately trained on the former governor, but the leader stopped the men from firing and returned the papers. When a man from Massachusetts said he was from St.

Louis, his Northern accent gave him away, and the bandit armed with a shotgun said, "I'll bet I can shoot his hat off, without touching a hair of his head." But the bandit didn't try it.

Reported the *Arkansas Daily Gazette*: "All of [the robbers] appeared to be jolly fellows and enjoyed the fun very much."[39]

On the other hand, the Northfield raid has little regard for history. In the movie, Clell Miller says he checked out the bank. The raid was likely the idea of Bill Chadwell, aka Bill Stiles, a native of Wright County, Minnesota, who had reportedly returned to his home state a year before the raid.[40] Chadwell and Pitts had been with the gang apparently since the 1873 train robbery at Adair, Iowa, which might have been a reluctant Jim Younger's first job.[41]

The movie has Chadwell and Charlie Pitts dying on the streets of Northfield. That's half right. Chadwell was killed, but Pitts made it as far as Hanska Slough, where he died in a shootout with the posse from Madeila. Clell Miller was the other bandit killed in Northfield.[42]

Two bankers are killed in the movie. Only Heywood was killed (by Jesse or, more likely, Frank, and not Clell Miller as shown in the movie). Alonzo Bunker was shot in the shoulder while fleeing the bank, but survived.[43]

Most definitely, the Pinkertons had not warned the citizens of Northfield that the James-Younger Gang might try to rob the bank, and the outlaws' desperate escape did not involve riding horses through plate-glass windows, though Jim Younger was shot through the jaw (at Hanska Slough, however, not in Northfield).[44] Townsmen noticed the strangers and grew suspicious when they rode into town. After Francis Howard saw the first three horsemen cross the bridge, he told Elias Stacy, "Stacy, those gentlemen will bear watching." When J.S. Allen tried to enter the bank, Clell Miller tried to stop him. Allen broke free, yelling, "Get your guns, boys. They are robbing the bank."[45]

The movie shows the outlaws traveling to Minnesota by train, which could be accurate, though accounts of their transportation method range from horseback to wagon to locomotive. They probably went to Minnesota in separate bands, not on one train as shown in the film.[46] The movie also has the outlaws, with the exception of Jesse, visiting a Missouri brothel before heading north. Possibly. They reportedly did hang out in one in St. Paul after arriving in Minnesota.[47]

The movie does accurately capture the tension between Cole and Jesse. Cole Younger and his brothers never implicated Frank or Jesse in the robbery. When Rice County Sheriff Ara Barton informed Cole that he might get a lesser sentence if he identified the slayer of Heywood, Cole wrote him a note, which read: "Be true to your friends if the Heavens fall."[48]

The Players

"I was filled with mixed emotions about playing Bob Ford," Nicholas Guest said. "Playing the role of a man responsible for killing a folk hero was not too easy. It took a lot of mental conditioning. It helped to know that John Carradine played the same role in 1939. I've taken a bit of kidding from his sons, David, Keith and Robert.... Yet I know that [by] playing a villain in films your career is helped and that made pulling that trigger a bit easier."[49]

For seven years, James and Stacy Keach — the film's executive producers — struggled to see their dream of telling the James-Younger Gang's story reach the screen. "Studios were shy of getting involved in a western-type project," James Keach said.[50]

Probably a key selling point came when brother actors signed on to play brothers. David (*Bound for Glory, Kung Fu*), Kevin (*Nashville, McCabe and Mrs. Miller*) and Robert Carradine (*The Cowboys, Coming Home*) played Cole, Jim and Bob Younger. James (*Comes a Horseman, FM*) and Stacy (*Doc, Fat City*) played Jesse and Frank James. Dennis (*Breaking Away, I Never Promised You a Rose Garden*) and Randy Quaid (*The Last Picture Show, The Last Detail*) played Ed and Clell Miller. And Christopher (*Girl Friends, Death Wish*—before finding a niche for his comic *faux* documentaries like *Best of Show*) and Nicholas Guest (*The Bell Jar*) played Charlie and Bob Ford.

"What's more logical than to have brothers playing brothers?" director Walter Hill said. "It's a perfect cast of form following function."[51]

Nicholas Guest watched as many old films as he could find that showed Jesse's death at the hands of Bob Ford.

Director and actors went out to re-imagine the story of the outlaws, and make a movie without the Western clichés. "Our film doesn't dwell on the Robin Hood mystique of the legend," James Keach said. "Instead we explore the interactions between the gang members, their relationships with friends and family."[52]

Added his brother: "You won't see any western film clichés in *The Long Riders*. For although we have mixed some fiction with fact in telling the story of this legendary band of outlaws, none of them comes off larger than life."[53]

Analysis

"What most critics fail to realize is that a movie is about a filmmaker's vision," director Walter Hill said.[54]

Hill often had a bleak but definitely cinematic vision. Perhaps best known for *48HRS.* (1982), he entered the movie business as an assistant director and writer, taking the director's chair for the first time for the brutal *Hard Times* (1975). *The Long Riders* was his first Western, but he has returned to the genre with *Geronimo: An American Legend* (1993) and *Wild Bill* (1995) on the big screen and a 2004 episode of HBO's series *Deadwood*—for which he won an Emmy as director — and the American Movie Classics miniseries *Broken Trail* (2006). Then again, as Hill points out, "All movies are Westerns."[55]

Hill had a wonderful vision of the James and Younger gang, and what helped it tremendously was the period music composed and arranged by Ry Cooder. Cooder had made a name for himself primarily as a slide guitarist in the late 1960s and as a highly regarded session player. He was credited with the guitar intro to the Rolling Stones' *Honky Tonk Woman*, but also released solo albums, including *Paradise and Lunch* (1974) which blended blues, gospel and Tex-Mex sounds. *The Long Riders* marked his first film composing; he followed with *Southern Comfort* (1981), *The Border* (1982), *Paris, Texas* (1984), *Geronimo: An American Legend* (1993), *Primary Colors* (1998) and many others. "Music is a treasure hunt," he told the *Christian Science Monitor* in 1999. "You dig and dig and sometimes you find something."[56]

He had excellent help from several musicians (Mitch Greenhill, Bill Bryson and Tom

Sauber earning credits for their on-screen performances). Warner Bros. Records released the soundtrack on album and tapes. Avon Books released a movie tie-in paperback novel adapted by screenwriter Steven Phillip Smith.[57]

"Just when everyone thought the Western was washed up as a movie genre, along comes Walter Hill's *The Long Riders* to remind us that applying such notions as 'dead' or 'alive' to types of movies is just plain silly," film critic Gene Siskel wrote for the *Chicago Tribune*.[58]

Filmed in Georgia, Texas, Northern California and at the Burbank Studios, *The Long Riders* had a wonderful feel and look to it. But it was more of a gimmick film — brothers playing brothers — moving from vignette to vignette to vignette with no sense of time's passage. And it really needed a more commanding presence than James Keach as Jesse James.

The Northfield robbery became a re-imagining of Sam Peckinpah's *The Wild Bunch*.

Certainly, Hollywood had come a long way from *Jesse James* (1939) and *Jesse James Rides Again* (1947), but as history and as movie entertainment, *The Long Riders* just didn't quite pull things off.

* * *

Washington Post (May 16, 1980): "*The Long Riders* appears to be a perfectly realized movie. An intelligent, unsentimental distillation of the decline and dissolution of the James Younger gang, it boasts beautifully modulated direction by Walter Hill, effective performances, and evocative period flavor in both externals and essentials, notably the depiction of the James Brothers, the Younger Brothers and their outlaw associates as an integral, albeit criminal, part of the rural American society of a particular time and place."

American Outlaws

(Warner Brothers, August 2001, 94 minutes)

CREDITS: *Director:* Les Mayfield; *Producer:* James G. Robinson; *Screenplay:* Roderick Taylor, John Rogers.
CAST: Colin Farrell (Jesse James); Scot Caan (Cole Younger); Ali Larter (Zerelda "Zee" Mimms); Gabriel Macht (Frank James); Gregory Smith (Jim Younger); Harris Yulin (Thaddeus Rains); Kathy Bates (Ma James); Timothy Dalton (Allan Pinkerton); Will McCormack (Bob Younger); Ronny Cox (Doc Mimms); Terry O'Quinn (Rollin H. Parker); Nathaniel Arcand (Comanche Tom); Ty O'Neal (Clell Miller); Joe Stevens (Loni Packwood); Barry Tubb (Captain Malcolm).

Synopsis

Four years of war have transformed a bunch of young Missouri farm boys into hardened, seasoned Confederate guerrilla warriors; they return to their homes near Liberty, Missouri (now under Federal rule), defeated, but not discouraged. "[N]one of them seem bothered by the fact that the South has just lost the war," the *New York Times* observed.[59]

Peace for Frank and Jesse James and the Younger brothers is short-lived, because here comes Rock Island Railroad man Rollin H. Parker, who works for railroad president Thaddeus Rains. The railroad is attempting to buy farms at ridiculously low prices as the

Top: Ma James (Kathy Bates) is glad to have her sons (Gabriel Macht and Colin Farrell) home in *American Outlaws* (2001). *Above:* Scott Caan was Cole Younger and Colin Farrell Jesse James in *American Outlaws* (2001).

railroad moves west. Rains is a powerful man, too. He has hired Allan Pinkerton, who formed the Secret Service during the war, to enforce the will of the railroad on poor Missouri farmers.

Frank, Jesse and their mother refuse to sell. Ma James is all for killing the railroad men. "The Lord says we can bury 'em out back in the orchard," she announces after a moment of prayer. "No one will ever find 'em." But the boys decide to organize other farmers to stop the railroad. Hotheaded Cole Younger, however, gets himself arrested and is sentenced to hang. Thus, Jesse leads a gang of young men — Bob and Jim Younger, Clell Miller, Loni Packwood, Comanche Tom and Frank James — to prevent the necktie party.

Cole is saved, but Jesse is badly wounded by Pinkerton, who gets run over by Jesse's horse. Jesse is brought to the home of Doc Mimms. It's also the home of Doc's beautiful daughter Zee.

The Army leaves Liberty, but that lets the railroad operate with impunity. Railroad men burn down much of the Younger farm, then blow up the James family home. Ma James dies in the arms of her boys.

Cole manages to get a list of banks that have railroad money, and the gang begins a war against the Rock Island. Jesse wants the gang to be called the James Gang, but bows to Cole's wishes for the James-Younger Gang. Later, when it's pointed out that there are three Younger brothers and only two James brothers, Cole suggests it should be the Younger-James Gang, but brother Bob argues against it. "Well, say we burst into a bank and we go, 'We're the Younger-James gang!' Now people are gonna be thinkin,' 'The younger James gang? Is there an older James gang? How come we never heard of the older James gang?' So people are tryin' to figure that out instead of raisin' their arms."

Crime is pretty much fun and games for the boys, but the Rock Island isn't amused. Pinkerton tells his employers: "My professional opinion is that you've managed to piss off the wrong bunch of farm boys this time."

As the boys continue robbing banks and trains, Rains insists Pinkerton bring those outlaws to justice, but the detective knows it won't be easy. "If I were to design the perfect outlaw band, this gang is what I would create."

Pinkerton sets up a trap, and the outlaws are ambushed while trying to rob a bank; Loni Packwood and Jim Younger are killed. Jesse decides to marry Zee and quit his outlaw ways. On their honeymoon, however, Jesse is captured by Pinkerton.

Rains has managed to get Jesse's trial set in Washington — where Jesse will most certainly be convicted — and Jesse is chained in a railroad car. The train heads east, but Jesse escapes, killing numerous guards before finding himself surrounded on the top of one of the passenger cars. At that moment, the James-Younger Gang arrives. Zee fires a cannon, which stops the train. The railroad men are defeated, Parker is killed, and Jesse lets Rains know that he can kill him at any time.

Pinkerton tells Jesse, "The railroad has no business in Tennessee. Therefore I have no interest in the state of Tennessee."

Jesse takes the hint. He rides off with Zee to start a new life in Tennessee.

The History

Producer James G. Robinson said that *American Outlaws* "is loosely based on the *story* of this real person."[60]

"*Loosely*" is stretching things.

Actor Colin Farrell put it better: "*American Outlaws* is very unconfined about being historically correct, or by having to try to be historically correct. This is a completely romanticized version of what went on back in the day."[61]

The movie opens during the Civil War, with Bob Younger serving in the guerrillas.

Jim Younger is the "kid." Actually, Bob Younger was the last-born son of Henry and Bursheba Younger. Jim was older, and it was Jim who had fought in the Civil War with Cole.[62]

Ma James wasn't living alone in the cabin with Frank and Jesse, and she wasn't killed when Pinkerton operatives raided the home in 1875. She outlived Jesse by decades, dying on February 10, 1911, shortly after visiting Frank in Oklahoma.[63]

Jim Younger wasn't killed during a bank robbery attempt. He spent twenty-five years in prison in Stillwater, Minnesota, and killed himself on October 19, 1902. He was fifty-four.[64]

About the only connections Jesse James had with the Chicago, Rock Island, and Pacific Railroad were a couple of robberies: 1873 near Adair, Iowa, the James-Younger Gang's first train robbery; and 1881 near Winston, Missouri. The railroad didn't really pursue the outlaws after the 1873 heist, but offered a reward, began putting armed guards on its trains, "and let it go at that." Yet railroad officials were concerned after the Winston robbery. Missouri Governor Thomas Crittenden even met with railroad brass in St. Louis on July 25, 1881, and a Chicago and Alton Railroad representative said he had heard a man in New York say that he would "be d-d if he'd pass through the state of Missouri. He'd go 500 miles around the state in case he had occasion to reach the other side of it."[65]

There has never been a Rock Island president named Rains. At the time this movie is set, the president would have been Charles W. Durant (the company president 1863 to 1866) or John F. Tracy (1866 to 1877).[66]

It wasn't a railroad robbery that began the Pinkerton National Detective Agency's pursuit of the James-Younger Gang. After the outlaws robbed the Obocock Brothers Bank in Corydon, Iowa, on June 3, 1871, the bank hired the agency to catch the bandits. Allan Pinkerton didn't go himself, however. He sent his son, Robert.[67]

One fact that is loosely right is when a newspaper publishes an account of one of the gang's robberies, reputedly written by Jesse himself. On January 31, 1874, when the outlaws robbed a train at Gads Hill, Missouri, one of the bandits handed engineer William Wetton or one of the passengers a press release before leaving, instructing that the report be telegraphed to the *St. Louis Dispatch*. It read:

> The most daring robbery on record. The southbound train on the Iron Mountain Railroad was robbed here this evening by five heavily armed men, and robbed of— dollars. The robbers arrived at the station a few minutes before the arrival of the train, and arrested the Agent, put him under guard, and then threw the train on the switch. The robbers are all large men, none of them under six feet tall. They were all masked, and started in a southerly direction after they had robbed the train, all mounted on fine blooded horses. There is a hell of excitement in this part of the country.[68]

The Players

James G. Robinson, chairman and chief executive officer of Morgan Creek Productions, wanted to make a Western aimed at the younger moviegoing public. He envisioned an "exciting and fun" movie.[69]

There was precedent. In 1988, *Young Guns*, a retelling of the Billy the Kid story with young "Brat Pat" actors Emilio Estevez, Kiefer Sutherland, Lou Diamond Phillips and Charlie Sheen, had grossed more than $44 million in the United States, prompting a sequel, *Young Guns II* (1990).[70]

"The James Gang is kind of like a rock and roll band out on the road on their first tour together," executive producer Jonathan Zimbert said. "This is something today's audience can relate to."[71]

Oh, brother.

Les Mayfield, whose first feature film, the comedy *Encino Man* (1992), had been a sleeper hit, was brought in to direct. Born in Albuquerque, New Mexico, Mayfield was a 1982 graduate of the University of Southern California's School of Cinema, and, really, hadn't directed anything decent — *Miracle on 34th Street* (1994), *Flubber* (1997), *Blue Streak* (1999) — since *Encino Man*. Mayfield said he grew up on Westerns, but what attracted him to the project was that the film might reinvent the genre. "We've put a new spin on an old tradition," he said.[72]

Dublin, Ireland's Colin Farrell was hired to play Jesse. He wasn't well-known to American audiences, but was pulling down more than $1 million per film. Although he had managed to shed much of his Irish brogue while preparing for *Tigerland* (2000), Farrell's selection left skeptics shaking their heads. "[A] lot of people thought we were out of our heads," Mayfield said.[73]

"If I was a 25-year-old American actor, would I be p****d off?" Farrell said. "I'd kind of be going, 'For f***'s sake, why can't we look in our own back garden?' I could understand that, I suppose. But, although I'm not aware of an Irish folk icon being played by an American, Tom Cruise did the movie *Far and Away*, Chris O'Donnell did *Circle of Friends* and Brad Pitt did *Devil's Own*. These were all big parts in big films that could have been played by Irish actors."[74]

Said Mayfield: "The idea of an Irish person playing Jesse James didn't seem right until I met Colin. Then I couldn't think of anyone else I'd rather have as the star of the movie. He personifies the spirit of the gentleman outlaw."[75]

Well, that's debatable. Farrell was good-looking, but unconvincing as a young Jesse James. He was perhaps not as wooden as Robert Wagner (1957's *The True Story of Jesse James*), but nowhere near as strong as Ray Stricklyn (1960's *Young Jesse James*).

Scott Caan, the son of actor James Caan, took on the part of Cole Younger. Caan had starred in *Enemy of the State* (1998), *Varsity Blues* (1999) and *Gone in Sixty Seconds* (2000). "When I heard they were making this movie, I wanted to be part of it," he said.[76]

Caan, however, preferred theater over film. The night after *American Outlaws* premiered in Los Angeles, Caan performed in a small North Hollywood theater in a play he had written titled *Almost Love*. That one grossed a mere $24; Caan laughingly said, "And that's split four ways."[77]

Caan's *Varsity Blues* co-star, Ali Larter, got the role of Zee Mimms. "At least five guys and one girl ... that's rough," Mayfield said. "But Ali stood up to them every day. She's feminine, but she's also very strong."[78] Added Farrell: "Well, she's got a bit of testosterone of her own! She can pack a punch." Farrell added, of course, that Larter never hit him, "but I think she would!"[79]

The best performance came from Welshman Timothy Dalton as Allan Pinkerton. Dalton, a Shakesperean-trained actor who had played James Bond in *The Living Daylights* (1987) and *Licence to Kill* (1989), researched Pinkerton. "I found a wonderful photograph of him with a gaudy checkered suit, in really bad taste I would say, and wearing a full grizzly beard and I thought 'That's my man.' I love the hat he wore, so I tried to copy that kind of image. He looked mad as a snake."[80]

Top: Jesse (Colin Farrell) has a lighter moment with his older brother Frank (Gabriel Macht) in *American Outlaws* (2001). *Above:* Alan Pinkerton (Timothy Dalton) thinks he has figured out a way to end the James-Younger Gang's crime wave in *American Outlaws* (2001).

Kathy Bates, an Academy Award winner for *Misery* (1990), had a cameo as Ma James, and impressed director and cast with her professional approach.

A month before filming began, much of the cast was brought in for "cowboy camp" hear Los Angeles for lessons in horseback riding, roping and shooting. It wasn't really a camp, Farrell said. "We hung out with a lot of cowboys, and drank a lot of bottles of Coors Light. And rode horses, and got taught how to ride. And we listened to the cowboys telling stories."[81]

Filming began July 17, 2000, near Austin in Wimberley, Texas, where a six-acre, back-lot-style Western town had been constructed. During the movie's sixty-five-day shoot, temperatures reached triple digits more than forty days. "It was so hot my hair extensions started to melt," said Canadian Nathaniel Arcand, who played Comanche Tom.[82]

Filming was also done at the Texas State Railroad Historical Park near Palestine, and at La Villita Plaza in San Antonio. The beach in St. Petersburg, Florida, doubled for Key West, where Jesse and Zee honeymoon. The steamboat scene was actually stock footage from Warner Brothers' *Maverick* (1994).[83]

The opening scene of a Civil War battle required up to 175 re-enactors every day. Most of them came from Texas, Oklahoma, Missouri and Indiana. That scene also had Jesse sticking the reins in his teeth and firing revolvers in both hands as he charges the Union forces.

"Some of that, I was actually on the back of a truck, sitting on a frigging saddle!" Farrell said. "You have no idea how stupid I felt."[84]

Filming was completed in early October, and the movie premiered on August 14, 2001. By October 21 the movie (budgeted at an estimated $35 million) had grossed less than $14 million.[85] It certainly would not be another *Young Guns*.

Analysis

Critics were united on this one:

Boxoffice: "*American Outlaws* is a western so devoid of a narrative, it plays like a prolonged version of the Wild West stunt show at Knott's Berry Farm."[86]

Entertainment Weekly: "...bogusly wholesome six-gun dud."[87]

(Naperville, Illinois) *Sun*: "You've not only seen this movie before — chances are you've already fallen asleep during it."[88]

New York Times: "*American Outlaws* may be simple, but it's also simple-minded...."[89]

San Francisco Chronicle: "This plot leaves ample room for viewers to sweat the small stuff, like whether Trevor Nunn's score is more Marines ad or deodorant commercial."[90]

Financially, critically and historically, *American Outlaws* was a disaster, an insipid retelling of the Jesse James legend, paling in comparison to the movie it wanted to mimic (*Young Guns*).

Young Guns wasn't a great movie, not even a great Western. But it had some charm — Emilio Estevez was convincing as a psychotic Billy the Kid — and a small bit of actual history. *American Outlaws* lacked charm, and was completely miscast. With the exception of Dalton, most actors seemed lost in their roles, as if they took their jobs just for a paycheck.

A dismal failure, *American Outlaws* could well be the worst movie about Jesse ever made.

* * *

Chicago Sun–Times (August 17, 2001): "For years there have been reports of the death of the Western. Now comes *American Outlaws*, proof that even the B Western is dead. It only wants to be a bad movie, and fails.... What happened to the rough-hewn American intelligence that gave us the Westerns of Ford, Hawks and Peckinpah? When did cowboys become teen pop idols?"

The Assassination of Jesse James by the Coward Robert Ford

(Warner Brothers, September 2007, 160 minutes)

CREDITS: *Director-Screenplay:* Andrew Dominik; *Producers:* Jules Daly, David Valdes, Dede Gardner, Brad Pitt, Ridley Scott.
CAST: Brad Pitt (Jesse James); Casey Affleck (Robert Ford); Sam Shepard (Frank James); Mary-Louise Parker (Zee James); Jeremy Renner (Wood Hite); Paul Schneider (Dick Liddil); Sam Rockwell (Charley Ford); Zooey Deschanel (Dorothy Evans); Pat Healy (Wilbur Ford); Ted Levine (Sheriff James Timberlake); Garret Dillahunt (Ed Miller); Michael Parks (Henry Craig); Brooklynn Proulx (Mary James); Kailin See (Sarah Hite); Joel Mcnichol (Express Messenger); Dustin Bollinger (Tim James); Joel Duncan (Deputy); Laryssa Yanchak (Ella Mae Waterson); Jesse Frechette (Albert Ford); Alison Elliott (Martha Bolton); James Carville (Governor Crittenden).

Synopsis

On September 7, 1881, as James Gang members gather in the Missouri woods to rob a train at Blue Cut, nineteen-year-old Robert "Bob" Ford tries to talk Frank James into letting him take part in the crime. "I honestly believe I'm destined for great things, Mr. James," he says.

Bob, whose older brother Charley has been recruited by the outlaws, hero-worships Jesse James to the point of obsession — and he gives Frank "the willies." Jesse, however, doesn't care who rides with him, and lets Bob join the gang.

An off-screen narrator (Hugh Ross) tells us that the gang has been robbing trains, banks and stagecoaches since 1867, but now, with all the original members except the James brothers either dead or in prison, the outlaws have been forced to fill their ranks with "petty thieves and country rubes."

In addition to the Fords, the gang includes Wood Hite, one of Jesse's cousins (a fact Hite is always holding over his colleagues), bumpkin Ed Miller, and poetry-spouting Dick Liddil.

The train is stopped and robbed, although the outlaws don't make much of a haul. Frank has had enough of Jesse and the gang — "My brother and me are hardly on speaking terms these days," Jesse tells Bob — and Frank finally leaves. The rest of the outlaws split up. Jesse keeps Bob around until Bob gets on Jesse's nerves. "I can't figure you out," Jesse tells him. "You want to be like me or you want to be me?"

Jesse sends Bob packing. Bob appears at the home of his sister Martha Bolton, who is renting rooms to Hite and Liddil. The latter two are at odds with each other, and that relationship is tested even more when the two travel to Kentucky, where Liddil has an affair with the beautiful young wife of Hite's father.

Four of the Blue Cut robbers have been arrested, and Jesse has become increasingly paranoid. He suffers tremendous mood swings, and is unpredictable. That paranoia causes him to kill Ed Miller, whom he suspects of betrayal. After Liddil and Hite have returned from Kentucky, Jesse goes searching for Jim Cummins, a former guerrilla who Jesse thinks

Writer-director Andrew Dominik talks with Brad Pitt during filming of *The Assassination of Jesse James by the Coward Robert Ford* (2007).

is out to get him. Bringing Liddil with him, Jesse arrives at the farm where Cummins lives. Cummins isn't there, and Jesse ruthlessly beats Albert, the teenage cousin of Bob and Charley. Afterward, Jesse sobs uncontrollably before riding away.

Back at Martha Bolton's home, Hite tries to kill Liddil. The two shoot each other while Bob watches nervously. With Liddil wounded in the leg and out of bullets, Hite puts his gun against Liddil's forehead, but before he can pull the trigger, Bob — in a spontaneous act — kills Hite.

If Jesse finds out that his cousin has been murdered, the Ford brothers and Liddil know, their lives will be short.

Jesse arrives, looking for one or two new recruits for his gang. After teasing Bob, he takes only Charley. As Bob becomes more and more disillusioned with his hero, he walks into a Kansas City police station and makes a pact with the law. First, he leads the authorities to Liddil, who is captured and arrested. Then he meets Governor Crittenden, who is determined to put the James Gang out of business. It's not just the reward Bob's after. "I've been a nobody all my life...." he says. "And ever since I can remember it, Jesse James has been as big as a tree."

Bob, brought into the gang, lives in the same house in St. Joseph with the James family and Charley Ford. The Ford brothers are nervous, waiting for Jesse to kill them, thinking he must suspect them of working with the law or killing Hite. Jesse's paranoia worsens, but he tries to make up for things by presenting Bob with a new Smith & Wesson revolver.

On April 3, 1882, Jesse reads in a newspaper about Liddil's arrest and confession. Jesse uncharacteristically takes off his revolvers and begins dusting a picture on the wall. He sees Bob's reflection in the picture as Bob draws the Smith & Wesson, but makes no attempt to defend himself. A bullet through the brain kills Jesse. As his wife Zee wails over his bloody body, the boys run down the street and telegraph authorities. Jesse's death is big news. A photograph of his corpse sells for $2 a print.

A year later, Bob and Charley are reenacting the death of Jesse James in a New York theater, Bob playing himself, Charley playing Jesse. He will reenact his act of treachery some 800 times. Charley becomes more despondent, begins to act more and more like Jesse on the stage, and audiences tire of Bob's betrayal.

Cries of "Murderer! Cur! Coward!" come from the audience, and Bob defends his actions with violence. He lands in jail. Eventually, Charley kills himself, and Bob winds up in Creede, Colorado, in 1892. "Why did you kill him?" a dancer he has befriended, Ella Mae Waterson, asks.

"He was going to kill me," he says, then answers truthfully that what he expected after killing Jesse was "applause. I was only twenty years old then, couldn't see how it would look to people. I was surprised by what happened. They didn't applaud."

Edward O'Kelley, longing for glory and revenge, enters Bob's saloon armed with a shotgun.

"There would be no eulogies for Bob," the narrator says. "No photographs of his body would be sold in sundry stores. No people would crowd the streets in the rain to see his funeral cortege...."

"Hello, Bob," O'Kelley says, and as Bob turns to face his assassin, the narrator tells us: "The shotgun would ignite, and Ella Mae would scream, but Robert Ford would only lay on the floor and look at the ceiling, the light going out of his eyes before he could find the right words."

The History

Based on Ron Hansen's powerful and well-researched literary novel, Andrew Dominik's screenplay remained faithful to the book (much of the narration is lifted directly from Hansen's text) and history.

There are some exceptions. At the beginning of the movie, we are told that the James Gang began its career in 1867. That leaves out the Liberty, Missouri, bank robbery of 1866, and that's all right. Nobody was ever convicted of that robbery, and some historians don't believe Jesse James was there. However, later in the movie, when Bob Ford is toying with the idea of visiting the victims of Jesse's crimes, George Wymore is mentioned. Wymore, a student at Liberty's William Jewell College, was an innocent bystander killed on the street during that holdup.[91]

I've found no documentation that says Dick Liddil was set up by Bob Ford, although that could have been the case. Around January 6, 1882, Sheriff James Timberlake led a posse to Martha Bolton's home. Liddil managed to escape capture and hid in a nearby field. With the law and possibly Jesse closing in on him, Liddil sent Bolton to Jefferson City, where she met Crittenden. On January 24, Liddil surrendered to Timberlake, agreeing — in order to avoid prosecution — to testify against Frank and Jesse.[92]

Ford did meet with Governor Crittenden on January 13, the night of the annual ball of the Craig Rifles. Ford and Liddil probably pointed law-enforcement officials to the Hite farm in Kentucky, because in early February, Clarence Hite was arrested there and returned to Missouri, where he pleaded guilty to the Winston train robbery.[93]

When Frank James leaves Jesse, the narrator says that Frank would be in Baltimore when he learned of Jesse's assassination. After the robbery of the Bank of Huntington, West Virginia, on September 6, 1875, Frank and Jesse did live in Baltimore with their families, but Frank was residing in Lynchburg, Virginia, when he first heard of Jesse's death.[94]

In the movie, before the Blue Cut robbery, Frank tells Jesse that the gang has a lot of timber to put on the tracks. The gang actually used rocks, and there weren't as many men in on the job — only six — as depicted in the film. Exactly who was there is uncertain, but Jesse and Frank James, Dick Liddil, Wood Hite and his brother Clarence, and Charles Ford, are suspected. Historian Carl W. Breihan said that Bob Ford and Jim Cummins were also there, but Breihan wasn't always trustworthy, and never documented his research.[95]

A group of young men from the area were arrested in connection with the crime. One of those even confessed, but William Wallace of Jackson County refused to prosecute. Nobody believed the boys were guilty.[96]

In the movie, Jesse wears a mask in the robbery; in reality, Jesse was the only bandit who *didn't* wear a mask. As he left the Pullman sleeper — only the second time the gang had robbed passengers — he said, "Goodbye. This is the last time you will ever see Jesse James."[97]

He lived up to his word. Jesse James never robbed another train.[98]

The Players

Ron Hansen's literary novel *The Assassination of Jesse James by the Coward Robert Ford* was published in 1983. "When I was starting to write the book, one of my colleagues said that the 19th century has really been influenced by two James families," Hansen said. "William and Henry James in the East, and Frank and Jesse James in the West. They shaped American consciousness.... I wanted to look at the intricacies between Robert Ford and Jesse James."[99]

It wasn't until 2004 that Dominik discovered the book while visiting a secondhand bookstore in Melbourne, Australia. "It knocked me out," Dominik said, and soon the property was optioned.[100]

Dominik, a New Zealand–born writer-director whose only movie had been the critically acclaimed *Chopper* (2000), and Brad Pitt had talked about working on a film together, and after reading the book and listening to Dominik, Pitt committed to the project.

Pitt had grown up in Missouri, the old stamping grounds of Jesse James. After drawing attention for a brief but star-making performance in *Thelma & Louise* (1991), Pitt followed with a string of successes, including *A River Runs Through It* (1992), *Legends of the Fall* (1994), *Se7en* (1995) and *Ocean's Eleven* (2001).

"The film picks up during the last year of his life, and he certainly was coming from a place of paranoia, most of it justified," Pitt said. "I'd argue that the paranoia consumed him and certainly was responsible for a lot of his erratic action."[101]

Regarding Jesse's death, Pitt said, "This is the thing that historians argue over ... that he had full knowledge of what Robert Ford or the Ford brothers were capable of and were after, and was taunting them and was going to take them out at a later time and kill them, and it was a bad gamble and a gamble he lost. The other argument is that he was unhinged, that he was weary of this life on the run and that it was actually a puppeteered suicide, unconscious or conscious."[102] Pitt said he filmed the scene both ways, "and let Andrew shape it out in the editing."[103]

Dominik discovered Casey Affleck while watching television with his girlfriend. "He looked like Bob Ford to me," Dominik said. "So I had Casey come in and read for the part. He was fantastic."[104] Affleck also appeared in movies with his older brother Ben Affleck, such as *Chasing Amy* (2007), *Good Will Hunting* (1997) and *200 Cigarettes* (1999), and in the Pitt–George Clooney comic-heist films *Ocean's Eleven* (2001) and *Ocean's Twelve* (2004).

"I thought Robert was kind of this kid who was uncomfortable in his own skin," Affleck said. "Playing him was a tricky balance. On one hand, this kid didn't know who he was, but he also felt like he was better than everyone else. He thinks if he can get close to Jesse, then at last Jesse will see what Robert is. But that doesn't happen, and he's crushed."[105]

The relationship between Bob Ford and Jesse James was a key in the film. "One of the

Casey Affleck received an Academy Award nomination for his performance in the supporting role of Robert Ford in *The Assassination of Jesse James by the Coward Robert Ford* (2007).

things I particularly like is how these characters struggle more with themselves than with each other," Dominik said. "Each is shaping a reality to suit his desires and anxieties, and they really do not connect with one another."[106]

The rest of the cast was filled with some incredible talent. Sam Shepard, a Pulitzer Prize–winning playwright who had been acting since the 1970s and earned an Oscar nomination for *The Right Stuff* (1983), played Frank James in what amounted to a cameo. Mary-Louise Parker, a Emmy and two-time Golden Globe–winning actress, played Jesse's wife. Her role might have been small, but her performance was outstanding. Sam Rockwell (Charley Ford), Jeremy Renner (Wood Hite), Garret Dillahunt (Ed Miller) and Paul Schneider (Dick Liddil) all nailed their parts.

"Honestly, I felt there were so many great people working on it," Affleck said. "I showed up on the set and felt like I had to rise to the occasion and be as good as I could be or I'd stick out like a sore thumb."[107]

The one odd bit of casting was putting Louisiana-born political consultant James Carville in the movie as Governor Crittenden. For a movie that strove to look and feel authentic, Carville's bald head and Louisiana accent stuck out like a sore thumb.

The movie was filmed from late August to early December 2005 in Canada (Alberta and Manitoba), and then Dominik and the studio began feuding over editing. Dominik's first cut came in at almost four hours, but he trimmed that to 160 minutes. Warner Brothers still didn't like it — but Pitt backed the director. Eventually, the studio went along with Dominik (or, rather, Pitt), and the movie opened in a limited release on September 23, 2007.

Reviews were mixed. The *Fresno Bee* said, "A bleached-out dreariness and lethargic pace drains this challenging film of much of its impact,"[108] while the *Detroit News* opined, "The one thing you're not supposed to do during a Western is doze off."[109]

Yet the *Chicago Tribune* called it "[t]he oddest major studio release of the year, and one of the most admirable,"[110] and *USA Today* said it "seamlessly melds a probing character essay with a lyrical Western epic."[111]

Without much of a push from Warner Brothers, it performed poorly at the box office. It did earn Affleck an Academy Award nomination as Best Supporting Actor. "…this movie really belongs to Casey Affleck," the *Washington Post* noted.[112]

Roger Deakins was also nominated for cinematography. "The movie has an almost hypnotic quality; its spare and often beautiful shots seem to sear themselves into the camera's lens," the *Seattle Times* reported.[113]

Dominik's screenplay won a Spur Award from Western Writers of America.

Most critics and viewers, however, either loved the movie, or hated it.

Analysis

For a movie lover or Jesse James buff, there is much to admire in *The Assassination of Jesse James by the Coward Robert Ford*. Affleck manages to steal the movie from Pitt with his chilling portrait of nerdy Bob Ford, and Roger Deakins's visuals turn this masterpiece into perhaps the best photographed Western since *She Wore a Yellow Ribbon* (1949).

Shepard and Parker, though underused, gave fine performances, and the supporting cast — especially Rockwell and Schneider — was excellent.

I would have liked to have seen a larger part for Shepard as Frank James, another actor instead of Carville as Crittenden, and more focus on the Ford brothers after Jesse's murder. Those misgivings aside, this is the best movie about Jesse James in both historical accuracy and entertainment terms.

That said, *The Assassination of Jesse James by the Coward Robert Ford* is more art film than Western, so it certainly won't appeal to all tastes. It's just too bad more people didn't see it.

* * *

New York Daily News (September 21, 2007): "The look and feel of the movie are as authentic as any Western since Robert Altman's *McCabe and Mrs. Miller*, and the performances by Pitt, as the contradictory James, and Affleck, as the troubled overachiever who finds infamy instead of fame, are dead-on. As is often the case, it took a foreign director — Dominic is an Aussie — to bring an aura of realism to an intrinsically American story. Good on ya, mate."

American Bandits: Frank and Jesse James
(Barnholtz Entertainment and Aro Entertainment, June 2010, 88 minutes)

CREDITS: *Director-Screenplay:* Fred Olen Ray; *Producers:* Fred Olen Ray, Kimberly A. Ray.

CAST: Peter Fonda (Marshal Kane); Tim Abell (Frank James); Jeffrey Combs (Ed Bass); George Stults (Jesse James); Michael Gaglio (Otis); Anthony Tyler Quinn (Burdette); Siri Baruc (Carrie); Laurie Eckstrom (Mary); Ted Monte (Tyler); Randy Mulkey (Jed); Reverend Simpson (Ian Patrick Williams); Doc Gable (Ron Harper); Christopher Weir (Cob); Peter Sherayko (Hank); Franc Ross (Harley); Patrick Gorman (Bartender).

Synopsis

The director of movies such as *Teenage Cavegirl* and *Tomb of the Werewolf* turns to a historical Western in a Jesse James movie that went straight to video and had little to do with actual history.

Sometime after the Civil War in an unnamed state or territory, Frank and Jesse James and three cohorts rob a federal paymaster, killing four Army soldiers in the process. Jesse's reckless — "Come on, Frank. I've always had a problem with authority," he yells before disobeying Frank's orders during the ambush — and Frank is cautious. The three other outlaws, led by Ed Bass, aren't trustworthy.

When a wounded soldier shoots Jesse in the shoulder (and is promptly shot to pieces), Frank tells the other members they will meet in four days at the ghost town of Gila Wells and split up the loot there. In the meantime, he has to get Jesse to a doctor. Ed Bass doesn't like this at all, but there's little he can do.

Frank brings Jesse to the church of the Reverend Simpson, a Southern sympathizer whose granddaughter, Mary, hates the Yankees almost as much as the James brothers do.

She gets the bullet out of Jesse's shoulder (Jesse screams during the surgery, but as soon as the bullet's out, he seems completely recovered). Believing that Jesse still needs a real doctor, Frank takes his brother to the nearest town.

Meanwhile, U.S. Marshal Kane suspects the James boys of robbing the $30,000 payroll and killing the guards. Kane's deputy, Burdette, is a good Union man but can sympathize with the defeated Rebels. "You're the man to bring them in," Kane tells him. "You think like they do." So Kane sends Burdette after the bandits. Alone. No posse. (Probably a budget issue.)

After examining Jesse, the town doctor suggests that Jesse rest a day or two before traveling on. Frank agrees and heads to Gila Wells, instructing Jesse to meet him there. After Burdette shows up at the Simpson church, Mary rides off to warn Jesse that a marshal is on his trail. (One would think that, after robbing a federal payroll, Jesse would know somebody would be coming after him.)

Over in Gila Wells, Frank is surprised to find the town isn't deserted. Four stagecoach travelers — a crazy old driver, a coward having second thoughts about marrying a pretty spinster, and a gambler on a long losing streak — have been left stranded by Kansas Jayhawkers. There might not be any lead or guns in town, but the bar's fully stocked. (I guess the Jayhawkers were good Kansas temperance men.) The coward, Jed, really wants Frank's horse so he can get away from having to marry Carrie. Naturally, Frank is soon smitten with Carrie.

Back in town, Jesse is falling for Mary.

After about forty minutes of sermons that defend the James boys, action returns to the movie — very briefly — when Burdette tracks down Jesse. "Am I wanted for anything?" Jesse asks. (Yeah, according to Marshal Kane, not only is Jesse wanted, he's wanted dead or alive.) Burdette's overconfident. He doesn't even have his gun drawn, and Jesse manages to wound him in the head before riding off to join Frank.

Back in Gila Wells, Frank agrees to let Jed have his horse, but the outlaw is more concerned for Carrie's welfare than her cowardly beau. Ah, but that's bad timing for Jed. He rides out of town after Ed Bass and the two other outlaws have arrived. Mistaking Jed for Frank, Ed kills the coward.

That sets up a showdown. Ed comes into town and gets the drop on Frank. But Jesse shows up and gets the drop on Ed. Only Ed's two colleagues have captured Carrie. The gambler, Tyler, sides with Ed. It's a stalemate. Ed sends his two pals out with Carrie to find the loot Frank has stashed away at an abandoned homestead.

Soon, guns are drawn. Tyler's killed. Jesse yells at Frank to rescue his girlfriend. Frank does, killing the two bad guys before they can harm Carrie. Jesse wounds Ed in the leg, but Ed manages to shoot Jesse. Before Ed can kill Jesse, however, Mary shows up with a rifle and puts a bullet in Ed's head.

Then Burdette arrives, getting the drop on Jesse. But Frank shows up to get the drop on Burdette. It's another stalemate. The brothers agree to give Burdette half the payroll (which he'll turn in), and the honor of having killed the Ed Bass gang. They're free to ride off with their true loves.

The History

It's pretty obvious listening to writer-producer-director Fred Olen Ray's comments on the DVD's audio track that he knew little about the true story of Jesse James. The brothers' father was not a doctor (he was a preacher, though their stepfather was a doctor) and Jesse James wasn't killed in North Carolina.

Yet Ray did some research. Frank James is depicted reading and quoting Shakespeare, and uses the alias Ben Woodson, all historically accurate. When Deputy Burdette tells Marshal Kane that the ex–Confederates can't vote or hold office, he's basically correct — in Missouri, at least. The state's 1865 Drake Constitution denied former Southern sympathizers the opportunity to vote, hold public office or be employed in any professional position.[114]

The movie isn't set in Missouri, however. The boys say they've been out of Missouri for a couple of weeks, and the setting of the movie is never identified. "I didn't want to get too tied down," Ray says in the audio commentary.[115] The movie was filmed in Canyon Country, California,[116] although there are stock images from Arizona and even Utah's Monument Valley.

The preferred six-shooter of the James boys (in the movie) is the 1875 Smith & Wesson Schofield .45. That might be true of Jesse, but Frank's weapon of choice was the 1875 Remington .44.[117]

Oh, and those love interests, Mary and Carrie? By 1875, Frank and Jesse were both married.[118]

The one payroll the James brothers robbed occurred near Muscle Shoals, Alabama, on March 11, 1881. They made off with only $5,240.18 — not $30,000 — and no one was killed. Army engineers (the payroll was for a crew working on a canal) did send one agent after the three road agents, presumed to be the James brothers and Bill Ryan. Like the movie's Deputy Marshal Burdette, the agent didn't capture Frank or Jesse, either.[119]

The Players

Fred Olen Ray has earned a reputation as a writer, director and producer of low-budget made-for-television and direct-to-video independent movies. Sometimes working under pseudonyms like Nichola Medina or Ed Raymond, Ray has turned out films with titles like *Bikini Chain Gang* and *Hollywood Chainsaw Hookers*— which you might expect from a guy who also is a professional wrestler, appearing under the name "Fabulous" Freddie Valentine. No stranger to Westerns, however, Ray directed (as Ed Raymond) *The Shooter* (1997), starring Randy Travis, Michael Dudikoff and William Smith. Some say *The Shooter* is Ray's best movie. Then again, how good does it have to be to be better than *Tarzeena: Jiggle in the Jungle?*[120]

With the exception of Jeffrey Combs (who has a great time as Ed Bass), most of the cast gives understated performances. Virginia-born Tim Abell, a former Army Ranger, is taciturn and menacing as Frank James. He can also pass for a brother of George Stults. The star of the TV series *7th Heaven* (2002–2007), Stults likely landed the role of Jesse because of an uncanny resemblance to Brad Pitt, who had played Jesse in *The Assassination of Jesse James by the Coward Robert Ford* (2007).

Easy Rider star Peter Fonda — son of Henry and brother of Jane — has enjoyed a mixed career, ranging from exceptional performances in exceptional movies such as *The Hired Hand* (1971) and *Ulee's Gold* (1997) to roles in some of the worst films ever committed to celluloid: *Open Season* (1974) and *The Cannonball Run* (1981). No stranger to B-films, having starred in campy drive-in hits such as *Dirty Mary Crazy Larry* (1974) and *Outlaw Blues*

(1977), Fonda appears in only three scenes in *American Bandits*, but dominates the DVD cover and got top billing in the closing credits. Wearing a scruffy beard — Fonda couldn't shave, Ray notes on the audio commentary, because of an accident resulting in stitches in his chin — Fonda was reserved as Marshal Kane.[121]

Kane's underling, Burdette, was equally underplayed by Anthony Tyler Quinn, whom Ray said he cast because Quinn resembles a young Lee Van Cleef.[122] Ray had directed Quinn in *Silent Venom* (2009). Indeed, many of the actors had previously worked with Ray, but suffice to say that the cast will never be mistaken for director John Ford's "Stock Company."

Analysis

An incredibly low-budget movie (you can count the horses on your hands), *American Bandits: Frank and Jesse James*— the title on the opening credits leaves out the surname — adds little to Jesse James film lore.

There's a lot of speechifying and little action. Tim Abell looks good in a Western — and might be the only actor in the production who could ride a horse — and Jeffrey Combs is fun to watch as Ed Bass. Actresses Siri Baruc and Laurie Eckstrom, however, are solidly wooden.

Where does this latest entry in Jesse James movies fit in? Well, it's not the worst and is leagues from the best, but might be the most boring Jesse James movie ever made.

* * *

www.justpressplay.net (May 2010): "...when you have *American Bandits* sharing shelf space with the likes of Andrew Dominik's haunting, lyrical elegy, *The Assassination of Jesse James by the Coward Robert Ford*, there is simply no reason to choose this version of the tale. Ever."

Chapter Nine

Euro Westerns, 1964–2009

"From 1963 to 1969," film historian Paul Simpson writes, "Italy made Westerns at such a rate that they manufactured the formula to death."[1]

Typically operating on a budget between $35 million and $50 million, and often filmed in Spain, Italy's "spaghetti Westerns" were often ultra-violent and short on plot. "No stories," writer-director Burt Kennedy once told legendary director John Ford, "just killing."[2]

The history of Italian Westerns dates to 1942, when *Una signora dell'ouest* was made. Although spaghetti Westerns featuring Wild Bill Hickok were popular in the 1950s, most Italian Westerns shied away from using historical characters in the 1960s. There were exceptions: actress Elsa Martinelli played Belle Starr in *Il mio corpo per un poker* (1968) and there are references to Confederate General Sibley's 1862 invasion of New Mexico Territory in *Il buono, il brutto, il cattivo,* better known in the United States as *The Good, the Bad and the Ugly* (1966).[3]

Jesse James showed up in at least two Italian Westerns in the 1960s, and made his way to France for 2009's *Lucky Luke*, the latter based on the 1983 comic book *Daisy Town*. Jesse almost made it into another French Western, *Un autre homme, une autre chance* (*Another Man, Another Chance*), but his scene didn't make the final edit.

Here's a brief look at Jesse James in the European Westerns that I could track down. There could be others.

Due mafiosi nel far west
(Also released as *Two Gangsters in the Wild West* and *Two Mafiamen in the Far West*)

(Fida Cinematografica, June 1964, 100 minutes)

CREDITS: *Director:* Giorgio Simonelli; *Producer:* Antonio Gentili; *Screenplay:* Marcello Ciorciolini, Giorgio Simonelli.

CAST: Franco Franchi (Franco Capone); Ciccio Ingrassia (Ciccio Capone); Fernando Sancho (Rio); Toni Di Mitri (Jesse James); Olimpia Cavalli (Calamity Jane).

Two Sicilian cousins, serving twenty years in prison for stealing mules, escape with the help of an American who sends them off to the West to find the gold mine that belonged to the Sicilians' grandfather.

In this comic Western, it seems that bandits killed the cousins' grandfather for the gold. Of course, the two Sicilians take over their mine, only to discover that Indians and outlaws might make keeping that mine difficult.

Solo contro tutti
(Also released as *Jesse James' Kid*; *One Against All*; *Son of Jesse James*; *A Man Alone*)
(Apolo Films, April 1965, 91 minutes)

CREDITS: *Director:* Antonio del Amo; *Assistant Producers:* Enrique F. Sagaseta, Adriano Merkel; *Screenplay:* Antonio del Amo, Pino Passalacqua.
CAST: Claudio Undari, billed as Robert Hundar (Bill James); Mercedes Alonso (Dorothy); Adrian Hoven (Allan); Raf Baldassarre (Bruce).

Jesse James's young son Bill (not Jesse Jr.) witnesses the murder of his father by Uncle Bob Ford. Twenty years later, he's tracking down his father's killer, now a wealthy rancher (going by the name Marshal) involved in a land-grabbing scheme.

Naturally, Bill James comes to the aid of a woman rancher, and is befriended by the ranch cook (who does his best, or worst, Edgar Buchanan impersonation). The movie borrows just about every cliché in the genre, not to mention other movies ranging from *Cimarron* (1931, 1960) to *Ben-Hur* (1925, 1959).

Belgian movie poster for the Italian Western *Son of Jesse James* (1965).

Un autre homme, une autre chance (Also released as *Another Man, Another Chance*)

(Les Films 13, September 1977, 130 minutes)

CREDITS: *Director-Screenplay:* Claude Lelouch; *Producers:* Georges Dancigers, Alexandre Mnouchkine.
CAST: James Caan (David Williams); Genevieve Bujold (Jeanne Leroy); Francis Huster (Francis Leroy); Susan Tyrrell (Debby/Alice); Jennifer Warren (Mary Williams); Richard Farnsworth (Stagecoach Driver).

In 1870 France, after Napoleon III has lost the Franco–Prussian war and left his country in ruin, Jeanne falls in love with a photographer, and the two head to America. Veterinarian David Williams lives nearby on a farm, and after a series of tragic events, David and Jeanne fall in love. Tony Crupi plays Billy the Kid. Christopher Lloyd plays Jesse James, but his scene wound up on the editing room floor. The French movie was filmed at Old Tucson Studios. Of director Claude Lelouch's overuse of hand-held cameras, critic Janet Maslin wrote, "The viewer is likely to feel seasick long before Miss Bujold makes her ocean voyage."[4]

Lucky Luke

(UGC YM, October 2009)

CREDITS: *Director:* James Huth; *Producers:* Said Ben Said, Yves Marmion, Sonja Shillito; *Screenplay:* James Huth, Sonja Shillito.
CAST: Melvil Poupaud (Jesse James); Jean Dujardin (Lucky Luke); Sylvie Testud (Calamity Jane); Alexandra Lamy (Belle); Michael Youn (Billy the Kid); Jean-Francois Balmer (Le gouverneur); Daniel Prévost (Pat Poker).

Lucky Luke can outdraw his own shadow, though he has never killed anyone. Now he's sent to return law and order to his hometown, Daisy Town, which is being run by the likes of Billy the Kid, Pat Poker, Calamity Jane and, yes, Jesse James.

Lucky falls in love with Belle, a saloon singer, along the way in this comedy Western that was originally filmed as an animated version in 1971.

CHAPTER TEN

Made-for-Television Movies, 1970–1999

Made-for-television movies have pretty much stayed clear of Jesse James, perhaps because of the oversaturation on the big screen.

Those that were made present a mixed bag, starting with traditional Western (*The Intruders*) and ending with fantasy Western (*Purgatory*). Jesse has made a cameo appearance in a movie about the Dalton brothers (*The Last Ride of the Dalton Gang*) and played a supporting role in the biopic of Belle Starr (*Belle Starr*), but, as of this writing, only two true made-for-TV biopics have been made about him.

The Intruders

(NBC, November 10, 1970, 100 minutes)

CREDITS: *Director:* William Graham; *Producer:* James Duff McAdams; Writer: Dean Riesner (from a story by William Lansford).

CAST: Don Murray (Sam Garrison); Edmond O'Brien (Col. William Bodeen); John Saxon (Billy Pye); Anne Francis (Leora Garrison); Gene Evans (Cole Younger); Edward Andrews (Elton Dykstra); Dean Stanton (Whit Dykstra); Shelly Novack (Theron Pardo); Stuart Margolin (Jesse James).

After the James-Younger Gang is put on the run after the disaster at Northfield, the residents of Madelia, Minnesota, fear the outlaws might be heading their way. They turn for protection to Colonel William Bodeen, a leading citizen, and the town marshal, Sam Garrison. There's just one problem: Garrison has lost his nerve. When Garrison deputizes his half-breed friend Billy Pye, that causes another clash — one that might prove even deadlier than the James-Younger Gang.

Although the movie claims to be "fact-based,"[1] there's little history to it. The real lawman of Madelia, Sheriff James Glispin, was a Civil War veteran who was known for solving disputes peacefully, but he definitely was no coward. He led the posse that killed Charlie Pitts and captured the Younger brothers. In 1880, he left Madelia, and later lived in California and Washington.[2]

Stuart Margolin, who would win two Emmy Awards playing the ex-con Angel in *The Rockford Files* (1974–79), is basically given a cameo as Jesse. The script is mostly predictable, with a few twists, but there's much to admire in this movie, too.

Ten. Made-for-Television Movies, 1970–1999

Don Murray helps John Saxon in a scene from *The Intruders*, a 1970 made-for-television movie set in Madelia after the James-Younger Gang's raid on Northfield (copyright 1983 Universal City Studios Inc.).

Murray does a good job in the lead role, and John Saxon is convincing as the half-breed (Saxon is Italian-American). There's a fine scene in which Sam Garrison blows his cool after the townsmen begin treating the captured Youngers as royalty.

I'm also a little curious about the name of actor Shelly Novack's character, Theron Pardo. Co-star Edmond O'Brien played a Theron Pardee in *Rio Conchos* (1964).

Not much history, but *The Intruders* is a pleasant way to kill a couple of hours.

The Last Ride of the Dalton Gang
(NBC, November 20, 1979, 146 minutes)

CREDITS: *Director:* Dan Curtis; *Producer:* Joseph Stern; *Writer:* Earl W. Wallace.
CAST: Cliff Potts (Bob Dalton); Randy Quaid (Grat Dalton); Larry Wilcox (Emmet Dalton); Sharon Farrell (Flo Quick); Matt Clark (George "Bitter Creek" Newcomb); Royal Dano (Pa Dalton); Julie Hill (Julie Williams); John Karlen (Charlie Powers); Bo Hopkins (Billy Doolin); Dale Robertson (Judge Isaac Parker); Jack Palance (Will Smith); Haris Yulin (Jesse James); Don Collier (Frank Dalton).

In 1934 Hollywood, oldtimers George "Bitter Creek" Newcomb and Emmet Dalton almost shoot it out over past differences. Which would have been pretty hard to do, in reality, since Newcomb was killed in 1895.[3] A writer calms the two men down, leads them to a saloon, and asks to hear their story, which Dalton decides to tell.

The youngest Dalton boys — Bob, Grat, and Emmet (actually, Emmett[4]) — become infatuated with bandits when their cousins, outlaws Jesse and Frank James and Cole

Members of the Dalton Gang ham it up for a photograph in *The Last Ride of the Dalton Gang* (1979), which had Harris Yulin (not pictured) making a cameo appearance as Jesse James.

Younger—stop at their Montgomery County, Kansas, farm in 1876. Historically, the Daltons were related to the Youngers, and not the Jameses.[5]

Years later, the three brothers try to follow in the footsteps of their lawman brother Frank, a deputy marshal for Judge Isaac Parker, but they're just too carefree and, well, easily led astray. Soon they're wanted men, pursued by railroad detective Will Smith, a fictitious creation.

Emmet's flashbacks show the mostly tongue-in-cheek career of the three wild ones and Flo Quick, Bob's true love. Of course, it's hard to be comic when dealing with the brothers' fatal attempt to rob two banks in Coffeyville, Kansas.

The story's pretty much hogwash. Sure, Bob and Grat Dalton were killed in the raid, along with two other gang members, and Emmett was wounded and served time in prison. But Judge Parker didn't show up after the bloodbath with a posse and outdraw and gun down a railroad detective named Smith.

That said, it's great to watch two old Western pros like Palance and Robertson facing down on the street. *The Last Ride of the Dalton Gang* is uneven yet fairly enjoyable, but *The Last Day* (NBC, February 15, 1975), in which Richard Widmark faces down the Daltons (Robert Conrad, Richard Jaeckel and Tim Matheson) is a better movie. Neither, however, is as fun to watch as director George Marshall's *When the Dalton Rode*, a highly inaccurate but rousing 1940 hit starring Randolph Scott, Brian Donlevy and Broderick Crawford.

Belle Starr

(CBS, April 1, 1980, 97 minutes)

CREDITS: *Director:* John A. Alonzo; *Producer:* Doug Chapin; *Writer:* James Lee Barrett.
CAST: Elizabeth Montgomery (Belle Starr); Cliff Potts (Cole Younger); Michael Cavanaugh (Jesse James); Gary Combs (Frank James); Fred Ward (Ned Christie); Jesse Vint (Bob Dalton); Alan Vint (Grat Dalton); Geoffrey Lewis (Reverend Meeks).

Why is a beautiful actress (Gene Tierney, Elsa Martinelli) always cast as Belle Starr, who was uglier than sin?

After 254 episodes as sweet housewife-witch Samantha Stevens on *Bewitched* (1964–72), actress Elizabeth Montgomery was obviously trying to shed her wholesome image. Whereas many actors and actresses are typecast after such a successful role, Montgomery was able to break away with shocking roles in *A Case of Rape* (1974), *The Legend of Lizzie Borden* (1975), *A Killing Affair* (1977) and *Act of Violence* (1979). So why not play the bandit queen?

Well, Montgomery just isn't convincing as Belle Starr. As entertainment, it's so-so. As history, it's bogus.

The film has Belle romancing Cole Younger, who rides with the James brothers and Ned Christie. It even has Belle taking part in a planned robbery at the Tulsa railroad with the Jameses, Cole and two Dalton brothers. It ends with Belle getting shot in the back at her ranch outside of Eufala, Oklahoma.

First, Belle did claim that Cole Younger was the father of her daughter, Pearl, but Cole always denied that.[6] Most definitely Cole did not try to rob a Texas bank with Frank and Jesse

James—and Ned Christie. Christie? Born in 1852, Christie didn't become wanted until 1887—when Jesse was dead, and Younger in prison. He wasn't killed on a Texas street during a bank robbery, but in present-day Oklahoma in a gunfight with marshals at his "fort" in 1892.[7]

Nor is there any documentation that the Jameses, Younger, and Bob and Grat Dalton tried to rob the Tulsa stockyard with Belle. Let's see, this crime would have had to have taken place before September 1876, when Grat would have been fifteen years old and Bob seven.[8]

In the film, Belle's son Ed informs the local marshal of his mother's plans to rob the stockyards. After the outlaws barely escape, Belle returns to her farm near Eufala to face her son, or husband. There, she's shot in the back and killed. It must have been a long ride back to Eufala. Belle wasn't killed until 1889.

About the only thing the movie got right is that Belle Starr was ambushed, and that her assailant was never identified.[9]

The Last Days of Frank and Jesse James
(NBC, February 17, 1986, 97 minutes)

CREDITS: *Director:* William A. Graham; *Producer:* Phillip Cates: *Writer:* William Stratton.

CAST: Johnny Cash (Frank James); Kris Kristofferson (Jesse James); Willie Nelson (General Jo Shelby); Marcia Cross (Sarah Hite); Gail Youngs (Anna James); David Allan Coe (Whiskeyhead Ryan); Andy Stahl (Dick Liddil); June Carter Cash (Mother James); Ed Bruce (Major Edwards); Darrell Wilks (Bob Ford); Meg Gibson, billed as Margaret Gibson (Zee); James Sinclair (Charlie Ford).

Instead of the "last days," this movie opens in 1877 as Frank and Jesse try to live the lives of gentlemen farmers in Tennessee. It focuses on the "last years" of Jesse's life, and follows with Frank's surrender and trial.

Country music legends Johnny Cash and Kris Kristofferson filled out much of the cast with Nashville friends, including Willie Nelson in a cameo as General Jo Shelby; David Allan Coe as a drunken outlaw; Ed Bruce as newspaper editor John Newman Edwards; even Cash's concert piano player, Earl Poole Ball, as "Squire Earthman." Yet I've always wondered how Cash's wife, June Carter Cash, felt about playing Frank and Jesse's mother. June was only two years older than her husband.

The *Chicago Sun-Times* called it "a dandy little yarn."[10] What it also is—surprisingly—is faithful to actual history, painting vivid portraits of the two outlaws, Bob Ford's motives for killing Jesse, and perhaps the most accurate movie depiction of Jesse's death.

There is some poetic license, of course. The movie opens in 1877 as the James families have settled in the Nashville area, but then Jesse persuades Frank to rob a bank in Huntington, West Virginia, with him. That crime actually took place two years earlier, on September 6, 1875. The movie has Dick Liddil and two Missouri boys, Jim and Bud McDaniel, joining the James brothers for the robbery. Bud McDaniel was dead by then, and Liddil didn't take part. Only four men robbed the Bank of Huntington: Former guerrilla Tom Webb and Tom McDaniel, brother of the late William "Bud" McDaniel, a former James-Younger Gang member, were positively identified. The two other bandits were likely two

Ten. Made-for-Television Movies, 1970–1999

Kris Kristofferson was Jesse James, Meg Gibson was Zee and John Jackson Routh played their son in *The Last Days of Frank and Jesse James*, a 1986 made-for-TV movie that, surprisingly, nailed several facts on the head.

of the following: Jesse James, Frank James, Cole Younger. Frank, however, later said that he wasn't there (what else would he say?) and that Clell Miller was. The robbery wasn't as violent as depicted in the movie, although Tom McDaniel was mortally wounded in a September 14–15 gunfight in Kentucky. Webb was later arrested in Tennessee.[11]

All facts go out the window after Frank is acquitted and begins seeking revenge on Bob Ford, but up until then, this is an amazingly strong retelling of the Jesse James legend.

Frank & Jesse
(HBO, April 22, 1995, 100 minutes)

CREDITS: *Director-Writer:* Robert Boris; *Producer:* Cassian Elwes.
CAST: Rob Lowe (Jesse James); Bill Paxton (Frank James); Randy Travis (Cole Younger); Dana Wheeler-Nicholson (Annie); Maria Pitillo (Zee); Luke Askew (Lone Rider); Sean Patrick Flanery (Zack Murphy); Alexis Arquette (Charlie Ford); Todd Field (Bob Younger); John Pyper-Ferguson (Clell Miller); Nicholas Sadler (Arch Clements); William Atherton (Allan Pinkerton); Mary Neff (Widow Miller); Richard Maynard (John Sheets); Jim Flowers (Bob Ford).

The "umpteenth retelling of the James Brothers legend" was supposed to go to the big screen, but the producers never could line up a distribution deal — possibly due to the big-screen flop of *Wyatt Earp* — so the movie wound up on HBO instead.[12]

The myth of Jesse saving the widow from foreclosure is repeated. So is the myth of the Northfield raid being a set-up by the Pinkertons, and the story of the gang not robbing the poor. During a train robbery, Frank tells a man with rough hands to keep his wallet: "We don't take money from the workin' man."

Frank's even-tempered. Jesse's a hothead. And Cole Younger, played by country singer Randy Travis, has a fine voice, singing "Auld Lang Syne." He also has only one brother, Bob, whom he mercifully kills after Bob is mortally wounded during the Northfield raid. (The real Bob died of tuberculosis in prison in 1889 at age thirty-four.) Brother Jim — not in this movie — died of a gunshot wound, but he shot himself in 1902.[13]

Travis comes across reasonably well. Bill Paxton is convincing as Frank. Rob Lowe is terrible as Jesse.

Jesse eventually sacrifices himself, turning his back on Bob Ford and holding out his hands as if he's on the crucifix, in order to save his brother. Jesse knows that if he's dead, the law will be more lenient on Frank.

Filmed in Arkansas, *Frank & Jesse* "includes some of the ugliest scenery ever seen in a western," the *Washington Post* noted.[14] It's also a pretty ugly movie.

Purgatory
(TNT, January 10, 1999, 94 minutes)

CREDITS: Uli Edel; *Producer:* Daniel Schneider; *Writer:* Gordon T. Dawson.
CAST: Sam Shepard (Sheriff Forrest/Wild Bill Hickok); Eric Roberts (Blackjack Britton); Randy Quaid (Doc Woods/Doc Holliday); Peter Stormare (Cavin

Guthrie); Brade Rowe (Leo "Sonny" Dillard); Donnie Wahlberg (Deputy Glen/Billy the Kid); J.D. Souther (Brooks/Jesse James); Amelia Heinle (Rose/Betty McCullough); Shannon Kenny (Dolly Sloan/Ivy); John Dennis Johnston (Lamb/ "Lefty" Slade); Saginaw Grant (Gatekeeper); Richard Edson (Knox); John Diehl (Badger); R.G. Armstrong (Coachman).

An outlaw band flees into the town of Refuge, where nobody carries a gun, drinks or cusses. Even the local lawman, Forrest, goes unarmed. Wow, what's not to like in a town like this if you're an evil killer named Blackjack Britton?

Ah, but young outlaw Sonny, an avid reader of dime novels, notices something peculiar about this town and its population. It turns out that the residents are dead criminals like Wild Bill Hickok, Doc Holliday and — of course — Jesse James, who are living in Purgatory. They must live in peace, or go straight to hell. So what happens when they have to defend themselves against a bad dude like Britton?

Gordon Dawson's script won a Spur Award from Western Writers of America (he was also nominated for a Writers Guild of America award), and the movie won a "Director's Award for Television Feature Film" in the Western Heritage Wrangler Awards competition from the National Cowboy and Western Heritage Museum in Oklahoma City.

Although an interesting concept, *Purgatory* is too long and probably would have worked better with fictitious villains. It could have been better handled as a *Twilight Zone* or *Night Gallery* episode.

Chapter Eleven

Television Series Appearances, 1953–2001

Television series brought Jesse James to the small screen.

In 1965, ABC even gave Jesse his own show, *The Legend of Jesse James* with Christopher Jones as a heroic (heartthrob) Jesse, Allen Case as Frank, Ann Doran as their mother and veteran Western screen villain Robert J. Wilke as Marshal Sam Corbett, who never managed to catch those pesky outlaws. Don Siegel produced it for 20th Century–Fox Television.

TV critic Cleveland Amory didn't care much for the show, writing, "The trouble is that the producers, having decided to give us an outlaw for a hero, then proceed in script after script to make him, if not an in-law, at least not all bad. And it's not easy to make, out of a robbing hood, Robin Hood."[1] Viewers didn't care much for it, either. The half-hour series lasted only thirty-four episodes before it was canceled.

Jesse (played by Stephen Nichols) also showed up during Phileas Fogg's quest to journey *Around the World in 80 Days*, a three-part NBC miniseries starring Pierce Brosnan that premiered on April 16, 1989.

Christopher Pettiet played Jesse as a young boy in the third and last season of ABC's *The Young Riders*. It told the fictional story of a bunch of teenage Pony Express riders that included William F. Cody (Stephen Baldwin) and James Butler Hickok (Josh Brolin), who were ramrodded by Teaspoon Hunter (Anthony Zerbe). In real life, Cody and Hickok were involved with the Pony Express, although Hickok was not a rider and some historians question if Cody actually rode for the Express. But Jesse? He was a Clay County farm boy during the Pony Express's eighteen-month run in 1860 and '61.

A look at Jesse's guest appearances in continuing TV series:

You Are There
"The Capture of Jesse James"
(CBS, February 8, 1953)

James Dean, before he became a Rebel Without a Cause, played a rebel with one as Bob Ford. The Emmy Award–winning series had host Walter Cronkite revisiting historic incidents. In the first season's second episode, John Kerr played Jesse. Sidney Lumet directed.

Stories of the Century
"Frank and Jesse James"
(Syndicated, February 7, 1954)

Jim Davis played Southwestern Railroad detective Matt Clark, who wound up helping track down some notorious "name" outlaws in a show that was often, surprisingly, fairly faithful to history. *Stories of the Century* won the Emmy in 1955 in the "Western or Adventure Series" category. In the third episode of the first season, Clark was assigned to bring Jesse James (Lee Van Cleef) to justice. Veteran William Witney directed.

Goodyear Television Playhouse
"Missouri Legend"
(NBC, October 7, 1956)

This was a prestigious series of live, one-hour plays filmed in New York. The first episode produced in color starred Robert Preston as Jesse James.

Tales of Wells Fargo
"Jesse James"
(NBC, July 1, 1957)

Dale Robertson, who had a big-screen turn as Jesse in 1949's *Fighting Man of the Plains*, played Jim Hardie in this series produced by Nat Holt. Frank Gruber served as story consultant. In the thirteenth episode from the first season, written by Western veteran Dwight Newton, Hardie went undercover, posing as a photographer, to bring in Jesse James (Hugh Beaumont). Character actress Olive Carey, in an excellent performance, played Jesse's mother

Playhouse 90
"Bitter Heritage"
(CBS, April 17, 1958)

James Drury, later to star on television's *The Virginian*, played Jesse James in a live episode that drew the wrath of the James family. James Ross, great-grandson of Jesse James, argued in the courts, "I understand that the right to privacy is the right to be left alone. We saw the show and it is not true or partly true. Does a man lose his right to privacy just because he has that name?" The judge didn't agree, saying, "If you're Jesse James, you are in the public eye."[2] The plot had a banker's daughter saving the James boys, who have been framed for a bank robbery. Franchot Tone played Frank.

Yancy Derringer
"Outlaw at Liberty"
(CBS, May 7, 1959)

Yancy (Jock Mahoney) and his pals headed to Missouri to prove that a friend was not guilty of murder. It turns out that Yancy's pal had been framed by Jesse James (Brett King). Lee Van Cleef, who had played Jesse in a *Stories of the Century* episode, plays Frank James this time.

Bronco
"Shadow of Jesse James"
(ABC, January 12, 1960)

Bronco Lane (Ty Hardin) tried to persuade Cole Younger (Richard Coogan) to quit and to turn over fellow outlaw Jesse James (James Coburn), who was proving to be one cold-blooded killer. Jeanne Cooper played Belle Starr, Lester Hellman was Bloody Bill Anderson, and Bill Tennant and James Westmoreland showed up as Cole's brothers Bob and Jim. Clearly the producers bought into RKO's logic that you can never have too many outlaws.

The Twilight Zone
"Showdown with Rance McGrew"
(CBS, February 2, 1962)

In this hilarious episode written by series creator and host Rod Serling, TV series cowboy Rance McGrew (Larry Blyden)—a tough guy on screen, but, in reality, a cowardly, inept egomaniac—was sent back in time, to be challenged by Jesse James (Arch Johnson). (It seems a bunch of dead outlaws didn't care for how they were being portrayed on McGrew's series.) In 1965, Serling tried his hand at a serious Western series, the underrated—and short-lived—*The Loner,* starring Lloyd Bridges, for CBS.

My Favorite Martian
"The Time Machine Is Waking Up That Old Gang of Mine"
(CBS, November 21, 1965)

Martin's (Ray Walston) time-travel machine short-circuits, transporting Jesse (Mort Mills) and Frank (L.Q. Jones) to Tim's apartment. The outlaws held Martin, Tim (Bill Bixby) and Mrs. Brown (Pamela Britton) hostage and tried to figure out how to use the machine for their own ends. Martin needed to save the day.

Hondo
"Hondo and the Judas"
(ABC, November 3, 1967)

Producer Andrew J. Fenady re-imagined the 1953 John Wayne movie *Hondo* for television. In the ninth episode of this short-lived series, Army scout Hondo Lane (Ralph Taeger) found out that his former Confederate commander William Quantrill (Forrest Tucker) wasn't dead. Quantrill was joined by several old bushwhackers, including Jesse James (Ricky Nelson) and Cole Younger (Richard Bakalyan). Quantrill planned to pull off a robbery—and to find out who shot him and left him for dead.

The Brady Bunch
"Bobby's Hero"
(ABC, February 2, 1973)

When young Bobby (Mike Lookinland) begins hero-worshipping Jesse James, Mike (Robert Reed) and Carol (Florence Henderson) set him straight by asking oldtimer Jethroe Collins (Burt Mustin) to explain to Bobby how Jesse cold-heartedly shot his father down. After Jesse (Gordon Devol) started murdering Bobby's family in a nightmare, Bobby decided to stop looking up to an outlaw. Likely the most famous of Jesse's TV guest shots.

Barbary Coast
"Jesse Who?"
(ABC, September 22, 1975)

This short-lived (thirteen episodes), lighthearted series starred a post–*Star Trek* William Shatner as government agent Jeff Cable and post–*The Virginian* Doug McClure as casino owner Cash Conover. "Jesse Who?," directed by Bill Bixby, involves crooks and a woman with larceny on her mind; they plan to rob a bank using a fake Jesse James (David Spielberg).

Little House on the Prairie
"The Aftermath"
(NBC, November 7, 1977)

Mary Ingalls got a lesson in outlaw history when Jesse (Dennis Rucker) and Frank (John Bennett Perry) showed up, using aliases, and were forced to take Mary hostage after a trigger-happy posse arrived. It turned out that Robert Ford (Tony Markes) was living in Walnut Grove, too. Funny, history tells us Ford grew up in Missouri, not Minnesota.

The Dukes of Hazzard
"Go West, Young Dukes"
(CBS, November 16, 1984)

Uncle Jesse (Denver Pyle) discovered an diary and saved the farm from Boss Hogg (Sorrell Booke) in a story told in flashbacks featuring the regular cast members playing their characters' ancestors. Paul Koslo played Jesse and Nick Benedict played Frank.

MacGyver
"MacGyver's Women"
(ABC, November 12, 1990)

Commitment in a relationship wasn't easy for MacGyver (Richard Dean Anderson), and when he fell asleep while watching a Western on video, he dreamed that he was in the Old West with a bunch of mail-order brides. He also dreamed up Jesse James (Wil Calhoun) and Billy the Kid (Russ Hamilton).

Earth 2
"The Enemy Within"
(NBC, January 8, 1995)

In this short-lived science-fiction series, Jesse (J.D. Garfield) and Frank (Clifford Happy) showed up in an odd sequence in a (virtual reality) town of New Pacifica. They "picked the wrong town to rob."

Lois & Clark: The New Adventures of Superman
"Tempus Fugitive"
(ABC, March 26, 1995)

Teaming up with H.G. Wells, Lois and Clark head back to 1866 in Wells's time machine to stop a bad guy, from the future, out to destroy baby Superman. Naturally, they run into Jesse (Don Swayze) and Frank (Josh Devane).

Legend
"Birth of a Legend"
(UPN, April 18, 1995)

In the pilot episode of this science-fiction Western with an accent on comedy, hard-boozing, womanizing writer Ernest Pratt (Richard Dean Anderson) has found success as creator of a dime-novel hero named Nicodemus Legend. Posing as his literary hero, Pratt teams up with an inventor, European scientist Janos Bartok (John de Lancie, best known as Q in *Star Trek: The Next Generation*). They head out to win the West. Jesse (Forrie J. Smith) and Frank (Monty Stuart) showed up along Pratt and Bartok's journey.

The Secret Adventures of Jules Verne
"Ballad of Steeley Joe"
(Sci-Fi, August 26, 2000)

Struggling writer Jules Verne (Chris Demetral) befriended Phileas (Michael Praed) and Rebecca Fogg (Francesca Hunt) and Passepoartout (Michel Courtemanche), fighting the League of Darkness and flying across the world in Fogg's dirigible, the *Aurora*. When Jesse (Kent McQuaid) hijacked the *Aurora*, Passepoartout created a steam-powered gunman, Steeley Joe, to help foil the bad guys.

Special Unit 2
"The Eve"
(UPN, October 31, 2001)

On Halloween night, a Link (basically, a monster, the missing link between apes and humans) resurrected four criminals from the dead, then crashed a Halloween party with the villains and took hostages. Of course, one of the dead bad guys was Jesse (Damon Johnson) in this show about a top-secret Chicago police unit fighting those pesky Links.

Chapter Notes

Introduction

1. Paul Andrew Hutton, email correspondence with author, March 20, 2008.
2. *New York Times*, April 9, 1951.
3. Paul Andrew Hutton, "Silver Screen Desperado: Billy the Kid in the Movies," *New Mexico Historical Review*, Spring 2007, pp. 149–50.
4. *Los Angeles Times*, August 25, 2001.
5. Ibid.

Chapter One

1. The account of the Liberty bank robbery is taken from Ted P. Yeatman's *Frank and Jesse James: The Story Behind the Legend* (Nashville: Cumberland House, 2000), pp. 85–86; William A. Settle Jr.'s *Jesse James Was His Name* (Lincoln: University of Nebraska Press, 1977), pp. 33–36; Marley Brant's *Jesse James: The Man and the Myth* (New York: Berkley, 1998), pp. 46–54; Robert J. Wybrow's "*Horrid Murder and Heavy Robbery*": *The Liberty Bank Robbery, 13 February 1866* (London: English Westerners' Society, 2004), pp. 1–13; Jack B. Wymore's *History of the Jesse James Bank Museum in Liberty, Missouri: Scene of the First Bank Robbery in America and First Outlaw Event in the Career of Jesse James* (Liberty, MO: Jesse James Bank Museum pamphlet, no date); the *Liberty* (Missouri) *Tribune*, February 16, 1866.
2. *Liberty Tribune*, February 16, 1866.
3. Ibid.
4. Cole Younger, *The Story of Cole Younger* (St. Paul: Minnesota Historical Society Press, 2000), pp. 51–52.
5. Phillip W. Steele, *Jesse and Frank James: The Family History* (Gretna, LA: Pelican, 1997), pp. 34–50.
6. Steele, *Jesse and Frank James*, pp. 34–35; Yeatman, *Frank and Jesse James*, p. 25.
7. Steele, *Jesse and Frank James*, pp. 35, 39; Yeatman, *Frank and Jesse James*, pp. 25–27.
8. Yeatman, *Frank and Jesse James*, pp. 25–26.
9. Settle, *Jesse James Was His Name*, p. 7.
10. Yeatman, *Frank and Jesse James*, p. 26.
11. Yeatman, *Frank and Jesse James*, p. 26; Settle, *Jesse James Was His Name*, p. 8.
12. T.J. Stiles, *Jesse James: Last Rebel of the Civil War* (New York: Vintage Books, 2003), pp. 30–31; Settle, *Jesse James Was His Name*, p. 8; Yeatman, *Frank and Jesse James*, p. 27.
13. Yeatman, *Frank and Jesse James*, p. 27; Steele, *Jesse and Frank James*, pp. 62–64.
14. Patricia L. Faust, editor, *Historical Times Illustrated Encyclopedia of the Civil War* (New York: Harper & Row, 1986), pp. 66–67, 408, 502–03; Dyer, Robert L. *Jesse James and the Civil War in Missouri* (Columbia: University of Missouri Press, 1994), pp. 8–9.
15. Faust, *Historical Times Illustrated Encyclopedia of the Civil War*, pp. 501–02; Dyer, *Jesse James and the Civil War in Missouri*, pp. 11–12.
16. Yeatman, *Frank and Jesse James*, pp. 30–32.
17. Yeatman, *Frank and Jesse James*, p. 33.
18. Brant, *Jesse James: The Man and the Myth*, p. 27.
19. Brant, *Jesse James: The Man and the Myth*, pp. 27–28; Yeatman, *Frank and Jesse James*, pp. 38–41; Stiles, *Jesse James: Last Rebel of the Civil War*, p. 88.
20. Brant, *Jesse James: The Man and the Myth*, p. 37; Yeatman, *Frank and Jesse James*, p. 41.
21. Settle, *Jesse James Was His Name*, p. 23; Yeatman, *Frank and Jesse James*, p. 44; Michael Fellman, *Inside War: The Guerrilla Conflict in Missouri During the Civil War* (New York: Oxford University Press, 1989), p. 25.
22. Stiles, *Jesse James: Last Rebel of the Civil War*, pp. 100–03, 115–27; Settle, *Jesse James Was His Name*, pp. 26–28; Faust, *Historical Times Illustrated Encyclopedia of the Civil War*, p. 123.
23. Yeatman, *Frank and Jesse James*, p. 58.
24. Faust, *Historical Times Illustrated Encyclopedia of the Civil War*, p. 606; Settle, *Jesse James Was His Name*, p. 29.
25. Settle, *Jesse James Was His Name*, p. 31; Brant, *Jesse James: The Man and the Myth*, p. 40; Stiles, *Jesse James: Last Rebel of the Civil War*, pp. 154–55.
26. Settle, *Jesse James Was His Name*, p. 32; Brant, Marley, *The Outlaw Youngers: A Confederate Brotherhood* (Lanham, MD: Madison Books, 1992), p. 62.
27. *Los Angeles Times*, November 22, 1914.
28. Settle, *Jesse James Was His Name*, p. 34.
29. Settle, *Jesse James Was His Name*, pp. 34–35; Yeatman, *Frank and Jesse James*, pp. 88–91, 93–94.
30. Yeatman, *Frank and Jesse James*, pp. 95–96; Settle, *Jesse James Was His Name*, pp. 38–39; Brant, *Jesse James: The Man and the Myth*, pp. 74–75.
31. Settle, *Jesse James Was His Name*, p. 39; Yeatman, *Frank and Jesse James*, pp. 96–97.
32. Settle, *Jesse James Was His Name*, pp. 43–44; Brant, *Jesse James: The Man and the Myth*, p. 84.
33. Brant, *Jesse James: The Man and the Myth*, p. 86.
34. Yeatman, *Frank and Jesse James*, pp. 102–04, 344–45; Brant, *Jesse James: The Man and the Myth*, pp. 87–88.
35. Settle, *Jesse James Was His Name*, pp. 47–48.
36. Settle, *Jesse James Was His Name*, pp. 49–50, 59–60, 70, 75–76; Brant, *Jesse James: The Man and the Myth*, pp. 107, 120.
37. Brant, *Jesse James: The Man and the Myth*, pp. 133–34; Yeatman, *Frank and Jesse James*, pp. 133–36.
38. Yeatman, *Frank and Jesse James*, p. 145.
39. Brant, *Jesse James: The Man and the Myth*, pp. 147–48, 150–51; Steele, *Jesse and Frank James*, p. 55.
40. Brant, *Jesse James: The Man and the Myth*, pp. 165–66.

41. Yeatman, *Frank and Jesse James*, pp. 164–65; Brant, *Jesse James: The Man and the Myth*, p. 172.
42. Brant, *Jesse James: The Man and the Myth*, pp. 177–83.
43. Brant, *Jesse James: The Man and the Myth*, p. 184; Robert Barr Smith, *The Last Hurrah of the James-Younger Gang* (Norman: University of Oklahoma Press, 2001), p. 160, 178, 180; John Koblas, *Faithful Unto Death: The James-Younger Raid on the First National Bank, September 7, 1876, Northfield, Minnesota* (Northfield, MN: Northfield Historical Society Press, 2001), pp. 138–41.
44. Brant, *Jesse James: The Man and the Myth*, pp. 200–01, 206, 208–12.
45. Settle, *Jesse James Was His Name*, p. 111; William H. Wallace, *Speeches and Writings of Wm. H. Wallace with Autobiography* (Kansas City: Western Baptist Publishing, 1914), pp. 276–78; Stiles, *Jesse James: Last Rebel of the Civil War*, p. 367.
46. Yeatman, *Frank and Jesse James*, p. 266.
47. Settle, *Jesse James Was His Name*, p. 115; Yeatman, *Frank and Jesse James*, pp. 266–67.
48. Yeatman, *Frank and Jesse James*, p. 268.
49. Ibid.
50. Yeatman, *Frank and Jesse James*, pp. 268–69; Settle, *Jesse James Was His Name*, p. 117.

Chapter Two

1. Yeatman, *Frank and Jesse James*, p. 279.
2. Gerald S. Petrone, *Judgment at Gallatin: The Trial of Frank James* (Lubbock: Texas Tech University Press, 1998), pp. 68, 71, 167, 192–94.
3. Settle, *Jesse James Was His Name*, p. 173.
4. Settle, *Jesse James Was His Name*, pp. 180–88.
5. Yeatman, *Frank and Jesse James*, pp. 275–91.
6. Paul Trachtman, *The Gunfighters* (Alexandria, VA: Time-Life Books, 1974), pp. 88–89.
7. John Koblas, *The Great Cole Younger & Frank James Historical Wild West Show* (St. Cloud, MN: North Star Press, 2002), page xx.
8. Brant, *Jesse James: The Man and the Myth*, p. 257.
9. Jon Tuska, *The Filming of the West* (Garden City, NY: Doubleday, 1976), pp. 3–5; George N. Fenin and William K. Everson, *The Western: From Silents to the Seventies* (New York: Penguin, 1977), p. 9.
10. Fenin and Everson, *The Western*, p. 9.

Chapter Three

1. Yeatman, *Frank and Jesse James*, p. 368. Yeatman got the title of the 1908 movie wrong; it's *The James Boys in Missouri*. He also got the year of *Jesse James as the Outlaw* wrong; that movie was released simultaneously with *Jesse James Under the Black Flag* in 1921.
2. Arnie Bernstein, email correspondence with author, February 9, 2010.
3. David Kiehn, *Broncho Billy and the Essanay Film Company* (Berkeley, CA: Farwell Books, 2003), p. 10.
4. Hal Erickson, All Movie Guide, www.allmovie.com.
5. David Kiehn, email correspondence with author, February 20, 2010.
6. Kiehn, *Broncho Billy*, p. 299.
7. *Trenton Evening Times*, April 7, 1908.
8. (Frederick, Maryland) *Daily News*, April 16, 1908.
9. (Elyria, Ohio) *Evening Telegraph*, June 5, 1908.
10. *The Life of Jesse James*, film herald, circa 1910.
11. Kiehn, email correspondence with author, February 20, 2010.
12. Felicia Hardison Landre, *The Enchanted Years of the Stage: Kansas City at the Crossroads of American Theater, 1870–1930* (Columbia: University of Missouri Press, 2007), p. 149.
13. Yeatman, *Frank and Jesse James*, p. 300.
14. *Kansas City Star*, February 10, 1902.
15. Settle, *Jesse James Was His Name*, p. 176.
16. Landre, *The Enchanted Years of the Stage*, p. 149.
17. Erickson. All Movie Guide, www.allmovie.com.
18. Larry Langman, *A Guide to Silent Westerns* (Santa Barbara, CA: Greenwood Press, 1992), p. 232.
19. Ibid.
20. *The Life of Jesse James* movie herald.
21. Erickson. All Movie Guide, www.allmovie.com.
22. Kiehn, *Broncho Billy*, p. 10.
23. Rick Montgomery and Shirl Kasper, *Kansas City: An American Story* (Kansas City: Kansas City Star Books, 1999), p. 176.
24. Robert Loerzel, "Reel Chicago" (*Chicago Magazine*, May 2007), www.chicagomag.com.
25. Biographical data come from imdb.com, wikipedia.com, *Broncho Billy and the Essanay Film Company* and "Reel Chicago," *Chicago Magazine*.
26. Loerzel, "Reel Chicago."
27. Arnie Bernstein, *Hollywood on Lake Michigan: 100 Years of Chicago & the Movies* (Chicago: Lake Claremont Press, 1998), p. 39.
28. Kiehn, *Broncho Billy*, p. 10.
29. J.W. Williamson, *Hillbillyland: What the Movies Did to the Mountains and What the Mountains Did to the Movies* (Chapel Hill: University of North Carolina Press, 1995), p. 386.
30. Bernstein, *Hollywood on Lake Michigan*, p. 39; Kiehn, *Broncho Billy*, p. 10; Kiehn, email correspondence with author, February 20, 2010.
31. Bernstein, *Hollywood on Lake Michigan*, p. 39.
32. Kiehn, *Broncho Billy*, p. 10; Kiehn, email correspondence with author, February 20, 2010.
33. Kiehn, email correspondence with author, February 20, 2010.
34. Edward De Grazia and Roger K. Newman, *Banned Films: Movies, Censors & the First Amendment* (New York: R.R. Bowker, 1982), p. 177; Frank Walsh, *Sin and Censorship: The Catholic Church and the Motion Picture Industry* (New Haven, CT: Yale University Press, 1999), p. 7.
35. De Grazia and Newman, *Banned Films*, pp. 177–78.
36. Kendall R. Phillips, *Controversial Cinema: The Films That Outraged America* (Santa Barbara, CA: Praeger, 2008), pp. 55–56.
37. Gregory D. Black, *Hollywood Censored: Morality Codes, Catholics and the Movies* (New York: Cambridge University Press, 1996), p. 11.
38. De Grazia and Newman. *Banned Films*, p. 178.
39. Stephen Prince, *Classical Film Violence: Designing and Regulating Brutality in Hollywood Cinema, 1930–1968* (New Brunswick, NJ: Rutgers University Press, 2003), p. 13.
40. *Moving Picture News*, September 23, 1911, quoted in Nanna Nerhoeff, *The West in Early Cinema: After the Beginning* (Amsterdam: Amsterdam University Press, 2006), p. 386. The author notes, "Since this was published three years later, it is not clear if it is about the Essanay title from 1908 or about another version."
41. Gerald R. Butters Jr., *Banned in Kansas: Motion Picture Censorship, 1915–1966* (Columbia: University of Missouri Press, 2007), p. 50.
42. *Belleville* (Kansas) *Telescope*, October 26, 1911.

43. Jody W. Pennington, *The History of Sex in American Film* (Santa Barbara: Praeger, 2007), p. 2.
44. De Grazia and Newman, *Banned Films*, p. 179.
45. Kiehn, *Broncho Billy*, p. 10; Kiehn, email correspondence with author, February 20, 2010.
46. Bernstein, *Hollywood on Lake Michigan*, p. 39.
47. Kiehn, email correspondence with author, February 20, 2010.
48. André Gaudreault, *American Cinema 1890–1909: Themes and Variations* (New Brunswick, NJ: Rutgers University Press, 2009), p. 207.
49. Fenin and Everson, *The Western*, p. 57.
50. Elizabeth Gilliam Beckett, Clay County Historic Sites Director, email correspondence with author, November 6, 2009.
51. (Stevens Point, Wisconsin) *Gazette*, November 22, 1911.
52. (Stevens Point, Wisconsin) *Gazette*, November 22, 1911; Kelly Segrave, *American Films Abroad: Hollywood's Domination of the World's Movie Screens from the 1890s to the Present* (Jefferson, NC: McFarland, 1997), p. 6.
53. (Stevens Point, Wisconsin) *Gazette*, November 22, 1911.
54. (Xenia, Ohio) *Daily Gazette*, May 15, 1911.
55. (Lebanon, Pennsylvania) *Daily News*, November 14, 1911.
56. Ibid.
57. *Racine Daily Journal*, July 12, 1911.
58. *Belleville* (Kansas) *Telescope*, October 26, 1911.
59. Fenin and Everson, *The Western*, p. 57.
60. *Daily News* (Frederick, Maryland), September 4, 1914.
61. Ibid.
62. Ibid.
63. Nancy Samuelson, email correspondence with author, June 19, 2010.
64. Ibid.
65. Scott Cole, email correspondence with author, June 11, 2010.
66. Trachtman, *The Gunfighters*, p. 87.
67. Settle, *Jesse James Was His Name*, pp. 163–64; Yeatman, *Frank and Jesse James*, p. 299.
68. Yeatman, *Frank and Jesse James*, pp. 299–300.
69. Koblas, *The Great Cole Younger & Frank James Historical Wild West Show* (St. Cloud, MN: North Star Press, xx; Yeatman, *Frank and Jesse James*, pp. 302–11.
70. Yeatman, *Frank and Jesse James*, pp. 312–13; Koblas, *The Great Cole Younger & Frank James Historical Wild West Show*, pp. 179–91.
71. Eric James, email correspondence with author, June 12, 2010.
72. Koblas, *The Great Cole Younger & Frank James Historical Wild West Show*, p. 211.
73. *Los Angeles Times*, November 22, 1914; Samuelson, email correspondence with author, June 19, 2010.
74. Yeatman, *Frank and Jesse James*, p. 318.
75. Ibid.
76. *Washington Post*, March 16, 1913.
77. *Washington Post*, July 28, 1914.
78. Steele, *Jesse and Frank James*, p. 46.
79. Koblas, *The Great Cole Younger & Frank James Historical Wild West Show*, p. 218.
80. www.learnaboutmovieposters.com. William R. Kane, *1,001 Places to Sell Manuscripts* (Ridgewood, NJ: Editor, 1915), p. 230; Peter Stanfield, *Hollywood, Westerns and the 1930s: The Lost Trail* (Exeter, England: University of Exeter Press, 2001), p. 183; Langman, *A Guide to Silent Westerns*, p. 300.
81. *Moving Picture World*, August 21, 1915, p. 1,329.
82. Cass Warner Sperling, Cork Millner and Jack Warner, *Hollywood be Thy Name: The Warner Brothers Story* (Lexington: University Press of Kentucky, 1998), p. 52.
83. Ibid.
84. Anthony Balducci, *Lloyd Hamilton: Poor Boy Comedian of Silent Cinema* (Jefferson, NC: McFarland, 2009), p. 188.
85. Kane, *1,001 Places to Sell Manuscripts*, p. 230; Balducci, *Lloyd Hamilton*, p. 189.
86. *American Globe Protective Financier*, October 1915, p. 8.
87. www.imdb.com. It's interesting to note that, at this writing, *The Near Capture of Jesse James* is not listed on the website www.silentera.com.
88. Balducci, *Lloyd Hamilton*, p. 189.
89. Faust, *Historical Times Illustrated Encyclopedia of the Civil War*, p. 302.
90. *Kansas City Star*, July 25, 1920.
91. H.H. Crittenden (compiler), *The Crittenden Memoirs* (New York: Putnam's, 1936), p. 333.
92. Ibid.
93. Laura James, *The Love Pirate and the Bandit's Son: Murder, Sin, and Scandal in the Shadow of Jesse James* (New York: Union Square Press, 2009), p. 154. James says Coates was from Hollywood, but other sources, including the *Kansas City Star* and Jesse E. James's wife Stella, say Coates came from New York.
94. www.imdb.com.
95. Quoted in James, *The Love Pirate and the Bandit's Son*, p. 155.
96. Stella Frances James, *In the Shadow of Jesse James* (Thousand Oaks, CA: Revolver Press, 1990), p. 137.
97. James, *The Love Pirate and the Bandit's Son*, p. 157.
98. Samuel Anderson Pence, *I Knew Frank ... I Wish I Had Known Jesse: Family, Friends and Neighbors in the Life and Times of the James Boys* (Independence, MO: Two Trails Publishing, 2007), p. 402.
99. Faust, *Historical Times Illustrated Encyclopedia of the Civil War*, p. 302.
100. Homer Croy, *Jesse James Was My Neighbor* (Lincoln: University of Nebraska Press, 1949), pp. 135, 144.
101. James, *The Love Pirate and the Bandit's Son*, pp. 155–56.
102. Williamson, *Hillbillyland*, p. 108.
103. *Kansas City Star*, July 25, 1920, August 1, 1920; Pence, *I Knew Frank*, p. 402.
104. *Santa Fe New Mexican*, November 8, 1920.
105. James, *The Love Pirate and the Bandit's Son*, p. 155.
106. James, *The Love Pirate and the Bandit's Son*, p. 103.
107. Yeatman, *Frank and Jesse James: The Story Behind the Legend*, pp. 292 96, 315.
108. *Sun-Journal* (Lewiston, ME), August 5, 1989.
109. James, *The Love Pirate and the Bandit's Son*, p. 153; James, *In the Shadow of Jesse James*, p. 95; *Kansas City Star*, July 25, 1920.
110. *Kansas City Star*, July 25, 1920, August 1, 1920.
111. *Kansas City Star*, August 1, 1920.
112. Ibid.
113. Brant, *Jesse James: The Man and the Myth*, p. 259; James, *In the Shadow of Jesse James*, p. 136; James, *The Love Pirate and the Bandit's Son*, p. 154.
114. Williamson, *Hillbillyland*, p. 108.
115. James, *The Love Pirate and the Bandit's Son*, p. 154.
116. James, *In the Shadow of Jesse James*, p. 95.
117. Williamson, *Hillbillyland*, p. 109; James, *In the Shadow of Jesse James*, p. 96; Brant, *Jesse James: The Man and the Myth*, p. 260.
118. James, *The Love Pirate and the Bandit's Son*, pp. 156–57; Brant, *Jesse James: The Man and the Myth*, p. 260.

119. Settle, *Jesse James Was His Name*, p. 177; Brant, *Jesse James: The Man and the Myth*, p. 260; James, *The Love Pirate and the Bandit's Son*, p. 158.
120. Crittenden, *The Crittenden Memoirs*, p. 333.
121. James, *In the Shadow of Jesse James*, pp. 94–97.
122. James, *In the Shadow of Jesse James*, p. 137; James, *The Love Pirate and the Bandit's Son*, p. 158; www.imdb.com.
123. James, *The Love Pirate and the Bandit's Son*, p. 154.
124. James, *The Love Pirate and the Bandit's Son*, p. 158.
125. Since no copy of the movie is known to exist, the plot is pulled from *Western Gunslingers in Fact and on Film* by Buck Rainey (Jefferson, NC: McFarland, 1998); *More Than a Cowboy: The Life and Films of Fred Thomson and Silver King* by Edgar M. Wyatt (Raleigh, NC: Wyatt Classics, 1988); *Hillbillyland: What the Movies Did to the Mountains and What the Mountains Did to the Movies* by Jerry Wayne Williamson (Chapel Hill: University of North Carolina Press, 1995); *The Filming of the West* by Jon Tuska (Garden City, NY: Doubleday, 1976); and *The New York Times* (October 17, 1927).
126. Wyatt, *More Than a Cowboy*, p. 196.
127. Williamson says that in the movie, Jesse's mother is "maimed through the villainy of Slade, guardian of the girl he loves." (*Hillbillyland*, p. 109).
128. Wyatt, *More Than a Cowboy*, p. 196.
129. Settle, *Jesse James Was His Name*, p. 177; Wyatt, *More Than a Cowboy*, p. 194.
130. *Portland* (Maine) *Express*, July 15, 1927, quoted in Wyatt, *More Than a Cowboy*, p. 194.
131. Carl W. Breihan, *The Man Who Shot Jesse James* (South Brunswick, NJ: A.S. Barnes, 1979), p. 21.
132. James, email correspondence with author, April 30, 2010.
133. Tuska, *The Filming of the West*, p. 139.
134. Wyatt, *More Than a Cowboy*, p. 196.
135. *New York Sun*, October 17, 1927.
136. *Los Angeles Times*, November 13, 1927.
137. *Los Angeles Times*, December 30, 1928.
138. Wyatt, *More Than a Cowboy*, pp. 44–72; www.imdb.com.
139. Tuska, *The Filming of the West*, pp. 137–38.
140. Wyatt, *More Than a Cowboy*, p 41; www.imdb.com.
141. Wyatt, *More Than a Cowboy*, p. 77.
142. Wyatt, *More Than a Cowboy*, p. 72; Cari Beauchamp, *Without Lying Down: Frances Marion and the Powerful Women of Early Hollywood* (Berkeley: University of California Press, 1998), p. 212; James, *The Love Pirate and the Bandit's Son*, p. 261.
143. www.imdb.com.
144. Laura James says Josephine James was up for the role of Jesse's mother (*The Love Pirate and the Bandit's Son*, p. 261). Edgar Wyatt says the daughters were Jessie Estelle James and Ethel Rose James (*More Than a Cowboy*, p. 196), and Williamson also says Jessie was up for the part of Zerelda Samuels (*Hillbillyland*, p. 110).
145. *New York Times*, October 17, 1927.
146. James H. Pierce, *The Battle of Hollywood* (Kansas City, MO: House of Greystoke, 1978), pp. 27–28.
147. Pierce, *The Battle of Hollywood*, p. 28.
148. Wyatt, *More Than a Cowboy*, p. 196.
149. Pierce, *The Battle of Hollywood*, p. 28.
150. Wyatt, *More Than a Cowboy*, p. 195; Beauchamp, *Without Lying Down*, p. 217.
151. *Photoplay*, October 1927, quoted in Wyatt, *More Than a Cowboy*, pp. 195–96; *Los Angeles Times*, November 13, 1927.
152. *Photoplay*, October 1927, quoted in Wyatt, *More Than a Cowboy*, pp. 195–96.
153. Wyatt, *More Than a Cowboy*, p. 194.
154. Wyatt, *More Than a Cowboy*, p. 195; *Variety* (September 14, 1927), p. 5.
155. Beauchamp, *Without Lying Down*, p. 217.
156. *New York Times*, October 17, 1927.
157. Michael R. Pitts puts the gross at $1.5 million in *Hollywood and American History: A Filmography of Over 250 Motion Pictures Depicting U.S. History* (Jefferson, NC: McFarland, 1984), p. 177.
158. Tuska, *The Filming of the West*, p. 139.
159. Beauchamp, *Without Lying Down*, p. 224.
160. Wyatt, *More Than a Cowboy*, p. 196. Pitts also writes that *Jesse James*'s box office failure "set the star's career on a downhill side" (*Hollywood and American History*, p. 177).
161. Williamson, *Hillbillyland*, p. 110; James, *The Love Pirate and the Bandit's Son*, p. 262.
162. Tuska, *The Filming of the West*, p. 140; *The New York Times*, December 27, 1928.
163. Wyatt, *More Than a Cowboy*, p. 97.
164. Wyatt, *More Than a Cowboy*, p. 112.

Chapter Four

1. Steele, *Jesse and Frank James*, pp. 62–67.
2. Yeatman, *Frank and Jesse James*, pp. 53, 119.
3. Yeatman, *Frank and Jesse James*, pp. 22–23.
4. Stiles, *Jesse James: Last Rebel of the Civil War*, pp. 323–35.
5. Breihan, *The Man Who Shot Jesse James*, p. 21; Stiles, *Jesse James: Last Rebel of the Civil War*, p. 357.
6. Stiles, *Jesse James: Last Rebel of the Civil War*, pp. 3–4, 374–75.
7. Breihan, *The Man Who Shot Jesse James*, p. 60.
8. Larry Bradley (compiler and editor), *Jesse James* (Noel, MO: McDonald County Press, 1970), p. 32; Yeatman, *Frank and Jesse James*, p. 327.
9. Yeatman, *Frank and Jesse James*, pp. 326–27.
10. David Quinlan, *The Illustrated Guide to Film Directors* (London: B.T. Batsford, 1983), p. 157; www.imdb.com.
11. *New York Times*, March 23, 1938.
12. Bradley, *Jesse James*, p. 3–5.
13. *Kansas City Times*, August 20, 1938.
14. *Jesse James* pressbook (1951 reissue), p. 1.
15. Quinlan, *The Illustrated Guide to Film Directors*, pp. 165–66; www.imdb.com.
16. *New York Times*, September 4, 1938.
17. *Kansas City Times*, August 20, 1938; Bradley, *Jesse James*, p. 10.
18. *New York Times*, September 4, 1938.
19. Bradley, *Jesse James*, pp. 7, 12.
20. Bradley, *Jesse James*, p. 12.
21. *Kansas City Times*, August 25, 1938.
22. Tom Weaver, *John Carradine: The Films* (Jefferson, NC: McFarland, 1999), p. 22.
23. *New York Times*, September 4, 1938.
24. Ibid.
25. *Kansas City Times*, September 10, 1938.
26. *New York Times*, September 4, 1938.
27. *Kansas City Times*, August 24, 1938.
28. Ibid.
29. Henry Fonda as told to Howard Teichmann, *Fonda: My Life* (New York: New American Library, 1981), p. 134.
30. www.imdb.com.
31. www.allmovie.com, www.imdb.com.
32. Robert Nott, *Last of the Cowboy Heroes: The West-*

erns of Randolph Scott, Joel McCrea, and Audie Murphy (Jefferson, NC: McFarland, 2004), pp. 9–13, 28, 153, 168.
33. Bradley, *Jesse James*, p. 43.
34. Bradley, *Jesse James*, p. 43; *Kansas City Times*, September 5, 1938.
35. Bradley, *Jesse James*, p. 45; *Kansas City Times*, September 5, 1938.
36. Fonda as told to Teichmann, *Fonda: My Life*, p. 305.
37. Ibid.
38. Bradley, *Jesse James*, p. 53.
39. Undated newspaper clipping, courtesy of Robert Nott; Bradley, *Jesse James*, p. 33; *New York Times*, January 15, 1939.
40. Ibid.
41. Undated newspaper clipping, courtesy of Robert Nott.
42. "Hollywood" by Ed Sullivan. Undated newspaper clipping, courtesy of Robert Nott.
43. Bradley, *Jesse James*, p. 53.
44. *Kansas City Times*, September 22, 1938.
45. *Kansas City Star*, July 21, 1968; www.imdb.com.
46. www.idsfilm.com.
47. Tuska, *The Filming of the West*, p. 361.
48. John H. Lenihan, *Showdown: Confronting Modern America in the Western Film* (Chicago: University of Illinois Press, 1980), p. 93.
49. Yeatman, *Frank and Jesse James*, p. 270.
50. *St. Joseph Gazette*, April 4, 1882; Yeatman, *Frank and Jesse James*, p. 275.
51. Yeatman, *Frank and Jesse James*, p. 287.
52. Stiles, *Jesse James: Last Rebel of the Civil War*, p. 395; Smith, *The Last Hurrah of the James-Younger Gang*, p. 198.
53. Yeatman, *Frank and Jesse James*, p. 283.
54. Stiles, *Jesse James: Last Rebel of the Civil War*, p. 380; Petrone, *Judgment at Gallatin*, p. 68.
55. Yeatman, *Frank and Jesse James*, p. 285.
56. Petrone, *Judgment at Gallatin*, p. 167.
57. Yeatman, *Frank and Jesse James*, pp. 230–35, 287–88.
58. Yeatman, *Frank and Jesse James*, p. 289–90.
59. Tuska, *The Filming of the West*, p. 362.
60. Quinlan, *The Illustrated Guide to Film Directors*, pp. 176–77.
61. Tuska, *The Filming of the West*, p. 362.
62. Quinlan, *The Illustrated Guide to Film Directors*, pp. 176–77.
63. www.imdb.com.
64. *The Return of Frank James* pressbook (1956 reissue), p. l; www.imdb.com.
65. www.imdb.com; www.allmovie.com.
66. Gene Tierney and Mickey Herskowitz, *Self-Portrait* (New York: Wyden Books, 1978), p. 43; www.imdb.com.
67. Tierney and Herskowitz, *Self-Portrait*, pp. 43–44; www.imdb.com.
68. Tierney and Herskowitz, *Self-Portrait*, p. 44.
69. Ibid.
70. *The Return of Frank James* pressbook, p. 1.
71. Tierney and Herskowitz, *Self-Portrait*, p. 44.
72. Ibid.
73. Tierney and Herskowitz, *Self-Portrait*, p. 44; www.imdb.com; www.allmovie.com.
74. Tuska, *The Filming of the West*, p. 363.

Chapter Five

1. Tuska, *The Filming of the West*, p. 460.
2. Brant, *Jesse James: The Man and the Myth*, p. 136.
3. Yeatman, *Frank and Jesse James*, p. 141.
4. Ibid.
5. Settle, *Jesse James Was His Name*, p. 76; Brant, *Jesse James: The Man and the Myth*, pp. 133–37; Stiles, *Jesse James: Last Rebel of the Civil War*, pp. 281–83; Yeatman, *Frank and Jesse James*, pp. 135–36.
6. Quinlan, *The Illustrated Guide to Film Directors*, p. 159.
7. *New York Times*, July 7, 1998.
8. Howard Kazanjian and Chris Enns, *The Cowboy and the Senorita: A Biography of Roy Rogers and Dale Evans* (Guilford, CT: TwoDot, 2004), p. 68.
9. Tuska, *The Filming of the West*, p. 461.
10. Bobby J. Copeland and Richard B. Smith III, *Gabby Hayes: King of the Cowboy Comics* (Madison, NC: Empire Publishing, 2008), p. 20.
11. Copeland and Smith. *Gabby Hayes*, p. 51.
12. Associated Press obituary, July 18, 1980. Courtesy of Boyd Magers, *Western Clippings*.
13. *London Independent*, December 11, 2001.
14. Tuska, *The Filming of the West*, p. 141.
15. *Los Angeles Times*, March 3, 1940.
16. Kazanjian and Enns, *The Cowboy and the Senorita*, p. 68.
17. *Los Angeles Times*, February 29, 1940.
18. *Boxoffice*, October 5, 1940, p. 32.
19. Richard Maurice Hurst, *Republic Studios: Between Poverty Row and the Majors* (Metuchen, NJ: Scarecrow, 1979), p. 122.
20. William K. Everson, *A Pictorial History of the Western Film* (New York: Citadel, 1969), p. 141.
21. *Washington Post*, August 16, 1941.
22. Brant, *The Outlaw Youngers*, p. 56.
23. Brant, *The Outlaw Youngers*, pp. 29–35; John J. Koblas, *Bushwhacker! Cole Younger & the Kansas-Missouri Border War* (St. Cloud, MN: North Star Press, 2004), p. 155.
24. Brant, *The Outlaw Youngers*, p. 8; www.allmovie.com.
25. Brant, *The Outlaw Youngers*, p. 96.
26. Faust, *Historical Times Illustrated Encyclopedia of the Civil War*, p. 502.
27. Stiles, *Jesse James: Last Rebel of the Civil War*, p. 233.
28. Mark Boardman, email correspondence with author, May 19, 2010.
29. Koblas, *Faithful Unto Death*, p. 16.
30. Brant, *The Outlaw Youngers*, pp. 270–81; Smith, *The Last Hurrah of the James-Younger Gang* (Norman: University of Oklahoma Press, 2001), pp. 209–10; Koblas, *Faithful Unto Death*, p. 169. Smith calls her Miller, but Brant and Koblas call her Muller.
31. Younger, *The Story of Cole Younger by Himself*, p. 99.
32. Quinlan, *The Illustrated Guide to Film Directors*, p. 89.
33. *Sydney Morning Herald*, November 17, 1941.
34. www.imdb.com, www.arlingtoncemetery.net.
35. www.imdb.com.
36. www.imdb.com.
37. *London Independent*, September 10, 1994, www.tcm.com, www.imdb.com, www.allmovie.com.
38. Barry Gifford, *Wild at Heart* (New York: Grove Weidenfeld, 1990), p. 75.
39. Croy, *Jesse James Was My Neighbor*, p. 247.
40. Croy, *Jesse James Was My Neighbor*, pp. 247–51.
41. Cole, email correspondence with author, May 14, 2010.
42. Brant, *Jesse James: The Man and the Myth*, pp. 222–23.
43. Copeland and Smith, *Gabby Hayes*, p. 20.

44. Cheryl Rogers-Barnett, *Cowboy Princess: Life with My Parents Roy Rogers and Dale Evans* (Lanham, MD: Taylor Trade Publishing, 2003), p. 85.
45. Copeland and Smith, *Gabby Hayes*, p. 56.
46. *London Telegraph*, June 29, 2009.
47. Raymond E. White, *King of the Cowboys, Queen of the West: Roy Rogers and Dale Evans* (Madison, WI: Popular Press, 2006), p. 134.
48. Tuska, *The Filming of the West*, p. 461.
49. In *King of the Cowboys, Queen of the West*, White lists two other songs from this movie, *Where the River Meets the Range* and *Old Chisholm Trail* (p. 134), while www.imdb.com credits only *The Old Chisholm Trail* and Sol Meyer's *You for Me*. It is possible other songs were included and later edited out for television, but the DVD I viewed (copyrighted 2006 by Double D Distribution) had only one song, *Just for You*.
50. Tuska, *The Filming of the West*, p. 461.
51. Dalton Trumbo, *The Remarkable Andrew* (Philadelphia: J.P. Lippincott, 1941), p. 24.
52. Jon Meacham, *American Lion: Andrew Jackson in the White House* (New York: Random House, 2008), pp. 203–04.
53. Trumbo, *The Remarkable Andrew*, p. 245.
54. Robert M. Utley, *Billy the Kid: A Short and Violent Life* (Lincoln: University of Nebraska Press, 1989), p. 183.
55. Bob Thomas, *Golden Boy: The Untold Story of William Holden* (New York: St. Martin's Press, 1983), p. 42.
56. Carson City Convention and Visitors Bureau, www.visitcarsoncity.com.
57. Thomas, *Golden Boy*, pp. 41–42; Michelangelo Capua, *William Holden: A Biography* (Jefferson, NC: McFarland, 2010), pp. 30–31.
58. Ibid.
59. www.glamourgirlsofthesilverscreen.com.
60. Quinlan, *The Illustrated Guide to Film Directors*, p. 132.
61. *Lodi News-Sentinel*, January 15, 1941.
62. *Rocky Mountain News*, December 5, 2005.
63. Biographical information comes from Peter Hanson's *Dalton Trumbo, Hollywood Rebel: A Critical Survey and Filmography* (Jefferson, NC: McFarland, 2001); editor Helen Manfull's *Additional Dialogue: Letters of Dalton Trumbo, 1942–1962* (New York: Bantam, 1972); www.imdb.com; www.wikipedia.com; and the *Rocky Mountain News*, December 5, 2005, September 10, 2004.
64. *Time*, February 3, 1941.
65. Manfull, *Additional Dialogue*, pp. 342–43.
66. Manfull, *Additional Dialogue*, pp. 21, 56.
67. Hanson, *Dalton Trumbo, Hollywood Rebel*, p. 63.
68. www.imdb.com.
69. *Boxoffice*, January 17, 1942.
70. Lawrence J. Quirk, *The Films of William Holden* (Secaucus, NJ: Citadel, 1973), p. 63.
71. Michael F. Blake, *Hollywood and the O.K. Corral: Portrayals of the Gunfight and Wyatt Earp* (Jefferson, NC: McFarland, 2007), p. 48.
72. Tuska, *The Filming of the West*, p. 481.
73. Tuska, *The Filming of the West*, p. 481–82.
74. Blake, *Hollywood and the O.K. Corral*, p. 54; *Los Angeles Times*, December 29, 1931; *Los Angeles Times*, September 21, 1949; www.imdb.com; www.richarddix.org.
75. *Los Angeles Times*, June 10, 1943. The movie was previewed before its general release in September.
76. Quinlan, *The Illustrated Guide to Film Directors*, p. 12.
77. *New York Times*, October 1, 1943.
78. www.imdb.com, www.allmovie.com.
79. *Chicago Daily Tribune*, December 30, 1943.
80. Frank Gruber, *Peace Marshal* (New York: Bantam, 1958), p. 36.
81. Gruber, *Peace Marshal*, p. 11.
82. John W. Morris, Charles R. Goins and Edwin C. McReynolds, *Historic Atlas of Oklahoma, Third Edition* (Norman: University of Oklahoma Press, 1966), map 62.
83. Timothy Eagan, *The Worst Hard Time: The Untold Story of Those Who Survived the Great American Dust Bowl* (New York: Mariner Books, 2006), p. 35.
84. Ibid.
85. Eagan, *The Worst Hard Time*, p. 35.
86. Eagan, *The Worst Hard Time*, p. 34.
87. Walter Prescott Webb, *The Texas Rangers: A Century of Frontier Defense* (Austin: University of Texas Press, 1935, 1965), pp. 220, 567.
88. Rick Miller, *Sam Bass & Gang* (Austin, TX: State House Press, 1999), pp. 64–78.
89. Miller. *Sam Bass & Gang*, pp. 247–62.
90. Trachtman, *The Gunfighters*, p. 155.
91. Robert Barr Smith, *Daltons! The Raid on Coffeyville, Kansas* (Norman: University of Oklahoma Press, 1996), pp. xiii, xv, 133, 166, 169; Trachtman, *The Gunfighters*, p. 84.
92. Quinlan, *The Illustrated Guide to Film Directors*, pp. 317–18, www.imdb.com.
93. *Los Angeles Times*, September 15, 1945, www.imdb.com.
94. Nott, Robert, *The Films of Randolph Scott* (Jefferson, NC: McFarland, 2004), p. 129.
95. www.allmovie.com; www.imdb.com; *Los Angeles Times*, May 2, 1987.
96. www.imdb.com.
97. Bob Herzberg, *Savages and Saints: The Changing Image of American Indians in Westerns* (Jefferson, NC: McFarland, 2008), p. 65.
98. Nott, *The Films of Randolph Scott*, p. 121; Nott, email correspondence with author, May 20, 2010.
99. www.b-westerns.com, www.allmovie.com; Richard B. Jewell with Vernon Harbin, *The RKO Story* (London: Octopus Books, 1982), p. 205.
100. Jewell with Harbin, *The RKO Story*, p. 211.
101. Ibid.
102. Stiles, *Jesse James: Last Rebel of the Civil War*, p. 298.
103. Yeatman, *Frank and Jesse James*, pp. 194–98; Stiles, *Jesse James: Last Rebel of the Civil War*, p. 339.
104. *Mining and Metallurgy, Volume 1* (New York: American Institute of Mining, Metallurgical, and Petroleum Engineers, January 1920), p. 51.
105. Stiles, *Jesse James: Last Rebel of the Civil War*, pp. 252–54; Settle, *Jesse James Was His Name*, pp. 59–60.
106. William C. Cline, *In the Nick of Time: Motion Picture Sound Serials* (Jefferson, NC: McFarland, 1997), p. 61; www.uclabruins.com; www.allmovie.com; www.imdb.com.
107. Hurst, *Republic Studios*, pp. 77–108; www.imdb.com.
108. Jack Mathis, *Valley of the Cliffhangers Supplement* (Barrington, IL: Jack Mathis Advertising, 1995), pp. 3, 10, 98–99.
109. Hank Davis, *Classic Cliffhangers: Volume 2, 1941–1955* (Baltimore: Midnight Marquee Press, 2008), p. 175.
110. www.imdb.com; Clayton Moore and Frank Thompson, *I Was That Masked Man* (Dallas: Taylor Trade Publishing), pp. 100–01.
111. Moore and Thompson, *I Was That Masked Man*, p. 100.
112. Boyd Magers and Michael Fitzgerald, *Westerns Women: Interviews with 50 Leading Ladies of Movie and Tel-*

evision Westerns from the 1930s to the 1960s (Jefferson, NC: McFarland, 1999), p. 225.
113. www.imdb.com.
114. www.b-westerns.com; www.imdb.com; Moore and Thompson, *I Was That Masked Man*, p. 101.
115. Cline, *In the Nick of Time*, p. 88.
116. Moore and Thompson, *I Was That Masked Man*, p. 101; www.b-westerns.com; www.imdb.com.
117. *New York Times*, December 29, 1999.
118. Moore and Thompson, *I Was That Masked Man*, p. 100.
119. Moore and Thompson, *I Was That Masked Man*, p. 82. Actually, Moore remembers the scene with him driving the wagon, leaping off, then the wagon flipping toward him. That's not the way it happens on film, however.
120. Moore and Thompson, *I Was That Masked Man*, pp. 82, 99.
121. *New York Times*, May 4, 1947.
122. Ibid.
123. Hurst, *Republic Studios*, p. 120.
124. Brant, *Jesse James: The Man and the Myth*, p. 55.
125. Moore and Thompson, *I Was That Masked Man*, p. 104.
126. Mathis, *Valley of the Cliffhangers Supplement*, p. 106.
127. www.imdb.com, www.classicimages.com.
128. Moore and Thompson, *I Was That Masked Man*, p. 104.
129. Maurice Zolotow, *Shooting Star: A Biography of John Wayne* (New York: Pocket Books, 1975), p. 100.
130. Samuel Fuller with Christa Lang Fuller and Jerome Henry Rudes, *A Third Face: My Tale of Writing, Fighting, and Filmmaking* (New York: Alfred A. Knopf, 2002), p. 247.
131. Fuller, *A Third Face*, p. 245.
132. Fuller, *A Third Face*, p. 247.
133. Yeatman, *Frank and Jesse James*, pp. 253, 261.
134. Yeatman, *Frank and Jesse James*, p. 266.
135. Croy, *Jesse James Was My Neighbor*, p. 201.
136. Breihan, *The Man Who Shot Jesse James*, p. 238.
137. Croy, *Jesse James Was My Neighbor*, p. 224.
138. Breihan, *The Man Who Shot Jesse James*, p. 255.
139. Breihan, *The Man Who Shot Jesse James*, pp. 270–71.
140. Breihan, *The Man Who Shot Jesse James*, pp. 282–87.
141. Yeatman, *Frank and Jesse James*, p. 292; Breihan, *The Man Who Shot Jesse James*, pp. 286–90.
142. Johnny D. Boggs, *Arm of the Bandit: The Trial of Frank James* (New York: Signet, 2002), p. 304.
143. Croy, *Jesse James Was My Neighbor*, pp. 226–29; Breihan, *The Man Who Shot Jesse James*, pp. 270–89; *Boxoffice*, November 20, 1948, p. 128.
144. *Christian Science Monitor*, March 9, 1949.
145. Information on Lippert and his companies come from material provided by Boyd Magers of *Western Clippings* magazine and the Robert L. Lippert Foundation website, www.robertllippertfoundation.com.
146. *New York Times*, November 8, 2009; Fuller, *A Third Face*, pp. 243–45.
147. Fuller, *A Third Face*, p. 245.
148. Fuller, *A Third Face*, p. 246.
149. Fuller, *A Third Face*, p. 247.
150. *The Washington Post*, March 23, 1992; *New York Times*, March 23, 1992; www.imdb.com.
151. www.imdb.com.
152. *Los Angeles Times*, January 29, 1949.
153. *Los Angeles Times*, September 23, 1948.
154. Fuller, *A Third Face*, pp. 247–48.
155. Fuller, *A Third Face*, p. 248.
156. Fuller, *A Third Face*, p. 247.
157. *Los Angeles Times*, January 29, 1949.
158. *New York Times*, April 2, 1949.
159. Brian Garfield, *Western Films*, p. 201.
160. Cline, *In the Nick of Time*, p. 42.
161. www.allmovie.com; www.imdb.com.
162. Ibid.
163. Michael G. Fitzgerald and Boyd Magers, *Ladies of the Western: Interviews with Fifty-one More Actresses from the Silent Era to the Television Westerns of the 1950s and 1960s* (Jefferson, NC: McFarland, 2006), p. 195.
164. Cline, *In the Nick of Time: Motion Picture Sound Serials*, p. 115; www.imdb.com.
165. Mathis, *Valley of the Cliffhangers Supplement*, p. 114.
166. www.b-westerns.com.
167. Paul Andrew Hutton, "Silver Screen Desperado," p. 161; *New York Times*, May 4, 1947.
168. Hurst, *Republic Studios*, p. 113.
169. Jack Mathis, *Valley of the Cliffhangers* (Northbrook, IL: Jack Mathis Advertising, 1975), p. viii.
170. Faust, *Historical Times Illustrated Encyclopedia of the Civil War*, p. 427.
171. Younger, *The Story of Cole Younger*, p. 43.
172. *Fighting Man of the Plains* pressbook.
173. Yeatman, *Frank and Jesse James*, pp. 109–10, 219–21; Carl W. Breihan, *The Day Jesse James Was Killed* (New York: Signet, 1979), pp. 62–63; Stiles, *Jesse James: Last Rebel of the Civil War*, pp. 264–65; Settle, *Jesse James Was His Name*, pp. 49–50, 70–71, 133.
174. *Fighting Man of the Plains* pressbook.
175. Interview with Wm. B. Shillingberg, September 2, 2009.
176. *Fighting Man of the Plains* pressbook.
177. Nott, *Last of the Cowboy Heroes*, p. 18.
178. *Fighting Man of the Plains* pressbook.
179. Nott, *The Films of Randolph Scott*, p. 121. Scott must have liked Marin. They worked on eight films together, more than Scott worked with any other director, before Marin's death in 1951 at age 52.
180. Quinlan, *The Illustrated Guide to Film Directors*, p. 198.
181. Biographical data came from Nott's *Last of the Cowboy Heroes*, The *Illustrated Guide to Film Directors* and imdb.com.
182. *Fighting Man of the Plains* pressbook.
183. Ibid., www.imdb.com.
184. *Fighting Man of the Plains* pressbook.
185. Ibid.
186. *Topeka Capital Journal*, August 1, 2002.
187. Richard S. Brownlee, *Gray Ghosts of the Confederacy: Guerilla Warfare in the West, 1861–1865* (Baton Rouge: Louisiana State University Press, 1958), p. 125.
188. Bob Herzberg, *Shooting Scripts: From Pulp Western to Film* (Jefferson, NC: McFarland), p. 65.
189. *New York Times*, November 17, 1949.

Chapter Six

1. *Boxoffice*, July 29, 1950, p. 23.
2. Boyd Magers, telephone interview with author, August 19, 2008.
3. Biographical information on Donald Barry's career is pulled from Internet sources such as Internet Movie Database (www.imdb.com) and All Movie Guide (www.allmovie.com), interviews with Boyd Magers and Jon Tuska, and various newspaper accounts from the 1950s to 1980.

4. Magers, telephone interview with author, August 19, 2008.
5. Internet Movie Database says 5'4½." His Associated Press obituary reports 5'8½." In an interview with Boyd Magers, Barry said he was 5'9."
6. Magers, telephone interview with author, August 19, 2008.
7. Tuska, *The Filming of the West*, p. 451.
8. Magers and Fitzgerald, *Westerns Women*, p. 26.
9. Nott, *The Films of Randolph Scott*, p. 193.
10. Information on Lippert and his companies came from material provided by Boyd Magers of *Western Clippings* magazine and the Robert L. Lippert Foundation website, www.robertllippertfoundation.com.
11. Magers and Fitzgerald, *Westerns Women*, p. 9.
12. The Donald Barry Productions were *The Dalton Gang, Square Dance Jubilee, Tough Assignment* (all 1949) and *Gunfire* and *Train to Tombstone* (both 1950). Barry also starred in, but did not produce, Lippert's *Red Desert* (1949) and *I Shot Billy the Kid* (1950). Those films also show Barry's choices of non–traditional characters. He's the antiheroic Billy in *I Shot Billy the Kid*, while *Square Dance Jubilee* is a Western musical and *Tough Assignment* is about modern-day cattle rustling.
13. Magers, telephone interview with author, August 19, 2008.
14. *New York Times*, May 13, 2004.
15. *Los Angeles Times*, March 8, 1970.
16. Magers and Fitzgerald, *Westerns Women*, p. 44.
17. As quoted in Buck Rainey, *Western Gunslingers in Fact and on Film* (Jefferson, NC: McFarland, 1998), p. 89.
18. Breihan, *The Man Who Shot Jesse James*, pp. 270–83.
19. Brant, *The Outlaw Youngers*, pp. 8, 30.
20. "The Trial of Clelland Miller for Bank Robbery, Corydon, Iowa, October, 1872," transcript, Prairie Trail Museum, Corydon IA; Brant, *Jesse James: The Man and the Myth*, pp. 77–78, 89–90, 102–03, 238–43.
21. Yeatman, *Frank and Jesse James*, pp. 201, 203, 263–64.
22. Yeatman, *Frank and Jesse James*, p. 85; Brant, *Jesse James: The Man and the Myth*, p. 74.
23. Croy, *Jesse James Was My Neighbor*, p. 247.
24. Ibid., p. 250.
25. Ibid.
26. *New York Times*, March 23, 1992; *Washington Post*, March 23, 1992.
27. Ray Hagen and Laura Wagner, *Killer Tomatoes: Fifteen Tough Film Dames* (Jefferson, NC: McFarland, 2004), p. 62.
28. Hagen and Wagner, *Killer Tomatoes,* pp. 50–64; www.imdb.com.
29. Hagen and Wagner, *Killer Tomatoes*, p. 63.
30. Bob Larkins and Boyd Magers, *The Films of Audie Murphy* (Jefferson, NC: McFarland, 2004), p. 45.
31. Koblas, *Bushwhacker!*, pp. 72–73.
32. Koblas, *Bushwhacker*, p. 74; Faust, *Historical Times Illustrated Encyclopedia of the Civil War*, p. 606.
33. Younger, *The Story of Cole Younger by Himself*, p. 43.
34. Richard S. Brownlee, *Gray Ghosts of the Confederacy,* pp. 123–25; Settle, *Jesse James Was His Name*, pp. 24–25.
35. Koblas, *Bushwhacker!*, pp. 236–37; Settle, *Jesse James Was His Name,* pp. 26–27.
36. Koblas, *Bushwhacker*, p. 259; Brownlee, *Gray Ghosts of the Confederacy*, pp. 226–29; Fellman, *Inside War: The Guerrilla Conflict in Missouri During the American Civil War*, p. 135.
37. Brant, *The Outlaw Youngers*, p. 56.
38. Koblas, *Bushwhacker!*, pp. 119, 157.
39. *New York Times*, April 4, 1920.
40. Ramon F. Adams, *Six-Guns and Saddle Leather: A Bibliography of Books and Pamphlets on Western Outlaws and Gunmen* (Mineola, NY: Dover Publications, 1998), p. 167.
41. Nancy Ohnick, compiler, *The Dalton Gang and Their Family Ties* (Meade, KS: Prairie Books, 2005), p. 31.
42. Brownlee, *Gray Ghosts of the Confederacy*, p. 104.
43. Edward E. Leslie, *The Devil Knows How to Ride: The True Story of William Clarke Quantrill and His Confederate Raiders* (New York: Da Capo Press, 1998), pp. 186–88.
44. Koblas, *Bushwhacker!*, pp. 261–62; www.briandonlevy.com.
45. Stiles, *Jesse James: Last Rebel of the Civil War*, p. 101.
46. Hank Sheffer, *The Queen and Her Court: A True Story of Apacheland Movie Ranch* (Arizona?: Norseman Publications, 2007), p. 20.
47. *Christian Science Monitor*, January 5, 1951.
48. *Los Angeles Times*, April 13, 1950.
49. Sheffer, *The Queen and Her Court*, p. 20.
50. Larkins and Magers, *The Films of Audie Murphy*, p. 43.
51. Larkins and Magers, *The Films of Audie Murphy,* pp. 41, 44; Nott, *Last of the Cowboy Heroes*, p. 99.
52. Ivan Spear, "Anyone Who Hasn't Played Jesse James Please Step Up," *Boxoffice*, July 29, 1950, p. 23.
53. Spear, *Boxoffice*, July 29, 1950, pp. 22–23; Bernard F. Dick, *Hal Wallis: Producer to the Stars* (Lexington: University Press of Kentucky, 2004), pp. 116; www.imdb.com.
54. *Washington Post*, December 14, 1950.
55. Larkins and Magers, *The Films of Audie Murphy*, p. 42.
56. Settle, *Jesse James Was His Name*, p. 26.
57. *The Great Missouri Raid* pressbook, p. 2.
58. *The Great Missouri Raid* pressbook, p. 3. Some sources say that *The Great Missouri Raid* is based on Gruber's novel *Broken Lance* but that novel was actually the basis for *Warpath* (1951), starring Edmond O'Brien.
59. Settle, *Jesse James Was His Name*, pp. 26–27.
60. Settle, *Jesse James Was His Name*, pp. 27–31, 91.
61. Stiles, *Jesse James: Last Rebel of the Civil War*, pp. 185–86.
62. www.wikipedia.org.
63. Yeatman, *Frank and Jesse James*, pp. 86, 106–07.
64. Stiles, *Jesse James: Last Rebel of the Civil War*, pp. 352, 357, 359, 371.
65. Settle, *Jesse James Was His Name*, pp. 116–19, 140–43, 152.
66. *The Great Missouri Raid* pressbook, p. 2.
67. Quinlan, *The Illustrated Guide to Film Directors*, pp. 79–80; www.imdb.com.
68. Macdonald Carey, *The Days of My Life* (New York: St. Martin's Press, 1991), pp. 171–72.
69. Macdonald Carey, *The Days of My Life,* p. 171; www.imdb.com.
70. Macdonald Carey, *The Days of My Life*, pp. 145–46, 171.
71. *The Great Missouri Raid* pressbook, p. 2.
72. *The Great Missouri Raid* pressbook, p. 3.
73. Macdonald Carey, *The Days of My Life*, p. 156.
74. Macdonald Carey, *The Days of My Life*, p. 171.
75. Ibid.
76. Settle, *Jesse James Was His Name*, pp. 29–30; Koblas, *Bushwhacker!*, pp. 270–80; Brant, *The Outlaw Youngers*, p. 63.
77. Brant, *The Outlaw Youngers*, pp. 62–63; Younger, *The Story of Cole Younger by Himself*, p. 50.

78. Younger, *The Story of Cole Younger by Himself*, p. 50.
79. Koblas, *Faithful Unto Death*, p. 168.
80. Stiles, *Jesse James: Last Rebel of the Civil War*, pp. 203–04; Koblas, *Faithful Unto Death*, p. 75. Historians argue about who killed Heywood, some saying Frank, others pinning it on Jesse. I believe it was Frank.
81. *Los Angeles Times*, September 10, 1948.
82. *London Independent*, March 1, 2002.
83. Ibid.
84. Ibid.
85. Douglas Brode, *Shooting Stars of the Small Screen: Encyclopedia of TV Western Actors, 1946-Present* (Austin: University of Texas Press, 2009), p. 53; Darwin Porter, *Howard Hughes: Hell's Angel* (New York: Blood Moon Productions, 2005), p. 518.
86. Brode. *Shooting Stars of the Small Screen*, pp. 62–63; www.imdb.com; www.allmovie.com.
87. *New York Times*, April 10, 2000.
88. Franklin Jarlett, *Robert Ryan: A Biography and Critical Filmography* (Jefferson, NC: McFarland, 1990), pp. 6–7, 23; www.imdb.com.
89. Jarlett, *Robert Ryan: A Biography and Critical Filmography*, p. 56.
90. Boyd Magers, email correspondence with author, June 11, 2010.
91. *Los Angeles Daily News*, June 15, 1951.
92. *New York Times*, August 10, 1951.
93. *Los Angeles Times*, September 10, 1948.
94. Ben Cooper, interview with author, November 8, 2008.
95. Faust, *Historical Times Illustrated Encyclopedia of the Civil War*, pp. 22, 501.
96. Ibid., pp. 632, 735–37.
97. Cooper interview with author, November 8, 2008.
98. Ibid.
99. Michael Fessier, "The Woman They Almost Lynched," *The Saturday Evening Post*, January 6, 1951.
100. Nott, email correspondence with author, July 1, 2010; www.imdb.com.
101. Magers and Fitzgerald, *Westerns Women*, p. 242.
102. Ibid.
103. Magers and Fitzgerald, *Westerns Women*, pp. 128–29.
104. www.imdb.com; www.allmovie.com; www.variety.com.
105. Magers and Fitzgerald, *Westerns Women*, p. 128.
106. Magers and Fitzgerald, *Westerns Women*, p. 242.
107. Cooper interview with author, November 8, 2008; Nott, email correspondence with author, July 1, 2010; Hurst, *Republic Studios*, p. 27.
108. Magers and Fitzgerald, *Westerns Women*, p. 129; Cooper interview with author, November 8, 2008.
109. Stiles, *Jesse James: Last Rebel of the Civil War*, p. 373.
110. Smith, *The Last Hurrah of the James-Younger Gang*, p. 178.
111. Breihan, *The Man Who Shot Jesse James*, p. 187.
112. Breihan, *The Man Who Shot Jesse James*, p. 282.
113. www.creede.com.
114. Boardman, email correspondence with author, June 9, 2010.
115. Smith, *The Last Hurrah of the James-Younger Gang*, pp. 110, 121.
116. Stiles, *Jesse James: Last Rebel of the Civil War*, pp. 185–86.
117. Smith, *The Last Hurrah of the James-Younger Gang*, pp. 30, 163–66; Stiles, *Jesse James: Last Rebel of the Civil War*, p. 312; Koblas, *Faithful Unto Death*, p. 17.
118. Settle, *Jesse James Was His Name*, p. 32.
119. *New York Times*, March 23, 1953.
120. *Los Angeles Times*, May 7, 1953; www.allmovie.com; www.imdb.com.
121. Barbara Payton, *I Am Not Ashamed* (Los Angeles: Holloway House, 2008), p. 8.
122. Payton, *I Am Not Ashamed*, p. 143; *Los Angeles Times*, May 11, 1967.
123. *Los Angeles Times*, May 11, 1967; www.imdb.com.
124. Payton, *I Am Not Ashamed*, p. 164.
125. Payton, *I Am Not Ashamed*, p. 165.
126. Payton, *I Am Not Ashamed*, p. 8.
127. *New York Times*, May 11, 1967; *Los Angeles Times*, May 11, 1967.
128. Richard W. Haines, *Technicolor Movies: The History of Dye Transfer Printing* (Jefferson, NC: McFarland, 2003), p. 59.
129. Yeatman, *Frank and Jesse James*, pp. 333–39.
130. Yeatman, *Frank and Jesse James*, p. 289.
131. Smith, *Daltons!*, p. 37, 72, 83–89; Trachtman, *The Gunfighters*, p. 84.
132. Trachtman, *The Gunfighters*, pp. 84–85; Smith, *Daltons!*, pp. 90–91.
133. Yeatman, *Frank and Jesse James*, p. 292.
134. www.imdb.com.
135. Ibid.
136. www.allmovie.com; www.imdb.com.
137. *Variety*, January 22, 1954.
138. Quinlan, *The Illustrated Guide to Film Directors*, p. 49.
139. Brant, *Jesse James: The Man and the Myth*, pp. 131–32.
140. Phillip W. Steele and George Warfel, *The Many Faces of Jesse James* (Gretna, LA: Pelican Books, 1995), pp. 14, 22.
141. *Meridian* (Mississippi) *Star*, September 3, 1954.
142. Ibid., September 3, 1954; September 5, 1954.
143. Ibid.
144. *Boxoffice*, August 14, 1954.
145. www.tcm.com, from the MPPA/PCA Collection at the AMPAS Library.
146. *Hattiesburg* (Mississippi) *American*, September 3, 1954; *Meridian* (Mississippi) *Star*, September 3, 1954; September 5, 1954.
147. *Boxoffice*, September 11, 1954.
148. *Meridian* (Mississippi) *Star*, September 3, 1954; September 5, 1954.
149. *Variety*, August 4, 1954; July 31, 1967.
150. *Los Angeles Times*, August 12, 1973; www.imdb.com.
151. Magers and Fitzgerald, *Westerns Women*, p. 26.
152. www.imdb.com.
153. *Los Angeles Times*, July 18, 1980.
154. www.imdb.com; www.allmovie.com.
155. Brant, *Jesse James: The Man and the Myth*, pp. 72–75.
156. David Nevin, *The Expressmen* (Alexandria, VA: Time-Life Books, 1974), pp. 216–20.
157. Yeatman, *Frank and Jesse James*, p. 251.
158. www.imdb.com; www.allmovie.com.
159. Brian Garfield, *Western Films* (New York: Rawson Associates, 1982), p. 250.
160. William C. Cline, *Serials-ly Speaking: Essays on Cliffhangers* (Jefferson, NC: McFarland, 1994), p. 155.
161. Hagen and Wagner, *Killer Tomatoes*, pp. 92–100; Nott, email correspondence with author, June 10, 2010; www.imdb.com.
162. *Variety*, www.variety.com, April 4, 2003; *Los Angeles Times*, March 6, 2003.

163. *Los Angeles Times*, March 6, 2003.
164. Garfield, *Western Films*, p. 250.
165. *Los Angeles Times*, March 6, 2003; *Variety*, www.variety.com, April 4, 2003.
166. Ibid.
167. *Los Angeles Times*, October 14, 1956.
168. Koblas, *Faithful Unto Death*, pp. 71, 74–75.
169. *Los Angeles Times*, October 14, 1956.
170. Koblas, *Faithful Unto Death*, p. 145.
171. Brant, *Jesse James: The Man and the Myth*, p. 8.
172. Koblas, *Faithful Unto Death*, p. 102; John Koblas, *Minnesota Grit: The Men Who Defeated the James-Younger Gang* (St. Cloud, MN: North Star Press, 2005), pp. 29, 54.
173. Smith, *The Last Hurrah of the James-Younger Gang*, p. 166.
174. George Huntington, *Robber and Hero: The Story of the Northfield Bank Raid* (St. Paul: Minnesota Historical Society Press, 1986), p. 51.
175. David Paul Thelen, *Paths of Resistance: Tradition and Dignity in Industrializing Missouri* (New York: Oxford University Press, 1986), p. 72.
176. Koblas, *Minnesota Grit*, p. 54.
177. Koblas, *Faithful Unto Death*, pp. 17, 26, 81.
178. Stiles, *Jesse James: Last Rebel of the Civil War*, p. 352.
179. Stiles, *Jesse James: Last Rebel of the Civil War*, pp. 364, 370; Yeatman, *Frank and Jesse James*, p. 290.
180. Settle, *Jesse James Was His Name*, p. 114.
181. Settle, *Jesse James Was His Name*, p. 113.
182. Stiles, *Jesse James: Last Rebel of the Civil War*, p. 370.
183. Stiles, *Jesse James: Last Rebel of the Civil War*, pp. 362, 370; Yeatman, *Frank and Jesse James*, p. 264.
184. Settle, *Jesse James Was His Name*, pp. 76, 85.
185. Yeatman, *Frank and Jesse James*, p. 267.
186. Yeatman, *Frank and Jesse James*, p. 270; Settle, *Jesse James Was His Name*, p. 119.
187. Settle, *Jesse James Was His Name*, pp. 171–72; Ronald H. Beights, *Jesse James and the First Missouri Train Robbery* (Gretna, LA: Pelican, 2002), p. 118.
188. *New York Times*, March 23, 1957.
189. R. Philip Loy, *Westerns in a Changing America 1955–2000*, p. 201.
190. Lenihan, *Showdown*, p. 141.
191. Fenin and Everson, *The Western*, p. 338.
192. *New York Sun*, September 19, 2007.
193. Lawrence Frascella and Al Weisel, *Live Fast, Die Young: The Wild Ride of Making* Rebel Without a Cause (New York: Touchstone, 2005), p. 269.
194. *New York Times*, September 16, 2007.
195. www.imdb.com; www.tcm.com.
196. Robert J. Wagner with Scott Eyman, *Pieces of My Heart: A Life* (New York: Harper Entertainment, 2008), p. 118.
197. Frascella and Weisel, *Live Fast, Die Young*, p. 269.
198. Frascella and Weisel, *Live Fast, Die Young*, pp. 269–70.
199. Wagner and Eyman, *Pieces of My Heart*, p. 118.
100. Frascella and Weisel, *Live Fast, Die Young*, p. 270.
201. Frascella and Weisel, *Live Fast, Die Young*, p. 269.
202. Wagner and Eyman, *Pieces of My Heart*, p. 118.
203. Johnny D. Boggs, "The Reel, Not Real, Jesse James in Film," *True West* (April 2007), p. 25.
204. Stiles, *Jesse James: Last Rebel of the Civil War*, pp. 272–73; Yeatman, *Frank and Jesse James*, pp. 126–27.
205. Ibid.
206. Yeatman, *Frank and Jesse James*, p. 251; Breihan, *The Man Who Shot Jesse James*, p. 21.
207. Breihan, *The Man Who Shot Jesse James*, p. 21.
208. Yeatman, *Frank and Jesse James*, pp. 114–15; Stiles, *Jesse James: Last Rebel of the Civil War*, pp. 253–55.
209. Stiles, *Jesse James: Last Rebel of the Civil War*, p. 289.
210. Stiles, *Jesse James: Last Rebel of the Civil War*, pp. 288–90.
211. Yeatman, *Frank and Jesse James*, p. 319; Brant, *The Outlaw Youngers*, p. 314.
212. *New York Times*, June 11, 1994; www.imdb.com.
213. Robert Vaughn, *A Fortunate Life* (New York: Thomas Dunne, 2008), p. 77.
214. www.imdb.com.
215. www.imdb.com.
216. Hurst, *Republic Studios*, pp. 25–28.
217. Hurst, *Republic Studios*, p. 24.
218. Gene Autry and James Garner are also sometimes given credit for cameos in the famous gunfight scene, but they are not in the movie.
219. Settle, *Jesse James Was His Name*, p. 55; Yeatman, *Frank and Jesse James*, p. 95.
220. Settle, *Jesse James Was His Name*, p. 69; Steele, *Jesse and Frank James*, p. 49.
221. Settle, *Jesse James Was His Name*, p. 121; Stiles, *Jesse James: Last Rebel of the Civil War*, p. 395; Yeatman, *Frank and Jesse James*, p. 275.
222. *New York Times*, May 18, 1959.
223. *Alias Jesse James* pressbook, p. 5.
224. www.imdb.com, www.tcm.com.
225. *Alias Jesse James* pressbook, p. 5.
226. www.whitehouse.gov.
227. www.imdb.com; *Alias Jesse James* pressbook, p. 5.
228. www.imdb.com; Quinlan. *The Illustrated Guide to Film Directors*, p. 204; *Los Angeles Times*, February 13, 1959.
229. *Los Angeles Times*, February 13, 1959.
230. Ibid.
231. Donald McCaffrey, *The Road to Comedy: The Films of Bob Hope* (Santa Barbara, CA: Praeger, 2004), pp. 81–83.
232. *Los Angeles Times*, March 18, 1959.
233. *New York Times*, May 18, 1959.
234. Settle, *Jesse James Was His Name*, pp. 8, 26; Yeatman, *Frank and Jesse James*, p. 29.
235. Faust, *The Historical Times Illustrated Encyclopedia of the Civil War*, p. 606.
236. Faust, *The Historical Times Illustrated Encyclopedia of the Civil War*, p. 676; Brant, *Jesse James: The Man and the Myth*, pp. 40–41.
237. Brant, *The Outlaw Youngers*, pp. 89–90.
238. Stiles, *Jesse James: Last Rebel of the Civil War*, pp. 196–97, 203–06, 218–20.
239. Settle, *Jesse James Was His Name*, pp. 33–34; Brant, *Jesse James: The Man and the Myth*, pp. 47–54.
240. www.imdb.com.
241. www.imdb.com; *New York Times*, August 25, 1960.
242. *New York Times*, August 25, 1960.
243. *London Independent*, May 29, 2002.
244. Ibid.; www.tcm.com.
245. Ray Stricklyn, *Angels and Demons: One Actor's Hollywood Journey: An Autobiography* (Los Angeles: Belle Publishing, 1999), pp. 136, 139.
246. Stricklyn, *Angels and Demons*, p. 136.
247. Stricklyn, *Angels and Demons*, p. 137; *London Independent*, May 29, 2002.
248. Stricklyn, *Angels and Demons*, pp. 137–38.
249. *New York Times*, August 25, 1960.

Chapter Seven

1. www.imdb.com.
2. Jeff Forrester and Tom Forrester, *The Three Stooges: The Triumphs and Tragedies of the Most Popular Comedy Team of All Time* (Los Angeles: Donaldson Books, 2004), p. 168.
3. www.imdb.com.
4. Ibid.
5. Ibid.
6. Ibid.
7. Stephen Cox and Jim Terry, *One Fine Stooge: Larry Fine's Frizzy Life in Pictures* (Nashville, TN: Cumberland House, 2006), p. 120.
8. Ibid.
9. Cox and Terry, *One Fine Stooge*, p. 121.
10. Cox and Terry, *One Fine Stooge*, p. 121; www.imdb.com.
11. Cox and Terry, *One Fine Stooge*, p. 140; *Hollywood Reporter*, January 8, 1965.
12. Cox and Terry, *One Fine Stooge*, pp. 166–69.
13. www.imdb.com.
14. Garfield, *Western Films*, p. 202.
15. James D. Horan, *Desperate Men* (New York: Bonanza Books, 1969), pp. 182–205.
16. Nott, email correspondence with author, July 7, 2010.
17. *New York Times*, June 27, 1965.
18. *Billy the Kid versus Dracula-Jesse James Meets Frankenstein's Daughter* pressbook.
19. *Billy the Kid versus Dracula-Jesse James Meets Frankenstein's Daughter* pressbook, p. 7; www.imdb.com.
20. *Billy the Kid versus Dracula-Jesse James Meets Frankenstein's Daughter* pressbook, pp. 7, 15; Robert Hofler, *The Man Who Invented Rock Hudson: The Pretty Boys and Dirty Deals of Henry Willson* (New York: Da Capo Press, 2006), p. 396; www.imdb.com; www.bmonster.com.
21. *Billy the Kid versus Dracula-Jesse James Meets Frankenstein's Daughter* pressbook, p. 15; www.imdb.com.
22. www.imdb.com; *Los Angeles Times*, March 14, 1966.
23. *Billy the Kid versus Dracula—Jesse James Meets Frankenstein's Daughter* pressbook, p. 15; www.imdb.com.
24. www.imdb.com.
25. Quoted in "Monstervision's Joe Bob reviews *Dracula* 1931," http://www.angelfire.com/mn/nn/Dracula1931.html.
26. Handbook of Texas Online, www.tshaonline.org.
27. Ibid.
28. *Boxoffice*, May 5, 1969.
29. Nott, *Last of the Cowboy Heroes*, p. 164.
30. Larkins and Magers, *The Films of Audie Murphy*, p. 216; *The Washington Post*, December 2, 2001; *Framework: The Journal of Cinema and Media* (Spring 2002).
31. Budd Boetticher, *When in Disgrace* (Santa Barbara, CA: Neville, 1989), p. 327; Don Graham, *No Name on the Bullet: A Biography of Audie Murphy* (New York: Viking, 1989), p. 309–10.
32. From Boetticher, *When in Disgrace*, p. 375; Larkins and Magers, *The Films of Audie Murphy*, pp. 218–19; and Wheeler W. Dixon, *Film Noir and the Cinema of Paranoia* (New Brunswick, NJ: Rutgers University Press, 2009), p. 69; Boyd Magers, telephone interview with author, August 19, 2008; Graham, *No Name on the Bullet*, p. 308.
33. Quoted in Dixon, *Film Noir and the Cinema of Paranoia*, p. 69.
34. Ibid.
35. Larkins and Magers, *The Films of Audie Murphy*, p. 218.
36. Graham, *No Name on the Bullet*, p. 310.
37. Ibid., p. 310; *Los Angeles Times*, December 13, 1992.
38. www.imdb.com, Larkins and Magers, *The Films of Audie Murphy*, pp. 216–19.
39. www.imdb.com; Larry Hedrick telephone interview with author, May 24, 2010.
40. Jim Kitzes, *Horizons West* (Bloomington: Indiana University Press, 1969), p. 127.
41. Nott, *Last of the Cowboy Heroes*, p. 166.
42. Larkins and Magers, *The Films of Audie Murphy*, p. 219.
43. Graham, *No Name on the Bullet*, p. 311.
44. Nott, email correspondence with author, May 24, 2010.
45. Nott, email correspondence with author, May 21, 2010. The quote comes from Drake Stutesman's September 2000 interview with Boetticher during the New York Film Festival, published in *Framework: The Journal of Cinema and Media* (Detroit: Volume 43, No. 1, Spring 2002).
46. Graham, *No Name on the Bullet*, p. 310.
47. Graham, *No Name on the Bullet*, p. 310–11.
48. Larkins and Magers, *The Films of Audie Murphy*, pp. 218–19; Nott, *Last of the Cowboy Heroes*, pp. 166–67; Nott, email correspondence with author, July 8, 2010.
49. Boetticher, *When in Disgrace*, p. 387.
50. *The Washington Post*, December 2, 2001.
51. Quoted in Nott, *Last of the Cowboy Heroes*, pp. 166–67.
52. Nott, *Last of the Cowboy Heroes*, p. 166.

Chapter Eight

1. *Los Angeles Times*, April 28, 1972.
2. Smith, *The Last Hurrah of the James-Younger Gang*, pp. 166–67.
3. Stiles, *Jesse James: Last Rebel of the Civil War*, pp. 288–90.
4. Croy, *Cole Younger: Last of the Great Outlaws* (University of Nebraska Press, 1999), p. 109; Brant, *The Outlaw Youngers*, p. 206; Smith, *The Last Hurrah of the James-Younger Gang*, p. 54.
5. Huntington, *Robber and Hero*, pp. 5–7; Smith, *The Last Hurrah of the James-Younger Gang*, p. 83; Koblas, *Faithful Unto Death*, p. 86.
6. Koblas, *Minnesota Grit*, pp. 81–83.
7. Koblas, *Minnesota Grit*, p. 50.
8. Koblas, *Minnesota Grit*, p. 84; Koblas, *Faithful Unto Death*, p. 88.
9. Smith, *The Last Hurrah of the James-Younger Gang*, pp. 116–17; Koblas, *Faithful Unto Death*, pp. 67–68.
10. Koblas, *Minnesota Grit*, pp. 33, 89–90; Koblas, *Faithful Unto Death*, p. 71.
11. Koblas, *Minnesota Grit*, pp. 21–22; Koblas, *Faithful Unto Death*, p. 71; Smith, *The Last Hurrah of the James-Younger Gang*, p. 98.
12. Koblas, *Minnesota Grit*, p. 24; Smith, *The Last Hurrah of the James-Younger Gang*, pp. 98–99.
13. Smith, *The Last Hurrah of the James-Younger Gang*, pp. 76–77; Koblas, *Minnesota Grit*, pp. 32–33.
14. Koblas, *Minnesota Grit*, pp. 34–35.
15. Koblas, *Minnesota Grit*, pp. 33–35.
16. Koblas, *Minnesota Grit*, p. 35; Koblas, *Faithful Unto Death*, p. 89.
17. *Los Angeles Times*, April 28, 1972; www.imdb.com.
18. *The Great Northfield Minnesota Raid* pressbook; www.imdb.com.
19. *The Great Northfield Minnesota Raid* pressbook; www.tcm.com.
20. *New York Times*, June 15, 1972.
21. *Minneapolis Star Tribune*, February 24, 2007.

22. *The Great Northfield Minnesota Raid* pressbook.
23. Ibid.
24. *Chicago Sun-Times*, November 6, 1988.
25. *True West* (April 2007), p. 25.
26. *Los Angeles Times*, April 28, 1972.
27. *The Great Northfield Minnesota Raid* pressbook.
28. Yeatman, *Frank and Jesse James*, p. 99; Stiles, *Jesse James: Last Rebel of the Civil War*, p. 213.
29. Yeatman, *Frank and Jesse James*, p. 139; Stiles, *Jesse James: Last Rebel of the Civil War*, pp. 352–53.
30. Yeatman, *Frank and Jesse James*, p. 218.
31. Smith, *The Last Hurrah of the James-Younger Gang*, p. 33.
32. Brant, *The Outlaw Youngers*, pp. 89–91.
33. Yeatman, *Frank and Jesse James*, p. 27; Stiles, *Jesse James: Last Rebel of the Civil War*, pp. 30–31.
34. Brant, *The Outlaw Youngers*, p. 116; Smith, *The Last Hurrah of the James-Younger Gang*, p. 37.
35. *The Long Riders* pressbook, p. 2.
36. Koblas, *Faithful Unto Death*, p. 16.
37. Brant, *The Outlaw Youngers*, p. 8.
38. Brant, *The Outlaw Youngers*, pp. 133–39.
39. Yeatman, *Frank and Jesse James*, pp. 109–10; Stiles, *Jesse James: Last Rebel of the Civil War*, pp. 242–43.
40. Koblas, *Faithful Unto Death*, p. 14.
41. Smith, *The Last Hurrah of the James-Younger Gang*, p. 39.
42. Koblas, *Faithful Unto Death*, pp. 78, 139.
43. Koblas, *Faithful Unto Death*, pp. 74–76.
44. Koblas, *Faithful Unto Death*, pp. 62–63, 143.
45. Koblas, *Faithful Unto Death*, pp. 62–63.
46. Koblas, *Faithful Unto Death*, pp. 22–23.
47. Koblas, *Faithful Unto Death*, p. 32; Smith, *The Last Hurrah of the James-Younger Gang*, p. 54.
48. Koblas, *Faithful Unto Death*, pp. 162–63.
49. Ibid.
50. *The Long Riders* pressbook, p. 2.
51. *The Long Riders* pressbook, p. 3.
52. *The Long Riders* pressbook, p. 2.
53. *The Long Riders* pressbook, p. 3.
54. *True West*, April 2008, p. 100.
55. *True West*, April 2008, p. 100; Quinlan, *The Illustrated Guide to Film Directors*, pp. 138–39; www.imdb.com.
56. *Christian Science Monitor*, July 30, 1999; www.imdb.com.
57. *The Long Riders* pressbook, p. 3.
58. *Chicago Tribune*, May 16, 1980.
59. *New York Times*, August 17, 2001.
60. *American Outlaws* pressbook, p. 3.
61. *Star Interviews*, January 1, 2001.
62. Brant, *The Outlaw Youngers*, pp. 8, 56.
63. Yeatman, *Frank and Jesse James*, p. 317.
64. Brant, *The Outlaw Youngers*, p. 281.
65. Stiles, *Jesse James: Last Rebel of the Civil War*, pp. 233, 250, 366–67.
66. www.rockrail.com.
67. Yeatman, *Frank and Jesse James*, pp. 99–100.
68. Yeatman, *Frank and Jesse James*, pp. 19–20; Stiles, *Jesse James: Last Rebel of the Civil War*, pp. 245–46; Brant, *Jesse James: The Man and the Myth*, p. 108.
69. *American Outlaws* pressbook, p. 3.
70. www.imdb.com.
71. *American Outlaws* pressbook, p. 3.
72. *American Outlaws* pressbook, pp. 3, 20; www.imdb.com.
73. *American Outlaws* pressbook, pp. 4, 15; *Star Interviews*, January 1, 2001; *Los Angeles Times*, August 13, 2001.
74. (London) *Sunday Mirror*, September 2, 2001.
75. Ibid.
76. *American Outlaws*, pressbook, p. 5.
77. *Los Angeles Times*, August 22, 2001.
78. Ibid.
79. *Star Interviews*, January 1, 2001.
80. *American Outlaws* pressbook, pp. 6, 19.
81. *Star Interviews*, January 1, 2001; *American Outlaws* pressbook, p. 8.
82. *American Outlaws* pressbook, p. 12.
83. *American Outlaws* pressbook, p. 12; *American Outlaws* DVD.
84. *Star Interviews*, January 1, 2001.
85. www.imdb.com; *American Outlaws* pressbook, p. 12.
86. *Boxoffice* magazine, August 16, 2001.
87. *Entertainment Weekly*, August 15, 2001.
88. (Naperville, Illinois) *Sun*, August 17, 2001.
89. *New York Times*, August 17, 2001.
90. *San Francisco Chronicle*, August 17, 2001.
91. Settle, *Jesse James Was His Name*, pp. 33–34.
92. Stiles, *Jesse James: Last Rebel of the Civil War*, p. 372.
93. Stiles, *Jesse James: Last Rebel of the Civil War*, pp. 372–73.
94. Yeatman, *Frank and Jesse James*, pp. 161–62, 270.
95. Yeatman, *Frank and Jesse James*, pp. 253–54; Brant, *Jesse James: The Man and the Myth*, pp. 214–15; Breihan, *The Man Who Shot Jesse James*, pp. 187–88.
96. Brant, *Jesse James: The Man and the Myth*, p. 216.
97. Stiles, *Jesse James: Last Rebel of the Civil War*, pp. 368–69; Settle, *Jesse James Was His Name*, pp. 111–12.
98. Stiles, *Jesse James: Last Rebel of the Civil War*, p. 369.
99. *Washington Post*, September 9, 2007.
100. Ibid.
101. *Chicago Sun-Times*, September 30, 2007.
102. *True West* (November–December 2007), p. 25.
103. Ibid.
104. *Washington Post*, September 9, 2007.
105. *Chicago Sun-Times*, September 30, 2007.
106. *New York Observer*, September 18, 2007.
107. *Chicago Sun-Times*, September 30, 2007.
108. *Fresno Bee*, October 19, 2007.
109. *Detroit News*, October 12, 2007.
110. *Chicago Tribune*, October 4, 2007.
111. *USA Today*, September 21, 2007.
112. *Washington Post*, October 4, 2007.
113. *Seattle Times*, October 5, 2007.
114. Brant, Marley, *The Outlaw Youngers: A Confederate Brotherhood* (Lanham, MD: Madison Books, 1992), pp. 62–63.
115. *American Bandits: Frank and Jesse James* DVD, audio commentary track (E1 Entertainment, 2010).
116. www.imdb.com.
117. Trachtman, *The Gunfighters*, pp. 45–47.
118. Settle, *Jesse James Was His Name*, pp. 69, 91.
119. Stiles, *Jesse James: Last Rebel of the Civil War*, pp. 359–360; Settle, *Jesse James Was His Name*, p. 133.
120. www.imdb.com.
121. *American Bandits: Frank and Jesse James* DVD, audio commentary track (E1 Entertainment, 2010).
122. Ibid.

Chapter Nine

1. Paul Simpson, *The Rough Guide to Westerns* (London: Rough Guides, 2006), p. 250.

2. Ibid.
3. Ibid., www.imdb.com, www.spaghetti-western.net.
4. *New York Times*, November 24, 1977.

Chapter Ten

1. MCA-TV press release #25620, October 15, 1970.
2. Koblas, *Minnesota Grit*, pp. 29–32.
3. Smith, *Daltons!*, p. 166.
4. Smith, *Daltons!*, p. 34.
5. Smith, *The Last Hurrah of the James-Younger Gang*, p. 11.
6. Younger, *The Story of Cole Younger by Himself*, p. 70.
7. Phillip Steele, *The Last Cherokee Warriors* (Gretna, LA: Pelican Books, 1987), pp. 70–103.
8. http://www.nps.gov/history/NR/twhp/wwwlps/lessons/99condon/99facts2.htm.
9. Smith, *Daltons!*, p. 24.
10. *Chicago Sun-Times*, February 14, 1986.
11. Yeatman, *Frank and Jesse James*, pp. 128, 154–59; Brant, *Jesse James: The Man and the Myth*, pp. 155–59; Settle, *Jesse James Was His Name*, p. 87; Stiles, *Jesse James: Last Rebel of the Civil War*, p. 303.
12. *Washington Post*, April 22, 1995.
13. Koblas, *Faithful Unto Death*, pp. 168–69.
14. Ibid.

Chapter Eleven

1. *TV Guide*, April 30, 1966.
2. James, *In the Shadow of Jesse James*, p. 107.

Bibliography

Books

Adams, Ramon F. *Six-Guns and Saddle Leather: A Bibliography of Books and Pamphlets on Western Outlaws and Gunmen*. Mineola, NY: Dover, 1998.

Balducci, Anthony. *Lloyd Hamilton: Poor Boy Comedian of Silent Cinema*. Jefferson, NC: McFarland, 2009.

Beights, Ronald H. *Jesse James and the First Missouri Train Robbery*. Gretna, LA: Pelican, 2002.

Beauchamp, Cari. *Without Lying Down: Frances Marion and the Powerful Women of Early Hollywood*. Berkeley: University of California Press, 1998.

Bernstein, Arnie. *Hollywood on Lake Michigan: 100 Years of Chicago and the Movies*. Chicago: Lake Claremont, 1998.

Black, Gregory D. *Hollywood Censored: Morality Codes, Catholics, and the Movies*. New York: Cambridge University Press, 1996.

Blake, Michael F. *Hollywood and the O.K. Corral: Portrayals of the Gunfight and Wyatt Earp*. Jefferson, NC: McFarland, 2007.

Boetticher, Budd. *When in Disgrace*. Santa Barbara: Neville, 1989.

Boggs, Johnny D. *Arm of the Bandit: The Trial of Frank James*. New York: Signet, 2002.

Brant, Marley. *Jesse James: The Man and the Myth*. New York: Berkley, 1998.

_____. *The Outlaw Youngers: A Confederate Brotherhood*. Lanham, MD: Madison, 1992.

Breihan, Carl W. *The Complete and Authentic Life of Jesse James*. New York: Frederick Fell, 1953.

_____. *The Day Jesse James Was Killed*. New York: Signet, 1979.

_____. *The Man Who Shot Jesse James*. South Brunswick, NJ, and New York: A.S. Barnes, 1979.

Brownlee, Richard S. *Gray Ghosts of the Confederacy: Guerrilla Warfare in the West, 1861–1865*. Baton Rouge: Louisiana State University Press, 1958.

Buel, J.W. *The Border Bandits: An Authentic and Thrilling History of the Noted Outlaws, Jesse and Frank James, and their Bands of Highwaymen*. Chicago: Donohue, Henneberry, no date.

Burt, Daniel S. *The Biography Book: A Reader's Guide to Nonfiction, Fictional, and Film Biographies of More Than 500 of the Most Fascinating Individuals of All Time*. Santa Barbara, CA: Greenwood, 2001.

Butters, Gerald R., Jr. *Banned in Kansas: Motion Picture Censorship 1915–1966*. Columbia: University of Missouri Press, 2007.

Capua, Michelangelo. *William Holden: A Biography*. Jefferson, NC: McFarland, 2010.

Carey, Macdonald. *The Days of My Life*. New York: St. Martin's, 1991.

Cline, William C. *In the Nick of Time: Motion Picture Sound Serials*. Jefferson, NC: McFarland, 1997.

_____. *Serials-ly Speaking: Essays on Cliffhangers*. Jefferson, NC: McFarland, 1994.

Copeland, Bobby J., and Richard B. Smith III. *Gabby Hayes: King of the Cowboy Comics*. Madison, WI: Empire, 2008.

Cox, Stephen, and Jim Terry. *One Fine Stooge: Larry Fine's Frizzy Life in Pictures*. Nashville, TN: Cumberland House, 2006.

Croy, Homer. *Jesse James Was My Neighbor*. Lincoln: University of Nebraska Press, 1949.

Davis, Hank. *Classic Cliffhangers: Volume 2 1941–1955*. Baltimore: Midnight Marquee, 2008.

De Grazia, Edward, and Roger K. Newman. *Banned Films: Movies, Censors & the First Amendment*. New York: R.R. Bowker, 1982.

Dellinger, Harold (editor). *Jesse James: The Best Writings on the Notorious Outlaw and His Gang*. Guilford, CT: Globe Pequot, 2007.

Dick, Bernard F. *Hal Wallis: Producer to the Stars*. Lexington: University Press of Kentucky, 2004.

Dixon, Wheeler W. *Film Noir and the Cinema of Paranoia*. New Brunswick, NJ: Rutgers University Press, 2009.

Dyer, Robert L. *Jesse James and the Civil War in Missouri*. Columbia: University of Missouri Press, 1994.

Eagan, Timothy. *The Worst Hard Time: The Untold Story of Those Who Survived the Great American Dust Bowl*. New York: Mariner, 2006.

Edwards, John N. *Noted Guerillas, or the Warfare of the Border* (originally published by Bryan, Brand, St. Louis, 1877). Independence, MO: Two Trails, 1996.

Everson, William K. *A Pictorial History of the Western Film.* New York: Citadel, 1969.
Faust, Patricia L. (editor). *Historical Times Illustrated Encyclopedia of the Civil War.* New York: Harper & Row, 1986.
Fellman, Michael. *Inside War: The Guerrilla Conflict in Missouri During the American Civil War.* New York: Oxford University Press, 1989.
Fenin, George N., and William K. Everson. *The Western: From Silents to the Seventies.* New York: Penguin, 1962, 1973.
Fitzgerald, Michael G., and Boyd Magers. *Ladies of the Western: Interviews with Fifty-one More Actresses from the Silent Era to the Television Westerns of the 1950s and 1960s.* Jefferson, NC: McFarland, 2006.
Forrester, Jeff, and Tom Forrester. *The Three Stooges: The Triumphs and Tragedies of the Most Popular Comedy Team of All Time.* Los Angeles: Donaldson, 2004.
Frascella, Lawrence, and Al Weisel. *Live Fast, Die Young: The Wild Ride of Making* Rebel Without a Cause. New York: Touchstone, 2005.
Fuller, Samuel with, Christa Lang Fuller and Jerome Henry Rudes. *A Third Face: My Tale of Writing, Fighting, and Filmmaking.* New York: Alfred A. Knopf, 2002.
Gaudreault, André. *American Cinema 1890–1909: Themes and Variations.* New Brunswick, NJ: Rutgers University Press, 2009.
Gifford, Barry. *Wild at Heart.* New York: Grove Weidenfeld, 1990.
Goldstein, Jeffrey H. (editor). *Why We Watch: The Attractions of Violent Entertainment.* New York: Oxford University Press, 1998.
Graham, Don. *No Name on the Bullet: A Biography of Audie Murphy.* New York: Viking, 1989.
Gruber, Frank. *Broken Lance.* New York: Bantam, 1954.
_____. *Fighting Man.* New York: Bantam, 1949.
_____. *Peace Marshal.* New York: Bantam, 1958.
Hagen, Ray, and Laura Wagner. *Killer Tomatoes: Fifteen Tough Film Dames.* Jefferson, NC: McFarland, 2004.
Hanson, Peter. *Dalton Trumbo, Hollywood Rebel: A Critical Survey and Filmography.* Jefferson, NC: McFarland, 2001.
Herzberg, Bob. *Savages and Saints: The Changing Image of American Indians in Westerns.* Jefferson, NC: McFarland, 2008.
_____. *Shooting Scripts: From Pulp Western to Film.* Jefferson, NC: McFarland, 2003.
Hofler, Robert. *The Man Who Invented Rock Hudson: The Pretty Boys and Dirty Deals of Henry Willson.* New York: Da Capo, 2006.
Horan, James D. *Desperate Men.* New York: Bonanza, 1969.
Huntington, George. *Robber and Hero: The Story of the Northfield Bank Raid* (originally published by the Christian Way Co., Northfield, 1895). St. Paul: Minnesota Historical Society Press, 1986.
Hurst, Richard Maurice. *Republic Studios: Between Poverty Row and the Majors.* Metuchen NJ: Scarecrow, 1979.
James, Laura. *The Love Pirate and the Bandit's Son: Murder, Sin, and Scandal in the Shadow of Jesse James.* New York: Union Square, 2009.
James, Stella Frances. *In the Shadow of Jesse James.* Thousand Oaks, CA: Revolver, 1990.
Jarlett, Franklin. *Robert Ryan: A Biography and Critical Filmography.* Jefferson, NC: McFarland, 1990.
Jewell, Richard B., with Vernon Harbin. *The RKO Story: The Complete Studio History, with All of the 1,051 Films Described and Illustrated.* London: Octopus, 1982.
Kane, William R. *1,001 Places to Sell Manuscripts.* Addison, 2008 (reprint of a 1915 book).
Kazanjian, Howard, and Chris Enns. *The Cowboy and the Senorita: A Biography of Roy Rogers and Dale Evans.* Guilford, CT, and Helena, MT: TwoDot, 2004.
Kiehn, David. *Broncho Billy and the Essanay Film Company.* Berkeley, CA: Farwell, 2003.
Kitzes, Jim. *Horizons West.* Bloomington: Indiana University Press, 1969.
Koblas, John J. *Bushwhacker! Cole Younger & the Kansas-Missouri Border War.* St. Cloud, MN: North Star, 2004.
_____. *Faithful Unto Death: The James-Younger Raid on the First National Bank, September 7, 1876, Northfield, Minnesota.* Northfield, MN: Northfield Historical Society Press, 2001.
_____. *The Great Cole Younger & Frank James Historical Wild West Show.* St. Cloud, MN: North Star, 2002.
_____. *Jesse James in Iowa.* St. Cloud, MN: North Star, 2006.
_____. *Minnesota Grit: The Men Who Defeated the James-Younger Gang.* St. Cloud, MN: North Star, 2005.
Langman, Larry. *A Guide to Silent Westerns.* Santa Barbara, CA: Greenwood, 1992.
Larkins, Bob, and Boyd Magers. *The Films of Audie Murphy.* Jefferson, NC: McFarland, 2004.
Leslie, Edward E. *The Devil Knows How to Ride: The True Story of William Clarke Quantrill and His Confederate Raiders.* New York: Da Capo, 1998.
Loy, R. Philip. *Westerns in a Changing America 1955–2000.* Jefferson, NC: McFarland, 2004.
Magers, Boyd, and Michael Fitzgerald. *Westerns Women: Interviews with 50 Leading Ladies of Movie and Television Westerns from the 1930s to the 1960s.* Jefferson, NC: McFarland, 1999.
Manfull, Helen (editor). *Additional Dialogue: Letters of Dalton Trumbo, 1942–1962.* New York: Bantam, 1972.

Mathis, Jack. *Valley of the Cliffhangers*. Northbrook, IL: Jack Mathis Advertising, 1975.

_____. *Valley of the Cliffhangers Supplement*. Barrington, IL: Jack Mathis Advertising, 1995.

McCaffrey, Donald. *The Road to Comedy: The Films of Bob Hope*. Santa Barbara, CA: Praeger, 2004.

Meacham, Jon. *American Lion: Andrew Jackson in the White House*. New York: Random House, 2008.

Miller, Rick. *Sam Bass & Gang*. Austin, TX: State House, 1999.

Montgomery, Rick, and Shirl Kasper. *Kansas City: An American Study*. Kansas City Star, 1999.

Moore, Clayton, and Frank Thompson. *I Was That Masked Man*. Dallas: Taylor Trade, 1996.

Morris, John W., Charles R. Goins and, Edwin C. McReynolds. *Historic Atlas of Oklahoma, Third Edition*. Norman: University of Oklahoma Press, 1966.

Neibaur, James L. *The RKO Features: Complete Filmography of the Feature Films Released or Produced by RKO Radio Pictures, 1929–1960*. Jefferson, NC: McFarland, 1994.

Nevin, David. *The Expressmen*. Alexandria: Time-Life, 1974.

Nott, Robert. *Last of the Cowboy Heroes: The Westerns of Randolph Scott, Joel McCrea, and Audie Murphy*. Jefferson, NC: McFarland, 2000.

_____. *The Films of Randolph Scott*. Jefferson, NC: McFarland, 2004.

Ohnick, Nancy (compiler). *The Dalton Gang and Their Family Ties*. Meade, KS: Prairie, 2005.

Pence, Samuel Anderson. *I Knew Frank ... I Wish I Had Known Jesse: Family, Friends and Neighbors in the Life and Times of the James Boys*. Independence, MO: Two Trails, 2007.

Pennington, Jody W. *The History of Sex in American Film*. Santa Barbara, CA: Praeger, 2007.

Petrone, Gerard S. *Judgment at Gallatin: The Trial of Frank James*. Lubbock: Texas Tech University Press, 1998.

Phillips, Kendall R. *Controversial Cinema: The Films That Outraged America*. Santa Barbara, CA: Praeger, 2008.

Pinkerton, Allan. *The Expressman and the Detective*. New York: G.W. Carleton, 1886.

_____. *Thirty Years a Detective*. New York: G.W. Carleton, 1885.

Pitts, Michael R. (compiler). *Hollywood and American History: A Filmography of Over 250 Motion Pictures Depicting U.S. History*. Jefferson, NC: McFarland, 1984.

Prince, Stephen. *Classical Film Violence: Designing and Regulating Brutality in Hollywood Cinema, 1930–1968*. New Brunswick, NJ: Rutgers University Press.

Quinlan, David. *The Illustrated Guide to Film Directors*. London: B.T. Batsford, 1983.

Quirk, Lawrence J. *The Films of William Holden*. Secaucus, NJ: Citadel, 1973.

Rainey, Buck. *Western Gunslingers in Fact and on Film*. Jefferson, NC: McFarland, 1998.

Rogers-Barnett, Cheryl. *Cowboy Princess: Life with My Parents Roy Rogers and Dale Evans*. Lanham, MD: Taylor Trade, 2003.

Segrave, Kelly. *American Films Abroad: Hollywood's Domination of the World's Movie Screens from the 1890s to the Present*. Jefferson, NC: McFarland, 1997.

Settle, William A., Jr. *Jesse James Was His Name*. Columbia: University of Missouri Press, 1966.

Sheffer, Hank. *The Queen and Her Court: A True Story of Apacheland Movie Ranch*. Apache Junction, AZ: Norseman, 2007.

Simpson, Paul. *The Rough Guide to Westerns*. London: Rough Guides, 2006.

Smith, Robert Barr. *Daltons! The Raid on Coffeyville, Kansas*. Norman: University of Oklahoma Press, 1996.

_____. *The Last Hurrah of the James-Younger Gang*. Norman: University of Oklahoma Press, 2001.

Sperling, Cass Warner, Cork Millner and Jack Warner. *Hollywood Be Thy Name: The Warner Brothers Story*. Lexington: University Press of Kentucky, 1998.

Stanfield, Peter. *Hollywood, Westerns and the 1930s: The Lost Trail*. Exeter: University of Exeter Press, 2001.

Steele, Phillip. *Jesse and Frank James: The Family History*. Gretna, LA: Pelican, 1997.

_____. *The Last Cherokee Warriors*. Gretna, LA: Pelican, 1987.

Steele, Phillip W., and George Warfel. *The Many Faces of Jesse James*. Gretna, LA: Pelican, 1995.

Stiles, T.J. *Jesse James: Last Rebel of the Civil War*. New York: Vintage, 2003.

Stricklyn, Ray. *Angels & Demons: One Actor's Hollywood Journey: An Autobiography*. Los Angeles: Belle, 1999.

Thelen, David Paul. *Paths of Resistance: Tradition and Dignity in Industrializing Missouri*. New York: Oxford University Press, 1986.

Thomas, Bob. *Golden Boy: The Untold Story of William Holden*. New York: St. Martin's, 1983.

Trachtman, Paul. *The Gunfighters*. Alexandria: Time-Life, 1974.

Trumbo, Dalton. *The Remarkable Andrew: Being the Chronicle of a Literal Man*. Philadelphia: J.B. Lippincott, 1941.

Tuska, Jon. *The Filming of the West*. Garden City, NY: Doubleday, 1976.

Utley, Robert M. *Billy the Kid: A Short and Violent Life*. Lincoln: University of Nebraska Press, 1989.

Vaughn, Robert. *A Fortunate Life*. New York: Thomas Dunne, 2008.

Verhoeff, Nanna. *The West in Early Cinema: After the Beginning*. Amsterdam: Amsterdam University Press, 2006.

Wagner, Robert J., with Scott Eyman. *Pieces of My Heart: A Life*. New York: Harper Entertainment, 2008.
Wallace, William H. *Speeches and Writings of Wm. H. Wallace with Autobiography*. Kansas City: Western Baptist, 1914.
Walsh, Frank. *Sin and Censorship: The Catholic Church and the Motion Picture Industry*. New Haven: Yale University Press, 1999.
Weaver, Tom. *John Carradine: The Films*. Jefferson, NC: McFarland, 1999.
Webb, Walter Prescott. *The Texas Rangers: A Century of Frontier Defense*. Austin: University of Texas Press, 1935, 1965.
White, Raymond E. *King of the Cowboys, Queen of the West: Roy Rogers and Dale Evans*. Madison, WI: Popular, 2006.
Williamson, Jerry Wayne. *Hillbillyland: What the Movies Did to the Mountains and What the Mountains Did to the Movies*. Chapel Hill: University of North Carolina Press, 1995.
Wyatt, Edgar M. *More than a Cowboy: The Life and Films of Fred Thomson and Silver King*. Raleigh, NC: Wyatt Classics, 1988.
Wybrow, Robert J. "*Horrid Murder & Heavy Robbery": The Liberty Bank Robbery, 13 February 1866*. London: English Westerners' Society, 2004.
Wymore, Jack B. *History of the Jesse James Bank Museum in Liberty, Missouri: Scene of the First Bank Robbery in America and First Outlaw Event in the Career of Jesse James*. Liberty, MO: Jesse James Bank Museum pamphlet, no date.
Yeatman, Ted P. *Frank and Jesse James: The Story Behind the Legend*. Nashville, TN: Cumberland House, 2000.
Younger, Cole. *The Story of Cole Younger* (originally published by the Press of the Henneberry Company, Chicago, 1903). St. Paul: Minnesota Historical Society Press, 2000.
Zolotow, Maurice. *Shooting Star: A Biography of John Wayne*. New York: Pocket Books, 1975.

Articles

"Audie Murphy Is President of New Production Firm." *Boxoffice*, May 5, 1969.
Beck, Henry Cabot. "The Curse of Idolatry." *True West*, November–December 2007.
Boggs, Johnny D. "The Real, Not Reel, Jesse James in Film." *True West*, April 2007.
_____. "The Vision of Walter Hill." *True West*, April 2008.
"Books: Counsel from Hollywood." *Time*, February 3, 1941.
"Continued from September Issue." *American Globe Protective Financier*, October 1915.
"Dot Farley in Standard Program Comedies." *The Moving Picture World*, August 21, 1915.
Fessier, Michael. "The Woman They Almost Lynched." *The Saturday Evening Post*, January 6, 1951.
Glelberman, Owen. "American Outlaws." *Entertainment Weekly*, August 15, 2001, www.ew.com.
Hughes, Albert Hilliard. "Outlaw with a Halo." *Montana: The Magazine of Western History*, Autumn 1967.
Hutton, Paul Andrew. "Dreamscape Desperado." *True West*, May 2007.
_____. "Silver Screen Desperado: Billy the Kid in the Movies." *New Mexico Historical Review*, Spring 2007.
"I Shot Jesse James." *Boxoffice*, November 20, 1948.
"Mississippi Premiere for *Jesse James*." *Boxoffice*, September 11, 1954.
"The Remarkable Andrew." *Boxoffice*, January 17, 1942.
Spear, Ivan. "Anyone Who Hasn't Played Jesse James Please Step Up." *Boxoffice*, July 29, 1950.
Stutesman, Drake. "Budd Boetticher Interview." *Framework: The Journal of Cinema and Media*, Volume 43, No. 1, Spring 2002.
"UA Will Distribute Four, in Color, in September." *Boxoffice*, August 14, 1954.
Warren, Holly George. "The Golden Age of the Western." *American Cowboy*, March–April 2003.
"Washington." *Boxoffice*, October 5, 1940.
Yeatman, Ted P. "Allan Pinkerton and the Raid on 'Castle James.'" *True West*, October 1992.

Archival Documents

"The Trial of Clelland Miller for Bank Robbery, Corydon, Iowa, October, 1872," Transcript, Prairie Trail Museum, Corydon IA.

Newspapers

Belleville (Kansas) *Telescope*
Boston Globe
Chicago Sun–Times
Chicago Tribune
Christian Science Monitor
Daily Gazette (Xenia, Ohio)
Daily News (Frederick, Maryland)
Daily News (Lebanon, Pennsylvania)
Dallas Morning News
Dallas Times Herald
Detroit News
Evening Telegraph (Elyria, Ohio)
Free Lance-Star (Fredericksburg, Virginia)
Fresno Bee
Gazette (Stevens Point, Wisconsin)
Hollywood Reporter
Jackson (Mississippi) *Daily News*
Japan Times
Kansas City Journal

Kansas City Star
Lawrence County (Mississippi) *Press*
Lewiston (Maine) *Sun-Journal*
Liberty (Missouri) *Tribune*
Lodi (California) *News-Sentinel*
London Independent
(London) *Sunday Mirror*
London Telegraph
Meridian (Mississippi) *Star*
Mt. Adams (Bingen, Washington) *Sun*
(Naperville, Illinois) *Sun*
New York Daily News
New York Herald-Tribune
New York Observer
New York Sun
New York Times
Rice County (Minnesota) *Journal*
Rocky Mountain News
St. Joseph Daily Gazette
St. Joseph Daily Herald
St. Joseph Weekly Gazette
St. Louis Globe-Democrat
Salina (Kansas) *County Journal*
San Francisco Chronicle
Santa Fe New Mexican
Seattle Post-Intelligencer
Seattle Times
Star Interviews
Sydney (Australia) *Morning Herald*
Topeka (Kansas) *Capital-Journal*
Topeka (Kansas) *Daily Capital*
Trenton (New Jersey) *Evening Times*
USA Today
Variety
Washington Post

Movie Pressbooks, Press Releases

Alias Jesse James. United Artists, 1959.
Billy the Kid versus Dracula — Jesse James Meets Frankenstein's Daughter. Embassy Pictures, 1965.
Fighting Man of the Plains. 20th Century–Fox, 1949.
The Great Missouri Raid. Paramount, 1950.
The Great Northfield Minnesota Raid. Universal, 1972.
Jesse James. Twentieth Century–Fox, 1951 (reissue).
The Long Riders. United Artists, 1980.
MCA-TV press release #25620, "World Premiere: The Intruders," October 15, 1970.
The Return of Frank James. Twentieth Century–Fox, 1951 (reissue).

Interviews, Letters

Beckett, Elizabeth Gilliam. Email correspondence (November 6, 2009; June 11, 2010).
Bernstein, Arnie. Email correspondence (February 9, 2010; February 21, 2010).
Boardman, Mark. Email correspondence (May 19, 2010; June 9, 2010).
Cole, Scott. Email correspondence (May 14–15, 2010; June 11, 2010).
Cooper, Ben. Telephone interviews (November 8, 2008; March 22, 2010).
Hedrick, Larry. Telephone interview (May 24, 2010).
Hutton, Paul Andrew. Email correspondence (March 20, 2008).
James, Eric. Email correspondence (April 30, 2010; June 11–12, 2010).
Kiehn, David. Email correspondence, February 20, 2010; June 6, 2010.
Magers, Boyd. Email correspondence (June 11, 2010).
_____. Telephone interview (August 19, 2008).
Nott, Robert. Email correspondence (May 20, 2010; May 21, 2010; May 24, 2010; June 10, 2010; July 1, 2010; July 7, 2010).
Shillingberg, Wm. B. Telephone interview (September 2, 2009).

Internet Sources

www.allmovie.com, All Movie Guide
www.angelfire.com/mn/nn/Dracula1931.html, Monstervision's Joe Bob reviews Dracula 1931
www.arlingtoncemetery.net, Arlington National Cemetery
www.bmonster.com, B Monster
www.chicagoparkdistrict.com, Chicago Park District (Broncho Billy Playlot Park (c/o Gill Park)
www.glamourgirlsofthesilverscreen.com, Glamour Girls of the Silver Screen
www.imdb.com, The Internet Movie Database
www.jessejames.org, Friends of the James Farm
www.learnaboutmovieposters.com, Learn About Movie Posters
www.lonepinefilmhistorymuseum.org, Museum of Lone Pine Film History
www.nmfilm.com, New Mexico State Film Office
www.nps.gov/history/NR/twhp/wwwlps/lessons/99condon/99facts2.htm, Determining the Facts: Reading 2: The Dalton Gang
www.richarddix.org, The Richard Dix Web Page
www.robertllippertfoundation.com, The Robert L. Lippert Foundation
www.rockrail.com, Rock Island Railroad
www.spaghetti-western.net, The Spaghetti Western Database
www.superstitionmountainmuseum.org, Superstition Mountain Museum
www.tshaonline.org, The Handbook of Texas Online
www.uclabruins.com, UCLA Official Athletic Site
www.visitcarsoncity.com, Carson City (Nevada) Convention and Visitors Bureau
www.whitehouse.gov, The White House

Index

Abell, Tim 223, 225, 226
Abbott & Costello 157, 183
Adair, Iowa 14, 40, 70, 128, 152, 153, 208, 213
Adams, Julie 115
Adventures of Frank and Jesse James (1948) 3, 94–97, 105
Adventures of Red Ryder (1940) 96, 114, 115, 154
Affleck, Casey 217, 221, 222
Alias Jesse James (1959) 4, 72, 141, 171–175, 188
Allen, J.S. 208
Allied Artists 124, 125
American Bandits: Frank and Jesse James (2010) 195, 223–226
American Outlaws (2001) 4, 195, 210–216
American Releasing Corp. 154
Anders, Merry 175, 178
Anderson, Bloody Bill 11, 13, 32, 121, 122, 123, 125, 128, 134, 169, 240
Anderson, Gilbert M. "Broncho Billy" (born Aaronson, Max) 26, 28
Anderson, Jim 169
Animal Humae Association 53–54
Another Man, Another Chance (aka *Un autre homme, une autre chane*, 1977) 227, 229
Apache Junction, Arizona 192
Appler, Augustus C. 21
Archainbaud, George 81, 84
Arness, James 173
Aro Entertainment 223
Arruza (1971) 191, 192
Askew, Daniel 14, 34, 163
The Assassination of Jesse James by the Coward Robert Ford (2007) 2, 5, 217–223, 225
Austin, Vivian 115, 154
Austin, Texas 14, 109, 216
Autry, Gene 65, 76

Bad Men of Missouri (1941) 68–72
Badman's Territory (1946) 85–90, 110, 119, 131, 133, 135
Ballard, Lucien 192
Baltimore, Maryland 220
Barbary Coast (1975) 3, 241
Barcroft, Roy 90, 92, 102, 105
Barnholtz Entertainment 223

Baron, Lita 150, 153
Barrett, Joyce Rhed 153, 154
Barry, Donald "Red" 3, 5, 63, 64, 66–67, 96, 112, 114, 115, 150, 153, 154
Barton, Ara 161, 208
Baruc, Siri 223, 226
Bass, Sam 85, 86, 87–88, 124
Bassham, Tucker 17, 162
Bates, Kathy 210, 211, 215
Baxter, Alan 68
Baylor, Hal 154, 157
Bean, Judge Roy 189, 191, 193
Beauchamp, D.D. 150, 171, 174
Beaudine, William 184, 186, 189
Belle Starr (1980) 3, 230, 233, 234, 240
Berke, William 112, 114
Bernstein, Arnie 23, 26
Besser, Joe 181, 183
Best, James 121, 125
Best of the Badmen (1951) 131–136
Billy the Kid (aka Antrim, Henry; Bonney, William H.; McCarty, Henry, etc.) 2, 5, 74–75, 79, 89, 106, 119, 124, 131, 135, 213, 229
Billy the Kid Returns (1938) 75, 119
Billy the Kid versus Dracula (1966) 186, 187, 188
Bird, Greenup 7
Bird, William 7
Black Bart (California outlaw Boyles, Charles E.) 156
Blake, Pamela 112, 113, 115
Block, Jake 27, 28
Blue Cut, Missouri 16, 100, 144, 217, 220
Boetticher, Budd 23, 115, 189, 191, 192, 193
Bogart, Humphrey 71, 80
Bolder, Cal 184, 185, 187, 188
Bolton, Martha 128, 217, 218, 219
Bond, Ward 126, 127, 129, 173
Bowers, William 171, 173
Brady, Scott 121, 125, 135
The Brady Bunch (1973) 3, 241
Brandon, Henry 166, 170, 171
Brennan, Walter 131
Britton, Barbara 97, 101
Broadwell, Dick 88
Brodie, Steve 85, 89
Bronco (1960) 3, 240

Brown, Harry Joe 44
Bryden, Bill 202
Buetel, Jack 131, 135, 150, 153
Bunker, Alonzo 160, 195, 196, 197, 199, 208

Caan, James 214, 229
Caan, Scott 210, 211, 214
Cagney, James 114, 145
Cameron, Rod 76, 77
Canutt, Yakima 94, 97, 102
Carbonara, Gerard 83
Carey, Macdonald 126, 127, 129, 130, 188
Carpenter, John (aka Forbes, John) 154, 155, 156, 157, 158
Carr, Mary 38, 41
Carradine, David 203, 206, 208, 209
Carradine, John 45, 52, 60, 62, 158, 164, 208
Carradine, Keith 203, 208, 209
Carradine, Robert 203, 208, 209
Carville, James 217, 222, 223
Case, Allen 238
Cash, Johnny 234
Castle, Peggie 150, 153, 154, 166
Castle, William 146, 149
Chadwell, Bill (alias Stiles, Bill) 15, 161, 195, 196, 197, 198, 199, 203, 204, 208
Christie, Ned 233, 234
Clements, Arch 33, 126, 128, 142, 143, 144
Coates, Franklin B. 32, 36
Coates, Phyllis 105
Coburn, James 240
Cody, William F. "Buffalo Bill" 21, 30
Coffeyville, Kansas 86, 146, 147, 148, 149, 233
Cole, Scott 30, 75
Collins, Ray 85
Columbia, Kentucky 14, 178
Columbia Studios 105, 144, 146, 147, 181
Combs, Jeffrey 223, 225, 226
Conti, Steve 112
Cooder, Ry 209
Cook, Elisha, Jr. 195, 201
Cooper, Ben 136, 137, 140, 141, 142
Cooper, Gary 53, 66, 145, 173, 178

Cooper, Jackie 55, 60, 61
Corey, Wendell 125, 126, 129, 130, 171, 173
Corinth, Mississippi 154
Corydon, Iowa 14, 34, 118, 206, 213
Courtright, William 38, 39, 41
Crabbe, Buster 3
Creede, Colorado 59, 99, 100, 112, 113, 114, 142, 143, 144, 149
Crittenden, Missouri Gov. Thomas 16, 19, 36, 59, 100, 156, 166, 168, 169, 213, 217, 218, 220, 222
Crittenden, Thomas T. 34, 36
Cronkite, Walter 3, 238
Crosby, Bing 173
Croy, Homer 74, 100, 119
Cummins, Jim 1, 217, 218, 220
Curtis, Tony 121, 125
Custer, George Armstrong 1, 3, 4

Dalton, Bill 88
Dalton, Bob 89, 146, 147, 148, 232, 233, 234
Dalton, Emmett 88, 146, 149, 232, 233
Dalton, Grat 68, 69, 146, 147, 148, 232, 233, 234
Dalton, J. Frank 74, 119
Dalton, Kit 121, 122, 123, 124
Dalton, Timothy 210, 214, 215, 216
Dalton Gang 69, 86, 88, 131, 146, 147, 148, 149, 232, 233
Dark Command (1940) 125
Darrell, Steve 94, 96
Darwell, Jane 45, 51, 52
Davis, Gail 173
Davis, Jim 137, 171, 173, 184, 188, 239
Dawson, Gordon 236, 237
Days of Jesse James (1939) 62–67, 75, 92, 114, 119, 158
Deakins, Roger 222
Dean, James 3, 164, 238
DeRita, Joe 181, 183
Dillahunt, Garret 217, 222
Dillinger (1945) 88, 135
Dix, Richard 81, 83, 84, 109, 178
Dix, Robert 175, 178
Dominik, Andrew 217, 218, 220, 221, 222, 223
Donlevy, Brian 45, 52, 76, 77, 79, 121, 123, 125, 136, 233
The Doolins of Oklahoma (1949) 55, 120, 129
Douglas, Gordon 126, 129, 131
Drake, Charles D. 134
Drake, Oliver, 154, 157
Drew, Ellen 76, 77, 79
The Duel at Silver Creek (1952) 170, 193
The Dukes of Hazzard (1984) 3, 242
Duvall, Robert 195, 197, 200, 201, 202
Dvorak, Ann 116, 120
Dwan, Allan 136, 140, 142

Earth 2 (1995) 242
Eckstrom, Laurie 223, 226

Edwards, John Newman 5, 14, 19, 21, 49, 50, 119, 169, 173, 234
Egan, Richard 121, 125
Embassy Pictures 184, 186
Enright, Ray 68, 71, 121, 126
Essanay Studios 23, 24, 26, 28, 29
Estevez, Emilio 213

Farley, Dot (aka Farley, Dorothea, and Farley, Dorothy) 31
Farrell, Colin 210, 211, 212, 214, 215, 216
Farrell, Tommy 112, 115
Fessier, Michael 139, 140
Fighting Man of the Plains (1949) 84, 106–111, 239
Film Booking Offices of America (FBO) 40, 41, 43, 44
Fine, Larry 181, 182, 183, 184
FIPCO Productions 189, 191
Fisher, Steve 136, 139, 140, 141
Fix, Paul 106
Fleming, Rhonda 171, 172, 173, 174
Fonda, Henry 2, 45, 50, 52, 53, 54, 55, 60–62, 225
Fonda, Peter 192, 223, 225, 226
Ford, Charles 17, 18, 21, 26, 47, 49, 57, 59, 97, 98, 99, 100, 112, 113, 114, 115, 116, 117, 118, 126, 127, 131, 158, 160, 169, 203, 204, 205, 209, 217, 218, 219, 220, 222
Ford, James Thomas 169
Ford, John 97, 145, 227
Ford, Robert 1, 8, 17, 18, 21, 23, 26, 34, 36, 39, 40, 47, 48, 49, 57, 58, 59, 62, 75, 92, 97, 98, 99, 100, 101, 102, 112, 113, 114, 116, 117, 118, 119, 126, 127, 128, 142, 143, 144, 146, 148, 149, 150, 151, 152, 158, 160, 163, 164, 166, 167, 168, 169, 191, 198, 203, 204, 205, 209, 217, 218, 219, 220, 221, 222, 223, 228, 234, 236
Ford, Wallace, 142, 145
Foster, Preston 97, 101, 102
Frank & Jesse (1995) 236
Frankovich, M.J. 90, 92
Fuller, Sam 5, 97, 99, 100, 101, 102, 114

Gads Hill, Missouri 14, 207, 213
Gallatin, Missouri 8, 13, 19, 59, 119, 129, 134, 156, 177
Garfield, Brian 146, 158
Garraway, Tom V. 150, 153
Gashade, Billy 21
Geray, Steven 184, 185
Gibson, Meg 234, 235
Gifford, Barry 72
Glendale, Missouri 16–17, 23, 26, 40, 162, 206
Glispin, James 161, 230
Goldstein (1965) 200
Goodyear Television Playhouse (1956) 239
Gordon, Leo 125
Granbury, Texas 74

Grant, Ulysses S. 140
Grayson, Kathryn 144
The Great Jesse James Raid (1953) 119, 120, 142–146, 175, 178
The Great Missouri Raid (1951) 84, 126–131, 173, 188
The Great Northfield Minnesota Raid (1972) 1, 5, 195–202
The Great Train Robbery (1903) 22, 26
Griffith, James 146, 149
Gruber, Frank 83, 84, 106, 109, 111, 126, 128, 129, 131, 239
Guest, Christopher 203, 209
Guest, Nicholas 203, 208, 209
Gunfire (1950) 5, 72, 112–116, 120, 144
Gustafson (Gustavson), Nicholas 15, 197, 199

Hadley, Reed 97, 100, 101, 116, 119, 137
Hall, Frank O. 119
Hansen, Ron 220
Hanska Slough, Minnesota 15, 49, 134, 144, 161, 196, 198, 208
Harrison, Missouri 70
Hart, William S. 40, 44, 49–50, 93
Hatton, Raymond 66
Hayes, George "Gabby" 63, 66–67, 72, 75, 85, 89
Healy, Ted 182, 183
Heisler, Stuart 76, 79
Hellman, Sam 60, 62
Hell's Crossroads (1957) 166–171, 175
Heywood, Joseph 15, 134, 160, 195, 197, 199, 200, 201, 208
Hill, Walter 1, 2, 202, 203, 205, 209, 210
Hilton, Arthur 116, 120
Hite, Clarence 17–18, 220
Hite, Wood 100, 128, 217, 218, 219, 220, 222
Hittleman, Carl K. 116, 119, 120, 184, 186
Hoffman, Harry 32, 33, 35, 36–37
Holden, William 76, 77, 79, 130
Holt, Nat 106, 109, 110, 126, 129, 130
Hondo (1967) 3, 241
Hope, Bob 4, 171, 172, 173, 174, 175
Hot Springs, Arkansas 14, 109, 207
Howard, Jerome "Curly" 183
Howard, Moe 181, 182, 183
Howard, Shemp 183
Hull, Henry 5, 45, 55, 60, 116, 119
Hunter, Jeffrey 158, 164
Huntington, George 161
Huntington, West Virginia 220, 234, 235
Huntsville, Alabama 19, 59, 129

I Shot Jesse James (1949) 5, 97–102, 114, 116, 117, 119, 120, 144, 201
In Old Oklahoma aka *War of the Wildcats* (1943) 91, 97

Index

Ingraham, Lloyd 38, 41
The Intruders (1970) 230–231
Ireland, John 97, 101, 102, 116, 117, 120, 125

James, Anna Ralston (wife of Frank) 14, 30, 114, 119, 128, 204
James, Frank: as actor 29–30; birth 8; death 30; impostors 30; joins Quantrill 10; marries Anna Ralston 14; protests *The James Boys in Missouri* 25; surrenders 19; trials 19–20, 59
James, Jesse: birth 8; death 18; impostors 74–75; marries Zee Mimms 14, 173; nicknamed "Dingus" 11, 144
James, Jesse Edwards (son of Jesse) 15, 23, 32–37, 41, 43, 173
James, Jo Frances (granddaughter of Jesse) 49
James, Mary Susan (daughter of Jesse) 18, 173
James, Robert (father of Jesse) 8–9, 177, 206
James, Robert (son of Frank) 119
James, Stella Frances McGown (wife of Jesse Edwards James), 36–37
The James Boys in Missouri (1908) 3, 23–28
The James Boys in Missouri (play by George Klimpt and Frank A.P. Gazzollo) 25
The James Brothers of Missouri (1949) 97, 102–106
Jergens, Adele 154, 157
Jesse James (1911) 28–29
Jesse James (1927) 23, 38–44, 92, 130
Jesse James (1939) 2, 5, 45–55, 62, 63, 97, 119, 131, 159, 166, 210
Jesse James as the Outlaw (1921) 3, 23, 32–37, 39
Jesse James at Bay (1941) 3, 72–76, 158
Jesse James Meets Frankenstein's Daughter (1966) 4, 184–189
Jesse James Rides Again (1947) 3, 90–94, 96, 97, 105, 106, 210
Jesse James Under the Black Flag (1921) 3, 23, 32–37, 39
Jesse James vs. the Daltons (1954) 146–150
Jesse James' Women (1954) 135, 150–154, 174, 175
Jewell, Isabel 85, 88
Johnson, Ben 89
Johnson, Nunnally 45, 48, 50–51, 55, 158, 164
Johnston, Joseph E. 140
Jones, Christopher 238
Jones, Jefferson 169
Jones, Spike 149
Jory, Victor 81, 85, 106, 108, 110, 189, 193

Kane, Joseph 63, 66, 72
The Kansan (1943) 81–84, 109, 178
Kansas Raiders (1950) 3, 79, 121–126, 204
Kaufman, Philip 1, 195, 198, 200, 201, 202
Keach, James 202, 203, 209, 210
Keach, Stacy 202, 203, 209
Keel, Howard 144
Kelly, Ed (aka Kelley, Ed; O'Kelly, Ed; O'Kelley, Ed) 59, 99, 100, 114, 219
Kelly, Nancy 45, 52–53
Kennedy, Arthur 68, 71
Kennedy, Burt 227
Kerry, Hobbs 15
Kiehn, David 24, 26
King, Brent 146, 147, 149
King, Henry 45, 51, 53, 55, 97, 131
King, Sarah "Kate" (aka Clarke, Kate) 121, 122, 124
Koblas, John J. 1, 206
Kristofferson, Kris 234, 235

Lamond, Don 181, 182
Lane, Nora 38, 49, 41, 43
Lang, Fritz 55, 60, 62
Lange, Hope 158, 165
Lapp, Richard 189, 193
Larter, Ali 210, 214
The Last Days of Frank and Jesse James (1986) 5, 234–236
The Last Ride of the Dalton Gang (1979) 3, 230, 232–233
Lawrence, Barbara 146, 149
Lawrence, Kansas 11, 35, 106, 109, 110, 122, 123, 139
Lee, Ang 2
Lee, Robert E. 124, 140, 177
Legend (1995) 242–243
The Legend of Jesse James (1965–1966) 238
Leslie, Joan 136, 140, 141, 142
Lexington, Missouri 13, 14, 109, 128, 144
Liberty, Missouri 1, 7, 8, 45, 47, 51, 92, 117, 119, 128, 177, 210, 219
Liddil, James Andrew "Dick" 17, 100, 127, 128, 131, 144, 162, 217, 218, 219, 220, 222, 234
Life and Adventure of the James Boys in Missouri (1914) 29 30
Lippert, Robert L. 97, 101, 102, 115, 119, 120, 144
Lippert, Robert L., Jr. 142, 144
Lippert Pictures 112, 115, 116, 120, 142, 143, 144, 145
Little House on the Prairie (1977) 3, 241
Lois & Clark: The New Adventures of Superman (1995) 242
Lone Pine, California 141, 192
The Lone Ranger 3, 93, 157
Long, Richard 121, 125
The Long Riders (1980) 1, 2, 5, 202, 202–210
Love, Montagu 38, 39, 41, 76, 77, 79
Lowe, Rob 236
Lucky Luke (2009) 227, 229
Luna Productions 31
Lupton, John 184, 188
Lynchburg, Virginia 59, 163, 220
Lyons, Cliff 54

MacGyver (1990) 3, 242
Mack, Wayne "The Great McNutt" 181, 183
Madelia, Minnesota 15, 230
Magers, Boyd 106, 114, 115, 125, 157, 193
Mammoth Cave, Kentucky 16, 109
Mankato, Minnesota 198
Manning, Anselm 161, 199
Manning, Jack 195, 201
Margolin, Stuart 230
Marin, Edwin L. 106, 110
Martin, Dewey 125
Marx Brothers 174
Maurer, Norman 181, 182, 183, 184
Maverick (1994) 216
Mayfield, Les 210, 214
McCoy, Arthur 169, 207
McCrea, Joel 125
McDaniel, Tom 234, 236
McDaniel, William "Bud" 234
McLeod, Norman 171, 173, 174
McNally, Stephen 166, 170
Meridian, Mississippi 153
Mesco Pictures 32, 36,
Meyer, Emile 175, 178
MGM 125, 149, 153
Miller, Alix 71
Miller, Clell 14, 15, 118, 144, 195, 196, 197, 198, 203, 204, 206, 208, 209, 212
Miller, Ed 18, 127, 128, 131, 203, 204, 206, 209, 217, 222, 236
Millican, James 106, 108, 126
Mimms, Zee (Zerelda James, wife of Jesse James) 4, 12, 14, 21, 34, 39, 97, 102, 128, 173, 175, 177, 201, 204, 210, 212
Mix, Tom 37, 40, 44, 93, 97
Monroe, Marilyn 157, 165
Montgomery, Elizabeth 233
Moore, Clayton 3, 92, 93, 94, 96
Moore, Pauline 63, 66, 67
Morgan, Dennis 58, 71, 72
Morris, Wayne 68, 71, 72
Muncie, Kansas 14, 152, 166, 168, 169
Murphy, Audie 3, 121, 124, 125, 189, 190, 191, 192, 193, 194, 204
Murray, Don 230, 231
Muscle Shoals, Alabama 16, 21, 59
My Favorite Martian (1965) 3, 240

Nashville, Tennessee 14, 18, 91, 148, 234
Neal, Tom 142, 145
The Near Capture of Jesse James (1915) 31
Neill, Noel 94, 96, 102, 105
Nelson, Willie 234
Newcomb, George "Bitter Creek" 88, 120, 232
Newman, Paul 3, 164
Nigh, Jane 106, 108, 110

Noel, Missouri 51, 52
Noonan, Tommy 97, 101, 119
Northfield, Minnesota 1, 15, 21, 34, 35, 48, 65, 91, 118, 129, 134, 144, 158, 160, 161, 162, 166, 186, 195, 196, 197, 198, 199, 200, 201, 202, 204, 206, 208, 210, 230, 231, 236
Nott, Robert 87, 89, 193

O'Brian, Hugh 116, 120, 173
O'Donnell, Jacklyn 175, 176, 178
Oklahoma! (Broadway musical) 76, 149
Old Tucson Studios, Arizona 192
Onyx, Narda 184, 185, 188
Otterville, Missouri 148
The Outlaw (1943) 55, 135
Outlaw Treasure (1955) 154–158
The Outlaws IS Coming (1965) 181–184
The Outriders (1950) 125
Owens, Francis Marion 40, 41

Palance, Jack 232, 233
Paramount 38, 39, 40, 42, 43, 76, 80, 83, 89, 125, 126, 130
Parker, Fess 173
Parker, Judge Isaac 233
Parker, Mary-Louise 217, 222
Parker, Willard 142, 143, 144, 145, 175, 178
Paso Robles, California 156
Paxton, Bill 236
Payne, John 140, 153
Payton, Barbara 142, 145
Peck, Gregory 51, 145
Pendleton, Steve (aka Pendleton, Gaylord) 112, 115
Penn, Arthur 3, 164
Pickford, Mary 41, 44, 186
Pierce, James 41–42
Pineville, Missouri 51–52
Pinkerton, Allan 128, 195, 210, 211, 212, 213, 214, 215
Pinkertons 14, 65, 91, 92, 128, 129, 163, 177, 195, 198, 202, 204, 205, 208, 213
Pitt, Brad 214, 217, 218, 220, 221, 222, 223, 225
Pitts, Charlie (aka Wells, Sam) 15, 35, 49, 144, 160, 161, 195, 196, 198, 199, 203, 204, 208, 230
Platte City, Missouri 18, 49
Playhouse 90 (1958) 239
Porter, Edwin Stanton 22, 26
Power, Tyrone 45, 50, 52, 53
Presley, Elvis 125, 164, 192
Preston, Robert 62, 131
Producers Releasing Corporation 3, 106
Purgatory (1999) 230, 236–237

Quaid, Dennis 203, 209
Quaid, Randy 203, 209, 235
Quantrill, William Clarke 10–11, 23, 26, 32, 35, 39, 42, 70, 106, 108, 109, 121, 122, 123, 124, 125, 126, 128, 132, 134, 136, 137, 139, 157, 159, 175, 176, 177, 181, 241
Quantrill's Raiders (1958) 125
Quinn, Anthony Tyler 223, 226

Randall, Anne 189, 193
Ray, Fred Olen 223, 224, 225, 226
Ray, Nicholas 158, 160, 164, 165, 166
Red Mountain (*Quantrell's Raiders*) (1951) 125
Reeves, George 81, 84
The Remarkable Andrew (1942) 76–81
Renner, Jeremy 217, 222
Reno Gang (train robbers) 70, 144
Republic Studios 3, 63, 67, 72, 90, 92, 93, 94, 95, 96, 102, 103, 104, 105, 106, 114, 125, 136, 141, 166, 170
The Return of Frank James (1940) 2, 55–62, 119
The Return of Jesse James (1950) 72, 116–120, 144
Return of the Bad Men (1948) 89, 110, 119, 131, 135
Revere, Anne 126, 129
Richards, Ann 85, 88
Richards, Keith 102, 105, 106
Richmond, Missouri 13, 100
Ride a Wild Stud (1969) 157, 181
Ride with the Devil 1, 2
RKO 85, 88, 110, 131, 135, 140
Roberts, Ollie "Brushy Bill" 74–75
Robertson, Cliff 1, 2, 195, 196, 202, 232, 233, 239
Robertson, Dale 106, 106, 107, 108
Robinson, James G. 210, 212
Rockwell, Sam 217, 222
Rocky Cut, Missouri 15
Rodriguez, Estelita 184, 188
Rogers, Roy 3, 63–67, 72, 73, 75, 76, 114, 173, 188
Ross, James R. (great-grandson of Jesse James) 4, 36
Roth, Eugene 102, 105
Royal, Lloyd 150, 153
Russell, William D. 131, 136
Russellville, Kentucky 13, 178
Ryan, Bill 16, 162
Ryan, Robert 89, 131, 135, 136, 164

St. Albans, Vermont 8
Ste. Genevieve, Missouri 14, 206
St. Joseph, Missouri 1, 18, 47, 59, 74, 97, 99, 100, 143, 144, 159, 160, 162, 163, 168, 218
St. Petersburg, Florida 216
Samuel, Archie (stepbrother of Jesse) 49, 66
Samuel, Dr. Reuben (second stepfather of Jesse) 9–11, 14, 48, 66, 123, 126, 128, 177, 206
Samuel, Zerelda Cole James (mother of Jesse) 4, 8, 9, 10, 11, 14, 21, 30, 39, 48, 66, 92, 123, 128, 129, 163, 177, 206

Samuelson, Nancy 29, 124
San Antonio, Texas 216
The Saturday Evening Post 139, 140
Savage, Ann 137, 140, 141
Savannah, Missouri 13
Saxon, John 164, 230, 231
Schneider, Paul 217, 222
Scott, Jeffrey 181, 182
Scott, Randolph 44, 45, 51, 53, 60, 69, 85, 89, 106, 107, 109, 110, 111, 131, 136, 192, 193, 233
Screen Guild 97, 101
Secret Adventures of Jules Verne (2000) 24
Shelby, Jo 59, 177, 204, 234
Shepard, Sam 217, 222, 223, 236
Sherman, Harry 81, 83
Sherman, William T. 140
Shumate, Harold 81, 83, 84
Siegel, Don 193, 238
Silver Creek, Mississippi 151, 152, 153
Simms, Benjamin (first stepfather of Jesse) 9, 206
Sitka, Emil 181, 183
Skelton, Red 157
Smith, Jefferson Randolph "Soapy" 100
Smith, Steven Phillip 202, 210
Son of Jesse James (aka *Jesse James' Kid*; *A Man Alone*; *One Against All*; *Solo Contro Tutti*, 1965) 181, 227, 228
Southwest City, Missouri 53
Special Unit 2 (2001) 243
Spoor, George K. 26
Stacy, Elias 208
Starr, Belle 85, 86, 87, 88, 175, 176, 177, 181, 183, 190, 203, 204, 205, 206, 227, 230
Starr, Sam 177, 204, 206
Starrs, James 148
Steele, Bob 3
Stirling, Linda 90, 92, 93, 96
Stone, Eleanor 60
Stories of the Century (1954) 3, 188, 239, 240
Storm, Gale 72, 73, 75, 76
Strange, Glenn 63, 67
Stricklyn, Ray 164, 175, 178, 179, 214
Stults, George 223, 225
Sullivan, Barry 125
Swain, W.I. 21

Tales of Wells Fargo (1957) 3, 239
Taliferro, Hal 96
Tamblyn, Russ 164
Taylor, Joan 106, 110
Texas State Railroad 218
Thomson, Fred 38, 40, 41, 42, 43, 44, 130
The Three Stooges 4, 181, 182, 183, 184
Thundercloud, Chief (born Daniels, Victor) 85, 89
Tibbs, Casey 189, 192
Tierney, Gene 55, 60–62, 88, 120, 233

Tierney, Lawrence 85, 88, 89, 131, 135
Timberlake, James H. "Henry" 100, 128, 217, 219, 220
A Time for Dying (1969) 3, 121, 180, 181, 189–194
Tone, Franchot 145
Topeka, Kansas 97, 99, 106
Totter, Audrey 136, 140, 141, 142
Travis, Randy 236
Trevor, Claire 131, 135
The True Story of Jesse James (1958) 158–166, 214
Trumbo, Dalton 63, 76, 79–80
Tuska, Jon 43, 54, 60, 62, 67, 76, 115
20th Century–Fox 45, 46, 51, 52, 53, 54, 55, 60, 63, 89, 106, 109, 112, 158, 164, 165, 166, 175, 178, 179, 180
The Twilight Zone (1962) 3, 240
Two Gangsters in the West (aka *Due mafiosi nel Far West*; *Two Mafiamen in the Far West*, 1964) 181, 227–228
Tyler, Tom 85, 131, 135

Under the Black Flag (book by Kit Dalton) 124
United Artists 81, 83, 150, 153, 171, 202
Universal/Universal-International 89, 92, 105, 121, 124, 125, 131, 195

Van Cleef, Lee 226, 239, 240
Vasquez Rocks, California 114
Vaughn, Robert 166, 170, 171
Vernon, Wally 112, 115
Vidor, King 3

Wagner, Robert 158, 164, 165, 166, 214
Wallace, Beryl 81, 83
Wallace, William H. 59, 162, 220
Wallis, Hal B. 125
Warner, Jack 31
Warner Bros. 68, 72, 80, 141, 145, 210, 216, 217, 222
Warren, James 85, 89
Watie, Stand 140
Wayne, John 4, 75, 97, 164
Webb, James 72, 74
Webb, Tom 234, 236
West, Adam 181, 183, 184
Wheeler, Henry 195, 196, 197, 198, 199
Whelan, Tim 85, 88
When the Daltons Rode (1940) 55, 69, 233
Whicher, Joseph W. 92, 169
White, Hugh 153
Wilcox, Frank J. 160, 195, 196, 197, 199, 202
The Wild Bunch (1969) 136, 192, 202, 210
Williams, Bill 106, 108, 110
Wimberley, Texas 216
Winston, Missouri 16, 18, 40, 59, 118, 213, 220
Woman They Almost Lynched (1953) 79, 125, 136–142, 154, 188
Woodell, Barbara 97, 102, 112, 116, 119, 142, 146
Woods, Harry 38, 63, 67, 92
Wyman, Jane 153
Wymore, George Clifford "Jolly" 7, 178, 219

Yancy Derringer (1959) 240

Yates, Herbert J. 66, 76, 114, 141, 170
Yeatman, Ted P. 23, 28
You Are There (1953) 3, 238
The Young Guns (1956) 164
Young Guns (1988) 213, 216
Young Guns II (1990) 213
Young Jesse James (1960) 112, 175–180, 181, 214
The Young Riders (1989–1992) 3, 238
Younger, Bob 8, 15–16, 49, 68, 69, 70, 71, 126, 131, 132, 133, 134, 158, 161, 165, 195, 196, 197, 198, 199, 201, 203, 204, 206, 209, 210, 212, 213, 236, 240
Younger, Bursheba Leighton Fristoe 70, 118, 206, 213
Younger, Cole 1, 8, 11, 13, 14, 15, 16, 22, 30, 33, 35, 49, 68, 69, 70, 71, 89, 109, 121, 122, 123, 126, 128, 129, 131, 132, 133, 134, 144, 151, 152, 158, 160, 161, 166, 168, 170, 175, 176, 177, 178, 181, 183, 195, 196, 197, 198, 199, 201, 202, 203, 204, 205, 206, 207, 208, 209, 210, 211, 212, 213, 214, 232, 233, 234, 236, 240, 241
Younger, Henry Washington 69, 70, 118, 206, 213
Younger, Jim 8, 15, 16, 49, 68, 69, 70, 71, 121, 122, 123, 158, 161, 177, 195, 196, 198, 203, 204, 206, 207, 208, 209, 210, 212, 213, 236, 240
Younger, John 203, 207
The Younger Brothers (1908) 28
The Younger Brothers (1949) 49, 55

Zanuck, Daryl F. 45, 50, 52, 60

www.ingramcontent.com/pod-product-compliance
Ingram Content Group UK Ltd.
Pitfield, Milton Keynes, MK11 3LW, UK
UKHW050539150426
5217IPUK00026B/1992